AF528282

COMPUTER-BASED LIBRARY INFORMATION SYSTEMS: DESIGNING TECHNIQUES (Revised Edition)

COMPUTER-BASED LIBRARY INFORMATION SYSTEMS: DESIGNING TECHNIQUES (Revised Edition)

Madan Mohan Kashyap

Edited by :
A. Neelameghan and K.N. Prasad

Published by
Ess Ess Publications
4837/24, Ansari Road
Darya Ganj
New Delhi-110 002

for

Sarada Ranganathan Endowment For Library Science
Bangalore

First Published **2006**

ISBN: 81-7000-484-5

Rs.1175/-

Published by:
Ess Ess Publications
4837/24, Ansari Road, Darya Ganj, New Delhi-110 002
Tel: 011-23260807, 41563444 Fax: 011-41563334
E-mail: info@essessreference.com url: www.essessreference.com

for

Sarada Ranganathan Endowment for Library Science
702, 'Upstairs', 42nd Cross, III Block, Rajajinagar,
Bangalore-560 010
E-mail: srels@vsnl.com Tel.:080-23305109

Printed in India at:
Printline, New Delhi

Dedicated with love to
my charming wife Saroj and my children and
grand children Ashali, Manika, Ajay,
Sudhanshu and Vivek

ROm poornamadah poorrnamidam poornaat poornam udachyate.
Poornasya poornam aadaaya poornam evavashishyate.
Om Shanti Shanti Shanti!S
(Isavasya Upanishad)

*ROm. That is **Whole** (or Complete), this is **whole** (or complete), from that **Whole**, the **whole** emanates. Taking away this **whole** from that **Whole**, the **Whole** still remains behind. Om. Peace, Peace, Peace.S*

If what we write, we do not read,
If what we read, we do not think about,
If what we think, we do not live.
Of what use is it all?
Dharma helps us translate
great ideas into action.
Dharma is to live righteously.

N **HDH Pramukh Swami Maharaj**

CONTENTS

FOREWORD

The Sarada Ranganathan Endowment for Library Science (SRELS), founded by Dr. S.R. Ranganathan in 1961, is registered as a Charitable Endowment with the Government of India (1963).

The aims of the Endowment briefly are:

* To improve the library and information services in India
* To train library and information service personnel
* To promote the provision of efficient library and information service
* To apply research results to library and information studies

The objectives of the Endowment are:

* Furthering the cause of library and information service
* Organising periodically courses of lectures on recent developments in library and information science and related fields by national and international experts
* Supporting the publication of these lectures and of other nascent ideas in the field of library and information science.

The Endowment is furthering these objectives by publishing a periodical entitled *SRELS Journal of Information Management (formerly, Library Science with a slant to Documentation (from 1964 to 1988), and Library Science with slant to Documentation and Information Studies* (from 1988 to 1999).

There are three *series* of lectures organized under the auspices of the Endowment:

1. Sarada Ranganathan Endowment Lectures. (1965-);
2. Dr. S.R. Ranganathan Memorial Lectures. (1973-); and
3. Curzon-Seshachalam Chimata Foundation Lectures. (2001-).

Computer-Based Library Information Systems Designing Techniques (Revised Edition) – The purpose of this book is, to give accounts of systems theory to help one to understand the process of systems analysis and design as well as design better information technology-based systems in libraries; to describe the methodology for conducting systems study; and, to explain the use and application of systems analysis and design tools and techniques. This book is written keeping in mind the practising librarians who are faced with the responsibility of evaluating library programs and procedures to identify the problem areas, that is, the situations where there are gaps or deviations between what is expected, what could or should be and find means to bridges the gaps. The second audience to whom thus book is addressed is the library and information science students who may join a course in Computer Application in Libraries, Library Systems Analysis and Design or Library Systems Study and Re-engineering Technique and Library Database Design and Development Approach.

The Endowment is grateful to Prof. M.M. Kashyap for allowing it to publish his book. The Endowment is also grateful to Prof. A. Neelameghan for editing the book.

K.N. Prasad
Executive Officer
Sarada Ranganathan
Endowment for Library Science

Acknowledgement

I thank the Sarada Ranganathan Endowment for Library Science (SRELS) for accepting to publish my book. I wish to thank specifically Prof. A. Neelameghan and Dr. K.N. Prasad for their efforts in editing and giving shape to the manuscript and advising me on some new materials added to this revised edition. I also wish to thank the staff of SRELS in particular Ms. S.K. Lalitha for preparing the print-ready copy for publication.

— M.M. Kashyap

Preface

It is proclaimed that we live in information age, though since time immemorial facts, data or information have always been important to man practically in all aspects of human enterprise. The present age is commonly accepted as information age because of unparalleled developments in the information technology that enable us to collect, process, and access information at rapid speed and at lower cost. Though, we agree that present era is of information and communication technologies and their immense output, yet it is also the era of information overload and misinformation, which is the product of extensive use of computers (hardware and software) supported by multimedia and telecommunication technologies (data, image, and voice networks). The mass of knowledge sources and transient information (including unreliable or distorted information) that we are producing these days in electronic form with the help of information technology and media need to be organised, processed, retrieved and made available to people, which is lasting, useful or purposeful. On the one hand, the information technology facilitates data creation, processing, storing and transmitting at greater speed, but, on the other hand, requires competent filtering and efficient handling and management of recorded information and knowledge available in various forms.

A library is an institution that is established by democratic society with a view to collect, preserve and to make available sources of documented knowledge to people for their self-education and learning. Fulfilling the requirements of the library members relating to the sources of recorded knowledge and information they need is the mission of a library, which is never going to change. Further, as an institution it is never going to be without walls. Even purely digital (electronic) library will have defined clientale and shall possess physical collection of electronic reading materials. A traditional library, digital library or mix type is supposed to provide relevant, meaningful or useful knowledge sources to its users, which they need. There has to be some methodology about it, some way of managing the library collection, and persons who know the right way of collecting and organising the sources of knowledge or information, providing bibliographic information about these sources and make physically available the items, the library users require. For this purpose, we need human experts or intermediaries who can extract, analyse, process, compress and repack qualitative and relevant information from the jungle of information, and make it available to library users, with the help of information technology or with out it.

The people who have been traditionally involved in organisation, processing and retrieval of recorded knowledge or information are known as librarians, documentalists, knowledge organisers or information scientists. They were the first information or knowledge management specialists who developed various theoretical approaches and techniques for organising, storing, and retrieving information about the sources of information on a given subject or field of study for the use of the library users.

With the coming of information technology, new brand of information technology professionals have arrived on the scene, who design and construct computer hardware, software and information systems of various domains. These specialists or information scientists have also built a theoretical base and created practical tools and techniques to construct information systems components.

In the present scenario computer-based library systems planning, design, development, and implementation strategy demands the convergence or unification of various library theoretical-approaches, tools, techniques, processes etc. and computer-based systems modelling and development techniques, in such a manner so that one can use and apply them more fruitfully and holistically. The convergence of computerised system development approaches and library methodologies, in the context of using electronic technology and its applications in the libraries, will enable us to achieve enhanced benefits or better results in our endeavour to develop better library systems and services on modern lines.

The use and application of computer technology in library and information science domain demands that we must have a fresh look at our traditional library tools and techniques, courses of studies, and teaching methodology and concentrate in these areas. There should be much interest to find the practical solutions to the problems faced in the implementation and use and application information technology in libraries and disseminate the findings. The library and information science is basically an applied science, and we must concentrate on applied areas and transfer of technology for library use to achieve the basic mission of a library.

We must also apply system approach and ***take holistic or gestalt type view of a library system*** while ***designing and developing computer-based library information systems and services.*** According to this approach one must examine, structure, design and implement the computer-based activities or functions of a library system holistically, keeping in view that though each sub-unit or subsystem of the organisation is functionally independent of all others, their computerised activities or functions get more intermixed or amalgamated. It implies, while designing computer-based library systems and services one need to look and structure its activities or transaction processing system not in isolation of each other, but as an interrelated and integrated whole.

We also need to improve the theoretical approaches, tools and techniques of library and information science, and interpolate the relevant theoretical and practical approaches of information technology to evolve new ones. We must identify and define the core area of library science and its peripheral domains, and make efforts to contribute and develop significant theoretical and practical knowledge base. We must move a step further from Ranganathan and improve the tools and techniques developed by him to meet the challenges of information technology and its application in library domain.

The computerisation of library systems and services is a highly complex process. The first prerequisites in seriously considering computerisation is to study examine or analyse the current operations and functions of the library, carefully and systematically. This step is taken, first, to identify the functions, tasks or processes that may be automated; second, to explore various ways and means so that the automation of the identified libraryoperations or task systems may lead to significant improvement in the library services, at the least cost. It involves a systematic critical examination of existing ways of doing library work and to develop more effective and easier methods to provide library services with the aid of information technology.

The systematic analysis of a library system may reveal to us the areas that need to be automated and those that simply are showing bad results partly due to either careless handling by the staff and/or ambiguities in the procedures and policies of the library. Often, the weakness or ineffectiveness in a manual system is not because it is manual but rather due to the way in which tasks are defined and the workload is organised and handled by the staff. Nevertheless, the results of the analysis help us to formulate the exact ideas regarding what we need or expect from the automated systems and design them accordingly.

Because of the increasing complexity, any modern library needs professional staff that must prove their capabilities in solving problems of a complex nature and improve effectiveness of the library system. For this purpose, they must involve themselves in high level planning and sound decision-making, instead of being merely capable of solving problems concerning daily administration, (e.g., in the running and control of day-to-day library operations). They must show proficiency in constructive planning, problems solving and decision making. They must possess requisite technical knowledge and expertise to ensure wise allocation and use of resources, and to develop and introduce innovative methods and measures to improve library effectiveness under ever changing and difficult environmental conditions.

The management of a modern complex organisation demand that librarians must not simply depend only on firsthand experience or on a heuristic approach (i.e., a trial and error approach based upon common sense), but must also rely on scientific and analytic approaches in solving library problems and designing and developing effective systems and services. They must set goals for specific jobs to be accomplished, analyse the problems being faced by them objectively, look for various alternative solutions or courses of action, choose the best or most suitable one from among the alternatives available to them and implement the chosen course of action. Later, they should evaluate the results of their actions to find out what must further be done or what further changes are desirable to implement the system.

Viewed from the above perspective, one systematic and scientific method of solving organisational problems is the systems approach (also known as systems analysis and design technique or systems re-engineering technique). This incipient and evolving methodology is based on systems thinking or systems philosophy and employs pertinent concepts from General Systems Theory in solving real-world problems of applied or practical nature. The tenets of systems theory are specifically used to design and develop information technology based library systems.

The systems analysis and design is a powerful systems management and re-engineering technique that is widely used these days:

— to recognise the problems causing ill-conditions, disruptions or malfunctioning of an organisation, and

— to conceive and design an explicit framework for improving or bringing the effectiveness and efficiency of the organisation to an optimum level. That is, to bring it closer to the way in which it should be functioning.

The entire attempt is carried out:

— to improve the procedures, quality of work, economy in human efforts.

— to bring improvement in the use of materials, equipment and work force,

— to bring improvement in the functional relationships in the organisation, and

— to augment faster decision making and a healthy work environment.

The library systems analysis, design and development technique involves the study of a present library system with a view to identify and define the exact problem (issue) by way of collecting all the facts about the problem, analysing or examining the collected facts critically and dispassionately, finding possible solutions to the problem or options for change, evaluation of alternative solutions, selecting and implementing the one that is most suitable, assess the results and take corrective measures or bring modification in the implemented system's solution, if necessary.

With the support of library systems analysis and design technique librarians can streamline library operations, eliminate unnecessary or overlapping procedures, articulate or design new and better library techniques, and improve the general effectiveness of their libraries.

The expertise in systems analysis and design technique and the related tools is prerequisite if one has to design computer-based library information systems (also called computer-based library management systems and services) or to re-engineer the exiting working system.

The term library information system or management system refers to the computer-based library functional or transaction processing system designed to provide bibliographic services to library members, to support the e-library staff to carry out their operational and management activities and decision functions. Information is resource, produced by information systems. Information systems of a library (one comprehensive information system or a federation of information systems) produce two kinds of information. Fist kind is bibliographic information that is vital to the library users and a second kind is management information that facilitates the operation and management control of the library system and is vital for the library staff to carry out their day-to-day activities.

Systems design is the general and detailed specification of computer solutions selected during systems analysis process. Computer programmers to develop application programs and database administrators for database systems implementations typically use the systems design specifications.

To develop computer programs about a process or system to be computerised, one has to break down the process into simple logical steps, taking care that every condition and every possible action has been specified. This is necessary so that a programmer can translate the algorithms of the systems or processes into a symbolic language for computer processing. The detailed logical statements or instructions showing how a particular library operation is to be carried out can be prepared by a librarian, who is not only well versed with the processes of a library, but also possesses expertise in library systems analysis technique and tools such as survey methodology, statistical methods, structured techniques including decision-table construction methodology and various diagramming techniques.

The purpose of this book is, therefore: to give accounts of systems theory to help you to understand the process of systems analysis and design as well as to design better information technology-based systems in libraries; to describe the methodology for conducting systems study; and, to explain the use and application of systems analysis and design tools and techniques. This book is written keeping in mind the practising librarians who are faced with the responsibility of evaluating library programs and procedures to identify the problem areas, that is, the situations where there are gaps or deviations between what is expected, what could or should be and find means to bridges the gaps. The second audience to whom thus book is addressed is the library and information science students who may join a course in Computer Application in Libraries, Library Systems Analysis and Design or Library Systems Study and Re-engineering Technique and Library Database Design and Development Approach.

In keeping with the foregoing, in this book we discuss:

— What systems philosophy is?

— The systems classes and their characteristics.

— Systems concepts and a view of the library as a system,

— Systems analysis and design methodology: A systematic approach for the design and re-engineering of library systems

— Computer based library information or management systems.

— Prototypical design of a library subsystem, as case study.

— Important methods and tools required for conducting system analysis and development studies.

This book is about an applied technique, so the question may arise in the mind of some as to why start with the topics theoretical in nature namely, systems philosophy, system classes and fundamental systems concepts. Systems analysis and design (re-engineering or development) is not purely a practical activity, but very much an art. We start with the basics and if you understand the basic systems concepts and philosophy, you will be able to apply effectively and with confidence, the practical tools and techniques we introduce.

In this revised edition we made certain changes, wherever they were necessary, and introduced an additional chapters.

M. M. Kashyap

"... I find the book very strong in covering various systems analysis, techniques, with examples drawn from automated library systems. This is really quite excellent. I believe this will be very useful in teaching the subject in library and information science schools. The discussions will also be found very useful by systems librarians and also computer systems specialists developing library automation systems and solutions.

The book will also be found very useful by digital library specialists in improved understanding of traditional library automated systems, particularly the systematic view of the library, a perception often lacking among many digital library developers, particularly those with strong computer science background. Fortunately, it is being increasingly acknowledged that digital libraries need to imbibe many features of traditional library systems. - thus the initial chapters of this book will be very useful to those developing digital libraries as well".

Dr. T.B. Rajashekar
Associate Chairman
Nastional Centre for Science Information
Indian Institure of Science, Bangalore.

A
Systems Philosophy

1 INTRODUCTION

Man has an innate urge to know, to find out how and why the world is as it is. To gain knowledge of the world around us, nature has provided us with the forceful means of observing the world (our senses) and for thinking about the world rationally (our brain mechanism). To understand and explain the complexities of the world or to gain knowledge about the various phenomena of the world, man has also developed certain theories or philosophical approaches, such as, speculative, positivist, reductionist or elementalist modes of thinking. The systems philosophy is one such philosophical approach or paradigm. It is a way of thinking or looking at the empirical world according to which one may view the individual phenomena of the world as interrelated, interconnected systems, integrated wholes rather than isolated ones.

According to systems philosophy, any entity (abstract or concrete) consists of interconnected and interrelated elements or units that form an organised complex whole. Besides, the entities or phenomena of the world exhibit certain "uniqueness of characteristics as a whole, they cannot be simply reduced to the properties of their individual parts" [**Laszlo**, 16; See also **Laszlo**, 14]. For example, an atom is other than the sum of the component particles taken individually and added together. A nation is other than the sum of individual beings composing it. The taste of water, for example, is a property of water, not of the elements hydrogen and oxygen that combine to form it.

Systems thinking rejects the concept of dualism of body and mind, man and nature, individual and society, atom and molecule, and cell and organ, and provides an integrated conception of the universe as a dynamic organisation of many levels, e.g., cells (systems) making up a living organism at macro-level (suprasystems) compared with the micro-level (subsystems) of molecules making up the cell, exhibiting a complexity of details, yet within the ambit of a harmony. However, the claim is that things work in quite different ways at different levels. For example, chemistry cannot explain biology and biology cannot explain chemistry completely.

The systems approach postulates that objects or phenomena of the empirical world are regarded as a system composed of interrelated, interdependent and dynamically linked components (subordinate entities) that create a whole entity, encompassed by an environment (or suprasystem), and interfacing with other related objects (or systems) composed of multitudes of sub-wholes (subsystems). Atoms are composed of elementary particles. Molecules comprise a multitude of atoms. Cells are composed of a multitude of molecules and organs of cells. Our society consists of a multitude of people in some form of interaction and intercommunication. A system in one perspective is a subsystem in another perspective. In brief, systems philosophy postulates that one must regard the living or nonliving objects of the empirical world as purposeful or purposive systems, which are coherently organised wholes composed of interacting, interdependent and integrated sub-wholes, interfacing with other related wholes, and which are enclosed by an environment or suprasystem.

This scientific approach "contrasts with the ***classical method (Newtonian)*** in science, which regarded any object of scientific investigation as a collection of isolated parts and tried to derive the properties of the whole object directly from the properties of its parts without considering any possible interaction between the parts." [**Klir**, 12] The classical (Newtonian) method in science, also known as analytical or atomistic based on ***mechanism***[1] and ***reductionism*** (or *elementalism*) was successful in explaining the phenomena of the physical world, but did not explain fully biological or social phenomena that display "***organised complexity***"[2] and a structure coupled with varied interaction.

Because of the failure of the mechanistic, reductionistic or elementalistic approach to account for the characteristics of living beings fully, a new organismic, holistic or integrative approach that could account for the phenomena of living systems has come to the fore. This approach proceeds according to the principle of *irreducibility* of the complex to simple or of the whole to its parts. The integrated object is deemed to have attributes that are not found in its constituent parts, and it has its own purpose and mode of action that cannot be derived from those of its elements or parts. The systems approach embodies this new method of thinking. Its approach is applicable specifically to the realm of biological and behavioural world as also to the realm of the physical world.

Systems philosophy is not new, in the sense that ancient Indian philosophers had proposed the concepts of 'holism' or 'unity' in diversity. Aristotle argued, "A whole is more than the sum of its parts".

The German Philosopher **Hegel** (1776-1831) said [**Schoderbeck**, 21]:

1. The whole is more than the sum of the parts.
2. The whole determines the nature of its parts.
3. The parts cannot be understood if considered in isolation from the whole.
4. The parts are dynamically interrelated or interdependent.

Ancient Indian seers (*Rishis*) believed: "In this universe all things are connected. There is one integrated existence. The moment you effect the slightest change in the order of things, you effect equal change within your own selves".

We find that systems philosophy, as it stands today, has evolved progressively, from the philosophical contributions of ancient Indian philosophers and western philosophers like Plato and Aristotle, and through the scholastic metaphysics of the Middle Age and the scientific outlook of the 17th Century.

The 'modern' discussion on this philosophy started in the later 19th and early 20th centuries with the emergence of the school of biology known as '*organismic*' school of thought and had a significant impact on its development. Oganismic biologists considered the 'organism' as the irreducible object to which a purely analytical or mechanical approach cannot explain away. In biology, the so-called organismic concepts were chiefly directed against mechanism. "In the controversy with mechanism the supporters of organismic concepts proceeded upon the assumption that integrative characteristics (those belonging to the whole), are not reducible from elementalist considerations." [**Blauberg**, 4]

2 GENERAL SYSTEMS THEORY

2.1 Introduction

The debate initiated by organismic biologists during the second half of the 19th century continued throughout the 20th century. Its modern form is known as ***systems theory*** or ***thinking***. The first tentative exposition of systems thinking was given by **C.D. Broad** in his work: ***The mind and its place in nature,*** 1923; by **J.C. Smuts** in his work: ***Holism and evolution***, 1926; and, by **J.H. Woodger** in his work: ***Biological principles***, 1929. Philosophers, such as, **F.H. Bradley** [5] and **Alfred North Whitehead** [27] and many other scientists and scholars belonging to different fields of study also contributed to the development of systems philosophy. Later, **Ludwig Von Bertalanffy**, a renowned biologist, in the mid 1940's pioneered a generalised organism thinking (the system theory of the organism, as he called it) and later thinking concerned with systems in general. In 1954, he spearheaded the General Systems Theory Movement and also helped to found the Society for the Advancement of General System Theory, later renamed as the Society for General Systems Research [*cf.*, **Von Bertalanffy**, 22-26]. It may be appropriate to mention here that some consider **Alexander A. Bogdanov** (1873-1928), a Russian scientist, is the originator of the truly generalised systems theory. Bogdanov developed the ***general theory of systems organisations*** a basic and original work and published it in Russia under the title ***'Tektologia'***, Vols. 1-3 (1912-27), several years before Von Bertalanffy proposed thc theory restricted to biology and aimed at what we would consider a synthesis between the two opposing biological theories 'biological mechanism' and 'vitalism' he christened 'organismic biology', and published in 1928. [*cf.*, **Mattessich**, 18]

General systems theory is an interdisciplinary field of study elaborating models, principles and laws that apply to all systems irrespective of their particular kind, the nature of their component elements and the relation and '*forces*' involved between them. In the broadest sense, it refers to a collection of general concepts, principles, methods, tools, techniques and issues associated with systems.

General systems theory provides a basis for understanding and integrating knowledge from many specialised fields. In the past, traditional knowledge had developed along well-defined subject matter lines; systems theorists suggest that various fields of knowledge have had continual evolution towards a parallelism of ideas. This parallelism provides an opportunity to formulate and develop principles that hold for the study of all phenomena or objects in general. General systems theory provides the over all broad view from which we may look at all types of phenomena or objects (Concrete or Abstract) as systems. The entire work going on in the General Systems Theory can be broadly divided into two channels: one, the development of systems philosophy *per se* and second, the application of systems thinking with in other domains.

Explaining exactly how this theory relates to a specific problem in a specific discipline, **A. Orchard Robert** states: "a formulation of a problem is actually a point of view taken by an investigator concerning the problem. If he wishes to use a certain general systems theory, he must define a system on the underlying phenomena (i.e., take a point of view), which coincides with the system definition encompassed by the particular general systems theory. It is important to note that the *point of view* is one that looks at the original problem in its systematic aspects. The system which is eventually defined on it, takes into account only those basic traits of systems which are present in the collection of system definitions in the general systems theory being used; hence, the results of any investigation by use of the theory will, of necessity, yield information of a systematic nature only." [**Robert**, 20].

Systems philosophy, as it stands today, reintegrates "the concept of enduring universals with transient processes within a non-bifurcated, hierarchically differentiated realm of invariant systems, as the ultimate actualistics of self structuring nature. Its data come from the empirical sciences; its problems from the history of philosophy; and its concepts from modern system research" [**Laszlo**, 15]

The systems movement has opened new vistas for viewing man and nature in a new perspective. It has exercised its influence on the directions, methods of the study and designs of specific systems in various fields of modern science, technology and practical activity. The systems approach, which is a way of tackling a problem based on systems thinking, is being increasingly applied to problem solving, scientific investigations, analysing and designing man-made systems. One can also use this approach for planning and management of human activity systems or organisations. When a person applies the *systems vision* or *approach* in analysing, evaluating and designing a system, or solving a system's problem, he provides himself with a fitting theoretical framework. This framework helps him in visualising the entirety of a problem and seeking the complete solution of the issue in hand. His attention is focused on interactions, interrelationships and integration factors of all elements of a system even when a change in only one or a few of its parts is contemplated.

In brief, systems approach demands that one should consider the following factors while planning a project, designing a system, or solving a problem:

a. The whole is primary and the parts are secondary.

b. Integration is the condition of the interrelatedness of the many parts within one.

c. The parts so constitute an indissoluble whole that no part can be affected without affecting all other parts.

d. Parts play their role in the light of the purpose for which the whole exists (i.e., Objectives of the total system are more important than the objectives of its elements).

e. The nature of a part and its function is derived from its position in the whole and its behaviour is related by the part relationship.

f. The whole is any system, simple or a complex configuration of energy like a single piece of an element, no matter how complex.

g. Everything should start with the whole as a premise and parts and their relationships should evolve. [Luchsinger, 17]

2.2 The System Picture of the World and Systems Classes

According to systems thinking the world consists of a hierarchy of interconnected and interrelated unitary wholes called *systems*. A pebble, a mountain, a forest, a galaxy, a cell, a man, an animal, a family, a nation, a state, a university, a hospital, a city, a library and so on, all are systems. Each of these entities or individual objects exhibits behaviour and is considered to be related in some way to the environment of the other associated entity or phenomenon; that is, with other individuals or systems with which it comes into contact or into some relationship. Each entity or individual system is thought of as consisting of a structure-complex of individual sub-systems of the order below it. Based on the systems hypothesis, several attempts have been made by systems theorists to survey the whole of the world in systems terms, and to describe and classify the possible types of systems. So far, there is no generally accepted classification of systems, and many suggestions reflect a particular outlook, interest or purpose. Nevertheless, the general idea about classes of systems and their specific features and characteristics are useful, which we shall discuss in the next part of this chapter.

Out of the various attempts made to describe and classify possible types of systems, the more significant ones are the general accounts of systems types given by **Boulding** [6] and **Checkland** [7]. Both have tried to view the whole world in systems terms.

2.3 Boulding's Hierarchy of Systems Complexity

Keneth E. Boulding [6] provides the systems picture of the world by arrangement of individual 'objects' or 'units' of empirical studies or disciplines into a hierarchy of systems, by their degree of complexity. Boulding singles out nine levels in such a hierarchy, starting from the static structures and ending with the 'transcendental systems', which, in his words, include 'the ultimate and absolutes and the inescapable unknowable' (*Refer* **Table 1,** given below, for details).

2.4 Checkland's Classes of Systems

Checkland identifies five classes of systems, namely; (i) Natural Systems, (ii) Designed Physical Systems, (iii) Designed Abstract Systems, (iv) Human Activity Systems, and (v) Transcendental Systems - Beyond knowledge.

i. Natural Systems

This class includes all animate and inanimate beings, objects and phenomena of nature perceived or inferred from observation and existing independently of the observer. These range from the subatomic system of nuclei as described by physics, through the physical framework of this and other planets and living systems (including man) observed on the earth, to the galactic systems at the other extreme. According to **Checkland** [9], "The natural systems are the evolution made, irreducible wholes which an observer can observe and describe as such, being made of other entities having natural relationships. They are '*irreducible*' in the sense that meaningful statements can be made about them as wholes, and this remains true even if we can describe their components and the relationships between the components with some precision. Carbon-dioxide is not reducible in this sense to carbon and oxygen, in that (i.e., in carbon dioxide) however, much we know inter-atomic distances and bond angles, carbon dioxide remains a higher level whole having properties of its own."

We can further subdivide the natural systems according to criteria, whether they are living or non-living. Living systems are

Table 1

Level	Characteristics	Objects	Relevant Discipline
1. Frameworks	Static structure	Crystals; Bridges; Cells; Plants.	The accurate description of static structures/ frameworks of the object or phenomenon (e.g., the patterns of atoms in a crystal, the anatomy of a gene, etc.). The beginning of the organised theoretical knowledge in any field.
2. Clockworks	Pre-determined motion; Simple equilibrium; Clocks; Machines; The solar system; Modern view of the atom; Simple dynamic system.	Physics; Astronomy; Classical Natural Sciences	
3. Control mechanism.	Close-loop control. Transmission and interpretation of information is essential part of the system	Thermostat, homeostasis mechanism in organism.	Control theory; Cybernetics.
4. Open systems	Structurally self-maintaining in the midst of a throughput of material and energy.	Flames; Cells.	Theory of metabolism.
5. Genetic-Societal	Organised whole with functionally dependent parts (roots, leaves, seeds etc.). Equifinal of blue printed growth. No highly specialised sense organs and information receptors. Reproduction.	Plants	Botany (Lower organism)

Level	Characteristics	Objects	Relevant Discipline
6. Animal Kingdom.	A brain to guide total behaviour. Ability to learn. Increased mobility. Teleological behaviour and Self-awareness. Specialised information receptors (eyes, ears, etc.)	Birds and Beasts	Zoology.
7. Man	Self-consciousness. Self- reflexive quality. He not only knows. but also knows that he knows, i.e., possessing knowledge of knowledge. Phenomena of language and symbolism.	Human beings.	Human Biology; Psychology.
8. Socio-cultural systems	Roles. Channels of communications.	Transmission of values Families; Clubs; Nations; Libraries.	History; Sociology; Anthropology. Behavioural Sciences.
9. Transcendental systems.	The Ultimates, Absolutes, and the inescapable. Unknowable.	God? Atma (Soul)?	Spiritualism; Mysticism.

Note In the table above

1. Complexity increases from level 1 to 9.
2. Emergent properties arise at each defined level; that is, the more complex systems at higher levels manifest more characteristics than the sum of the characteristics of their units or parts at lower level.

those endowed with biological functions such as birth, death and reproduction. They are open systems and use inputs of food or fuels from the environment to restore their energy and to repair breakdowns in their structure. They have a decider - the essential critical component or subsystem that control the entire system, causing its subsystems and components to interact. Further, their subsystems are integrated together to shape into dynamic, self-regulating, developing, reproducing unitary systems, with purposes and goals. Every physical system that does not have the characteristics of a living system is a nonliving system, such as a mountain, a pebble, an atom, a river, and so on. They are closed systems, do not exchange energy with the environment, and have the tendency to rundown or to decompose.

NOTE: *Sometimes one uses terms such as birth and death to describe lifelike processes of nonliving systems, although they have no life in biological sense as found in the plant and animal cells. However, one can well understand the implication or meaning of the terms, when we make such statements, in the context of a nonliving system. What we mean is that the system has taken birth (i.e. created by nature or man) or has decayed, disintegrated or decomposed.*

ii. Designed Physical or Concrete Systems

This class includes man-made systems, the class stretching from hammers, clocks, and carts to space rockets. People design these systems to serve some given human purpose or because of the need for them in some human activity system.

iii. Designed Abstract Systems

Man, as a designer not only designs physical artefacts but also can construct conceptual or abstract systems, such as logic, number systems, poems, or philosophies. They represent the ordered conscious product of the human mind. Although they are in themselves abstract systems, one can capture, portray or provide picture of them in designed physical systems such as books, films, and records of all types. In an abstract system the elements are created by defining, and relationship between them are created by assumptions (e.g., through axioms and postulates). [*cf.*, **Ackoff**, 1]

Further, they exist because of a man's positive act related to some objective. The objective may be elucidation or the enlargement of knowledge about something, or to fulfil an inner urge to express the inexpressible. All abstract systems are non-living and man-made systems.

iv Human Activity Systems

A human activity system is a purposeful system that expresses some purposeful human activity. At one extreme is a very simple system consisting of one man wielding a hammer at some one or to accomplish something else, and at the other extreme, are the very complex national or international political systems. What every system of this class has in common is that it consists of several activities linked together as a whole and fulfils some human purpose or mission. A human activity system is basically constituted of human and what every member of a system has in common is that he/she may be involved in some or several activities of the system linked together and carry out his/her activities jointly with others with a view to fulfiling some human purposes or mission, common to all. There are innumerable numbers of human activity systems observable in the world. The range covered by this class of system is very large indeed.

The concept of human activity system, as explained by **Checkland,** is crucially different from the concept of natural and designed systems. These latter systems, once they are created or originate 'could not be other than what they are' but human activity systems can manifest only as perceived by human actors who are free to attribute meaning to what they perceive.

Ackoff points out, "both organisms and organisations (human activity systems) are purposeful systems; organisms do not contain purposeful elements. The elements of an organism may be state maintaining, goal seeking, multigoal seeking, or purposive, but not purposeful. Thus, an organism must be variety increasing. An organisation, on the other hand, may be either variety increasing or decreasing (e.g., the ineffective committee). In an organism only the whole can display will; none of the part." [**Ackoff**, 1]

v. *Transcendental Systems*

Systems, beyond natural, designed physical, designed abstract and human activity systems belong to this category. Transcendental systems are the systems beyond knowledge or the systems relating to the phenomena (i.e., God, Ghost, and Soul) beyond human experience or knowledge. Though perhaps, not beyond potential knowledge or intuitively be aware of their existence.

After providing the general accounts about systems types as specified by **Boulding** and **Checkland** we may now describe various categories of systems, based on different criteria for classification.

3 TYPES OF SYSTEMS

Classification is the first step in developing a theory or to understand the characteristics of things. To use the systems approach as a method for analysing and designing complex systems, such a system must be characterised and classified. In the following sections of the book we describe in detail the various recognised classes of systems or types of systems and their characteristics.

3.1 Conceptual or Abstract Systems

An abstract system is one in which all the elements are concepts; languages, philosophic systems and number systems are examples.

NOTE: It may be noted that numbers are concepts but the symbols that represent them, that is, the numerals are physical objects. Numerals, however, are not the elements of a number system. The use of different forms of numerals to represent the same number does not change their value. Whether we choose Devanagari form or Roman form to represent those numbers, their values remain the same.

By defining we give shape to the elements of an abstract system and relationships among them are formed by assumptions (e.g., axioms and postulates). Such systems, therefore, are subjects of study of formal sciences. All abstract systems are nonliving and man-made systems. [*cf.*, **Ackoff** 1; **Miller**, 19]

vi. *Abstracted Systems*

Very often when we use *models* or *abstract or theoretical description* of physical entities, situations or operational problems, we may call them abstracted systems. (*cf*., **Miller**, 19.)

3.2 Concrete or Physical Systems

A concrete system is one; at least two of whose elements are physical objects [cf., **Ackoff**, 1]. A concrete system is a non-random accumulation of matter energy in a region in physical space-time, which is organised into interacting, interrelated subsystems or parts.

The subsystems (units, components, parts or members) of these systems are also concrete systems (*cf*., **Hall and Fagen**, 10, **Miller**, 19). In case of concrete systems, to establish the nature or properties of their elements and nature of relationships that exist among their parts requires empirical research. Such systems, therefore, are the subject of study of the so-called '*non-formal sciences*'. The concrete systems can be natural or man-made.

3.3 Natural and Man-Made Systems

Systems are either natural or man-made. Natural systems are part of nature and purposive. One can further subdivide the natural systems according to whether they are living or non-living. Man-made systems are either *abstract* or *concrete*. An *abstract system* is an orderly arrangement of components, all of which are concepts. For example, number systems, languages, are abstract man-made systems. A concrete system is one in which at least two components are objects. There are two main classes of concrete systems:

1. *Physical Systems*: A physical system comprise a set of physical components that operate together to accomplish an object, e.g., a computer hardware system, a railway track, and like.
2. *Human Activity Systems*: A human activity system or a social system is an organised group and co-ordinated group of people who operate together to achieve common purpose or goal, e.g. social organisations, such as a library, a university and so on.

3.3.1 Natural systems

Any entity of the universe that does not owe its existence to conscious human planning and execution is a natural system — including human beings and many social (multi-persons) organisations in which he /she participates. It is part of the universe, not man-made, which an observer elects to treat as a whole entity having emergent properties. Further, natural systems can be (i) living, such as plants, animals, and human beings. They are open systems, exist in dynamic environments and use inputs of foods or fuels to restore their own energy and repair breakdown with their supra-systems and subsystems. Natural systems can also be (ii) nonliving such as mountain, pebble, atom, river, and so on. They are closed systems, do not exchange energy with environment when in a state of equilibrium, and have the tendency to run down or to degrade.

3.3.2 Man-made systems

A man-made entity, which a designer or observer elects to treat as a whole having emergent properties. Designed systems may be concrete (e.g., clock, computer, railway engine) or abstract (e.g. mathematics, language, Vedanta philosophy). Man-made systems display many properties of natural systems and are often their replications or extensions of great magnitude or scale. These are designed by man to be more adaptive, in the sense that they help man to cope with his environment. Part man-made and part natural systems include production systems, socio-technical systems and other human activity systems.

3.4 Open and Closed Systems

Systems have also been categorised as *closed* and *open* systems. **Von Bertalanffy** [22-26] first introduced the concepts of open and closesd systems and later elaborated by many other authors. This classification may be regarded as a primary one in systems theory.

According to Bertalanffy, a system is called *closed* if there is neither *inflow* nor *outflow* of matter in it (only possible energy exchange is considered). As opposed to this, there are continual input and output of both energy and matter in an open system.

Further, *open systems* demonstrate characteristics of purposiveness, arrive at final state or condition from different initial conditions and different ways, maintain themselves in steady state, can avoid increase of entropy, and may even develop towards states of increased order and organisations.

Later on, **Klir** and **Valach** [13] bifurcated the notion of the closed system into those of absolutely closed systems and the relatively closed systems (i.e., closed against certain influences). According to them:

a. An ***absolutely closed system*** is one that has no environment; that is, in whose case no interaction between the system and the environment is to be considered or no outside system impinges on it.

b. A ***relatively closed system*** is one in which the ways the environment acts on the system and the system acts on the environment are strictly defined.

c. An ***open system*** is one in which one considers all possible effects of the environment and vice-versa.

However, observing that it is impossible to imagine a system capable of receiving and responding to any number of inputs of the environment or vice-versa, **Miller** [19] points out that no system is completely closed or open, systems are either relatively open or relatively closed; and defines open systems and closed systems in the following terms:

"***Open system***: Most concrete systems have boundaries, which are at least partially permeable, permitting sizeable magnitudes of at least certain sort of matter-energy or information transmission to cross them. Such a system is an open system. Such inputs can repair system components that break down and replace the energy that is used up".

"***Closed system***: A closed system is a concrete system with impermeable boundaries through which no matter-energy or information transformations of any sort can occur is a closed system. No actual concrete system is completely closed, so concrete systems are either relatively open or relatively closed. Whatever matter-energy happens to be within the system is all there is going to be. The energy is gradually used up and the matter gradually becomes disorganised. A body in a hermetically sealed casket, for instance, slowly crumbles and its component molecules become intermingled. Separate layers of liquid organs in a container move towards random distribution. Gravity may present entirely random arrangement".

However, **Katz** and **Kahn** [11] present a comprehensive picture of the common characteristics of open systems. According to them open systems have the following attributes:

1. ***Importation of energy*** : Open systems import some forms of energy from the external environment. For example, a cell receives oxygen from the blood stream; the body similarly takes in oxygen from the air and food from the external world. Similarly, we find that social organisations must draw a renewed supply of energy from the society or from the environment. No social structure is self-sufficient or self-contained.
2. ***The throughput*** : Open systems transform and import some form of energy from the external environment. For example, the body converts starch and sugar into heat and action. The organisation creates a new product, or processes materials, educates and train people, or provides a service. These activities entail some reorganisation of input.
3. ***The output*** : Open systems export some product into the environment whether it is the invention of an inquiring mind or a bridge constructed by an engineering firm. Even the biological organisms export physiological products such as carbon dioxide from the lung that helps to maintain plants in the immediate environment.
4. ***Cycle of events*** : The pattern of activities in the energy exchange has a cyclic character. The product exported into the environment by one system furnishes the sources of energy for the repetition of the cycle. For example, the carbon dioxide,

which humans and animals breathe out or export in to the environment is converted by the plants into oxygen, which again becomes energy input for animals and human beings, who breathe it in.

3.3.1 Open systems

The open system is one that has an environment with which it exchanges energy or matter and information. That is, it *inputs* some form of *energy* or *matter* and *information* from the environment and *transforms* (or *throughputs*) the energy or matter available to it in some way, and *outputs* some products into the environment. Further, the pattern of activities of the energy exchange has a *cyclic character* - that is, it gets re-energised from sources in the environment. So, an open system can be defined as one that is highly dependent upon environment or external forces, and whose growth and/or survival depends on constant interchange with environmental factors. [*cf.*, Von Bertalanffy, 29-32; Klir, 14; Katz and Kahn, 11]

Open system also shares the characteristics of negative-entropy feedback, steady state, differentiation, Equifinality and teleology [*cf.*, Von Bertanlanffy, 29, 30, 32; Koehleer, 15; Katz and Khan, 11). We explain these concepts below:

i. ***Negative-entropy*** **:** Open systems resist the tendency towards disorder and move towards increased organisation - a state of greater organisation or negentropic state. This action results from a favourable balance in the exchange of energy and information between the system and environment.

ii. ***Feedback*** **:** Feedback is informative input a special energetic input. It is a kind of signal to the system about environmental conditions and about the functioning of the system in relation to its environment. The feedback enables the system to correct its own malfunctioning due to changes in the environment or otherwise and thus, maintains its steady state or homeostasis. This is a dynamic rather than a static balance or equilibrium. Feedback is an essential requisite for effective control of the system in order to regulate its components in interaction so that the systems objectives are finally realised. A system changes due to feedback, which are of several types, such as:

Positive feedback (i.e., the amplifying processes that take the system ever farther from its original state).

Negative feedback (i.e., counteracting processes that stabilise the system).

Feedforward (i.e., anticipating and correcting processes that anticipate and help to correct discrepancies or take the system forward).

The feedback can be deterministic, probabilistic, or random.

iii. ***Steady State***: A steady state is condition of dynamic equilibrium. In this state a system maintains its structure as invariant or stable, despite fluctuation in environmental conditions. Open systems maintain steady state (*dynamic equilibrium or homeostasis*) through the continuous inflow of materials, energy and information. In a steady state, the amount of energy consumed in system co-ordination or in the system functioning or work is precisely replaced or substituted by new energy or resources drawn from the environment. Further, in the presence of a stimulus (feedback) from the external environment or internal environment, it re-establishes itself in a steady state either by modifying its own functioning or modifying the environment. For example, a living organism maintains a fixed level of blood sugar, blood protein, and fats in continuous and varying intake of foods, external condition of humidity and temperature may vary, but its body temperature remains the same.

Open systems can also adapt due to alterations in environmental conditions through elaboration. During adaptation the various functions of open system can become quite complex and often develop specialised parts to perform different functions. The process is known as differentiation.

Open systems are primarily complex systems that organise themselves to maintain the dynamic equilibrium or steady state. "The mechanism through which complex systems organise themselves is, to a large extent, through a set of interlocking feedback loops. *Part A* effects *part B*, and *part B* effects *part A* and then they continue to interact until each is in the region of stability under the conditions provided by the other. The law of requisite variety makes explicit the amount of control a given part can have on another part. In particular, the law of requisite variety shows that we can forget some powerful, unitary part of a system as a major (or the only) regulator of all the system. For instance, a dictator with life and death control over all of his or her own regulatory capabilities with a large secret police force, etc., in the process of achieving regulation over these aspects of the system, the dictator typically (and increasingly over the time) loses control over system aspects such as loyalty of the citizens, legitimacy of his/her rule and ability of the system to innovate, grow or change in a positive fashion decreases. And, as loyalty, legitimacy and ability to innovate decrease, the forces of regression grow. In this way the dictator's attempt to impose regulation upon the system sows the seeds of his or her own destruction." [*cf.*, **Clemson**, 7]

iv. ***Differentiation*** **:** To survive, open systems not only adapt to a changing environment but also move in the direction of elaboration and higher level of organisation or growth due to their built in resilience. Growth leads to differentiation of functions and to specialisation. Bertalanffy points out to the continual elaboration of a biological or living organism. He states, "In organic development and evolution, a transition towards a state of higher order and differentiation seems to occur. The tendency towards increasing complication has been indicated as a primary characteristic of living as opposed to inanimate nature." [*cf.*, 12] Thus, integration, synergistic behaviour together with the process of increased organisation and differentiation represents the special feature of open systems. In contrast, closed systems move towards entropy and disorganisation.

v. ***Equifinality*** **:** It is the ability of the open systems to reach a given state or condition by several different paths or means. Open systems arrive at a final state of condition through variations in process and from differing initial states or conditions due to inherent resilience and capability of adjusting itself with changing environment. For instance, the sea Urchin shows that a normal creature of the species can develop from a complete ovum form each half of the divided ovum or from the fusion produced or two whole ova. In contrast, "in any closed system, the final state is unequivocally determined by the initial conditions. If either the initial conditions or the process is altered, the final state will also be changed." (*cf.*, **Bertalanffy**, 31).

vi. ***Teleology*** **:** The empirical systems show three types of goal oriented behaviours: (a) purposive behaviour, (b) purposeful behaviour and (c) purposeless behaviour. The open systems exhibit purposeful behaviour and tend towards defined objectives, which may vary according to particular states of the system in time, and use processes of adaptation, differentiation, growth, feedback and organisation to move towards these goals. Basically three types of goal seeking behaviours are recognised among various types of systems. We define the three above stated systems behaviours defined below:

a) ***Purposive*** (or ***teleonomic***) ***behaviour*** pertains to non-living physical systems (natural or designed) which have a fixed or assigned purpose or which do not have objectives of their own. Such systems can be further split into three types, namely: states maintaining, goal seeking, and purposive. "While the first merely reacts due to change in environment (e.g., a simple thermostat system); the second responds by exercising choices of strategies, but not of goals (e.g., an automatic pilot); the third pursue different goals, without, however, selecting the goal to be pursued (e.g., a computer programmed to play checkers)." [*cf.*, **Mattessich**, 18]

b) ***Purposeful*** (or ***teleological***) ***behaviour*** pertains to open-living systems that can decide how they are going to behave. They display will, and thus choose their own goals, human, human organisations, and the like. **Ackoff** adds another type in this category. Namely, ideal seeking systems or purposeful systems, which attaining their goals move to select another higher mission, ever closer to perfection. Such a purposeful system "is one, which can change its goals under certain conditions, it selects ends as well as means and thus displays will. Human beings are the most familiar examples of such systems". [*cf.*, **Ackoff**, 2]

c) ***Purposeless behaviour*** is aimless behaviour, which is not directed towards the achievement of specific goals. [*cf.*, **Rosenblueth and others**, 25; **Rosenblueth and Wiener**, 26].

vii. ***Hierarchy*****:** Open systems are hierarchical, that is, they are both independent frameworks consisting of several integral lower level parts or subsystems and each is a dependent member of higher-level system or suprasystem. Therefore, the open systems are organised in hierarchies with each level made of several integral subsystems. For example, the cells making up a living organism are at a macro-level (supra-systems) compared with the micro-level of the molecules (subsystems) making up the cells (systems). However, things work in different ways at different levels.

3.3.2 Closed Systems

A close system is one that has no environment, that is. it has no interaction with the elements not contained in it. It is completely self-contained and its internal properties are well buffered against external intrusions. A relatively closed system is one that has least dependence upon environment or has small interaction with elements not contained in it. A close system (or relatively closed system) is characterised by an irreversible process a tendency towards static equilibrium. Further, unlike open systems, it cannot adapt to changes in environment and moves towards positive entropy* (loss of energy), that is, the energy is gradually used up and the system slowly becomes disorganised or inert. Thus, in any close system the amount of order (or organisation) can never increase and must eventually decrease.

Further, in close systems (or inanimate systems) the final state of the system is determined by its initial condition. Any change in the initial condition produces a change in the final condition.

NOTE : The concept of entropy derives from the second law of thermodynamics, which postulates that for a closed system, the quality 'entropy' must increase to the maximum until equilibrium is reached, i.e., a state of lesser organisation (or just randomness or another variant chaos). According to the second law of the thermodynamics, the general trend of events in physical nature is towards a state of maximum disorder and levelling down of differences, that is, the degradation of matter and energy in the universe to an ultimate state of inert uniformity, with this so-called heat death of the universe as a final outlook, when all energy is degraded into evenly, distributed heat of low temperature and the world process comes to a stop. [cf., **Lilienfeld**, 17; **Katz** and **Kahn**, 11].

In contrast, the living world shows in embryonic development, and in evolution, a transition towards higher order, heterogeneity and organisation. Living systems maintaining themselves in steady state can avoid the increase of entropy and may even develop towards states of increased order and organisation. For living systems, positive or maximum entropy means death or extinction of the species. For organisations or human activity systems, maximum entropy could also mean maximum conditions of disorganisation due to a lack of all-necessary information or feedback for running the system.

Having discussed the key concepts of the General Systems Theory, we will consider the library in the framework of systems thinking, in the next section of this Chapter, we shall provide a general definition, characteristics and a broad conceptual model of the library as a system that will be applicable for all types.

4 SUMMARY

The General Systems Theory provides an interdisciplinary approach, elaborating models, principles and laws that apply to all entities (natural or man-made). Application of the systems theory in the study and management of social organisations is considered as a major advance over the traditional approach. The traditional organisation theorists treat an organisation as a closed system consisting of isolated individual units, which can be managed or investigated in isolation. Whereas, the system theorists consider an organisation as an open system, which interacts with its environment and consists of interrelated, interdependent, and integrated units or subsystems.

The systems theory provides us a way to view the total organisation in interaction with its environment and to conceive the relationships among its internal components or subsystems. It demands that one should think for the wholeness properties of organisation, such as, integration, cohesion and its total environment. Thus, for applying the systems '*vision*', '*approach*' or '*paradigm*' in management or solving problems of an organisation, or analysing and evaluating its systems or processes for re-engineering, one needs to be equipped with a sound theoretical framework, which helps in visualising the exact problem of the system as a whole. The correct identification of the problem area helps in finding required solution..

The application of systems approach becomes particularly important when a major change in an organisation is undertaken. This approach guides us to see that the contemplated changes may affect all the units or segments of the organisation. Therefore, one takes a holistic view even while introducing changes in a unit of an organisation. The systems paradigm no doubt offers an effective framework to managers and systems analysts for the analysis and finding solutions to organisational problems, which are becoming increasingly more complex

References and Reading List

1. Ackoff, Russell L. Towards a system of systems concepts. *Management Science*, v.17; July, 1971; p.661-71.
2. —; Emery, Fred E. *On purposeful systems*. 1972. Tovistock Publication, London.
3. Blauberg, I. V.; others. *System theory, philosophical and methodological problems*. 1977. Progress Publishers, Moscow. p. 16
4. —; —. *ibid.* p. 23.
5. Bradley, F.H. *Appearance and reality*. 1962. Oxford University Press.
6. Boulding, Kenneth E. General system theory - the skeleton of science. *Management Science*. v.2(3); 1956; p. 197-208.
7. Checkland, Peter. *System thinking, system practice*. 1981. John Wiley, New York.
8. —. *ibid.* p. 47.
9. —. *ibid.* p. 113.
10. Hall, A. D. and Fagen, R. E. Definition of system. General Systems. *Yearbook for the Society for the Advancement of General Systems Theory*. v.1; 1956; p. 18-28.
11. Katz, D.; Kahn, R. L. Common characteristics of open systems. **In** EMERY (F E), Ed. *System thinking*. 1969. Penguin Books, Harmondsworth, Middlesex. p. 86-104.
12. Klir, George J. Preview: the polyphonic general system theory. **In** KLIR (George J), Ed. *Trends in general systems theory*. 1978. Ed 2. Harper & Row, New York. p. 1- 18.
13. —; Valach, Miroslav. *Cybernetics modelling*. 1967. Lliffe Books.
14. Laszlo, Ervin. *Introduction to system philosophy. Towards a new paradigm of contemporary thought*. 1972. Harper & Row, New York.
15. —. *ibid.* p. 12.
16. —. *The systems view of the world, the natural philosophy of the development of sciences*. 1972. Basil Blackwell, Oxford. p. 8.
17. Luchsinger, Vincent P.; Dock, Thomas V. *The systems approach: A primer*. 1975. Kendal/Hunt, Dubuque, Iowa. p. 16.
18. Mattessich, Richard. The system approach: Its variety of aspects. *Journal of the American Society for Information Science*. Nov.; 1982; p. 383-94.
19. Miller, James G. The nature of living systems. *Behavioural Science*. v. 16; 1971; p. 277-301.
20. Orchard, Robert A. On an approach to general systems theory. **In** KLIR

(G J), Ed. *Trends in general systems theory.* 1972. Interscience, New York. p. 205-50.

21. Schoderbeck, Peter P. Ed. *Management system.* Ed 2. 1957. Wiley, New York. P 55-56.

22. Von, Bertalanffy L. *General System Theory: Foundation, development, and application.* George Braziller, New York. 1968.

23. —. General System Theory. **In** *General systems: Yearbook of the Society of Advancement of General systems.* 1956; p. 1-10

24. —. The history and status of general systems theory. *In* KLIR (G J), ed. *Trends in general systems theory.* 1972. Wiley, New York, p. 21-38.

25. —. The open systems in physics and biology. *Science.* v. 111; 1950; p. 23-9.

26. —. An outline of general system theory. *British Journal of Philosophy of Science.* v. 1; 1950; p. 139-64.

27. Whitehead, Alfred North. *Process and reality.* 1929. Macmillan, New York.

FOOTNOTES

1. **Mechanism :** This is the philosophical view that all natural processes are explicable in terms of Newtonian mechanics and views that all biological processes may be described in physicochemical terms. Newtonian science regarded the universe as a giant mechanism obeying elementary deterministic laws of motion. Understanding it meant breaking down a complex set of phenomena or objects into elementary components. In other words, the mechanistic paradigm implies that one must try to understand or contrive a phenomenon by analysing it down to its constituents or at least its significant parts, by that making it *understandable* and *manageable*.

2. **Reductionism or Elementalism :** The method of inquiry that is essentially concerned with the search for the rudimentary, further indivisible and substantial parts or elements to which any object can be reduced and explained; that is, reduction of the complex phenomena to simple ones, of whole into its parts. It is a way of describing the world as "Simple Nature" and "Composite Nature" and shows how the latter could be reduced to the former **[Checkland**, 7 and **Blauberg**, 3].

   Emergent Properties : The general model of organised complexity is that there exists a hierarchy of levels of organisations (in nature or within objects), each one more complex than the one below, a higher level being characterised by *emergent properties* that do not exist at the lower level. Thus, the *principle of emergent properties* implies that whole entities exhibit properties that are meaningful only when attributed to the whole, not to its parts. That is, the whole (or integral) object is believed to have properties and qualities not to be found in its constituent parts. For example, the human consciousness cannot be reduced to the physiological properties of the human brain. Accordingly, we can say that every object (or system) exhibits properties (as a whole entity) that it derives from its parts.

B
Systems View of the Library

1 INTRODUCTION

To view the library as a system in a correct perspective requires familiarity with the basic ideas of the General Systems Theory. We have discussed the General Systems Theory, its principles and concepts in chapter A. Nevertheless, for sake of convenience, we shall review some of the principles and philosophy of the systems approach here.

2 SYSTEM

2.1 Systems Philosophy — W(holism). Synergism. Organicism. Gestalt

According to the theories or philosophies we presented in chapter A the whole (entity) is not just the sum of its parts. The whole has integrative and emergent (or holistic) properties possessed by none of the parts. The parts, which constitute a whole, though distinguishable, are interdependent. They have certain characteristics by their inclusion in the whole, and each part has the characteristics not possessed by the whole. Every one part of the whole is so related to every other part; that changes in that particular part causes a change in all the other parts and in the whole entity, object or phenomenon. In other words, the system behaves coherently as a whole. Holism is the opposite of elementalism, which views total (entity) as sum of its individual parts. Thus, according to w(holism) or systems philosophy a whole entity (phenomenon or system) cannot be simply comprehended from its parts. One can only explain, comprehended or visualised it properly in totality. The other terms used by scholars for this concept are, Organicism; Gestalt and Synergism. According to Organicism, a biological entity is an organic (or *organismic*) *entity* and is composed of many different parts, which all contribute to the way whole works. A *gestalt* is something that you think or see of that has particular qualities when you consider it as a whole, which are not noticeable or apparent when you consider only separate parts of it. A *synergy* is the act of working together so that combination of separate parts is more effective than if each acted alone. [*cf*., Lange 16; Angyal, 3; Blauberg 5; Ackoff 1]

2.2 Systems Approach

By approach we mean a step or steps taken in resolving a problem or setting about a task, and so forth. It is a method that one uses to investigate something; or a course of action that one follows to do something. Consequently, the systems approach implies a way of tackling a problem, or managing, improving or designing anything based upon systems (or holistic) philosophy.

Systems theory recognises that a complex organisation such as a library can be analysed as system that contains subsystems. These components of systems are also systems. In other words, the systems theory recognises there may be hierarchy of systems within systems and a complex system can be analysed by examining its smaller meaningful parts, which one can often further reduced into meaningful subparts. The systems approach is not simply an analytical one - "annihilating divisor" where the whole is broken down into its constituent parts or subsystems and than each of the decomposed elements or components is viewed or considered in isolation to understand or explain the whole. It is an analytic-synthetic, holistic or gestalt type of approach, attempting to view the total system with all its interrelated and interdependent parts in interaction. The whole system is not considered as a reconstituted one (the whole is equal to the sum of its parts); it is an integrated or undivided one (the whole is greater than the sum of its parts).

According to this approach the properties or functions of any complex being, phenomenon, or an organisation can be understood only by the organic character or structure of the whole and its parts, and by the relation of the parts to the whole. It emphasises relations among system components, and system and the surrounding environment.

The idea of (w)holism is contrary to the notion of reductionism, which presupposes that greater understanding can be gained by simply reducing complex structures into smaller parts. Instead it asserts that only by recognising the purpose and relationships that a part will have with the whole and with other parts, the parts as well as the whole can be understood.

2.3 Emergent Property

Associated with the concept of holism is the notion of emergent property or properties of a system. The emergent property or properties of a system are those properties that can result from the combination of subsystems and resources to form a system.

2.4 Environment

Environment is the set of factors or variables that have influence on the effective working of the system, but is not controlled by it. Environment and its properties are not part of a system, but a change in which can alter the state of the system.

Changes in its internal environment or external environment of the system stimulate the system to bring changes within the system. We find that stimulus for change in a human activity system comes from many sources. The source of stimulus or cause could be its environmental suprasystem or environment of its subsystems. The general (macro) environment for any human organisation includes technological, economic, legal, political and cultural factors. Components of specific (micro) environment of an organisation consist of users, suppliers, trade, staff unions, etc. Both macro and micro factors can bring change or lead to modification of goals, technical subsystems, structure, human relationships (psycho-social subsystem) and managerial processes of the organisation. The change at any point usually leads to many adjustments throughout the system.

2.5 Stability and Control

Stability, also known as homeostasis, is usually achieved by control. Maintaining stability or homeostasis means responding to constantly changing or hostile environments. There has to be a mechanism that enables a system or organisation to maintain a steady or healthy state when negative changes in environment occur. The system detects changes through feedback mechanism or information system and respond to changes.

2.6 System Boundaries

Any system has a boundary separating it from its environment. It may be either an open or a close system, depending upon how firm the boundary is. Systems' boundaries are limitations or perimeters that provide an interface with elements of the same or other systems. The idea boundary helps us to make the distinction between open and closed systems. The relatively closed system has almost rigidly impenetrable boundaries, whereas the open system has permeable or soft boundaries between itself and the broader suprasystem.

One can easily identify or define the boundaries of mechanical, physical or biological systems or their subsystems, as they are visible. For instance, we can define the physical boundaries of the human body very precisely. (e.g., the perimeters of human skeletal system, nervous system, respiratory system, and so on, are well defined). However, with human beings (as physico-social entities) and human activity systems such as organisations it is rather difficult to delineate their boundaries or fix the boundaries permanently. As they do not have precise physical boundaries, which one can see or touch. We can define their boundaries on the basis of their distinct functions, activities or tasks rather than based on physical structures. For example, a library system can divided into its functional subsystems and their boundaries fixed based on technical or managerial activities that are carried out in the library system as whole.

It may be observed that in a small library all the library activities may carried out by a single librarian for the whole unit, or a library may be constituted of two or more sub-units or sections in the form of one or more technical or service units controlled by **different unit Heads,** or any other way. A large library may be structured or organised into several departments and their units, which together support the total activities of the library system. The criteria selected to divide, delineate or organise a library system into physical sub-units may vary from one situation to other. However, overall functional subsystems of all the small or large library systems, more or less, remain the same.

Although the boundaries of human organisations or their subsystems are somewhat open or permeable and difficult to define, but at the same time one can reasonably and practically define them and provide a separating or filtering out function. The boundaries serve:

1. To '*homogenise*' the inputs, so that organisations can deal with them effectively. (For example, libraries set forth certain requirements for membership, universities generally require a certain percentage or marks or grade point average and course prerequisites for admission, thus homogenising the students as inputs),
2. To differentiate the internal structuring of the organisation or establishing its functional subsystems.
3. To describe the systems or their subsystems based on input-transformation process - output model of the organisation, and
4. To show the degree of autonomy and independence from environmental intrusion or it gets from its suprasystem.

2.7 Interface

Every system, to be a proper system, must somehow be distinguishable from the environment (or suprasystem) in which it resides. One must be delimit and border it in some way, having a perimeter or boundary that serves to define the domain of the system. External forces must pass through this perimeter to influence systems structure or behaviour; by the same token the output from the system must pass into the environment of (suprasystem). We call the points where external forces or inputs pass into the system or where internally generated forces or outputs pass into the environment (or suprasystem) as interfaces. Thus, interfaces are those boundaries where two systems or subsystems meet. It is the area of contact between one system and the other or between subsystems so that the input of one system becomes an output of the other.

3 LIBRARY AS A SYSTEM

3.1 Introduction

Modern theory of organisation, based on systems thinking, views an organisation as an goal seeking, open, socio-technical system bound by its supporting environment or supra social system. [*cf.*, **Cumming**, 8; **Emery** and **Trist**, 9; **Kast** and **Rosenweig**, 11; **Katz** and **Kahn** 13; **Miller**, 19; **Rice**, 23; **Seiler**, 27]

The notion of the organisation as an open system implies that it interacts with its external environment, is influenced by it, and in turn influences it. The organisation receives input from the external environment and through transformation processes (throughputs) produces outputs. In this sense, an organisation is something that accomplishes a set of operational processes; that is, something is operated upon in some way to produce something. That which is operated upon is called input, that which is produced is called output, and the operating entity is called system.

In addition, under this view an organisation is not simply a *technical or task system* (i.e., that set of activities through which its input, conversion, output processes are carried out) and *social system* (i.e., people working together or engaged in integrated set of tasks with mechanical or other means). Rather, it is the structuring and integrating of human activities (including their psycho-social behaviour) around varied technologies.

Organisation implies a manner in which people consciously co-ordinate their activities or work together in interdependent relationships to accomplish some human purpose or need. However, organisations are not natural like physical or biological systems. They are contrived systems comprising people, resources, concepts, procedures and integrated structures of these elements. Organisation are so designed or structured that people benefit from corporate efforts and are *anchored in the attitude, perceptions, beliefs, motivation, habit and expectation of human beings.*

We know that the library is a social organisation. As such, the library or an information organisation from the systems' perspective, is to be considered as an open, purposeful, socio-technical system, which interacts and exchanges resources with the environment (i.e., the society or community that constitutes its suprasystem) and achieves steady-state or dynamic equilibrium through the means of information inputs or feedback mechanisms.

As an open system it must respond to external and external environment, arrest entropy, display growth and achieve a higher level of organisation through external elaboration. It must possess the trait of Equifinality; that is, it must be able to accomplish its objective with diverse inputs and varying internal activities.

Thus, the library as a social organisation can be defined as an assemblage of interrelated, interdependent and interacting functional components (or socio-technical subsystems) comprising of men, money, materials, methods, procedures, ideas, information technology etc., established and unified by human design to form a coherent whole designed, to provide opportunities of independent learning and thinking to men or to meet the information needs of people, and is encompassed by its supra-social system.

The library as a human activity system performs specific functions. It finds, obtains, processes, systematically maintains, stores and makes accessible packages of information or recorded knowledge to its users to meet their information needs. Library systems provide information about information *per se* (which is the attribute or domain of respective science or discipline) or about the knowledge stored in various types of bibliographic items, to its users. A library as an information organisation serves society at large or a specific client group. The premise is that library systems are either subsystems of a given nation, community or society; or one of its social, economic, political or educational organisations or a super-unit, which constitutes its environmental supra-system. It must accomplish its goal or mission within the constraints that are the integral part of the environmental supra-system or the mother organisation. After this preliminary statement, let us now examine in detail the characteristics of the library as an open system in the light of the basic assumptions underlying the General Systems Theory.

3.2 An Open System Model of the Library

Viewed as an open system the library imports or inputs resources from the environment or suprasystem (i.e., from the society or its lower level units or parts) transforms the resources available to it by processes into outputs.

We show a schematic model of the library as a general open-transformation system in the following **Figure Chapter B.1.** Next we describe the features of the library system from the perspective of systems theory.

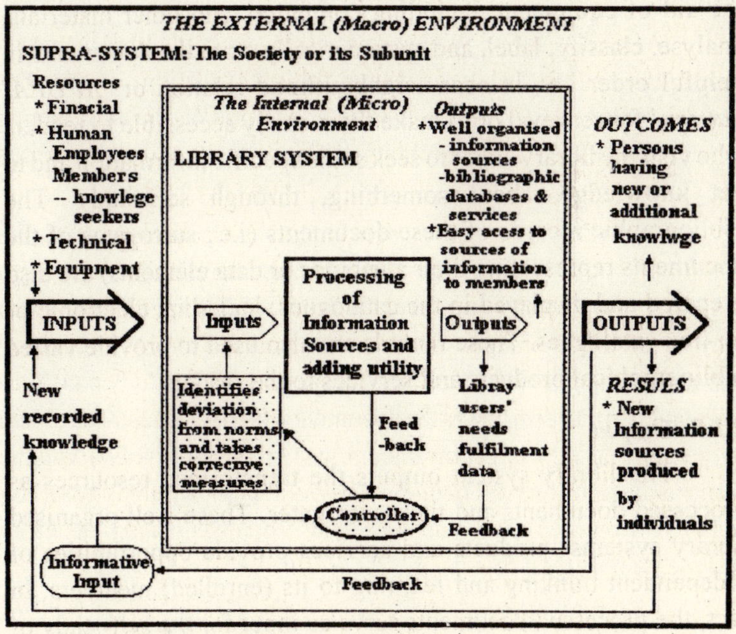

Figure B.1: A Schematic Model of the Library System

3.3 Characteristics of the Library as an Open System

3.3.1 Input

Input consists of all those elements or objects the suprasystem provides for or that enter the system from the environment and are converted by the system (i.e., from the society or its subsystems) as *money*, *information sources* (i.e., the documents of all types), *human resources*, *technology*, *equipment*, *information* (*feed back*) about environmental fluctuations and transforms these into output as information products and services.

3.3.2 Throughput

Library system moves the resources through it and transforms the key inputs unique to the system (i.e. documents), through technical operations, into products having added utility to its users. Transformation occurs when the staff using their technical knowledge (human energy) and synergistic behaviour with or without the aid of equipment, including computers and other materials, analyse, classify, label, and systematically store the documents in helpful order i.e., in near-neighbourhood relation or '*APUPA' pattern'* for retrieval or to make them easily accessible to readers who visit the library either to seek some specific information and to get knowledge, about something, through self-study. The bibliographic records of these documents (i.e., surrogates of the documents representing their attributes or data elements) are also prepared and displayed in the catalogues, including electronic or on-line catalogues. These records are also used to provide varied bibliographical products and services to the readers.

3.3.3 Output

The library system outputs the transformed resources as processed documents and their surrogates. These well-organised library systems' products and services provide opportunities of independent thinking and learning to its (enrolled) members. In fact, the processed documents serve as input for the self-study of library users. The library users read these documents and through intellectual process acquire knowledge, gather information and go out of the library system as better-informed or knowledgeable persons. We also find new publication obtained by a library system constitute major input to the system. These bibliographic items are catalogued, classified and finally constitute as value-added inputs to the system. The document added to the library collection from the output or input of the library circulation system, as and when lent out or returned. Library materials also form at times, permanent output of the system, when they become outdated or worn-out by use and discarded as waste products. Staff is selected, appointed, and when joins continued as input to the system. The library employees ultimately make up an output of the system, by way of retirement, dismissal or resignation. The library system can negative outcomes as well. For instance, the output from the library system may be that no document is made available to a reader on a topic his interest. Causes may be many — not available or found, misplaced, wrongly catalogued or classified. So the reader is hindered to complete his assignment, study or research works in time. This type of recurring phenomenon may result in the way of providing effective services to the library member or meet their demands up to optimum level.

3.3.4 Other Features of the Library as an Open System

The Library system also displays other characteristics of open system, namely: *a cycle of events*, *teleology* (i.e., *purposeful behaviour* or *goal directed behaviour*), *feedback mechanism* to achieve negative entropy and dynamic equilibrium, *growth* and *differentiation*, *hierarchy* and *Equifinality*.

A Cycle of Events: The library as an open system, from the system theory perspective, must have a cycle of events, that is, the products exported by it into the environment must furnish the source of energy or input for the repetition of the cycle of activities within the system. It is not difficult to observe the cycle of events in the library as an open system. We find that the library system acts as a catalyst to recycle the 'public knowledge' or 'objective knowledge' (the world 3 of Popper, [21]) into environment. Readers come to the library, get desired information or knowledge through open and easy access provided by the library to the recorded knowledge, packages of information or documents are collected, organised, and made available to the readers by various means by a library system. Among the users of the library some become authors and produce new knowledge as published documents. These documents form input to a library system through its acquisition subsystem and new cycle of events starts within the library system.

Teleology: According to systems theory, organisations are considered as purposeful systems; that is, they have a certain mission or purpose, which they strive to achieve or accomplish. We find that the library system is also teleological; that is, it has purposeful behaviour directed towards achieving its goal or mission. The purpose or mission of the library system is to make available the socialised or public knowledge through effective and efficient services and products. The primary missions or goals of the library are, to provide 'Every Reader His or Her Book', 'Every Book Its Reader' and to 'Save the Time of the Reader'.

Negative Entropy: According to systems theory the open-system resists the trend towards disorder by maintaining dynamic equilibrium by adapting to change in environment and moving towards better organisation, growth and differentiation. We find that a progressive library system, like any other open-system, maintains dynamic equilibrium, adapts or modifies its activities and operational goals to fit or adjust with the changing environmental conditions.

However, the pattern of functioning and adaptation is seen varying at different stages of the systems' life cycle. One finds that library systems decline over time, yet never meet their eternal death. They continue to operate despite their ill health and deficient outputs (see note below) till some dynamic manager or controller comes to the fore, rejuvenates them and puts them into gear through corrective and innovative measures. The lifecycle of any information organisation is seen moving in the form of clockwise and anti-clockwise movements of a watch-spring. That is, first moving towards increased organisation and then to decline, again moving towards increased organisation and then to decline, and so on. Briefly, we can say that a library system, grows, matures like a biological system, has a natural tendency to decline with age or due to the negligence or indifference of information but they never die. They get better or worst in a cyclic order.

Note: Normally, entropy, or running down of a library system occurs if the necessary financial and other resources are not pumped into the system. Alternatively, the resources are not converted into effective outputs or services due to bad information. Further, for a social system, such as library, the most important resource is human efforts and motivation. Thus decline in this effort and motivation of staff in the library system becomes as important cause of entropy as decline of financial and other sources.

Feedback: To check the entropy, the open system work by of informative inputs, which furnish the signals to the system about any environmental changes and about it's functioning in relation to the changed environment or otherwise. The feedback of such informative signals enables the open system to keep control over its components, to correct their functioning, adapt the system to changing conditions and maintain steady-state or dynamic equilibrium. The library system like any other open system is affected by an internal and external environmental shift and has the means through a feedback control mechanism to maintain a steady-state and adapt to changing conditions.

The library system gets two kinds of feedback of informative input:

One external informative input from its suprasystem, which has its own general social-economic environment.

Another internal informative input about its internal operations or environment.

For instance, from the external environment, the library system may get informative input about

a. New technology, which can be incorporated to improve the functioning of the system, and

b. About new publications, out of which certain items can be selected, purchased or obtained and added in the collection.

The library may also get informative input in the form of complaints from its readers or the community about the inadequacy of its collection, ineffective services, or unhelpful attitude of the staff, etc. This information, when used advantageously, contributes to an improvement in the system.

The internal feedback provides information about the performance-level of the systems' components; whether the staff is working in a cohesive manner, or there is a conflict or dissatisfaction among them. Based on analogous information, the decision-maker (i.e., the system's controller or manager) regulates or modifies the interacting components or activities in some way so the system's performance is kept at an optimum or desired level of performance, and systems' targets are achieved. The salient characteristics of good monitoring of feedback system are continuity and comprehensiveness.

Control is one of the major functions of a manager or controller of an organisation. Control implies making appropriate responses to disturbances and problem situations in an organisation at all level of activities, or functional units, by the respective controllers. The control is a corrective activity, which entirely depends on effective feedback system. In the control process judgement about performance of the system is made and corrective actions are taken. The essence of control is action that adjusts the systems performances or to bring it to its steady state and its basis is information or feedback.

Effective management and control are impossible without information. Systems approach assumes that to be effective library manager or controller, must actively seek the information that enables him to have best control on the system.

Thus, the role and purpose of library feedback mechanism is to monitor library activities and environment in which library operates to provide facts to the library manager so that he can make suitable decisions and take appropriate actions to maintain a library system in steady and healthy state. (*cf.*, Ramprasad, 22)

Growth, Differentiation and Hierarchy: One of the characteristics of open systems is that they have a tendency towards increased organisation and growth. Growth leads to differentiation of functions and specialisation so the open systems become more complex and often develop specialised components to perform different functions. (*Note*: the fifth Law of library science: *Library is a Growing Organism* is reflection of the library characteristics as open system. The first law: *Book for All* is the *mission of a democratic society*, alternatively *Books are for Use for All* is the purpose assigned to a book in a democratise society).In the next paragraph we list some indicators of differentiation of functions due to growth.

In a library system differentiation due to growth becomes evident when we create two divisions out of one division; say, we create two distinct divisions namely readers' services division and technical services. Further subdivisions of readers' services and technical services into subject units are another indication of differentiation and specialisation. We observe that the tendency towards differentiation and specialisation is in increase in many modern libraries due to the implementation information technology and developing new computerised information processing systems and services.

Equifinality: Open systems are further characterised by the principle of Equifinality. According to this principle an open system can achieve defined goals, objectives, end-states or conditions through variations in the process and from differing initial states or conditions. Equifinality is apparent in the library system. Each library system though, to some extent, provides the same services and the same types of materials. Each, however, has some difference in its procedures, say, documents may be processed using different cataloguing and classification systems in different libraries or different types of documents may be process or organised using different cataloguing and classification systems with in a library system. Different library systems have different inputs and processes but accomplish the same end-results or their goal or mission is the same. Often, library systems change their targets as well as means to achieve the goals.

4 THE ELEMENTS OF LIBRARY SYSTEMS

4.1 Introduction

Open Systems Theory leads us to regard the library as a human activity system and composed of a number of dynamic operational subsystems or components, in interaction with one another and with their environment. The subsystems are interconnected are interrelated with each other so that the energy and efforts used by each are in the direction of achieving the objectives of the total system. The implication of this axiom is that when we apply systems approach to manage or design a library system we have to be concerned with the interrelated parts (subsystems), which comprise the system and how these parts together accomplish the purpose for which system exists.

From systems theory viewpoint, a library or its subsystems can be visualised as consisting of the following set of primary elements. (An element of something is an important feature or quality that it has or need.) [*cf.*, Churchman 6; Kast and Rosenzweig 12].

Mission or Purpose: A human activity system or socio-technical system being an open teleological system has some mission or central purpose. By mission or central purpose we mean the reason or reasons for creation and continued existence of a system. The central purpose of a library system is to provide opportunity for self-education and learning to its clients or members by way of providing sources of documented knowledge (books, journals, etc.) and information (bibliographical or otherwise) according to their requirements. The central purpose of the library system is the reason of its existence or continuance in a democratic society.

The mission of the system directs the formation of goals, objectives and performance measures. Any organisational system has a long-term goal or goals and a short-term objective or objectives that can be explicit or implicit. The purpose, goal(s) and objective(s) of the system serve as the basis for constructing a measure(s) of performance.

Measure(s) of Performance: The success of an organisation

relates to the degree of goal attainment. The measures of performance are the means of finding out the degree up to which the system's purpose goal(s) and objective(s) are being accomplished. These are the yardsticks or the reference points to detect the success of a system from various perspectives. There are two classes of measures that can be applied to find out to what extent the purpose; goals or objectives are being achieved by a library system. These are effectiveness measures and efficiency measures. While effectiveness measure answers the question: *Are we doing the right thing to achieve the purpose of the system*? An efficiency measure provides an answer to the question: *Are we doing the thing the right way*?

Various approaches to measure the performance of libraries exist. Basically, a library system can be considered operating effectively and efficiently if it has the information sources required by its members, the members are satisfied or happy with its services, its internal processes and operations are cost effective and efficient, and it is away from staff problems or other strains.

Users or Clients: Users are the people whose interests are served by the system. Libraries are social systems designed to fulfil the need its members. The satisfaction of the library users is the ultimate standard of the measure of the performance of the library system.

Operational Subsystems and Interrelationships: A system consists of purposeful subsystems or components - the parts that make up the whole system. Each subsystem of a system in turn may be constituted of still smaller whole subsystems or components.

The technical cores or the task systems of a library system, which carry out system's core functional activities, generally constitute its subsystems. These subsystems together accomplish or co-produce library's work or transform its inputs into outputs.

The distinction between a subsystem and its component is arbitrary and depends on the nature of system under study and the person(s) studying the system. For a practical purpose, we will consider components to be basic elements of a subsystem. While a subsystem is investigated as system, its components are not.

Subsystems and their interrelations constitute the system structure. The break down of a system into its subsystems is context dependent. It is often an arbitrary process, since a subsystem can be broken down further to its subsystems, in many ways.

The systems approach requires that the systems analysts and designers consider the system as whole. A system may be too complex or too large for detail analysis. Therefore the system is subdivided or partitioned into subsystems. The process of division is continued until the subsystems are of manageable size. This partitioning process comprises a careful study of emerging boundaries and interfaces of the subsystems and deciding the hierarchical structure of the entire system. The hierarchical structure reflects how the purpose and goals of the whole system have been partitioned to sub-goals or objectives. Each subsystem has some specialised functions that contribute to the goals of the system, above it in the hierarchy.

Environment and its Constraints: The suprasystem in which the system exists. It comprises a set of elements, factors, or variables that are not part of the system as such, but change in, any of which can produce change in the state of the system. Environmental factors can be external or internal. A system is influenced or affected by external constraints imposed by its environment. Library systems, for instance, have to cope with financial limitations and non-availability of certain publications (may be out of print, rare or very costly) required by their users.

Feedback: Feedback is the key to an open system control. As the system becomes operational the information about the working of the system is to be fed back to the controller or manager of the system so the performance of the system must be assessed and if necessary, corrective measures must be taken by the controller or manager of the system.

Decision-maker or Controller: He is the person or committee who plays the central role in goal setting, planning, directing, controlling, and integrating or co-ordinating system's activities. He has the responsibility, bestowed with authority, to monitor the output of the system, check causes of negative deviation and bring positive changes in the system.

Designer or Systems Analyst: He is the person who keeps watch on the pulse of the system, helps the controller, manager or decision-maker in the review and evaluation of systems operations and services and suggests ways for possible improvements in the systems' output.

We describe in detail the elements of a library system as an open system corresponding to the above-described elements in the following sections. A schematic model depicting the elements of a library system is also shown in the Figure B-2:

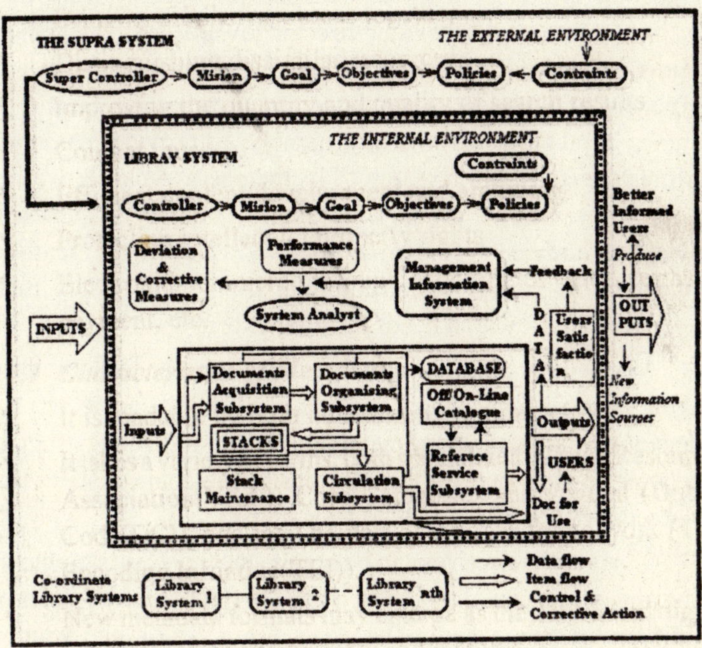

Figure B-2 : A Schematic Model of the Library and its Elements

* Mission

By mission or aim we mean the central purpose or reason for creation and continued existence of a human activity system. For example, the central purpose of a library is to provide opportunities of self-study, education, research or getting information on something to its clientele by way of providing reliable information services and also sources of information or knowledge. Ranganathan has well defined the missions of a library system in the form of following Laws of Library Science: Every Reader His or Her Book, Every Book its Reader, and Save the Time of the Reader. (I think Ranganathan's Laws namely, 'Book for All' or 'Books are for Use' reflect the missions or axioms of a democratic society, i.e., (supra-system of a library system).

* Goals, Objectives and Policies

As information organisations or library systems in systems' perspective, are teleological or ideal-seeking open systems, they must have purposeful behaviour directed towards the achievement of aims, goals and objectives. Primarily, a library system is a component of a society, a nation or any organisation created or designed to achieve his mission, namely, to provide maximum facilities for study and research to its members. As such, we can generally say, that the primary function of a library system is to provide free and easy access to recorded knowledge to the members of it supra-system (or to its potential users) and satisfy their educational and research needs to fuller extent.

Missions or aims are ultimate objectives set forth by ideal seeking open-systems, which perhaps can never be achieved; but endeavour to pursue them and may achieve them after a long struggle. The goals on the other hand, are the desired outcome or states and the objectives specific targets to be achieved.

Goals and objectives can be seen as more precise statements of the aim or mission of a system. They are future desired states or conditions of the system. The goals are a long-range wanted outcomes, whereas the objectives are short-range targets and attainable.

Objects are specific targets directed towards goals. Most objectives are defined at the subsystem level. That is, each library unit, such as classification and cataloguing unit, a circulation unit, and other units of a library system will have their own objectives, though collectively they serve the broad objectives or goals of the system. After goal and objectives of each unit are defined, the policies, or the guidelines to be followed to carrying out the day-to-day library tasks, are adopted.

A policy is a set of rules that govern some task or function (or a set of activities) performed by the system. For instance, libraries have documents' circulation policies for determining whether to lend out or not a document type to a particular member type.

* Measures of Performance

Performance measures are the means of finding out the degree to which the systems are effective in providing services to their end users or could achieve their set goals and objectives. The performance measures are the yardsticks that explicitly show in quantitative and qualitative terms what is barely acceptable, below average, above average or an exceptional system's performance [*cf.*, **Athey** 4]. These are the indicators or yardsticks with the help of which systems' controllers, managers or analysts can measure progress or regress, effectiveness or ineffectiveness, efficiency or inefficiency of the systems, in quantitative and qualitative terms. Based on their findings, they can introduce effectual measures to improve the systems, if need be.

To measure exactly the outputs and the beneficial effects of library systems and services, we must define adequately and precisely the expected benefits or outputs. The standard measures or indicators of expected performance must also be stipulated. Basically, higher is the performance or output of a system the better are the interests of the users served.

There are many performance-evaluation models and techniques developed to help the library managers and systems analysts to assess the performance of the library systems. These techniques also help us to establish the standards of performance or yardsticks against which one can measure the outcome or benefits of the specific systems and services. Systems research techniques developed by the scientists in the field of behavioural sciences and other fields also help us to study the performance of library systems, and to re-engineer theirs functional systems or processes. At times, one may have to conduct many types of studies - managerial, financial, staff, services, etc., by means of questionnaires, empirical observations, and sometimes even through experimentation.

* Users or Library Members

The governments and other organisations establish library systems to provide the opportunities of self-learning to the people and their members, correspondingly. As such, library users, including all its potential members, are very crucial components of library systems. They are the reason for which information organisations or library systems are conceived and established. Thus one can best judge or determine the goodness or effectiveness of any information organisation or library system by the extent to which it provides for the fulfilment of its users' informational or self-learning needs and interests.

* Library Functional Subsystems

These are core components of the system, which co-produce the outputs of the library system or co-achieve the objectives of the total systems. Each library system can consist of smaller functional units or task subsystems that convert their inputs into outputs or perform specific processing operations on the inputs. Input is an event, such as a library member's request for a bibliographic item or items, which triggers one or more actions, or a series of activities. For instance, the member's request for items may lead to actions such as, searching of the items in library stacks, checking documents circulation records, and reservation or recall of items, if issued out. Alternatively, if one does not do not find the item listed in library catalogue or holdings, the request may eventually lead to purchase, order, receipt of item and bill, making stock entry of the item, technical processing the item, and ultimately making the item available to the member.

While each subsystem is functionally independent of all others, no system exists by itself or in isolation from other systems. The outputs of one subsystem can be the input of another; or the two functional subsystems or transformation subsystems can jointly convert an input into an output.

In fact, a network of systems within systems exists throughout the library system. They are organised in hierarchical order conforming usually, though not always, to the traditional organisation chart-lines (tree structure), and ranging from very large and general systems at the top of the hierarchy too very small and specific systems at the bottom level of hierarchy. Systems approach recognises that the subsystems of a library system at any level must be considered a system in its own right having it own objectives, policies, functional systems, management control, environment and so forth.

Note: *A subsystem is* always charged with the responsibility for an identifiable subset of the whole systems objectives).

Further, subsystems of a given level communicate vertically (i.e., information flow occurs vertically) up with higher-level systems, vertically down with lower-level systems, and horizontally among themselves.

The subsystems and their interrelationships constitute the system structure. The breakdown of a system to its subsystem is often an arbitrary process, since a subsystem can be broken down further to its subsystems. This is actually the essence of systems analysis.

A library system consists of following basic functional units or subsystems:

1. Library Technical Subsystem, which can be subdivided into
   * ***Bibliographic Documents Acquisition Subsystem*** encompasses the activities relating to selection, ordering, receipts and inventories of digitised and non-digitised bibliographic items.

* ***Bibliographic Document Processing Subsystem***, involving activities relating classification and cataloguing bibliographic documents, creating their catalogues (bibliographic database or online catalogues), and release of processed documents for the use of library users.

2. Library Services Subsystem, which is comprised of

* ***Bibliographic Items Circulation Subsystem***, encompasses bibliographic items lending, recall and reservation activities.
* ***Bibliographic Items Shelving and Maintenance Subsystem***, involving bibliographic items shelving, binding and withdrawal (from stock) activities.
* ***Digitised Information Sources Handling System***, involving electronic storage and access of digitised ***bibliographic items.***
* ***Reference*** Services Subsystem, which carries out all the essential activities to satisfy the information needs of the library users. It is concerned with the processing the queries of library members relating to the holding of the library or information sources in general, by way of searching bibliographic databases and supplying the information about the bibliographic items of interest to library users. It also provides specialised information services to the library users, such as current awareness service, and obtains documents on interlibrary loan for use of readers.
* ***Bibliographic Information system*** – involving electronic storage and access bibliographic information about library holdings of all types of bibliographic items, including digitised packages of information.

3. Library Administrative Subsystem, which is constituted of

* **Finance, Account and Budgeting Subsystem**, which handles financial resources of the library system - finds,

obtains, gets, manage, monitors, the funds of library systems.

* **Personnel Administration Subsystem,** which handles human resources. Concerned with selection, appointments, salary, retirements, and other activities connected with the employees of the library system.
* **Equipment & Outfits Acquisition and Control Subsystems,** which acquires, maintain and distribute equipment, materials, hardware etc. required by for running the library system.
* **Library Development and Control System,** which monitors performance of a library system as a whole. Identifies system's problems and takes steps to remove the problems, re-engineers the subsystems. Review and improve library policies, rules, methods, techniques, and procedures. The supervision, control and development of the library system as a whole or its subsystems are possible due to existence of an information system for management and control. Each functional system of a library system handles the various activities within its framework and their respective staff gets data, facts or information from the library information subsystem intermeshed with each functional subsystem. The information or data provided by the library information system, as a whole or its subsets help the library staff in decision making and taking appropriate actions to regulate the activities of the library system as whole and its functional subsystems. Each functional system have its own information system constituting the sub set of library information system for management

The supervision, control and development of these functional systems are possible due to existence of information system for management and control. Functional system or units handle the most basic activities of a library system. The staff members of each functional system get facts or receive information from the library information system for management. This information or data help them in decision making and taking appropriate actions to regulate the activities of the functional system. Each physical functional system or unit may have its own information system.

In the Figure Chapter B-3 we illustrate a hierarchical partitioning of a library system into levelled sets of subsystems. The hierarchical division of a complex system is a key element of structured analysis, design, and programming of computer applications. We structure a system if it hierarchically partitioned into subsystems, and the interfaces with one another is defined. The hierarchical structure also reflects how the purpose and goals of the whole system have been partitioned to sub-goals. Each subsystem has a specific function that contributes to the goals of the system above it in the hierarchy.

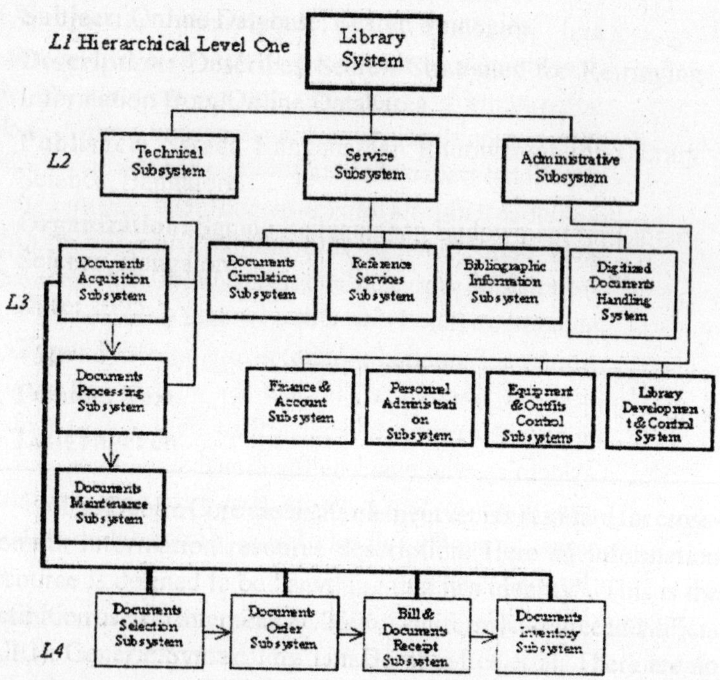

Figure B-3: Hierarchical Structure of a Library System (Illustrative)

Primarily, libraries are information organisations that are concerned universe of knowledge or information sources of all types and are composed of a network of people, structures, technical operations (functional systems), machines, equipment and other technologies that input the (raw) sources of information or documents of various types, convert them into well-organised resources or holdings and provide information services and products according to the needs of library members - the end users of the systems as outputs. The traditional library system, humans perform the required technical or processing operation (i.e., organised set of activities, tasks or operations performed on inputs to convert them into outputs). If one uses a computer system for some or all library works, a computer-based library system results. In such a system humans and computer(s), usually share responsibility for doing the work. In this context, the human performer must have the knowledge of computer technology besides library techniques or technology.

Thus, we find that a library system consists of a network of men (i.e. psychosocial subsystems), functional subsystems, library techniques, auxiliary technology, equipment and machine systems. (By library techniques we refer to the techniques used or process involved in the transformation of inputs into outputs and the intellectual technique or specialised knowledge required for true performance of a job or task unique to a library system).

The building blocks of a library system or an organisation are the functional units or subsystems, composed of a decision-maker (or a decision centre), staff who carries out unit day to day activities and their products.

In accomplishing tasks men use materials, machines, equipment, specialised knowledge and technology. The psychosocial system component of a human activity or social system is composed of individuals' group in social relation (or interaction). Further, "it consists of individual behaviour and motivation, status, and role relationships, group dynamics and influence subsystems. It is also affected by sentiments, values, attitudes, expectations and aspiration of the people in the organisation. These forces set the organisational climate within which the human participants perform their roles and activities" [28].

Intermeshed with its functional (or task) systems and psychosocial subsystem is the organisation structure and feedback mechanism. The organisation's structure provides formalisation of relationships between the functional, psychosocial and information systems. Structure involves the ways in which the tasks of the library or information organisation are divided (differentiated) and co-ordinated (interlinked, coupled or integrated). In the formal sense, the structure of an organisation is set forth by the manager or controller of the system by way of mission, policies, rules, functions and procedures statements, by way of positions and job descriptions and often depicted in the form organisation charts. The description of an organisation or human activity system is also concerned with a pattern of authority, communication (data flow) and workflow within the organisation or system.

Only, a well-structured functional unit or system (i.e., a set of logically related operations for accomplishing a job or converting systems inputs into outputs) does not give optimum results. The optimum results, outputs of an operating functional, or task subsystem also depend upon how a job is psycho-socially organised. To obtain optimum results an appropriate compromise is to be found between the need of a task system and psychosocial needs of those who operate it. Thus, a composite socio-technical system is 'jointly optimised'. There is, however, a third independent aspect, which is 'economic validity', which in turn refers to the constraints imposed by optimum output requirement and limited resource inputs. The task of the systems analyst and library manager or controller is collective optimisation of all the three aspects.

*** Interconnections between Library Functional Subsystems**

One can divide a library system into subsystems in many ways, and interconnections between functional subsystems are often described as the extent to which they are interfaced or integrated. The interfaces are the points where the entity types - information items (documents), book orders, readers' requests, being processed in one subsystem are transferred to another subsystem for further processing or use through the system. These are also the points of data transfer or points of information flows from one subsystem to another. This pertains to the activities (or events) that occur in the system and the entities involved.

Each activity (event) that occurs within a library system or in its subsystem (unit) triggers one or more data transactions. Each transaction is made into a record (i.e., converted into a source document or form describing important facts). For instance a member's make a request to get a bibliographic item on interlibrary loan we create an interlibrary loan request form, to record certain facts or data about that activity. Facts or data, such as - what item is required and by whom, what actions were taken to process the request, when were they taken, who were involved, how much expenditure was involved and so on. These transactions may be recorded manually (on forms) or electronically (on electronic worksheets, records, files). The records of transactions are called data. This data is captured and processed to provide supportive information to both operational and management level staff. Virtually any type of information can be produced if this data is maintained and processed electronically using computers. This is the task of a transaction processing system. It records and stores most data required by the operational staff of a library system and it also generate most reports and documents needed by library users and various levels of library staff.

There is no absolute indicator to detect whether two functional subsystems of a library system are interfaced or integrated. In an integrated library system (or sub systems) the *internal operations and / or resources are closely linked*, whereas it is not true in case of two or linked or interfacing systems (or subsystems). For example, a computerised library system is considered integrated if all its functional or transaction processing systems share same database. For example, monograph acquisition subsystem, serial acquisition subsystem, order subsystem, membership subsystem when *integrated* may share same database. Whereas, these system are developed or structured as two independent (though loosely linked, or interconnected and interrelated) modules then each one will have its own distinct database may not be share their databases. As interfacing systems, at least one system will use information from the other. For example, monograph acquisition system may seek information about a particular volume of a monograph belonging to a series been on order or is being available in the library at a particular point of time from the serial system's catalogue or database, not sharing same catalogues or database.

Among interfaced or linked systems (or subsystems), data or information about activities, events or transactions in one system (or subsystem) are transmitted to the other system (or subsystem) occasionally or on the basis of specific provision or demand. Within integrated or linked systems, we can reproduce from or show data of one subsystem into other subsystem. For example, the information, whether a particular document or bibliographic item available in a library is on loan or issue to some library member or not, will be instantaneously shown, if, say, circulation system and bibliographic information systems are integrated or linked. Subsystems of a library system are also considered as an integrated one if their work is carried out under the direction of one controller or Head, though functionally they may not be integrated, but this is a different issue.

We also observe that from one interfaced functional subsystem to another subsystem of a library, say from the document acquisition subsystem to classification and cataloguing subsystem, and later to circulation subsystem two types of flows occur:

1. One type is the flow of processed physical objects, such as a document, an invoice, and a form, on which some feature, quality, quantity, or some value is either added or modified by people. For example, we write or affix the value of the attribute accession number on a book or its tag after acquisition and before it is transferred to the classification and cataloguing system for technical processing. We later add the data value named call number to bibliographic item during technical processing. A technical person using a classification system

and having expertise in the classification area assigns the value named call number. We also appended the value of call number on a tag affixed on the physical unit or on the back page of a document, before it is transferred to circulation system for use,

2. The other type is the flow of facts, data or information through a system about events that occur and about the entities - people, resources, and other objects associated with the system or the things that system processes, produce or handles. The data is frequently captured and stored for later use on physical data stores such as forms, registers, and files. This data is processed to provide supportive information to both the operational and managerial level staff. To perform a typical library activity we need specific data or information. For example, to place order for a document we need bibliographic details about the document.

* **Library Transaction Processing Systems**

A *transaction processing system* (TPS) or a *data processing system* (DPS) is a part of a library functional or task subsystem. Transactions are records or data of events that occur in an organisation, such as user's request for book, book purchase orders, book supplies, receipt of vendors' invoices and book loans. Transaction processing systems process data transactions and provide operational information needed to operate the library activities daily.

In a library task or functional system two types of transactions or data processes occur - *input transactions* and *output transactions*.

Input transactions involve capturing and storing of data. Examples of input transactions are members' requests to purchase documents, vendors' bills and supplies, and the like. All these transactions input data into the system.

Output transactions are responses, further actions or confirmation of actions to those who eventually receive those conformations. The examples of output transactions are the purchase orders generated and sent to the suppliers of books, for the item(s) requested by members or selected for purchase, or the letters generated to inform the members about the action taken on their request.

We collect and store data about, objects, actions, events, and transactions (i.e., results of action) and sometime control and decisions made as a part of a library activity or a task subsystem. For example, a task subsystem, such as library documents circulation system or book order system is generally concerned with record keeping or handling data or information every time we take certain action or carry out certain transaction, say we issue a document, receive a bill, or make payment of a bill. Some consider task systems to be separate from their corresponding data processing systems, actually both activities are interrelated. To produce information, we must capture data. The data relating to library activities are very vital and support most information needs of library staff to take timely action to accomplish a task or take a decision. The management reporting is the natural extension of library task subsystems or their corresponding data processing systems. Data captured and stored during transactions processing can be used to produce information of value to the end users (library staff), especially senior library managers.

NOTE: *The type of data for management and control that originate from functional or transaction processing systems can be of the type: (i) information or data about the transactions, activities carried out in a subsystem, such as number of books ordered, or to be processed etc., (ii) information or data about the monitoring of physical movement of items or entities (e.g., movement of invoice from one section too other - from its receipt in the library to till its payment is made or acknowledgement of its payment from the supplier is received or not), (iii) information or data regarding outputs, use of items, results of actions or activities called events (e.g., Number of documents issued in a day or month etc.), and (iv) about the identity of the persons who are responsible or carry out the actual transactions and actions, or decide what action(s) may be taken in a given situation(s).*

We also find that different transactions carried out or activities performed in a library system have varying degree of frequency of operations. Frequencies of operation could be continuous (e.g., inquiries on a reference desk), daily (e.g., Posting of letters), weekly (e.g., sending reminders for non-receipt of issues of serials other than daily news papers), monthly (e.g., payment of salary to staff), and periodic (e.g., stock taking).

*** Library Environment and Constraints**

The environment includes forces that are more indirect in their effect on a system. These forces have significant impact on a library system and usually change the magnitude and direction of the system, though slowly. Library systems as open-systems are affecting both by external and internal environment, also called the general (macro) environment and specific immediate (or micro) environment respectively. The general or external environmental factors which influence information organisations or libraries are the national, state, regional education policies, the rapid growth of information and communication technology, the astronomical expansion of recorded human knowledge, the increasing cost of publications, the spreading aspirations of men to be more knowledgeable, and the limiting financial resources. We find that when resources of a suprasystem become scarce, the library has to bear the maximum impact. It suffers a disproportionate cut in financial input, generally being at a low level of priority for funding purposes.

The components of internal (or micro) environment include users, staff and their unions, book suppliers, etc. Both internal and external environments can bring change or lead to the modification of objectives, task systems, human relationships and managerial processes of the information organisations.

For survival and prosperity, the library systems must increase their social relevance by demonstrating in concrete terms by producing the expected benefits. In this context, one must measure capabilities and outputs of library systems not only to find how good their services are but what social benefits, in tangible terms, the systems are providing to the society. If library system is found lacking in providing efficient and effective services, we must consider what should be done to improve the situation and to fulfil the desired social expectations.

* **Decision-maker or Controller of the Library System**

He is the person or team (group of people), whose function is

a to assure that the necessary resources are obtained and used efficiently and effectively in the accomplishment of system's objectives;

b to keep system's activities under control; and

c to direct the system in such a way that the desired results are achieved.

He, via his expertise, authority and other resources, can bring changes in the objectives, structure and functioning of library systems' components or subsystems, can take regulatory steps, if the system deviates from its desired performance level, can take positive steps to increase the performance-level or utility of the system. He is the person or committee who has the authority to take decisions to change the system according to changed circumstances. He can introduce new operations and services based on the findings of a systematic systems study.

Performance or outcomes of systems normally depend on the management style of the decision-maker or manager. The open systems theory demands the library manager should not be authoritarian but an open-minded person. He should create congenial and healthy work conditions or environment, encourage his staff to do their best, look after their interests, and provide them opportunities for maximum exercise of creativity and self-direction in their work [*cf.*, Speller 28]. He should also maintain balance between two dimensions:

i. Autonomy of sub-units versus fusion of the systems as an integrated whole, and

ii. Stability of operations versus adaptation to changing conditions.

Too much autonomy (independence or freedom) to the systems' units or subsystems often results in the lack of total purpose, loss of cohesion or synergy. Too much centralisation (or consolidation of power) results in loss of flexibility and initiative by the units or subsystems. It leads to loss of initiative and morals in the units. They develop the attitude of passing the buck and much red tape. Too much stability in an organisation or system makes it increasingly obsolete, outdated and redundant much, rapid a pace of adaptation or change results in chaos, sense of direction. and a shortfall in the system's output and massive inefficiency.

Effective management of a library system requires that we must define and delineate their sphere of activities. That is, we must properly delineate their boundaries and domains of activities, and must give autonomy to the operational subunits, limited by the requirement of systems' cohesion /integration. This requires that the controller of each level or lower unit must focus his attention on the holistic aspect of their system (i.e., maintain cohesion and integration among their subunits) and that they should not meddle in details of those units' operations or in day to day functioning of their subunits.

*** Library Systems Analyst and Designer**

Library systems analyst and designer is a person whose is concerned with the conducting of systematic systems study of a library system to keep watch on the deviations in the performance of the system; that is, what is expected and what actually is the output or performance of the system. He is concerned with analysing the library system, finding its drawback, if any, and suggests modifications or solid redesign for making it more efficient and effective to the management. The library systems analyst and designer is an "agent of change", suggest way and mean to solve library problems and undertake systems development projects.

Problems, opportunities and directive from higher authorities usually trigger library development projects. Problems exist when the current system runs down for some reason. Opportunities are chances to improve a system despite absence of problems. Directives are decisions imposed on a system by the management.

With the coming of computer technology, library managers have become more concerned in developing computer-based library systems and services in place of manual systems and services. In such a situation, the responsibility of a library system analyst and designer is to study the problem and set forth the needs. A systems analyst finds out that how computer systems, library methods or procedures, and staff can best solve the problem. Essentially, the systems analyst study the current library systems, specify computer-based systems solutions, set up the one approved, and provide support to the one implemented. The system analyst is the principal link between library staff and computer programmers or vendors. He normally works for the computer-based systems and every organisation develops its own structure to set up computer-based systems. Although the name may vary, there are four centres of activity: Development centre, information centre, database (administration) centre, and a computer centre.

* **Library Feedback System or Information System For Management**

Information is vital for an organisation. All organisations generate data that reflect their activities, transactions, or tasks performed. This data is collected, processes and maintained by the information system of the organisation. The information system of an organisation acts as a feedback system that provides to the managers and supporting staff of the organisation with the facts and forecasts necessary for day-to-day work and decision-making, short-run (or tactical) planning, strategic (or long term) planning and development of the organisation. [Ahituv, *et al,* 1: P9]

A library is a knowledge-based system, which acquire, organise, safe guards, give access to sources of knowledge and information in all forms, free of charge, to its clients, by way of systematically organising the sources knowledge or documents and bibliographic information about them. It also assists and instructs the library members in the use of the library collection to which they have access. In a library system, in addition to bibliographic information, another type of information is also generated, namely, the organisational information required to carry out day-to-day library activities, management control, and tactical and strategic planning. Consequently, we can say that a library information system is a special type of information system, which unlike the information systems of other organisations, not only handles and produces organisational information useful to the library staff to carry out their functional and managerial activities, but also handles and produces bibliographic information useful to the library users.

A library information system, thus, can be defined as subsystems of a library system as a whole that constitute two (intermeshed) subsystems namely:

* Bibliographic Information System for Library Users, and
* Information System for Library Management.

The end users of the bibliographic information system are the library members, where as the end users of the information system for management are the staff members working in the library system.

Bibliographic Information system

The library bibliographic information system constitutes of series of activities whose end product is a library catalogue. A traditional or computerised library catalogue contains metadata or bibliographic data about the knowledge sources or bibliographic items available in a library system. Broadly speaking these activities are concerned with acquisition, classification, indexing, and cataloguing of the bibliographic items and are core professional activities that are primarily executed by the professional library staff.

Traditionally we design and put into operation a library bibliographic information system to serve as instrument

- To *identify* and *locate* the bibliographic items available in the libraries, whose one or more attribute, such as author, collaborators, title, subject and so on are known to them.
- To *show him* what bibliographic items or works the library has
  - a. By a given author or authors.
  - b. On a given subject.
  - c. Belonging to a series.
  - d. Published by a given publisher.
- To *assist him* in the choice of a bibliographic item, as to its
  - a. Edition
  - b. Date of its publication
  - c. Language and script
  - d. Physical attributes – in printed or book form, in brail, digital, multimedia form, and so forth.

However, with the coming of digital documents, additional dimensions have been added to this system. The computer based library information system not only holds processes and provides bibliographic information about bibliographic items; it also contains the digital documents as well. Bibliographical information about them and the documents itself are made accessible online.

Information System for Library Management

To carry out any activity, to do work or to accomplish something we need certain facts, data or information. For example, we need certain facts or data to purchase a book or any equipment. Therefore, every library work practice or activity involves handling, processing or management of entities or objects or things and dealing with their data or information. We therefore, must understand the relationship between the library work practices or activity systems and the information system for management. The information system for management supports the library staff to carry out day-to-day system's activities. In any library work practice or task system two types of input and output are involved: (i) Input of physical entities or objects - bibliographic items and like, and output of physical entities as processed items, and (ii) informative input and output about entities being processes or handled and the transactions or processes being carried out in the system by the staff.

For example, in a library we find that a book purchase slip or form is given by a user at the reference desk, which is first processed or attended to at that end, and later forwarded to the order processing unit for further action, if necessary; where formal purchase order is prepared and sent to the vendor or book supplier. The purchase requisition slip tells (provides data or information) to the person at the reference desk or to the order unit, about what document is needed, and by whom. Preparation of purchase order and to forward order to the supplier and the maintenance of the record about the actions taken is the duty or job of the order unit (or subsystem) staff. Later, library forwards the purchase order, the physical output of the order unit, to the vendor by post or electronically where it starts an activity for the supply of the document and bill to the library. The purchase requisition slip, order slip and the purchase order forwarded to the vendor are part of information flow necessary for finding and getting a book (physical object) by the library for its user.

We may also point out that the library operations follow events that occur in relation to entities. The event such as, a request from a library member, regarding getting a monograph on a loan, shall be followed by number of operations. This event or transaction - issuing the book to the member - will require that we keep data about the monograph that the library issue to a member, such as to whom the monograph has been issued, date of issue or return, and so forth. Thus, a library functional or transaction processing subsystem (manual or computerised), such as library documents circulation system is usually concerned with record keeping or handling data or information every time we take certain actions or process transactions, say we issue a document, receive a bill, or make payment of a bill. We keep record of this data in some form and make available to the library staff to carry out their daily activities (work), or take certain decision and actions.

As a matter of fact, each functional system of a library system is a highly structured system based on detailed specification of how a specific function or activities of a library system should be carried out to transform specific physical inputs into outputs, processing bibliographic information as well as the bibliographic items; and, there by appending new features, qualities or values to them and to their records and generate information necessary for doing repetitive tasks, planning and decision making. Some consider library task or functional systems to be separate from their information systems. However, to do work we need facts, data or information. As such, all library functional systems, manual or computerised, are concerned with in capturing data about daily library transactions and to support information need of staff.

Further, all functional or task systems handle two types of information: (1) transactional information and (2) status information. The *transactional information* usually passes from one unit (subsystem) of an organisation to another (e.g., from a reference desk to the order unit), or from one organisation to another organisation, (e.g., from a library to bookshop or vendor and vice versa, A transaction relates to the occurrence of an event that causes a specific action(s) and specific work to be performed and each version of the transaction serves as an initiator of some physical activity or action and provides basic data for preparation of the later transaction. *Status information* either represents the status of a transaction, or reflects the status of the resource or entity affected by a transaction (e.g., Number of orders placed, supply due date, amount of budget committed, and so forth).

Both *transactional information* and *status information* (also called *operational information*) are necessary for having an effective control over the day-to-day working of the library. The status information and the data collected during transaction processing, with added value, is also used the produce information for management and decision-making and is called management information system. Unlike operational information, technical and supervisory staff uses the *management information* for solving unusual problems or decision-making situations and short and long range planning.

These days, computerised library functional or transactions processing systems collect and store data in digital data stores about objects, transactions, actions or events (i.e., results of action) and sometime controls decisions made as a part of a computerised library activity or a task subsystem. The computerised transaction processing cycle consists of three stages:

Source Data Capturing or Collection. This is an initial stage and the recording of source data may be done on a worksheet or a form. In a library system, traditionally, performance of an activity or occurrence of an event or transaction (source data) is recorded on a printed form, register or paper.

Data Input - Comprising of data *conversion, verification* and *validation*. Data *conversion* is a process of transforming data from a human-readable medium - document, worksheet or form (also called a source document or a *date store*[1]) - to a computer readable medium (data store). One capture data from a source document and entered (input) it through a keyboard of a small computer or on-line terminal in the computer data store. The data entry activity may introduce errors. It is therefore necessary to check or verify the data transcribed to a computer-readable form. Validation is a computerised process applied to individual characters and fields and/or combination of several fields from the transaction record.

Retrieval and Reporting (or Display) of Information. It involves processing and updating of files, internally by the computer system

An on-line functional or transaction processing system can provide immediate data validation or immediate updating, processing and immediate reporting, or all the stages combined. In an on-line environment, the user (a library member or a staff member) can directly access the data, data records, data files and computer programs via local or remote terminals and communication lines.

During processing library transactions, each subsystem or transaction processing system of library information system collects and stores data or information, which may be required to manage library functions in electronic form. This data or information constitutes the database of the system and a source for providing specialised information to management for planning and decision-making. The subsystems of library information system interact with one another and often share the same data or database. Each of the subsystem of computerised library information system is made up of certain procedures or application subsystem, which can be further partitioned into lowest-level modules or processes, as shown in the Figure Chapter B-4. For example, a document acquisition information system includes procedures namely document selection, order, order receipt, and accession. Lowest-level processes or program modules of a Bill Receipt and Payment application subsystem could be - Get bill input data (create bill record), process bill payment, and produce output.

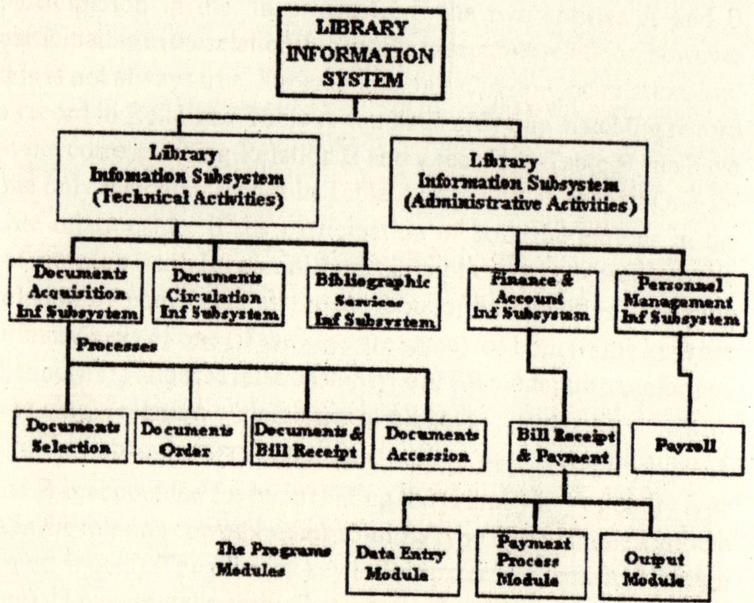

Figure B-4: The hierarchical structure of a library Information System

4.2 Information Technology Based Library Systems

With the arrival of information and communication technology, forward looking professional librarians and library managers have become more concerned in developing computer-based library information systems and services. In a computer-based library system, a computer interfaces with a human via a data. The humans capture data, input the data into computer, which processes it, and displays the results. The computer informational output or displayed results are analysed and interpreted by staff for some purpose, say to take some decision and succeeding actions, which are taken on the basis of decisions arrived at; or to perform certain tasks in connection with their work. In other words, the computer receives the data, process it, store it, and send back (output) the data as processed information, which is used by people for some purpose.

In a manual system, human performs the all the activities of functional systems of an organisation, such as a library or a business enterprise. Each operation, transaction, event or activity, which occurs within a system or subsystem, triggers one or more actions or operations. Traditionally we keep data or information about each operation, transaction, action or event in the form of a record (i.e. converted into a source document or form describing important facts or data) and filed in a file cover or cabinet, for future retrieval. These stored data or records help the staff to perform routine tasks or activities and to take decision in situations that are more complex. *If we use information technology* for some or all library works, a computer-based system results. In such a system humans and computer(s), usually share responsibility for doing the work and computer-based records of the functional activities, transactions or events that occur with in library functional systems, and about objects (or entities) associated with the system are maintained.

These days, in some libraries almost all library activities are computerised and in some few of the library activities are automated. Soon, we may also have library expert systems for carrying out technical processing such as classification (For example, *refer to*

Pannigrahi, 2003.) and other work practices of a library system. We design and implement computer-based *library information processing systems* (*also called transaction-processing systems* or simply *library information systems*) to support the operational, management, and decision-making functions of library staff and to provide bibliographic information and services to the library members. In a computer-based library system, a professional librarian works as a *system manager*, *systems analyst*, *databases administrator* and *information processor*, and so forth.

As a *systems analyst*, he is concerned with conducting systematic systems study of the system and its subsystems, keeps watch on the deviation in their expected performance or outputs. If he observes any deviation in its performance or any drawback(s), then he tries to identify the causes of deficient outputs, find solutions to remove the deficiency or deficiencies, and suggests modifications or a sound redesign for making it more efficient and effective, to the library management.

As a *database administrator*, he is responsible for appropriate capture of library data (both bibliographic or non-bibliographic), the correct input of the data in the computer, proper processing and storage of data, authorising access to the database to the legitimate users, and co-ordinating and monitoring its use.

As an *information analyst and processor* or *knowledge worker*, he conducts subject analysis of bibliographic items, produce subject headings and class numbers that represent the contents of the items, feed this data in the computer, and also acts as intermediary between the library users the bibliographical *information* system for retrieving relevant *information* for their use.

In the beginning a number of libraries and information centres in India and abroad developed computer-based bibliographic information systems in place of traditional card catalogues for identification and location of documents available in the libraries or to serve as an index to various types of bibliographic items available in their collections. These systems are referred to as *on-line catalogues, on-line public assess catalogues (OPACs)*, or *on-line catalogue databases*. Some libraries do not use the term catalogue at all and prefer the names such as *information storage and retrieval system, information retrieval system*, or merely *information system*.

However, currently computerised library *information* systems (or library management systems) are being build up not only to serve the purpose of an on-line catalogue, but also as a systems that serve as *information* system for management that support library staff to carry out their work as well as provide bibliographic and reference services to library users. A computerised library *information* system incorporate near total library activities or functions - such as, monographs acquisition, serials acquisition and control, membership registration, documents circulation control, bibliographic information system, financial control, personal management, feedback system (information system for library management) and so on. The subsystems of computerised library information system designed to carry out these activities are called transaction processing system or functional systems of a library and named as, document acquisition system, serial control system, documents circulation system, financial system, personnel management system, and so forth. These subsystems are very often considered distinct from a bibliographic information system designed to provide bibliographic information to library users. This actually is not the correct view.

We must also distinguish and clearly perceive the relationship between *library information system* as whole (also called *library management system*) and its subsystems, namely the *bibliographic information system*, which generate and produce bibliographic information for the use of *library members* and the *information system for management* that supports work practices and information need of library staff for effective management and control. The end users of a bibliographic information system are library members, whereas the end users of an information system for management are the staff members working in the system, and both the systems constitute subsystems of a (integrated, federal or comprehensive) computerised library information system. A computerised library information system in turn constitutes a subsystem of a library system or organisation as a whole.

Primarily, a computerised library information system (LIS) constitute of a set of library transaction processing (or functional) systems designed to provide

* Bibliographic information and services to the library members
* Operational and status information to the library staff to carry out their day-to-day activities,
* Management information to senior library staff for planning, management and control.

It also includes a computer (hardware and software) as one of its components.

The scope or extent of computerised library information systems varies from library to library. One can develop an integrated or comprehensive computerised library information system incorporating near total library activities, functions, or a stand-alone computerised transaction-processing system for each of the major functional activity of a library system. However, the most effective kinds are those that incorporate near total library functional activities. It may be pointed out that each library functional area is not an isolate unit and concerned or deal with its own domain, but they are closely linked with each other and as a whole fulfil the information needs of library users and staff. As such developing a unified or integrated library information system or one that has potential to incorporate all functional systems is the best choice.

Thus, we can be defined a computer-based library information system as *a set of library functional systems encompassing*

* Library work practices or procedures,
* Information technology – computer technology (hardware and software) and communication technology, database management system and a corporate database (it is not simply a bibliographic database but much more),

* Work force – staff, and
* A database or a set of linked databases data shared by multiple applications - it is not only a bibliographic database but also much more.

All geared together for accomplishing the library objectives to provide

* Bibliographic and other type of wide-ranging information to library members,
* Online access to digitised information sources and services[2] available in the library system, networks of library systems and on Internet to the library users for their learning, self study and research, and
* Information to library staff and management for effective control and management of library affairs.

To sum up what has been stated above, we can say that a computerised library information system constitute *a group*[3] of interconnected library functional or transaction processing systems and specialised management information systems, which serve as a tool

* in the performance of library work practices, by way of providing operational information to the library staff,
* to make available bibliographic information to the library members about the library holdings, and
* to provide complete information support to all levels of library staff – directors, managers, supervisors, middle managers, professional and technical staff, necessary for:
    * ***Day-to-day operations and decision-making***.

      That is, information that is usually useful to the library staff for carrying out day-to-day work, operational control or for routine processing of the transactions. For example, facts such as status of book orders, bills, and other matters must be available to them to carry daily work efficiently. Such information helps the staff to take day-to-day decisions such as: What book orders are pending? For whom orders may be placed today. Which book orders are overdue? For whom necessary reminders need to be sent today? And so forth.

* ***Tactical planning and decision-making.***

  Tactical planning and decision making is concerned with short-run planning: staff recruitment, redeployment, promotion, the annual budgeting process, and like. A responsibility of making such plans and deciding the ways of achieving desired results depend upon level of manager, the organisation structure and management approach.

* ***Strategic or long terms planning.***

  Strategic decisions involve cost and risk and are usually made by or endorsed by a chief executive or board of directors, or the equivalent. Decisions are quite forward-looking and relatively unstructured, i.e., they may not be based on hard facts. These decisions will often be significant for the whole library system.

Specialised Library Information Systems for Management

A specialised library information systems for management (or management information system) is a computer based application that provide informational output to the library managers to monitor and improve the day-to-day library work, as well as to support the problem solving and decision-making needs of top management. Different types of specialised *computerise management information systems* can be developed to help library managers to accomplish structured, semi-structured, and unstructured tasks[4] involving corresponding decision.

A library management information system supplement library functional or transaction processing systems with management reports, provide the decision maker with decision-oriented information to identify a problem and its possible solution. The library management information system is often composed of three applications or modules: (i) Structured Decision Support System (SDSS), (ii) Decision Support System (DSS) and (iii) Expert Systemes

i The *Structured Decision Support System (SDSS)* is a module or application of the management information system that helps library management by producing structured, summarised reports on regular or recurring basis for operational and executive control.

ii The *Decision Support System (DSS)* is a module or application of management information system that supports decisions of the management control and strategic planning. DSS differs from transaction processing system (TPS) and structured decision support system (SDS) is that they do not always support an on going process and assist decision-making in less structured environment. [**Neumann** and **Hadass**, 20]. The DSS system provides the decision maker with tools to access the data and analyse it to identify a problem, its possible solutions, selecting and implementing the solution that is most relevant or applicable. The decision support systems are some time called **executive support systems (ESS)**. Decision support systems

iii The *Expert System* (ES) is a programmed decision-making module or application of the management information system. It captures and reproduces the expertise or knowledge of an expert, problem solver or decision maker and simulates the thinking, assessments or actions of that person.

Structured Decision Support System (SDSS)

The structured support system (SDSS) is an application or a module of a library management information system (LMIS) that provides detail and summarised information in the form management-oriented statements, financial reports and analyses, forecasting, and so forth, to the library managers. Specifically, it is a set formalises rules and procedures designed and used with the help of information processing technology for making available to the library managers, technical and supervisory staff the accurate and timely information for taking right decisions while carrying out their planning, control and operational responsibilities. It provides information by converting data form a task (or transaction) processing systems and from a shared database that store data from many sources into information for monitoring, managing and controlling performance of library system. It make available to the library managers detailed information, summary information, statements, analysis and reports for management oriented reporting and operational control. These reports are generated in a prearranged format at regular interval or predetermined schedule.

Decision Support Systems (DSS)

A decision support system (DSS) is a special type of computerised information system that supports manager, analysts and other professionals in non-routine decision making tasks. A decision support system (DSS) helps them by providing information, models or tools for analysing information for planning, problem solving or making decision in complex situations. DSS is basically a specialised LMIS designed to support a manager's skill at all stages of decision making process viz. identifying the problem, defining the courses of action, and selecting the most appropriate course of action out of defined courses of action. A decision support system is some times called executive information system (EIS). The data extracted from the operational database and conventional files as well as the data and information generated by management information system are stored in data warehouse. Managers with DSS tools access the data warehouse to generate variety of information for resolving unstructured decisions.

A decision support system does not replace structured-decision support system (SDS). It supplements SDS and supports decision making in semi-structured and unstructured situations. The key element of a DSS is a modelling process. A model is a mathematical representation of a real life situation. One can computerise a mathematical model. Like any computer program, the model can use inputs and produce outputs. The inputs to model are called independent variables, because they can change. The outputs are called dependent variables because they depend upon the inputs. Using a computer model to reach a decision about a real life situation is called simulation. You plan the independent variables - the inputs - and examine how the model behaves based upon the dependent variables - outputs - it produces.

Consider the following example. Suppose you have the task of deciding which documents need to be purchased for your library. You have many factors before you to consider or weigh up: The price, subject interest of the user, the standing of the publisher, the year of publication, standard of exposition, the assessments score or rating value given by experts, and so on. These are all independent variables - the data that will be fed into the computer model and analysed based on some criteria to decide whether the item need to be purchased or given preference over other documents.

Expert Systems

An expert system (ES) makes the knowledge of experts available to others in situations where they require expert knowledge, or support of knowledgeable people or professionals engaged in design, development and application in a well-defined area. We can implement expert systems using artificial intelligence technology (AI). AI captures, stores, and provides access to experts reasoning. Expert systems are computer programs, using Artificial Intelligence (AI) based logical programming, designed to emulate the reasoning process of an experienced professional. These are also known as knowledge base systems. Here the concept knowledge refers to a particular domain of expertise say, library classification. This expertise could include highly technical or specialised information not be normally expected to be available otherwise. Knowledge Engineering is the discipline that deals with the way the knowledge base is organised so that it becomes available in the most useful manners possible. The term engineering refers to practical approach of using knowledge of an expert to solve problems.

A knowledge base contains all the facts, rules and procedures related to specific field for solving problems in that field. Usually the knowledge engineer interviews the expert who describes many cases he has handled or problems he has solved. From these interviews relevant knowledge is extracted, formalised and structured. The knowledge engineer has to make the ideas so explicit that the computer can accept them. For example, an object is defined first assigning a unique name to it, then its attributes are specified and finally values are assigned to these attributes. In an expert system, a knowledge base comprising declarative, procedural and heuristic knowledge is created. The knowledge in the system is represented in the following ways: tree representation, semantic networks, production systems, frames, lists, and predicate logic.

A knowledge base alone does not make an expert system. The system must possess another component called inference engine, which directs the application of the knowledge for problem solving. It decides which heuristic search technique is to be used and to determine which and how the rules of the knowledge base are to be applied in solving problems. The inference engine performs all such tasks that give the system semblance to human intelligence.

References and Reading List

1. Ackoff, Russell L. Towards a system of systems concepts. *Information Science*. v.17; July; 1971; p. 661-71.
2. Ackoff, Russell L; Emery, Fred E. *On purposeful systems*. 1972. Tovistock Publication, London.
3. Ahituv, Niv; Others. *Principles of information systems*. Ed 4. 1994. Wm C Brown Communication, Dubuque, IA.
4. Angyal, Andras. *Foundation for science of personality*. 1941. Harvard University Press. p. 243-61.
5. Athey, Thomas H. Systematic systems approach: an integrated method for solving systems problems. 1982. Prentice Hall, Englewood Cliff, New Jersey. p. 133.
6. Blauberg, I V. System and wholeness concept. **In** NAPPELBAUM (E L), and others, *tr*. *Systems research methodological problems*. 1984. Pergamon Press, Oxford. p. 49-61.
7. Churchman, C West. *The design of inquiring system; basic concepts and systems and organisations*. 1971. Basic Book, Inc., New York. p. 43.
8. Clemson, Barry. *Cybernetics: a new information tool*. 1984. Abacus House, Tunbridge Wells, Kent. p. 40.

9. Cumming, Thomas G. Ed. *Systems theory for Organisation development.* 1980. Wiley, Chichester.

10. Emery, F E; Trist, E L. Socio-technical systems. **In** CHURCHMAN (C W) and VERHULST (M), *eds. Information science model and techniques.* 1960. v 2. Pergamon Press, London. p. 93-9.

11. Hall, A D; Fagen, R E. *Definition of system. General Systems: Yearbook for the Society for the Advancement of General Systems Theory.* v.1; 1956; p. 18-28.

12. Kast, Fermante E; Rosenzweeig, James E. *Organisation and management: A system and contingency approach.* Ed 4. 1985. McGraw-Hill, New York.

13. –; –. *abid.* p. 114-5.

14. Katz, D; Kahn, R L. Common characteristics of open systems. **In** EMERY (F E), *ed. System thinking.* 1969. Penguin Books, Harmondsworth, Middleses. p. 86-104.

15. Klir, G J; Valach, Miroslav. *Cybernetic modelling.* 1965. Lliffe Books.

16. Koehler, W. Closed and open systems. **In** EMERY (F E), *ed. Systems thinking.* p. 56-69.

17. Lange, Oskar. *Wholes and parts: A general theory of system behaviour.* 1965. Pergamon Press, Oxford.

18. Lilienfeld, Robert. *The rise of system theory: an ideological analysis.* 1978, John Wiley. New York. p. 20.

19. Mattessich, Richard. The systems approach: its variety aspects. *Journal of the American Society for Information Science.* v 33; Nov, 1982; p. 383-94

20. Miller, James G. The nature of living systems. *Behavioural Science.* v. 16; 1971; p. 277-301.

21. Neumann, S; Hadass, M. DSS and strategic decisions. *California Information Review.* v. 22, 2; 1980; p. 74-88.

22. Panigrahi, P K. Use of logic programming in developing an artificial Intelligence based Automatic Classification System. *Iaslic Bulletin.* v. 48, 2; June, 2003; p. 2003.

23. Popper, K R. *Objective knowledge: an evolutionary approach.* Callaredon Press. Oxford. p. 74.

24. Ramprasad, Arkalzad. On the definition of feedback. *Behavioural Science.* v. 28; 1987; p. 4-13.

25. Rice, A K. Productivity and social Organisation. The Ahmedabad experiment. 1950. Tavisstock, London.

26. Robert, A. Orchard. On an approach to general systems theory. **In** KLIR

(G J), *ed. Trends in general systems theory*. 1972. Interscience, New York. p. 205-50.

27. Rosenblueth, Arturo; Others. Behaviour, purpose and teleology. *Philosophy of Science*. v. 10; 1943; p, 18-24.
28. Rosenblueth, Arturo; Wiener, Norbet. Purposeful and non-purposeful behaviour. *Philosophy of Science*. v. 17; 1950; p. 316-26.
29. Seiler, J. *Systems analysis in Organisation behaviour*. 1967. Irwin, Homewood, 111.
30. Speller, Benjamin F. Living in an open system the individual and the library Organisation. *Journal of Library Administration*. v. 5; 1984; p. 41-52.
31. Von Bertalanffy, Ludwig. *General System Theory: Foundation, Development, Application*. George Braziller, New York. 1968.
32. –. General System Theory. General systems: Yearbook of the Society of Advancement of General systems. v.1; 1956; p. 1-10.
33. –. The history and status of general systems theory. *In* KLIR (G J), *ed. Trends in general systems theory*. 1972. Wiley, New York, p. 21-38.
34. –. The theory of open systems in physics and biology. *Science*. v. 111; 1950; p. 23-29.

FOOTNOTES

1. **Note :** Traditionally we record or store the data connected to transactions or processes on paper forms and after recording date the library staff keep the processed form in a box, in a file folder or in file cabinet and the like. Forms, registers, boxes, file folders and file cabinets are traditional data stores. When we computerised library tasks, activities or processes, the system works precisely as before. Computer places the records of transactions in computer files or databases, which are stored or recorded on digital mediums.
2. **Note:** *Today a library contains both digitise and non-digitised sources of information or bibliographic documents. In a library, the digitised bibliographic items (electronic documents) are acquired, processed, organised and store much like non-digitised bibliographic items. However, we need computers to access, scan, and display or read their contents or reproduce hard copies. Digitise documents are unlike non-digitised documents. One can scanned or read non-digitised documents without the aid of computers.*
3. **Note:** *The term group is used to stress that the interrelationships among various information systems comprising a whole library information system do exist, but are not so tight as to impede independent development of each system and integrating them at an appropriate time.*

4. **Note :** ***Structured tasks*** *are those, which we can specify exactly, how they are performed. The decisions and actions involved in a structured task can be well understood and predicted or programmed. The managers can usually define the* ***information*** *requirements to support the structured decision and actions comprising a structured task. For example, we can provide a check or rule to help a counter assistant decide whether to issue a particular bibliographic item to a member. We know that only certain types of items can be reissued (e.g., Those reserved cannot be reissued) and to whom. We can define what type of information one needs for taking appropriate decision and course of action in a given situation. In a semi-structured task, the* ***information*** *requirement and procedures are mostly, known, but not all the variables can be considered at the outset. For certain variable we do not know when need for decision-making will arise, and we do not know the nature of such a decision. The decisions involving unknown variables is normally taken by the person concerned based on his judgement and experience.*

   An **unstructured task**, at the outset, is poorly understood, as the pertinent **information**, the method of using the **information**, and the criteria for deciding which way the task can be done properly, cannot be exactly specified. Unstructured task involving unstructured decisions and actions can be performed from experience, intuition, heuristic (rules of the thumb), trial and error method, and using both qualitative and quantitative **information**. Decision support systems are primarily developed to support the unstructured task or decisions. (The classical model of decision-making used by managers is known as the Simon model, which we shall discuss later).

C
Library Systems Analysis and Design Technique

1 INTRODUCTION

The systems analysis and design technique is a systematic method of analysing the objectives, interrelationships, and interdependence among various components of a system and finding what problems, deficiencies, or weaknesses exist in the system under study. What are the causes of these situations and what courses of action can be taken to resolve the problems or remove the deficiencies? It is a methodology of designing new systems or improving an existing one, if those examined are found wanting. This method of inquiry is based on system philosophy and embodies systems approach or strategy in designing or improving man-made systems, including a mission oriented human activity service system. *Systems analysis and design technique*, *systematic systems study*, *systems engineering*, *systems research*, and *systems analysis are the terms* very often interchangeably used, with slightly different emphasis, to describe the practical application of systems philosophy for understanding and modelling complex systems.

Systems philosophy or theory speculates that a phenomenon of an empirical world is a system composed of interrelated, interdependent and integrated components (subsystems or subsets), encompassed by environment (or supra-system) and interfacing with other related systems (or phenomena). The behaviour or properties of the (whole) system or phenomenon under investigation is derived from the behaviour or properties of its components, considering all possible interactions of the components (i.e., the subsystems comprising the system) and examining how these parts or subsystems together accomplish the purpose for which the system has been established.

Systems thinking or approach is in divergence to classical scientific method or approach that regards an entity or object of scientific investigation as an assembly of isolated components and attempts to derive the characteristics of the whole entity or object directly from the properties of its component parts, without considering possible interdependence and interactions among the parts. This scientific approach is being increasingly applied to problem solving, planning and management of human organisations. This scientific investigation approach is correlated with and requires the use of relevant concepts from the general system theory developed by Ludwig Von Bertanlaffy and his collaborators. [*Von* Bertanlaffy, 1968]

When a system study of a library system or an information organisation is carried out, the aim is:

* to detect its problem(s) or the causes of deviation in the performance of the system — between what is expected and what actually happens, and;
* to suggest appropriate solution(s) to remedy the situation and to bring significant improvement in the system, or,
* to devise and apply appropriate design of the system selected to correct or overcome the deficiencies of the system or design a new one.

Systems improvement refers to the process of identifying the gaps between expected performance of a system or its subsystems and ensuring that the system or its subsystems act according to expectation. It implies that the design of the system has been set and the system does not appear to operate as initially intended, or yield predicted results, or there is a gap between what is expected and needed and what actually exits.

During this process efforts are made:

* in tracing the causes of departures of the system from its established operational norms, and

* to find how the system can be made to yield better results — the results that come closer to the established norms.

The method found most suitable to improve the system or removing the causes of its deviation from the desired results is implemented. In this approach, one keeps the basic system design or framework intact and proceeds in an evolutionary mode; that is, in step by step progression for introducing modifications, as opposed to making major or fundamental radical alterations in the system.

In contrast, the concept systems design implies bringing fundamental change or transformation in the whole system and creation of almost new phoenix-like system configuration or design, which is more effective and efficient. In this case, the very nature of the system and its role in the context of the larger system is questioned. [Von Gigch, 1978: p 1- 31].

Systems analysis and design is, thus, a way of tackling a problem, managing, improving or designing man-made systems based upon systems (holistic) philosophy. This approach has opened new vistas for viewing and management of human organisations and can be applied to solve a very wide-variety of complex organisational problems. One can effectively use this approach to investigate the causes of deficient output of a library system as a whole or its subsystems and improving their performance by removing the factors that are causing the malfunctioning, or to plan and develop new systems and services.

Looking from system philosophy perspective, a library can be viewed as an open socio-technical system — a complex, but organised assemblage of people, machines, documents, procedures, and other resources geared to meet the information need of people. As an open socio-technical system, a library is often under stress due to environmental change and uncertainty often.

Varieties of environmental conditions or internal problems demand continuous monitoring of its working conditions and to bring stability or improvement in its functioning. Libraries must respond to the changing circumstances by adjusting their course of action or functional activities to achieve and maintain desired level of performance, and check their back slide or increase entropy. The regress may have set in due to some unsuitable or improper environmental conditions, or undesirable contacts or influences. As open systems, they must also endeavour to improve their processing systems and services by way of introducing innovations or new technology.

Library managers have to be alert to take right decisions whenever they have either to solve library problems or to introduce new ways and means to improve the performance of libraries. Managers have to base their decisions upon a thorough understanding of the network of interrelationships and interdependencies that exist in library systems. What makes their task very challenging is that libraries are complex open systems and the demands for continual adjustment and change, due to their very compelling and critical dynamic fast changing educational and socio-technical environment. In this context conducting system study of libraries using systems analysis, design and development tools and techniques, is very helpful.

The systems analysis of a library system is carried out to understand the present system, to learn how it works and how it meets needs of users. The results of this investigation show us: how effective or efficient the present system is? What and why there is a deficiency or a problem? The findings lay the groundwork for improvement of the system.

By studying the existing system, an analyst can gain general background knowledge into how the system is currently working and how much effective and efficient it is. The result of systems analysis provides him a framework to suggest the way and means to improve the library systems and services or to design a new one. The systems analysis also provides benchmark against which the proposed designs or solutions can be compared or for establishing how much the new design or solutions are better in terms of cost, accuracy, reliability, etc. The system design is the process of developing a plan for improved system, based upon the results of systems analysis.

The library systems analysis and design is a specific way of proceeding to find out the solution to library problem(s). The basic objective of the library systems analysis and design is to study in depth the aims and objective of a library system, interrelatedness of its components or subsystems and to find the causes for the deviation of their performances. It may form the basis to develop or design new systems or techniques that will correct or overcome the existing library problem(s), make more effective use of the available resources and enable the organisation to attain its goals as efficiently and effectively as possible.

Problems, environmental requirement, mandates from higher management, or when the library managers see and seize opportunities to improve the systems usually triggers library systems development projects. The librarian or library management gives directives to the systems analyst to take necessary actions in this direction.

Problems are undesirable situations that prevent the system from fully achieving its purpose or desired results. For example, one may encounter difficulties in operating the current system at maximum level of efficiency may be due to increase in the workload, or due to financial crunch, or lack of other resources. Other indicators of problem situations can be:

* Increase in the number of users' complaints and staff problems.
* Significant deviation in the performance or output of its operating subsystems.

Opportunities are chances to improve a system despite absence of problems. For example, management is always receptive to adopt new procedures, techniques or new cost effective technology.

Environmental mandates are decisions imposed on a system by the management due to some environmental circumstances, external influences or technical reasons. For example, due to extraordinary increases in the cost of published materials, services and products the management may give directives to adopt cost-effective measures. In addition, management may dictate support to a new policy formulated by someone higher up in the authority or due to some other reason. For example, management may decide to participate in an interlibrary co-operation and computer-based networking program, at regional, national or international level. The agenda for the co-operative ventures may be relating to bibliographic data generation, consolidation, distribution and speedy information transfer. The purpose being, to provide more extensive, prompt and easy access to the bibliographic databases of other library systems as well as databases of commercial enterprises (book seller, publisher and agencies providing indexing and abstracting services), spread over several locations, to the library users and staff.

Systems study project in a library system may be triggered by any one or more of the many factors listed above and may lead to bringing about significant changes in the system's functioning or in its subsystem's design.

The systematic systems study of a library may be carried out on current short run operational problems or for developing and implementing long run or future oriented strategies to improve the system. Current short run operational problems can be — (a) excessive operational cost, (b) management dissatisfaction with the performance of a unit and so on. Long run strategies may have to be developed because of changing environment, or to introduce cost saving technology, systems or services.

The systems analysis and design technique is primarily, an on-going library management or problem solving technique. As indicated earlier it is a method of tackling a problem, managing, designing or developing man-made systems based upon systems (holistic) philosophy or approach. One can use this technique very effectively to investigate the causes of deficient outputs of a library system (as a whole) and it its subsystems. Using this technique one can improve their performance by way identifying and removing the factors that are causing the malfunctioning of operative systems, or by designing and implementing better systems and services. [Kashyap, 1993]

Thus, the objective of library systems analysis and design is:

1. to systematically examine in detail the aims and objectives of a library system, working of its and staff functional subsystems, its environment and constraints, requirements of library users, their comments, complaints or problems, if any,
2. to find out the causes of the problems the system and its subsystems are facing, or the reasons of deviations in system's and subsystems' outputs from the norms, and
3. to suggest ways to bring about improvement in the present working condition of the system and its subsystems, or to develop a new, more effective and efficient manual or computer-based library subsystems and services.

A person who has expertise and whose responsibility is to conduct systematic systems studies of library systems is known as library systems analyst. The library systems analyst analyses, designs and develops library task systems (functional systems or applications) and plays a very important role in the development and implementation of library systems and services, both manual and computerised.

Library systems analyst can be any professional librarian whose job is to study the current library system, using various survey and research techniques, and specify improved or new systems and services for implementation. For this purpose he/she interviews the library users to identify their needs and wants, and discuses with the library staff to find out how they are doing their jobs, the type of difficulties they are facing in their work, and so forth. As an end result, he describes in precise terms the problems, functional requirements and constraints of the system, using techniques like logical flowchart, data-flow diagrams, and decision table.

In case one is carrying out the systems analysis of a library system to introduce computerisation in library systems then computer systems analysts, programmers, and database administrators make use of the final product of the systems study to develop library application programs, structured designs of programs or system and logical databases design of an information system, respectively. The functional specifications of a system in precise terms — the input to be supplied, the output needed, and the algorithms (step by step procedure) involved also helps the library staff to do their jobs, manually or using computers, correctly and efficiently.

These days in libraries, computers are used to collect and store enormous bibliographic data, process library transactions with speed and accuracy, and to provide timely and accurate bibliographic information to library users, as well as to library managers for effective management and control of library systems and services.

The library systems analyst identifies the requirements of end users, especially sophisticated library users and senior staff members, develop specifications for procedures that meet these requirements; defines the applications and problems that one need to solve with the aid of computer technology and provide this information to the computer systems analyst or the application programmer and the person involved in the design, use and maintenance of the database of the library system, known as database administrator.

From the foregoing, we can sum up that the library systems analysis and design is a technique of systematically examining the library systems and their problems, and specification of appropriate solutions to bring improvements in the present systems or to make them more effective by way of introducing innovation, including a computer-based solution. It is a scientific method of investigation based on system philosophy or thinking.

After this brief introduction we can now describe the role and function of a systems analyst and explain the systems analysis process in detail.

2 THE LIBRARY SYSTEMS ANALYST / DESIGNER

2.1 Introduction

The library systems analyst or designer normally does both analysis and design of a system (Occasionally, the term *systems designer* is also used in place of systems analyst). He/she finds out the requirements of the end users—especially sophisticated library users and senior staff members — and develops new or improved library systems and procedures (manual or computerised) on the basis of identified requirements of the end users.

The library systems analyst also examines the problems, functional activities, and services of a library system and determines how best information technology can be used to improve library activities and services. He/she provides this information to the computer systems analysts or the application programmers and the persons involved in the design, use and maintenance of computerised library systems, known as database administrators.

To design and manage a computerised library information system and database is generally the responsibility of the library database administrator. He/she is a professional who identifies the data to be stored in the library database and choosing appropriate structures to represent and store this data with help of application software or a database management system. Administering computerised database system is also the responsibility of a database administrator (DBA). He/she is responsible for efficient capture of library data, the input of that data into the computer, processing and storage of that data, authorising access to the database, and co-ordinating and monitoring its use.

A computer systems analyst or an *application programmer* is a person concerned with the structural design of the computer program or system; that is, with the appropriate subsystems, sub-programs, or modules of the whole hardware and software and their interconnections.

Computer specialists and programmers frequently do not understand library applications. Here is where the library system analyst plays a very vital role in information technology decisions of a library. The *library systems analyst* is the one who detects the users' needs, and provides functional requirements or systems specifications to the computer systems designers and application programmers. They set up the specifications of library operations provided by the library systems analysts as program or application software. Software in its most elementary form is the creation of stand-alone programmes for well-defined single or many library applications, tasks or functions. Developing a library program involves three basic steps: defining the problem, devising a plan to solve it and translating the solution into a language that the computer can understand.

A systems analyst often deals with unstructured problems. He acts as the interface among many different types of system users, both technical and non-technical, such as library executives, supervisory and professional staff, library users, computer systems vendors, application programmer, systems programmer, library database administrator and facilitates the library computer applications by co-ordinating the efforts of the professionals.

The Library Systems Analyst {also called Systems Manager, Library Information System Manager (LIS manager) or Electronic Data Processing Manager (EDP manager)}, very often heads the computer systems department of a library. The function of this department is to manage the computer system and co-ordinate the computer related activities and services of all the other departments of a library system.

We also find that in some libraries one person performs all the tasks outlined above. In other libraries, the library systems manager generally has a team of highly skilled professionals. Depending upon the organisation, the systems manager would be helped by specialists like system analysts, programmers, database administrators, and library professionals.

2.2 Know How and Skills Required of a Systems Analyst

Essentially, the library systems analyst studies the problems and needs of library users and staff to decide how people, library methods and information technology can be best integrated to accomplish library functions. He/she is a trained professional who uses both systems approach and scientific methodology to find the causes of systems inefficiency and ineffectiveness (or efficiency and effectiveness), makes use of quantitative or statistical methods wherever applicable, and qualitative factors such as judgement, creativeness, heuristic and experience to maximise the effectiveness of the system. Thus, he/she bases the conclusion of the findings on scientific evidence; that is, based on data or fact gathered about the system under controlled conditions, analysed and interpreted in a reasonably rigorous manner.

The role of library systems analyst or systems manager is complex and demanding one in an organisation. He/she requires basic knowledge and proficiency about library applications and information technology, systems management practices, systems analysis and designing methodology, project scheduling and execution techniques, work force management approaches, and of course must possess good communication and interpersonal skills. He/she is the one responsible for utilising the people, resources and power of computers and makes the library capable of delivering the best possible computer-based services to library users.

The library systems analyst or systems manager should have a creative and analytical mind, and must be:

* Proficient in problem solving and analytical skills. (i.e., he/she must be able to apply scientific techniques or approaches to solve library problems. Must possess communication ability, be expert in maintaining interpersonal relations, and have decision-making skill (that is, capability in selecting the right course of actions to solve a problem).
* Familiar with library functions, operations and applications, computer technology, communication technology, and some programming languages.

He/she also needs a thorough understanding of:

* The organisational structure and working of the library system under study. These facts enable the systems analyst to identify the problem in proper perspective.
* Problem solving methodology, which enables examining the problem critically, break it into smaller components, find the causes and effects of the problem, the various aspects of the problem and then re-engineer the system to solve the problem.
* Basic systems concepts and principles. Systems concepts and principles help to adapt to new and different situations, and methods as they become available.
* Systems analysis and design methodologies. Methodologies are specific approaches or strategies for applying specific tools and techniques in an effective manner to successively re-engineer or design systems.
* Interpersonal relation and communication skills.

Initially, a systems analyst may not know enough about the library system to be investigated and the specific problems the system is facing. Therefore, data has to be collected about the present operating condition of the library systems and about the objectives and functions of the library system and its subsystems. He/she must talk to library executives, technical and supervisory staff and library users to find out their needs and expectations; ask questions from the concerned system staff, such as: What is being done? Why it is being done? How is it being done? Who is doing it? What is the major bottleneck or problems involved in doing it? What is not being done that should be done? To get such data, he/she is highly dependent upon library staff and its members. For this purpose, the systems analyst requires human relation skills and communication ability, both to express orally and in writing.

Library systems analyst has to accomplish much of his work through other people. Hence, his abilities to work with and communication with, and understand others are crucial. Effective communication is necessary not only to get correct facts, analyse them and think through a way to solve the system's problems but also to express the results of his findings very clearly and exactly, so that no body is in any doubt about what he meant.

The library systems analyst must be able to convince library management how the use and application of information technology can benefit the library and its operations. For this reason, he must have working knowledge of information technology and techniques. He must also keep informed about the latest developments in information technology. The information technology is changing fast. This technology is moving towards databases, objects oriented tools, client server architecture, and wide area networks. The knowledge about the recent developments in technology will help him/her to apply the technology to re-engineer or improve the library systems in a better way by using his/her professional expertise.

Library systems analyst needs to be proficient in one or more high-level programming languages, like Pascal. Sophisticated applications are being built with object-oriented languages as C ++ or Java. In particular Java has become popular because of its use and applicability to the Internet and World Wide Web.

3 LIBRARY SYSTEMS ANALYSIS AND DESIGN PROCESS

3.1 Introduction

Library systems analysis and design is a systems development or problem solving technique, consisting of a series of interrelated activities. Using this technique, the systems analyst analyses/ critically examines existing library systems, procedures, methods, hardware and software, to understand fully the activities and the objectives of the library systems, to study and improve library systems, or alternatively design more effective and efficient library systems and services.

To comprehend the full details of an entire library system or make its work practices and functional activities transparent, we need to decompose the system into smaller subsystems and functions. (Work practices are the methods used with or without the aid of equipment, etc., to do work. These includes the policies, procedures and processes (i.e., step by step instructions for accomplishing a task or the steps a system goes through to convert inputs into outputs.). In addition, one must find out in which way the staff co-ordinate, communicate, decide and perform tasks in an organisation.

By analysing and decomposing the procedures, processes and operations of library subsystems into series of logical decisions and actions we can obtain a greater level of detail. This detailed analysis enables us to identify and describe the inputs, step-by-step process (structured operations), and outputs (products and reports) to be produced.

The result of this analysis is a report giving a total detailed picture of functional systems of a library system and recommendations for setting up improved systems. The detailed descriptions of processes and procedures, also help the library staff to execute the proposed processes and procedures—both manually or using computers—as well as to carry out their functions efficiently and effectively.

The need to conduct systematic systems study of a library system arises when the manager of the system *recognises either the opportunities to improve the system or identifies existence of a complex problem.* Using this methodology, one may come up with the most satisfactory solution to the problem and the logical basis in support of choosing the right course of action.

Recognition of a problem may arise in different ways. Often, library managers try to anticipate the problems they are likely to meet and deal with them before they develop into major crises. To this end they set up library performance measures, standards, or criteria for measuring expected outputs. Using these tools one can identify deviance between the actual and intended outcomes of the system. If necessary, one starts investigation to determine the source of deviation and possible course of action that need to be taken to remedy the situation. Some problems are identified as a result of monitoring the external and internal environment of the library system. It helps to pick up possible early warning of events, which may impact upon the library system's output or functioning, both favourably and unfavourably.

Often in this absence of formal efforts to anticipate problems or change in environment of a library system, result in system difficulties or crises, suddenly. As such, one must develop a formal and structured approach to the acquisition, compilation and analysis of information about the conditions or changes in external and internal environment of the system, if one has to resolve library problems satisfactorily. For this reason, the library management establishes a systems study department/unit in an organisation to monitor the working of ongoing system, which is headed by a systems analyst. The systems analyst other members of his unit conduct the systems studies either to resolve the problems faced by the library management and other staff in day to day running of the system efficiently, or to design and implement new systems and services, whenever need be.

The strategy used by systems analyst to conduct system study, for resolving library problems or re-engineering library systems and services, is known as library systems analysis and design methodology. It is basically a library system development or problem solving method, which consists of series of interactive activities.

The analyst needs to know what work is being performed, how much work is being performed and how much time is taken per unit work. These quantitative data are important in order to find out the cost of present systems, to determine whether the systems are cost effective and appraising the suitability of present work methods. This data serves as benchmark to develop and implement improved or new library methods, procedures and systems, manual and computerisation.

4 PHASES OF LIBRARY SYSTEMS ANALYSIS AND DESIGN STUDY

4.1 Introduction

The library systems analysis and design (also called library systems study) involves series of interactive activities or cyclic steps, based upon systems approach or thinking [*cf.*, Chapman, 1970; Fitzgerald and Fitzgerald, 1973; Gouch and Srikantaiah, 1978; Liston, 1971; Smith, 1980; Wasserman, 1980; Whitten and others, 2001]

These activities can be broadly divided into the following four phases:

1. ***Preliminary investigation phase***

During this phase we determine the exact nature of the problem and outline a rough plan to continue with the study. It involves identification and specification of the apparent problems in precise terms and establish scope, preliminary requirements, constraints, budget and schedule of the proposed project.

2. ***Analysis phase***

During this phase, we try to understand and critically evaluate the existing system. The focus is on data gathering and data analysis. Efforts are made to ascertain the system's goals, objectives, environment and work practices in clear terms; the problems the system is facing or operations that need to be improved are identified, and the requirements of workers and users of the system are also explored and examined.

3. ***Design phase***

This phase involves planning and development of a new system, or re-engineering the current system. The emphasis is on the design and development of alternative systems or approaches to solve the problem, and recommend the most suitable design or solution.

4. ***Implementation phase***

This entails construction, testing, review and implementation of the new or improved system or services, recommended for implementation. This phase also involves training the staff for running the system and services. Ongoing technical support for maintenance and improvement of the implemented system at later stages is also required and provided.

We give below explanations of systems study phases, which is followed by detailed account in the later sections:

* **Phase 1: Preliminary Investigation**

This preliminary investigation — also called the problem diagnosis, preliminary survey, project planning, feasibility study, or system survey — is the initial investigation stage of systems study. During this phase the analyst collects general facts about the problem or system under study to detect the *true nature of the problem* and what to do about it. Very often, what appears to be a problem turns out to be, on a closer look, only a symptom. For example, suppose you are examining students' complaints about non-availability of certain textbooks in textbook collection of the library. Your brief study may reveal that the source of the problem is not in the textbook section or in the working of library system, as you first thought. It reveals that the cause of the problem lies in the detached role-played by the teaching department in building up the collection. The department did not suggest or forwarded recommendation to the library for acquiring the newly added course books. The department should have forwarded the recommendation to the library, according to practice, either immediately after the new course of study was approved or much before the classes started.

Thus, the aim of the initial inquiry is *to define the nature and scope of the problem* in exact terms. Establishing, the nature and scope of the problem is a critical element of an inquiry. The boundaries of the problem must clearly be delimited, so that it is possible to solve it within available budget and schedule.

During this phase, the analyst *outlines a rough plan on how to go on with the project*. He/she sets the project's goals, specifies technical constraints, possible solutions of the problem, and assesses the cost and feasibility of the project.

In this phase of the systems study the systems analyst performs many of the steps that will be performed in the systems analysis phase, but with much less thoroughness. The output of this initial survey or investigation is an assessment report or feasibility report that presents findings and recommendations. It usually includes:

- The Project name.
- The nature, scope and objectives of the project.
- General description of the proposed system solutions (this can be a proposal for the development of a new or modified system).
- Preliminary cost-benefit analysis that helps to find out whether the project is feasible or not. What resources should be committed to the project and what should be the possible plan of action, if a project is undertaken.

The management reviews the findings and project plan. The proposals are either accepted or rejected. Alternatively, management may ask for further probe or revision. If the management decides to give go ahead signal to the systems analyst, then a detailed systems analysis and evaluation study of the library system is carried out.

* **Phase 2: Systems Analysis and Evaluation**

The purpose of systems analysis is to understand the existing system and to establish system requirements. To understand the system implies gathering all the data or fact about it; this data must be organised and analyses. Data gathering is time-consuming and requires much hard work and patience. The final product of this phase of study is a report delineating a set of functional requirements and system's specifications (also called as functional specifications) and describing in precise terms the input, the processes involved, and output expected by the users.

During this phase, the analyst studies and analyses the current system in detail. The nature of information that is required by the systems analyst for the purpose of defining the problem could be organised as followed:

1. Background information of the library system — the origin and history of the library system.
2. Objectives, policies, and other structural aspects of the organisation.
3. Resources — human, physical and financial.

4. Communication channels, control systems.

In addition, he/she collects facts on how well the current system is functioning. Information about the needs of users - wants and expectations of the library users - is also collected. Impression or idea about the perception, attitudes, and level of involvement of staff of the library system is also obtained. The system analyst also may identify reasons for dissatisfaction among the library users and staff.

Most of the information may be obtained from library records, such as annual reports, budget estimates, etc. Talking to individuals or by observing people at work, or administering questionnaires one can also obtain certain types of information and clarifications, which normally one cannot obtain from the library records or other sources.

After discussion with staff at all levels in the library and its users, the analyst finally arrives at the specifications of the end-users' requirements. After having identified the requirements, possible solutions to the problem are figured out and whether it is feasible to implement the possible solutions is checked.

The analysis of the system makes us understand how the existing system works. It is only after understanding how a system operates and determining where it fails; we can specify the exact nature of the problems, their causes and effects. We can also formulate the possible solutions. The results of this study phase are presented in the form of written document which will include problem statement, end-users' requirements, systems specifications, and the candidate solutions or changes to be done in the systems based on end-users requirements or identified problems and updated feasibility assessment of the project.

The feasibility study involves consideration of various constraints within which the proposed solutions are to be implemented. The cost estimates and resources required to implement the solutions are determined. The cost and the benefits of each solution are also established.

Based on the findings of the analysis phase the management may cancel the project or give directive to continue to the next phase of the system study work.

* **Phase 3: System Design and Development**

This phase is an inventive or creative stage of a system development process. You consider the end-user requirements to be met and design new operations, methods or processes to be implemented. This is the phase when you plan to re-engineer existing system or design a new one. During this phase, the analyst determines new operations, methods, processes and design of working systems. Very often, a limited working system or subset of a system — a prototype is developed, to get an idea of what system, process, or procedure might be like before it is fully developed.

The system analyst documents the specifications of the proposed alternative designs, giving estimated cost and cost-effectiveness or cost-benefit analysis of each alternative design. He/she ultimately presents the specifications or report of the study to the management for review, with the recommendations to implement one that is most cost effective. If the management accepts the design proposals, further steps are undertaken.

* **Phase 4: System Implementation, Maintenance, and Re-valuation**

In this phase a detailed design is developed based on the prototype designed earlier. Also, construct or install the new system, procedure, or the application, test the system, and modify if need be. The role of the system analyst changes from system development to system support, once the system becomes operational. It implies maintenance, periodic evaluation and further improvement of the system.

5 THE LIBRARY SYSTEMS DEVELOPMENT

5.1 Life Cycle

As mentioned above the four phases of the library systems development or systems analysis and design process constitute a series of interactive activities or cyclic steps. Consequently, this systems investigation process is also called systems development life cycle (SDLC) [Figure: Chapter C-1]. The detailed description of the phases and the cyclic steps involved are given in the following sections.

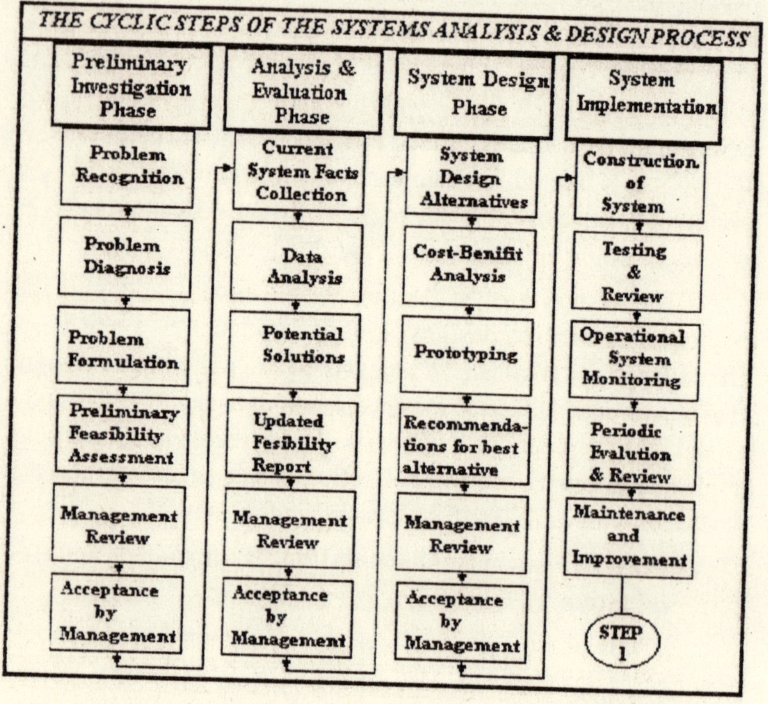

Figure C-1: Systems Analysis, Design and Development Cycle

5.2 Cyclic Steps of Systems Analysis and Design Process

(1) Preliminary Investigation or Feasibility Study Phase

As stated earlier, the library systems development analysis and design process commences when the library management becomes aware of a problem or opportunity and directs the systems analyst to appraise or assess the system and propose ways of improving or re-engineering it, or develop a new one.

Before actual initiation of a library system study project, the systems analyst often conducts a preliminary study of the system. The major purpose of this activity is to collect data needed to detect and state the problem in exact terms, and to decide what steps one needs take to understand and resolve the problem of the system.

During this phase one makes an attempt:

- to recognise the deficiencies in the system, if any and to define the system's problem clearly by pinpointing the causes of unsatisfactory performances, excessive cost of operation, and missing functions, and so forth
- to find out and specify the possible solution of the problem, or the systems or services that need to be improved or developed as a possible solution to the problem; or to determine and stipulate the best way to achieve the objective of the management's request
- to assess the feasibility of the proposed solution or system and to decide whether the further detailed study is necessary or desirable and, if so,
- to set goals to remove these deficiencies—the set goals must be realisable within the constraints of the organisation
- to estimate the cost, time, personnel, and other resources required for carrying out the project, and
- to furnish a work plan for conducting the study along with appropriate advice and justifications for the consideration of management for approval.

This initial fact finding involves consultation not only with the top management but heads of the sections, staff involved with carrying out the systems activities, users of the system who will be affected by the changes to be brought in the working of the system.

The outcome of this activity is a report that contains the following items:

a. Definition of Problem.

b. Feasibility assessment.

c. Project's plan, which includes statement of objectives of the project or plan, broad specification of the proposed solution or system, possible costs, personnel required, and a schedule for completion.

During the feasibility study, the individual systems analyst or group conducting the study often uncover alternative methods of achieving the objectives of the project. These alternative methods are reported to the management. A feasibility study also enables us to find out a general workable solution to the stated problem and state the plan for carrying out the workable solution as a formal feasibility report.

The major purpose of the feasibility study is to establish whether a project should be undertaken, and if so how one can best carry it out and complete it. The systems analyst conducts the feasibility study, prepares the report and submits it to the management for review and final decision.

A feasibility study is really a system study done on a small scale, it requires nearly all the steps necessary to analyse and evaluate a system, but the steps are not carried out in full detail. The steps involved are:

(1) To define the goals and scope of the feasibility study.

This involves recognition and definition of the problem as perceived by management, to have an idea about the objectives, constraints (time, budget, are personnel) imposed by the management, in finding a feasible solution.

(2) To study of the current situation.

This involves conducting a brief survey of the organisation to gather information about the current situation. Start by collecting background and general information. Interview key persons, find out the requirement of users (both library staff and library members) and then get into detail of pertinent process.

The background information should provide the systems analyst, conducting the feasibility study, sufficient knowledge about the type of operation or activities involved, as well as information about the organisational structure, finance, volume of operations, and organisational policies and objectives. Finally the study must give a clue to the cause(s), of the current problem(s), or in what way the innovations can be introduced.

(3) To find out the possible alternative solutions, with variations in features and costs.

At this stage the systems analyst must figure out and offer one or more alternative solutions. One must be able to tentatively assess the costs, benefits, and relative utility of each alternative. Each solution must be considered, only if found reasonably viable to be carried out.

(4) Preparation of the feasibility report and submission to the management for approval.

At this stage the systems analyst prepares feasibility study report that includes his finding and recommendations for further actions, and submits it to the management for review and final decision. The report contains:

a. The scope of the study, including a statement of objectives and constraints of the study.

b. Brief description of current system(s).

c. Description of the current problem(s) and constraints. Identify deficiencies by pinpointing missing functions, unsatisfactory performances, and excessive cost of operation and so forth.

d. Statement whether the project sounds reasonable from a financial and technical standpoint.

e. Specification of the goals set to remove the problems or deficiencies — Give description of tentative workable solutions, realisable within the constraints of the organisation. Account of the characteristics of each alternative solution and their cost and benefit analysis.

f. Recommendations regarding the chosen or proposed solution. One needs to justify and describe what the proposed system will achieve (Recommended solution should be the one that best meets the management's or the library users' needs and is flexible enough to meet future needs). The estimated cost, other resources required, and the timetable for design and development of the system.

When management approves the initial or introductory library system development plan or project, in the next phase, the system analyst conducts the analysis and evaluation of the working system in detail, with a view to identifying the exact system problems, functions, feature, constraints and the future needs of the users. The objective of this phase is also to determine and formulate future requirements of the system and outline the proposal or plan to improve the existing system or design and develop a new system.

(2) Systems Analysis and Evaluation Phase

Once the preliminary phase, also called *problem definition*, or *planning phase*, which involves identification and specification of the problem in exact terms and preparation of the proposals for the system study project, is over, and the management approves the proposals. The system analyst undertakes the detail analysis and evaluation of the system, which constitutes the second phase of the system study.

This phase — also called by some as feasibility study phase — is an in-depth fact finding phase and solution(s) searching phase under which the detailed survey and critical assessment of the present system are carried out, with a view:

- To find out the current operating conditions of the system, based on a thorough understanding of present methods, procedures used,
- To ascertain how effectively, efficiently, and at what cost, the present system meets the requirements of the library users,
- To establish and report to the management, after evaluating

the present methods, procedure, personnel, equipment and services of the system - What steps need to be taken? Whether to retain the existing procedures with minor changes, reorganise some operations, increase or decrease staff, or design and implement a completely new system and services, and if so,

- To take necessary steps in this direction, and develop prototype systems, services, or operations for implementation, and recommend one for implementation that best meets the needs or is most cost effective.

During this phase a detailed fact finding or in depth survey of the system is conducted by the analysts to obtain all possible information as necessary to get a clear picture of the system under investigation and the current demands on the systems. During this phase the information collected would cover the system's objectives, policies, functions and procedures, structure, personnel, method of control, external and internal environment, output, financial and other resources, hardware and software, equipment, and user requirements.

Without a clear understanding of the nature of the existing system, it is not possible for the systems analyst to decide on what to look for to detect the exact nature of a problem. Secondly, in spotting the bottleneck and to discover whether they are caused by inadequate skill or training of the staff carrying out the operations, or due to the weakness and complexity in operations, or by backlog or by other factors, the system analyst will be in a better position to propose operational alternatives to the existing processing systems, and ultimately design and implement new or improved cost effective systems.

Current System's Study Approach and Data Gathering Methods

Generally, to study the current system or collect facts about the system, system analysts apply the top-down approach. The analyst starts by collecting background information about the requirements of the organisation and the users of the system through planned discussions with the key staff members of the library system and interviewing selected library users. Next step should be getting information about organisational structure; human, financial and other resources; details of processes — volume of operations and transactions; relationships with the environment (users, trade union, supra-system, book trade, other libraries, etc.); organisational and financial policies and objectives, etc.

Gathering data is time-consuming and expensive. There is no standard procedure for gathering data, but there are certain well-established methods of collecting and analysing data, such as:

* Interviews
* Questionnaires
* Observation
* Sampling
* Written documents

Systems analysts use *structured systems analysis methodologies* such as **Decomposition Diagrams, Data Flow Diagrams, Flow Charts, Decision Tables, Structured English**, etc., — to understand the processes of the system and relation between system components and provide structured description of processes, procedures and data flow through the system. Process models, in various forms, help system analysts, librarians, and technical staff to visualise library processes and redesign or develop a new one to improve efficiency of the workflow. To model data about a library system, system analysts use **entity relationship diagrams (ERDs). Object-Oriented Analysis and Design** has also emerged as a model-driven approach that introduced object diagrams that document a system in terms of its objects and their interactions. These methodologies use their own tools and standards and help us to understand and build models of the systems. One can build models both for existing systems — to better understand those systems — and for the proposed systems or designs. A model is graphic representation, pictogram or a physical replica of the entity. These models show not only what a system is or does, but also how the system is physically set up.

Modelling techniques can be used along with automated tools. Systems analysts draw system models with general-purpose graphics software such as, *Microsoft Word, Corel Draw or Corel Flow.* Repository–based CASE or modelling tools such as *System Architect, Visible Analysis* or *Rational ROSE* are also used

The objective of this phase of study is to have a complete knowledge of the present conditions and problems of the system. The systems analyst investigates deeply into the structure of the system to obtain a better understanding of its nature, its working and objective, and to find the problem area(s) and to think about on how to regenerate it. Attention is focussed on in identifying all the characteristics of the system and on gaining detailed information, using appropriate data gathering and data analysis techniques, about each of the following aspects of the system:

(1) Mission, goals, objectives and policies

(2) Organisational structure

(3) The requirements of the system

The requirements of the system are the demands placed on the system from all sources — library members, staff, management and its internal and external environment.

(4) Current operating conditions of the system and its functional units.

The analyst must collect facts to obtain a working knowledge of the functions or operations of the system. One must find out about the steps involved in various library operations and collect information about inputs, processes, and outputs of the subsystems of the system from the staff, library manuals and the forms used. This information helps to construct the procedures or processes and depict them in the form of flow charts and flow of data in processes with the aid of data flow diagrams. Survey of the equipment used is also necessary to establish the proper use and efficacy of the equipment.

Detailed survey and work measurement of the individual jobs in the system, helps on checking whether the job descriptions of each job match the function to required.

(5) ***Outputs***

The outputs are the end products of the system — information products, reports, records prepared or results of action taken on the system to meet the demands being placed on it.

(6) ***Inputs***

The inputs are the resources — documents, finance, personnel, hardware and software, equipment — raw materials or data required to produce outputs.

(7) ***Cost of the system and its subsystems.***

Besides understanding fully the functions, operations (i.e., detailed activities of its subsystems) and the objectives of the present system, the systems analyst needs to know how much work is being done and how much time and money are spent per unit of work. These quantitative data are important:

- In finding the present cost of an operation or system, known as cost unit. For example, during acquisition and technical processing of a document in a library, an individual title, monograph, or serial can be regarded as a cost unit at each stage of the process. Certain costs are incurred as each sub-process is completed, and this cost can be aggregated to give the operation cost for an acquisition subsystem's cost centre or technical processing system's cost centre or for both. [*cf.*, Wilkinson, 1980; Pierce and Taylor, 1978];
- In determining the cost-effectiveness of an operation or subsystem, in appraising the suitability of present methods or systems, and using the data as benchmark in comparing them with possible alternatives considered for replacements;
- In measuring the effect of work elimination or personnel requirements; and

- In spotting bottlenecks in operations, etc.

After critically examining the collected data, the present design or working of the system is evaluated to detect the extent of deviation from the given objectives, performance norms or from expected results.

At this stage of the study the analyst not only identifies the exact causes of deviation of the system from the normal behaviour or course to be followed but he/she can work out the ways to make the system achieve the desired results.

The analysis and evaluation of the system are also necessary to detect the present operating cost. A complete cost picture will provide a base or benchmark to make realistic comparative studies of proposed new systems and services.

After collecting relevant data, analysing and assessing it, the systems analyst not only can pinpoint and define the problem areas, but also to visualise and outline alternative solutions to the problems. The result of this study is presented as a feasibility report to the management for approval. The contents of the report are:

- Project name.
- Description of the problem.
- Functional specifications and evaluation of the current system, including a brief description of the current system and its deficiencies — missing functions, causes of failure, unsatisfactory performance and so forth.
- A statement of the goals set to remove the deficiency and the performance requirement of the new or alternative system.
- General description of the proposed system solution or design (this can be a new or a modified system).
- Evaluation of the feasibility of the proposed system and description of the identified alternative solutions or designs. It involves evaluation and testing of alternative solutions, models, or designs for their technical feasibility, operational capability, cost effectiveness, schedule probability by the

systems analyst and modified, if necessary. Finally systematically recording the findings for and presentation before, the library management

Technical feasibility indicate the technical resources and expertise required. Whether the staff handling the system has the technical expertise to build and implement the system. What steps need to be taken to train the staff to make them competent to handle the system. *Operational capability* means finding out whether the solution will fulfil the users' requirements and how well it will work when implemented. *Schedule probability* means to find out whether the solution can be designed and implemented within acceptable time period.

Only after the analyst is satisfied he/she presents the findings to the management in a well-documented form, for approval and implementation.

Once the management approves the system development project, the next phase of the system development process, namely system design phase begins. Before taking this attempt, it is necessary that the system analyst prepares a project management plan that helps to monitor, direct and control the project efforts effectively and efficiently, so that one could complete it within the stipulated time. Preparing an effective *project management document or plan* is must before one launches any system development project. It helps in the development of the system at a minimum cost and within a specific time frame. The system analyst can use project management tools and techniques such as *Gantt Chart* and PERT (*Project Evaluation and Review Technique*) for preparing a project management plan. Project Management Software, such as *Microsoft Project*, *Artemis Management System* etc., can also be used to plan a project, develop its schedule and budget estimates, monitor its progress and cost, generate reports and bring effective changes during the process of its execution, if necessary.

Once the project management plan is complete, the actual system development process is started, which involves system design and implementing phase.

(3) *Systems Design Phase*

This phase is an inventive, creative or a discovery stage of a system study. The system analyst, with the active collaboration of library staff and management prepares and presents a detailed design of the proposed alternative systems and services. At this stage, the analyst must consider the problem to be solved and the requirements to be met and generate new operations, methods or library technical subsystems' design, for re-engineering the existing one or to install absolutely new ones.

System design is the process of developing a plan for an improved system or to design a new system, based on the result of the systems analysis. For instance, the analysis phase may reveal that the newly enrolled students have to wait for a long time to get them registered as members in all the divisions and department libraries of a university library system. The new system design may involve a plan to change the existing manual registration process, or to design a computerised system replacing the existing manual system, or to integrate the existing computerised membership system module with the proposed integrated library information system in the future.

The design phase of the systems study includes nearly all the elements of the analysis phase, but varying in objective and approach. It involves:

1. Determination or confirmation of the requirements of the proposed new or redesigned system.
2. Establishment, specification and recommendations for remodelling system's structure and operations (inputs, processes, outputs).
3. Redefinition of job descriptions.
4. Redesigning of forms and reports.
5. Recommendations for addition of new and/or replacement of obsolete equipment.
6. Improvement and/or provision of workspace.

During the designing stage, the systems analyst first develops some working models or prototypes of the alternative solutions or designs. Prototypes are then evaluated to provide the library management pros and cons (positive or negative features) of each the solutions or designs. Each alternative solution or design is examined under certain criteria. The criteria for evaluation and measurement of efficiency and effectiveness of proposed solutions or designs can be their relative operational, technological and economic benefits. The systems analysts make use of quantitative and qualitative techniques, statistical and modelling to forecast possible outcomes for each alternative.

After evaluation of the prototype or experimental working models, the systems analyst creates detailed design of any one found most suitable. He/she documents the specification of the design and estimated cost and gives along with it the cost-effectiveness and cost-benefit analysis of each alternative for the benefit of the management review.

In this phase the systems analyst redefines the objectives of the system, based on the identified new requirements or demands placed on the system, and explores alternative solutions, models or designs for achieving the newly defined objectives of the system. The relative utility, cost-effectiveness or outcomes of the proposed models or designs are also noted. It requires a detailed examination of alternative designs regarding their performance, proficiency, cost and other attributes. Subsequently, he/she submits the final proposal or recommendations along with implementation plan, stating relative efficiency and effectiveness of the alternative designs or models to the library management for selection of the one found most appropriate, with recommendation. The chosen model or design is usually the one that best meets the needs, easy to install and cost effective.

The *logical analysis*, thus presented, helps the decision-maker to make the choice considering the *ramifications*. An implementation plan that focuses on all necessary tasks, constraints, cost, and other parameters affecting project implementation and schedule, is also provided. After considering the proposal, the management may approve the proposal, reject or ask for modification.

(4) Systems Implementation, Testing, Maintenance and Re-evaluation Phase

After the proposal is approved then the process of actual development and implementation of the proposed system design begins. At this stage a system installation plan and schedule, is developed, the design specifications are also verified before the new design of the system or application is actually physically implemented.

After installation the system, process, or application is tested and re-examined. If need be, the necessary changes are made before it is made operational. The process of consolidation, monitoring and review of installed system is continued.

The necessary training of the staff is undertaken. They must learn how to work with the system. Library members must also receive hands-on training to learn to use the system, particularly, if it is a computerised one. Important tools in training are the staff manual and user manual — the documents prepared to aid and staff and end-users not familiar with the system.

Maintenance is an on going activity and begins only after the initial development effort is complete. Some consider it a separate phase. However, monitoring of the on going system is necessary.

6 THE TOOLS OF SYSTEMS ANALYSIS AND DESIGN

There are several tools and techniques used by a systems analyst during the distinct phases of a systems development life cycle. In this section, we will give a brief description of such tools and technique. These techniques enable the systems analyst to analyse the complex system, think clearly about the new system design and communicate or document the findings in clear terms. We will also explain these tools and techniques in detail, in the later part of the book.

6.1 Fact-Finding Techniques

Effective use and application of data collection and analysis tools and techniques are crucial during a system study and development project. A systems analyst does fact-finding during every phase of the systems development cycle — initial survey phase, analysis and evaluation phase, design phase, and the designed system implementation phase. The analyst collects facts about library members, staff, system components, processes, library collection, finance, and other resources. The common fact-finding techniques used by systems analysts are observation, questionnaires, interviews, sampling, and extracting data from *written documents* — these include internal data sources of institutions, such as office records, written procedures, manuals, various official reports, forms and documents, etc.

Selecting the appropriate method (or methods) will depend upon the nature and complexity of the problem under study, the facilities available, the extent of accuracy required, the time span of study, and other costs and resources associated with and availed for data gathering. Each method has its advantages and disadvantages. For example, *questionnaires* have the advantages of obtaining data more efficiently in time and cost wise as compared to obtaining data by interview method. *Interviewing* has the advantage of flexibility for adapting, and changing questions as the analyst proceeds with the interviews. One can formulate questions that can draw very significant information. Gathered data are analysed and represented using statistical tools and techniques. [*cf.*, Kashyap, 1984; 1969; 1984; 1986]

One of the important survey research design decisions pertains to sampling. Sampling, also called *survey sampling* or *population sampling*, deals with the method for selecting and observing (*measuring*), including collecting data — may be through interviews or questionnaires — from or about, a part (sample) of the population, to make inferences about the whole population. Population refers to the entire group of people, events or things of interest that the analyst or researcher wishes to investigate.

The reasons for using a sample rather than collecting data from the entire population are fairly obvious. In investigations involving a very large number of elements (members) of the population, it would be practically impossible to collect data from, or to test, or examine every element. Even it were possible, it would be prohibitive in view of the time, costs, and other resources required for conducting the study.

A sample survey can have several advantages over a complete census: (i) economy, (ii) feasibility, (iii) speed and timeliness, and (iv) quality and accuracy. On the other hand, a complete census survey has special advantages in some situations:

- It is easier to secure complete data from or for a small number of elements; units or population.
- One can secure better compliance and response from people.
- Bias of coverage may be easier to check and reduce.
- Sampling statisticians are not required [*cf.*, Yates, 1953 - p 2; Zarkovich, 1961 - V 1, Chap. A and B]

As pointed out, in *sampling design*, we are basically concerned with two aspects: a *selection process*; that is, the methods or rules and operations by which some members of population are included in the sample, and an *estimation process* for computing the sample statistics, which are the *sample estimates* of population values; that is, the size of the sample necessary to generalise the findings from the sample data to the total population. Besides the sample design, the other important aspects or steps involved in the general survey process, (also called survey research or survey design) are:

(a) The definition of the survey variables.

(b) The methods of observation, measurement, data collection and data processing.

(c) The method of analysis to reduce the survey data to meaningful results or inferences.

(d) The use of survey results in finding solution to the problem or formulating hypotheses.

We shall discuss these data gathering techniques, in detail, in an other chapter of the book.

6.2 Structured Analysis and Systems Specification Methodologies

There are several structured analysis and system specification techniques also called activity analysis and data flow analysis methods. These techniques are used in structured system development to represent systems in graphic form and to develop models for existing and proposed systems [*cf.*, DeMacro, 1979; Gane and Sarson; Yourdon, 1979; Yourdon and Contantine, 1979]. Models (also called logical models, physical models or implementation models in different settings or contexts) show not only what system is or does, but also how a system is physically implemented. These models help us to (i) describe the processes of the system and relationships among the system components, and (ii) depict flow for specific entities (forms, documents and other items), and flow of data through the system.

Processes represent operations; actions or work performed by people on certain items (forms, bills, books, etc.) with or without the aid of machines (especially computer programs) on incoming data flows to produce outgoing data flows. The depiction of processes and how they interact or interface with one another is termed process modelling. The interaction between processes takes the form of flow of processed items and data between them. A representation of flow of items or data and processing performed on the items or data is called process model. Process models are graphically represented as flow charts and data flow diagrams. A graphical representation in which symbols are used to show operations, activities or processes in sequence is called a flow chart. A graphic representation of the movement and transformation of data within a system or an organisation is named as data flow diagram (DFD). (Also known as data flow graph, or data flow graph or bubble charts.)

Using these methods and their tools we can furnish structured description of processes and develop computer programs. We briefly describe below, some of the tools and techniques used for structured description of processes (i.e., logical progression of library operations) and flow of data thorough the system

6.3 Flowcharts

Flowcharts are one of the earliest of diagramming techniques for representing a detailed logic of systems procedures or programs. A flowchart presents a visual map of a program or procedure and shows the basic input, output, and processing components for a program or procedure. The processing components are the steps involved in doing work. The flow chart uses arrows to represent the direction of the program flow and boxes and other symbols to display actions.

Flowcharts help the analyst or programmer to breakdown the system into smaller workable segments and aid the analysis and sequencing alternative paths in the operation. Flowcharts usually bring to light new area of the problem that needs further study and evaluation.

Using standard flowcharting symbols, we can draw various types of flowcharts, such as, a systems flowchart, a program flowchart, and a process flowchart. A *system flowchart* shows the overall work flow of the system. A *program flowchart* is a detailed explanation of how each step of the program or procedure is actually performed. Programmers use program flowcharts to show the step-by-step sequence of instructions of the computer program. System analysts use program flowcharts (also called *logical flowcharts*) to show the step-by step sequence of decisions and actions within a procedure or operation. [*cf.*, ANSI, 1970; Chapin, 1970; Thomas, 1971]

6.4 Entity-Relationship Diagrams

We need data and information to run and manage a library system efficiently and effectively. Thus, systems analysts need to understand an organisation's data requirements to design the information system. Information systems provide appropriate and useful data and information required in running and managing the library system efficiently and effectively. Entity-Relationship Diagrams (ERD) are *data modelling tools* used to graphically depict an organisation's data, and design information systems of organisations.

All information systems capture and store data about various entities (no matter whether computers are used or not). Any entity represents a real world object or concept, such as monograph, serial, a library member or a library job. ERDs show the Entity-types — persons, objects, events, places, organisations and other systems with which the system interacts or is involved in running the enterprise and the relationships among these Entity-types. Entities are described by their properties, called attributes and the relationships among them. [*cf.*, Chen, 1976, 1983; Bachman, 1969; Martin, 1985; Martin and McClure, 1985]

6.5 Data flow Diagram (DFD)

A data flow diagram is a graphical presentation of the flow of data between processes and data stores or files in the information system. It is a systems analysis tool to show how data flows through a logical system or a process that works on or transforms data and the data stores (Data flows to and from data stores). The DFD delineates the *sources* that generate data, the *processes* which the data undergo, the *files* where the data is stored, and the *destinations* (also called *sinks)* of the information provided by the system.

A source is a data origin; an example is a bill sent to the library by a vendor. The vendor is a source of data. A sink or destination is the recipient of data; an example is the library member to whom bibliographic information is provided. A source or sink is represented by a *square*. Processes are the actions taken on the data — comparing, checking, filing, and so forth. A circle or bubble represents a process. A file is a repository of data — a disk or tape file, a set of papers in a file cover and so forth. An open-ended box in a DFD represents a file. The data flow traces the flow of data through the system processes. An arrow shows the direction of the data flow — a line with directional notation — also called *a vector*.

The data are identified by name written along side its corresponding arrow. An arrow must go to or come from a process circle, or bubble. In fact, the data flow shows how the processes are connected. [*cf.* De Marco, 1979; Gane and Sarson, 1979; Martin, 1982; Martin and McClure 1985; Yourdon, 1989; Yourdon and Constantine, 1979]

6.6 Decision Tables

Decision table is a tool for specifying complex policies and *decision-making* rules. A *decision table*, also called a *decision logic table*, is a tabular representation of: (1) Conditions - the factors to be considered in making a decision; (2) Actions - steps to be taken when certain combinations of conditions exists; and (3) Rules - specific combination of conditions and the actions to be taken under those conditions.

Decision tables are useful in cases that involve a series of interrelated decisions; and their use helps to ensure that no alternatives are overlooked. Programmers can code portion of a program right from a decision table. [*cf.*, Hughes, 1978; Kashyap, 1978, 1980; Pollock, 1971]

6.7 Structured-English

Structured–English is a tool for describing procedures or program logic in English-like terminology. It uses the vocabulary of English combined with logical constructs of a structured programming language (by structured we mean, it is highly organised). As this language is based on the principle of structured programming, process description in Structured-English is easy to convert to a structured computer program. Decision tables and Structured English complement one another to describe a single process. [*cf.*, De Macro, 1979; Gane and Sarson, 1979; Martin and McClure, 1982]

6.8 Systems Evaluation Techniques

The existing system's performance or utility of alternative system designs or models is gauged based on its operational worthiness, technical merits, and economic utility. Thus, the utility of a system; that is, how beneficial the new system design or model would be to an organisation is established on the basis of three criteria—*operational feasibility, technical feasibility and economic feasibility or viability.*

a) *Operational feasibility* of a system depends on its efficiency and effectiveness, that is, how good is the performance or output of the system. Performance measures or effectiveness criteria of a system are based on goals of the system and contains a strong cost element. One tries to find answers to questions such as:

   Does the system provide the end users and managers with timely, pertinent, accurate information?

   Does the system provide desirable and reliable services?

   Does the system make optimum use of available resources including people, time, etc.?

b) *Technical feasibility* implies the practicality of a specific technical solution and the availability of technical resources. It is also a measure of schedule feasibility. It addresses the following issues:

   Does the system encompass up-to-date technology?

   Is implementation of the proposed technology or solution pragmatic or possible?

   What ability is necessary to run the designed system?

   Can the staff have the required technical ability made available or trained?

   Can a project finish within the given time limit fixed by the management to complete a project?

c) *Economic feasibility or viability* is a measure of the cost-effectiveness and cost-benefit of a system or solution. The techniques used to establish economic feasibility of a system or solutions are known as Cost Analysis Technique and Cost-effective Analysis Technique.

6.9 Cost Analysis Techniques

Cost analysis technique is device of cost study or assessing basic cost (direct or indirect) for a task, cost unit or cost centres (i.e., system or service). Cost analysis of a system is carried using work measurement methods, such as time study, method study and work-study. (*cf.*, Barnes, 1968; Clements, 1975; Currie, 1972; Druschel, 1981; Gilder, 1976; Robert, 1985)

6.10 Cost-effective Analysis Techniques

Cost-effectiveness analysis is a method of finding either (a) the cheapest means of accomplishing a defined objective or (b) striking a balance between the cost of developing and operating a system and the benefits derived from the system or (c) achieving maximum results or value at least cost.

It is a measure of the efficacy with which various means will achieve a given level of performance of a system, judged to be satisfactory. It is a technique with which we can attempt to find out the costs and evaluate the relative effectiveness or performance level of library systems and services. [*cf.* Dumont and Dumont, 1981a, 1981b; Flowerdew and Whitehead, 1974; Lancaster, 1977, 1988; Orr, 1973; Standera, 1974; Robert, 1985]

6.11 Cost-benefit Analysis

Cost-benefit analysis is a technique that evaluates the social costs and social benefits of a project or system. [*cf.* Lancaster, 1977, 1988; Robert, 1985]

6.12 Job Evaluation Techniques

These are techniques to find out the requirements and specifications for a library managerial, professional or non-professional position. Job evaluation is "the process of analysis and assessment of the relative contents of jobs, to place them in an acceptable rank order that can be used as a basis for pay structure". [Dutton, 1976]

6.13 PERT/CPM Network Technique

The PERT (*Planning Evaluation and Review Technique)* and

CPM (*Critical Path Method) network techniques* are well-developed management tools, developed concurrently for the same purpose. The term *PERT/CPM* or network analysis refers to the general method of planning, scheduling and controlling of progress on various constituents of a project. One can use this technique effectively in the detailed planning and scheduling of library projects. [*cf.*, Kashyap, 1976; Dhirendra Rao, 1978; Pratap Lingam, 1981; Brophy, 1983]

References and Reading List

1. Ahituv, Niv; others. 1994. *Principles of information systems*. Ed 4. Wm C Brown Communication, Dubuque, IA.
2. Ansi. *Standard flow chart symbols and their use in information processing* (X.3). American National Standard Institute, New York, 1970.
3. Ansi/X3/Sparc, Database Management System Study Group. *Interim report*. American National Standards Institute, Washington, D.C. 1975.
4. Bachman, C. W. Data structure diagrams. *Database*. v. 1, 2; 1969; p. 4-10.
5. Barnes, R. M. *Motion and time study: Design and measurement of work*. Ed 6. John Wiley, New York, 1968.
6. Brophy, Peter. Critical Path Analysis: a library management tool. *Program*. v. 17, 4; 1983; p. 204-17.
7. Chapin, Ned. Flow Charting with ANSI standards: a tutorial. *Computing survey*. v. 2, 2; 1970; p. 119-143.
8. Chapman, E. A.; Others. *Library systems analysis guidelines*. John Wiley - Inter science, New York, 1970.
9. Checkland, P. B. Toward a system-based methodology for real world systems. **In** Beishon, J and Peters, G. *System behaviour*. Ed 2. 1976, p. 51-77.
10. Chen, Peter Pin-sen. The Entity-Relationship model - towards a unified view of data. *ACM Transaction on Database Systems*. v. 1, 1; 1976; p. 9-36.
11. –, ed. Entity-Relationship approach to information modelling and analysis. North-Holland, Amsterdam, 1983.
12. Clement, D. W. G. The costing of library service. *Aslib Proceedings*. v. 27, 3; 1975; p. 98-111.
13. Currie, R. M. *Work study*. Ed 3. Pittman, London, 1972.
14. Dhirendra Rao. M. K. PERT/CPM - its application to library and information systems. *Annals of Library Science and Documentation*. v. 25; 1978; p. 31-7.

15. De Macro, Tom. *Structured analysis and system specification.* Prentice-Hall, Englewood Cliff, NJ, 1979.

16. Dumont, P. F.; Dumont, R. R. A goal typology of system model of library effectiveness. *Journal of Library Administration.* v. 2, 1; 1981; p. 13-24.

17. Dumont, R. R.; Dumont, P. F. Measuring library effectiveness: a review and assessment. *Advances in Librarianship.* v. 9; 1981; p. 104-41.

18. Dutton, B. G. Job assessment and job evaluation. *Aslib Proceedings.* v. 28; April, 1976; p. 144-60.

19. Druschel, J. Cost analysis of an automated and manual cataloguing and book processing system. *Journal of Library Automation.* v. 14, 1; 1981; p. 24-19.

20. Fitzgerald, John M.; Fitzgerald, A. P. *Fundamental of systems analysis.* John Wiley, New York, 1973.

21. Flowerdew, A. D. J.; Whitehead, C. M. E. *Cost effectiveness and cost-benefit analysis in information science.* London School of Economics, 1974.

22. Ford, G. Performance measurement: Principle and practice. *IFLA Journal.* v. 15; 1996; p. 13-7.

23. Gane, Chris; Sarson, Trish. Structured systems analysis: Tools and technique. Prentice-Hall, Englewood Cliff, NJ, 1979.

24. Gilchrist, A. Cost effectiveness. *Aslib Proceeding.* v. 23, 9; 1971; p. 455-64.

25. Gilder, L.; Schofield, J. L. *Work measurement techniques and library management: methods of data collection.* University of Cambridge, Cambridge, 1976.

26. Gouch, Chet; Srikantaiah, Taverkara. *Systems analysis in library.* Clive Bingley, London, 1978.

27. Hughes, Marrion L.; Others. Decision tables: a tool for librarian. *Library Resources and Technical Services.* v. 22; 1978; p. 42-6.

28. Kashyap; M. M. The basic features of scientific method. *Library Herald.* v. 23; 1984; p. 61-73.

29. –. 1978. Decision making for library managers and systems analysts. *Journal Library and Information Science.* V. 3; 1978; p. 140-55

30. –. 1980. Decision Table: a tool of systems study. *Journal of Library and Information Science.* v. 5, 1; 1980; p. 44-51

31. –.Integrated database design for a library system: Employing library techniques developed by Ranganathan and CDS/ISIS database management system. *Journal of Library and Information Science.* v. 18, 2; 1993: p. 82-141.

32. –. Library systems analysis and design technique. *Journal of library and information science*. v. 17, 2; 1993; p. 128-42.

33. –. Network analysis: A library project management tool. *Journal of Library and Information Science*. v. 1, 2; 1976; p. 199-23

34. –. On-line library catalogues and standards for common application in a network environment: Paper presented to XVI IASLIC Seminar, Bombay, 1994. In *IASLIC SEMINAR (BOMBAY) (1995) (16). Net working of libraries: Problems and prospects*. v. 16; 1995; p. 1-25.

35. –. 1969. Planning of library survey. *Library Herald*. v. 11; 1969; p. 92-101.

36. –. 1984. Measurement theories and its application in library systems study. *Journal of Library and Information Science*. v. 9, 1; 1984; p. 17-35.

37. –. 1986. Method of testing reliability and validity of a measuring device developed for behavioural research. *ILA Bulletin*. v. 22; 1986; p. 10-18.

38. Klir, George J. Preview: the polyphonic general system theory. *In* KLIR (George J), *ed. Trends in general systems theory*. 1978. Ed. 2. Harper & Row, New York, 1978, p. 1-18.

39. Lancaster, F. W. *The measurement and valuation of library services*. Information Resources Press, Washington, 1977.

40. –. *If you want to evaluate your library*. University of Illinois, Champaign, 1988.

41. Laszio, Ervin. *Introduction to System Philosophy*. Harper & Row, New York, 1972.

42. Liston, David M.; Schoene, Mary L. A systems approach to the design of information system. *Journal of the American Society for Information Science*. v. 22; 1971; p. 115-22

43. Martin, James. *Strategic Data-planning Methodology*. Prentice-Hall Inc., Englewood Cliffs, NJ, 1982.

44. –; McCulre, Carma. *Diagramming Techniques for Analyst and Programmers*. Prentice-Hall, Englewood Cliff, NJ, 1985.

45. Orr, R. H. Measuring the goodness of library service: a general framework for considering qualitative measures. *Journal of Documentation*. v. 29, 3; 1973; p. 235-267.

46. Pratap Lingam, P. Library and information systems: planning scheduling and control through the PERT/CPM. *Library Science with Slant to Documentation*. v. 18; 1981; p. 248-62.

47. Pierce, A. R.; Tayjer, J. K. Model for cost comparison of automated cataloguing system. *Journal of Automation*. v. 11, 1; 1978; p.6-23.

48. Pollock, Solomon L: Others. *Decision Tables: Theory and Practice*. Wiley, New York, 1971.

49. Robert, Stephen A. Cost management for library and information services. Butterworth, 1985.
50. Smith, D. System thinking in library and information science. Bingley, London, 1980.
51. Standera, O. R. Costs and effectiveness. *Journal of the American Society for Information Science*. v. 25, 3; 1974; p. 302- 07.
52. Thomas, P. A. *Task analysis for library operations*. Aslib. London, 1971.
53. Von Bertanlaffy, Ludwig. General Systems theory: Foundation, Development, Application. Braziller, New York, 1968.
54. Von Gigch, John. *Applied General System Theory*. Ed. 2. Harper & Row, 1978.
55. Wasserman, A. T. Information Systems and Design Methodology. *Journal of the American Society of Information Science*. v. 31, 1; 1980; p. 5-25.
56. Wilkinson, J. B. Economics of Information: Criteria for Counting the Cost and Benefits. *Aslib Proceedings*. v. 32, 1; 1980; p. 1-9.
57. Whitten, Jeffery L.; Bentley, Lonnie D.; Dittman, Kevin, C. *Systems Analysis and Design Methods*. Fifth Edition. Tata McGraw–Hill Publishing Company Ltd., 2001.
58. Yates, F. *Sampling Methods for Censuses and Surveys*. Ed 3. Griffin and Company, London, 1953.
59. Yourdon, Edward. *Modern Structured Analysis*. Yourdon Press, Englewood Cliff, NJ, 1989.
60. –; Constantine, Lary L. *Structured Design: Fundamentals of A Discipline of Computer Program and Systems Design.* Yourdon Press, Englewood Cliff, NJ, 1979, p. 43-47.
61. Zarkovich, S. S. *Sampling Methods and Censuses*. V 1. Rome, FAO, 1961.

D
Computer-Based Library Information Management Systems Design

1 A LOOK AT INFORMATION SYSTEM

An **information system** is an open, purposive subsystem of an enterprise. It produces information and information products and services. The system has an input, process, and output cycle. It consists of at least three major components — data, transaction processing systems and people involved in the collection, management, dissemination and use of information. The people follow procedures or set rules to capture and process or manipulate data to produce information products and services useful to or needed by the end users in decision making, research or learning about something. Thus, the provision of an information system in an enterprise is always linked to decisions and actions, that is, deciding to do things, accomplishing them and recording the results of actions for future actions and decisions

An information system may or may not use information technology. However, when information technology is used, it helps to enlarge the capabilities of an information system. Computerised information systems store and process data and produce organisational information at greater speed. Information is resource that helps people to accomplish tasks, to understand things, or resolve problems.

Data is pool of observation, a collection of measurements, or some raw facts in isolation about an entity and include numbers, words, symbols, ideas, concepts, and oral verbalisation. By themselves, they are meaningless unless the relationship between them and the context from which they are derived is known. The data 'Rs. 285.00' means nothing if the user does not know that this is the cost (not a published price) of the book entitled Colon Classification paid by the library. Analysis and processing of data help us to discover new facts and/or new knowledge, concepts or interpretations necessary in management, research, learning etc. Thus by data, we mean known facts that can be recorded and that has implicit meaning.

Information is different from data. Data are raw, unprocessed or unevaluated facts that have little or no meaning in themselves; whereas, information is the data processed into an organised form that is meaningful to the recipient. In other words, information has value, otherwise it is data. Information shows its users something they did not know or confirms what they speculated or suspected.

Analysed or processed data i.e., Information plays an important role in improving the efficiency and effectiveness of human decision-making and problem-solving process. Further, the raw observations, facts or data when placed in meaningful context through data-processing operations, carried out by persons mentally or with the aid of computer processing, allow us to draw inferences (or intelligence) from them. To draw inferences a person depends upon his/her cognitive ability, wisdom, knowledge or expertise — the body of meaningful facts, information, truth accumulated by the person with the passage of time.

Based upon the definition of data and information, as given above, we can define **information processing** as an activity of handling or manipulation of raw data, or isolate items of facts and transforming these into meaningful data, facts or information organised in the form it can be used for some purpose. Aggregated or processed data or information; that is, the end products of information-processing operations, provide us understanding, knowledge, or intelligence and thus help us in decision-making or taking a right course of action or in understanding something.

2. FUNCTIONS OF INFORMATION-PROCESSING SYSTEM

An ***information-processing system*** carries out three basic functions (refer to Figure Chapter D-1):

1. Accept raw data - input function
2. Process or convert data into information — processing function, and
3. Produce and communicate information to users — output function.

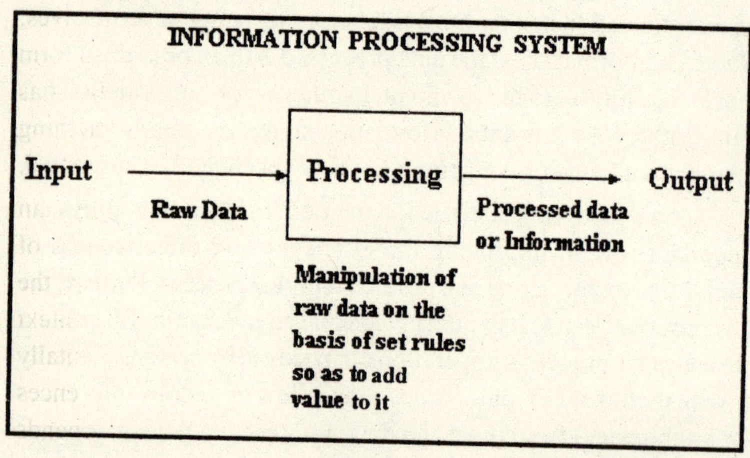

Figure D-1

Input is the 'start up' element on which the system operates or that which is changed by transformation process. It is referred to as raw data to be processed or used to make up finished products or output(s).

Output is defined as the result of an operation performed on data. In a very real sense, output stands for the outcome or the end product of conversion process of a system—the purpose (or the end result) for which the system has been set up.

Process is defined as the activity or set of activities that makes possible the transformation of input into output in useable form.

NOTE : *Inputs, processes, and outputs are also called systems parameters, because these are the essential conditions or properties by which all data-processing systems are described.*

The **computer information processing** involves handling of data or information in a logical and unchanging four-part sequence: *input, storing, processing* and *output*.

Input

The first part of electronic information-processing (EIP) sequence consists of three steps:

i. Gathering or Collecting of Relevant Data

It is the activity by which data are collected for entry into computer system. It involves collecting of data manually from source documents for later keying into a computer. For example, bibliographic data of a document may be first recorded on a worksheet for keying in a computer through terminal or through another input device.

ii. Verifying the Data for Accuracy

It is important to carefully check the data going into a computer for all possible errors. If the data submitted or fed into a computer is invalid or incorrect, the results or outputs will be useless.

iii. Encoding or Transcribing Data

Data are encoded or transcribed into the form that the computer can 'understand' and entered them into computer. (The act of putting previously recorded data into machine-readable form is called transcribing or encoding).

Storing

This operation places either raw (semi-processed) data or information (i.e., processed data) into some storage media. It can be stored either temporarily or permanently to be accessed and retrieved when needed. Quite often, an output of one operation becomes input of another. When this occurs, a cycle is created that can be repeated continuously until the major process is completed. During the intermediary step, the output may be stored temporarily in storage media.

Processing

This part of computer processing involves the actual work performed by the computer on the input to convert it into output. The processing portion may include any or all functions namely: (i) Classifying, (ii) Sorting and arranging, (iii) Comparing and analysing, (iv) Merging, (v) Computing, (vi) Summarising, (vii) Updating the data, and (viii) Storing for future use.

1. ***Classifying***: It means grouping the raw facts according to some pre-selected criteria or a characteristic that make sense to users. The operation involves identifying data or data records (i.e., a set of related items of data, treated as a unit) according to common characteristics or attributes, and placing them into specific categories. For example, records of ordered books might be grouped according to vendors or suppliers, with whom the orders have been placed and later regrouped according to subjects for calculating financial commitment under different subject allocations.
2. ***Sorting and Arranging***: This process involves sorting and then arranging the data items or records according to some logical sequence or rank. For instance, records of monographs on order may be arranged by their respective dates of order, or by author. The sequence of sorting items can be ascending (from lowest to highest values) or descending (from highest to lowest values). For example, starting from alphabet A to Z or Z to A.
3. ***Comparing and Analysing***: This operation involves matching or comparing a set of data or records with another set of data or records. For instance, to avoid duplication we need to know whether the selected documents are available in the library or not. For this purpose we compare book selection records of newly selected documents with the records of the documents in order file, processing file and a library catalogue

(holdings file). Matching process can also be used to analyse, search or retrieve specific data or information. For instance, if we need to retrieve information about the availability of specific document(s) in the library, the required or relevant information can be retrieved by scanning and matching the query (say a subject statement or name of an author) with the earlier posted records in the catalogues or documents holdings file and retrieve the relevant information. By this process, we detect such factors as the nature, proportion, relative value, relationship, and similarity of data.

4. ***Merging***: This operation involves combining one set of source data with other sets of source data. Often combinations of a match and merge, match and retrieve operation are performed. For instance, we match and merge the records of recently ordered documents along with the records of earlier ordered documents to create a single alphabetical file; or we search, match and retrieve the records of documents received from the supplier and make the book order file up-to-date.

5. ***Computing***: This operation entails arithmetic and/or logical manipulation of data; that is, reconstructing source data to create meaningful results through addition, subtraction, multiplication or division and with the help of comparison and logical operations. For instance, computations may be performed to find the total financial commitment of a book order and to calculate balance available and so forth.

6. ***Summarising***: This operation involves reducing a mass of data to a concise meaningful form. After input data have been fed into a data-processing system, the manipulated or processed results are presented in a detailed form or in a summary form (the type of output desired depends upon a decision-making or problem solving situation or job being executed, and is planned in advance). Very often, for decision-making and control purposes, it is not necessary to present all the facts, and only logically condensed data is required. For instance, we may provide only brief bibliographical data about

books while preparing a list of books on a specific topic for a reader or provide aggregated figures about the budget commitment to the librarian from the detailed book budget account record.

Updating: Updating is the process of modifying or changing the data stored in the computer. As old data become outdated, it may be deleted. If, new information becomes available, it is used to replace the old one or added to.

Storing: Storing is the process of keeping data (in this case processed data) in a storage medium in the form of electronic file. It can be stored either temporarily or permanently in an storage media to be accessed and retrieved when needed

In a computer system several methods are used for inputting, processing and updating data. The two main methods are **batch processing** (processing data transactions in-groups at convenient times — usually sometime later - and **transaction processing** (processing the transactions immediately, "*in real time*". A combination of these two techniques is also used.

Batch processing is a technique in which transactions are collected into groups, or batches, to be processed at a time when the computer may be more accessible. Real time processing (also called **transaction processing**) is a technique in which a transaction is processed fast enough for the results to be obtained and acted upon right away.

A computer-based file updating involves three primary files: an existing **master file**, a semi permanent set of related records, a **transaction file**, contain all changes to be made to the master file, and a **new up-to-date master file**. The new master file becomes the permanent repository of all data records relating to an entity type(s), such as library member, or loaned document, or a set of documents or bibliographic items available in a library at a given point in time. The transaction file contains all transactions that occur during a specific period. The data records found in the transaction file show what kind of updating is needed. Three common updating functions are: (1) *additions*, (transaction to create new records in the master file, say for new members enrolled by a library), (2) *revisions*, changing the value of a data field in a record or records of the master file, such as, phone numbers or addresses of library members (3) *deletions* (transaction with instructions to delete the master records, say of library members who quit or cease to be members of the library). In batch processing, with data from the transaction file, the existing master file is updated with the changes called for in the transaction file, not immediately or on-line, but sometime later, and a new master file is created. In real time processing, a transaction is processed immediately for the result to show up and acted upon right away. For processing to be real time, it must be **on-line**—that is, the terminals must be connected directly to the computer.

Output

It is an operation that consists of three steps. The first step involves *retrieving the processed information* from a computer storage device. The second step involves *converting the information* from the form that was used to store it, into a form the user can understand. The third and final step involves *communicating the information* to those who need it, when they need it. Usually, this is done through terminal display, or by providing a printed copy.

3 COMPUTER HARDWARE SYSTEM

A computer hardware system requires four components namely: (1) Input devices, (2) The central processing unit (3) output devices, and (4) the storage to carry out the above mentioned five functions or to handle four main aspects of data handling: input, storage, processing, and output.

The abstract combination of the four primary components comprising a computer hardware system is shown in Figure Chapter D.2:

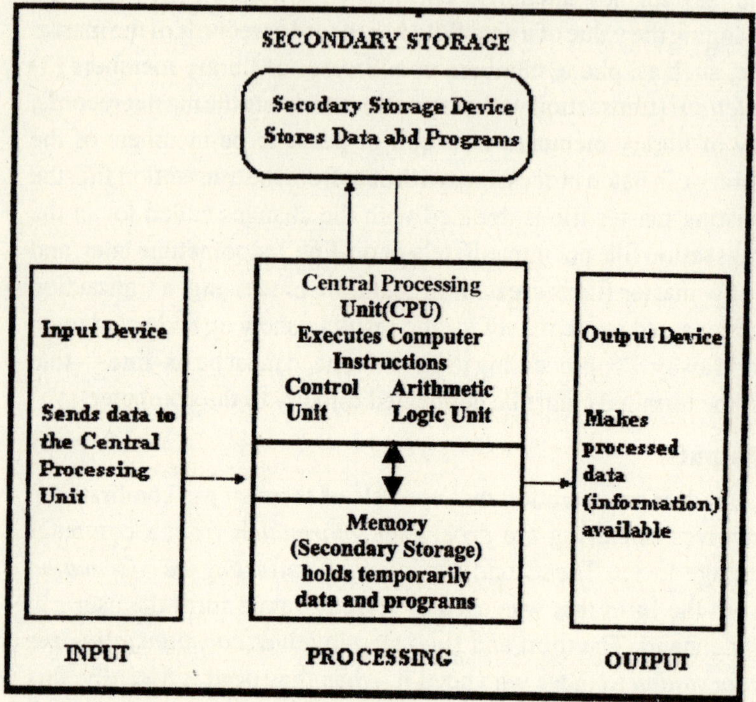

Figure D-2: Four primary components of a computer hardware system

Input Devices

The computer-input devices accept or send data in the form the computer can use. These devices convert mechanical, sound, or light signals into electronic signals. The most common way of entering data into a computer is with a typewriter like ***keyboard***. When a person strikes a keyboard key, say 'M', a specific pattern of an electronic signal is transmitted to the central processing unit, which it sees as the letter 'M', and stores it in a storage device. The other common ways of feeding input data into system are:

Pointing with or clicking a **mouse**. A mouse is an input device, which looks a little bit like a mouse, has a ball on its underside, is moved by hand over a flat surface. As the ball rotates, the mouse movement causes corresponding movement of *pointer* or ***cursor*** on the screen. Pressing buttons on the mouse lets you invoke commands.

Writing with a **pen-based input system**, this allows to input data by writing on a special tablet or pad

Speaking through **voice input system**, also called **speech** *recognition* **systems**, and

Scanning with **scanners**, such as *wand reader* and *bar code reader*, this use laser beams to read special letters, numbers, or symbols such as the zebra-striped bar codes printed on book jackets and on the packages of many other products.

The Central Processing Unit

The central processing unit (CPU), also called **a processor,** is a control centre of a computer hardware system and has the electronic circuitry that manipulates the raw data to produce output. The CPU has the capabilities:

(a) to add, subtract, multiply, and divide (i.e. to perform arithmetic functions on numeric data),

(b) make comparison; That is, compare two values or data to see if they are equal to or not equal; or if one value or data is greater than (>) or less than (<) the other (These values or data may be numeric or alphabetic or alpha-numeric),

(c) to organise, process, store and retrieve processed information or data. In processing the computer data performs such operations as classifying, arranging, comparing, sorting, calculating, summarising, updating data and storing results for future use, and

(d) to direct the entire computer system to carry out, or execute stored program instructions

The **central processing unit**, or **CPU** consists of two parts

1. The control unit, and
2. The arithmetic /logic unit.

The **control unit** of a CPU contains circuitry that uses electrical signals to direct the computer system to carry out, or execute, stored program instructions denoting the sequence in which the input, storage, processing and output tasks need to be performed by the computer system. The control unit communicates with the arithmetic/ logic unit and memory.

The **arithmetic/logic unit (ALU)** contains the electronic circuitry that executes all arithmetic and logical operations. It performs four kinds of basic arithmetic operations: addition, subtraction, multiplication, and division. It also performs logical operations. A **logical operation** is usually a comparison. The unit can compare letters, numbers, or special characters. The computer can then act on the basis of comparison. A logic unit can discern six logical relationships: equal to, less than, greater than, less than or equal to, greater than or equal to, and less than or greater than (that is, not equal to). Symbols called **relational operators** allows defining the type of comparison to be made. The most common relational operators are: = (equal to), <> (not equal to), < (less than), <= (less or equal than), > (greater than), and > = (greater or equal to).

Further, **Boolean expressions** can also be used to determine whether a set of one or more conditions is *true* or *false* and evaluate the truth-value. The operand of a Boolean expression can be one of the following:

* ***Relational expression*** *which compare two values and determines whether a given relationship exits, such as, mfn < 12.*
* ***Boolean functions*** *which return truth-value. The operand of a Boolean expression may be combined with the three Boolean operators - NOT, AND, and OR.*

Output Devices

The computer output devices show or produce the processed data in a form people can use easily. Once data has been entered into the computer, it is processed by the central processing unit and the results are displayed on a screen or printed as output. The output may, for example, appear as *soft copy* on a **Cathode Ray Tube (CRT)**, or may be produced as *hard copy*, as tangible and permanent output printed on paper. The most common output devices are video screens and printers. Each one takes bits' patterns from the computer system convert them into symbols or images that are comprehensible to people.

The most common type of screen is the **cathode ray tube**, or **CRT**.

Computer Storage

The storage or memory of a computer holds data to be processed and the instructions that indicate what processing is to be done. A computer may have several different kinds of storage. These types include:

i. *Limited Internal or Primary Storage:* Vary fast but **limited internal** or **primary storage**, also known as **main storage**; **main memory**, and **primary memory** — all these terms are used interchangeably. The primary memory is the part of the computer and holds data to be processed and the instructions that direct and control the operations of the computer while processing data.

Computer's primary memory holds the data after it is input to the system and before it is processed. It also holds the data after it has been processed but before it is released to the output device. In addition, it holds the programs needed by the central processing unit.

Although closely associated with the CPU, computer primary memory is separate from it. Most types of memory only store instructions or data while the computer is working. The data and instructions are destroyed when the computer is turned off. Part of the primary memory may also contain permanently stored instructions that tell the computer what to do when it is turned on.

Computer internal storage or memory components evolved from vacuum tubes to a magnetic core to semiconductors. Most modern computers use semiconductor memory made up of thousands of very small integrated circuits — pathways for electric currents—on silicon chip. Semiconductor storage has one major disadvantage: it is **volatile**, meaning that when power is turned off, every thing stored on it is erased. The two basic types of semiconductor memory chip in every computer are known as **random-access memory (RAM)** and **read-only memory (ROM)**. The terms RAM and ROM are actually a little misleading, since every chip, RAM or ROM provides random-access storage. That is, all areas of RAM or ROM can be accessed and the central processing unit can perform read and write operations at memory position at any time.

The real difference between the RAM and ROM is that, as the name implies, the contents of ROM can be read only and programs or data cannot be written on it. RAM is volatile, that is, when the power to the computer is shut off (accidentally or by design); every thing on RAM is lost. ROM is non-volatile — its contents do not disappear when the power is turned on.

ii. *External Storage:* Slower but very large **external storage**, also known as **auxiliary storage**, or **secondary storage**, is used for permanent or long-term storage of data and programs. The secondary storage is necessary because primary memory or storage can only be used temporarily. Secondary storage is non-volatile. It is much cheaper than semiconductor memory, but it is much slower.

iii. *Registers, Buffers and Cache Memo:* The **registers** are the fastest and costliest memory normally contained within processing units, for holding instructions or data values that are to be worked out immediately.

Registers

As mentioned above registers are temporary storage areas for holding instruction or data values to be worked immediately. It is the fastest and most costly memory, normally contained within the processing units. Registers work under the direction of the control unit to accept, hold, and transfer instructions or data and perform arithmetic or logical comparisons at high speed.

Cache Memory

Often, a computer's CPU must wait idly while data are being read from or written to the relatively slow secondary storage. Caching is a technique that uses a small amount of semiconductor memory, called a cache, to help in solving this problem of an idle CPU. Most computers use cache memory speed up processing.

Basically, the cache memory is a small amount of very high-speed semiconductor random access memory that stores data temporarily while they are in transit, in either direction, between primary and secondary storage. It serves as a buffer between access speeds of primary and secondary memories. The CPU deals only with the fast cache memory and continues processing while data are in transit to and from cache memory and the slower secondary storage.

Caching can also be used between the registers of the CPU, and the main memory. In this case, a small amount of high-speed semiconductor memory is used as cache, which the CPU searches before looking into slower main memory.

Buffers

A buffer is another special purpose memory. It may be part of the CPU or may be built into devices used to input or output data. Unlike a register, a buffer can hold more than one piece of data at a time. It acts as an intermediary between CPU and any input or output device. As these devices operate at much slower speed than the CPU, a memory is required for holding data temporarily. For example, a printer cannot print data as quickly as the CPU can transfer or send data. A buffer allows the data transferred by a CPU to be stored temporarily, thus freeing the CPU to do other tasks and for the printer to catch up.

Secondary Storage Devices

The two common means of secondary storage are magnetic disk and magnetic tape.

Magnetic Disk Storage

A **magnetic disk** is a plastic or a metal platter coated on both sides with magnetic oxide that looks like a Gramophone record, but it has smooth surfaces instead of the record's characteristic grooves. Magnetic disks are either floppy or hard. **Hard disk** is a metal platter coated with iron oxide and the **floppy disk**, (also called **diskette**), is a round piece of plastic coated with iron oxide.

Diskettes have been popular shortly after personal computers reached the market. It comes in two popular sizes: 5.25" and 3.5" are typical diameters. The 5.25" diskette can hold 360K to over 2MB of data. The 3.5" diskette can hold from 720K to 20MB data. Hard disks come in variety of sizes: 8", 5.25" and 3.5" are typical diameters. The more popular PC diskette is 3.25" or 1.44 MB capacity.

Programs or data written onto the disk remains there permanently or until it is overwritten. Data is stored in a set of concentric circles. Each circle is called a track. A typical disk has fixed number of tracks on each side and one can directly retrieve any data item recorded at any point on the surface, i.e., data can be accessed randomly. However, data can also be stored on it in such a manner that it can be accessed sequentially, using appropriate file organisation techniques.

The Disk Drive

A disk drive is a device that allows data to be read from a disk or write on a disk. The mechanism for reading or writing data on a disk is an **access arm**. It moves a read/write head into position over a particular track of a diskette or a hard disk.

To read or write a diskette is inserted into a disk drive. Whereas hard disks are assembled in a disk pack and we use hard disk drive to read and write on them. Therefore, a hard disk drive has a series of access arms, which slip in between the disks in the pack. Two read/write heads are on each arm, one facing up for the surface above it, one facing down for the surface below it. However, one read/write head can operate at any one time only.

Hard disk drives are of two types. One in which disks, or disk packs are fixed and constitute an integral part of the drive, and are called **fixed disk units**. Other types are called **removable-disk units** or **drives**. As the name implies, these drives are built in a way that the access arms can be retracted and then the disk pack or cartridges can be removed. In fixed disk units, however, the disks (or disk pack), access arms, and read/write heads are combined in a sealed module called **Winchester disk**. Many Winchester disks are permanently built into the drive, some are removable in that sense that the entire module can be lifted from the drive. The removed module however remains sealed and contains the disk and access arms.

Magnetic Tape Storage

A magnetic tape is a continuous plastic coated with magnetised material, usually iron oxide, wound into a reel. Tapes come in number of forms. Normally tapes are half-a-inch (1/2-inch) wide and are wound in the length of 500 to 800 metres, on a spool. Other forms of magnetic tape are: (a) 1.25 inch cartridges; (b) Cassettes; and (d) Digital audiotape (DAT), which uses helical recording technology. Data are stored as extremely tiny magnetic spots that are sensed electronically. The amount of data on a tape is expressed in compactness or density, which is the **number of character per inch (cpi)** or **byte per inch (bpi)** that can be stored on a tape. The amount of data that tape cartridge can hold may be expressed in megabytes or in gigabytes.

The Magnetic Tape Unit

Tapes are mounted on **tape drives** that have a mechanism to move the tapes over an electromagnet read and write head. When it is reading, the head detects the magnetised spots on the tape and converts them into electrical impulses, which are sent to the processor. In the reverse procedure; that is, while writing the head magnetises the appropriate spots on the tape. When the machine is writing the **erase head,** first erases any data previously recorded on the tape.

Tape technology used at home for video or music is now being used with computers. A **digital audiotape**, or **DAT**, uses **helical scan recording** technique. This technique uses a rotating read/write head to write data in diagonal tracks across the tape. The rotating read/write head spins vertically as it moves and places the data in a diagonal band that run across the tape rather than down its length. Some advantages of helical scan recording are high data density; fast recording, fast transfer rate, fast access data and long tape life.

The computer's five basic functions allow it to process data much as a person does — by collecting and manipulating data to derive desired results.

4 LIBRARY INFORMATION SYSTEM

4.1 Introduction

The library system is a human organisation that provides access to sources of knowledge and information to its clients by way of processing and organising information about them. The library as an enterprise selects, acquires, organises and stores for effective retrieval the packages of information or knowledge, in various physical forms and makes them available for use to its members. It also collects bibliographic and other types of information from commercial or non-commercial enterprises, such as libraries, bibliographic information systems, World Wide Web Pages and so forth, and reprocesses it for the use of its member. It also provides referral services and products indicating the relevant information sources (persons, institutions, publications, etc.) useful for getting information on specific area of study and research.

A library is a human enterprise whose information system is distinct from information systems that are typically a part of other enterprises. In a library system, in addition to bibliographic information, organisational information required by the library staff to carry out their activities and decisions making is also assembled and made accessible to them. Thus, a **library information system** constitutes of two major subsystems; one, which is concerned with keeping records or data about library activities and provides organisational information to library staff in their day to day work to function efficiently and effectively, and the other, which processes and organises information relating to the holdings of the library and their contents for the use of library members.

Library managers have to base their decisions on the basis of feed back they get from the organisational information systems or transaction processing systems of the library system and thorough understanding of the network of interrelationships and interdependencies that exist among the library functional systems and staff. What makes their task very challenging is that libraries are complex open systems and the demands placed on library systems for continual adjustment and change, due to their dynamic fast changing educational and socio-technical environment are compelling.

After the advent of information and communication technologies, computer-based functional systems and services are replacing the traditional manual task systems and services of the library systems. Information technology can accomplish programmable tasks more quickly than traditional manual systems. However, human intervention is needed to ensure checks and balances for continuously updating the library processes and techniques, so that the related 'computer programmes' or 'applications' are in alignment with the dynamically changing external and internal environment of a library system.

These days, to help the management and staff to manage the library functional systems efficiently and effectively or to carry out their activities at high level of proficiency information technology based library information systems or library management systems are being developed.

A **computer-based library information system** or **library management system** is a system that includes the computer system (hardware and software) as an additional component. It is an arrangement of people, processes, data (database) and information technology (hardware and software) that are geared together to support day-to-day library operations, as well as sustains the information need of the library staff to perform their day-to-day activities, effectively and efficiently, and provide bibliographic information to the library users. It processes operational and management information required by the library staff and generate the information needed by the library members, to identify and locate the documents available in the library, which is the basic mission of a library information system.

The computerised library information system can also be seen as a computer that interfaces a person or user via the data. The person captures data, input data and uses or interprets the displayed or printed results (computer outputs). The computer receives the data, stores it, processes it and sends it back (in printed form) or displays it on the screen. Data or a database is the link between the computer and person or end user. To accomplish a particular task, both computer and person require specific instructions. The computer's instructions take the form of computer programs. The instruction for persons takes the form of procedures followed by the person to accomplish tasks. Computer programs are a set of instructions for the computer to follow; as procedures are instructions to people to follow.

As pointed out earlier, a computer-based library information or management system consists of two major interrelated subsystems, namely (i) bibliographic information system and (ii) organisational information system or information system for management. The use of information technology also enables us to develop and install specialised management information systems, as components of library information systems besides transaction processing systems. The specialised management information systems are the applications that provide for higher management–oriented information to the library managers, used by them for effective management control, short term and long term strategic planning.

4.2 Types of Computer-based Library Information Systems for Management

Different types of computer based library information systems for management can be developed to help library managers, technical and administrative staff to accomplish structured, semi-structured, and unstructured tasks involving corresponding decision making. These are known as: (a) **library transaction** or **data processing systems (TPS)** (b) the **information management systems (MIS)** or the **structured decision support system (SDS)**, and (c) the **decision support system (DSS)**. All these information systems help library managers as well as administrative and technical staff at different levels to do their work efficiently. The relationship of these information systems for management and at various levels of library staff are shown in the Figure Chapter D.3 below:

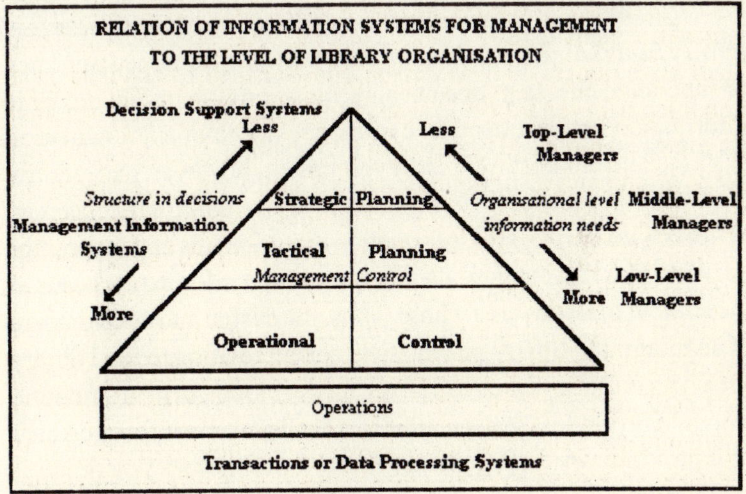

Figure D-3

The subsystems or modules of a **library information system for management** that provide operational information to support daily library operations are called **library functional systems** or **transaction processing systems (TPS)**. The subsystem or module of the library information system for management that produces structured information for management, control and decision making purposes is called as **management information system** or **structured decision support system (SDSS)**. The **structured decision support system (SDSS)** helps management by producing structured, summarised reports on regular or recurring basis for operational control and management control. The subsystems or modules of the library information system for management that are interactive computer-based facilities and support decisions of the management control and strategic planning are called **decision support system (DSS)**. DSS differs from TPS and SDSS is that it does not always support an ongoing process and assist decision-making in less structured environment.

5 COMPOSITION OF A COMPUTERISED LIBRARY INFORMATION OR MANAGEMENT SYSTEM

5.1 Introduction

Traditionally, for a library system, ***discrete computerised library functional or transaction systems*** were developed patterned on functional lines (e.g., documents acquisition system, bibliographic information system (electronic catalogues), documents circulation system, and so forth. This development however had certain limitations because each library functional area is not only concerned or deals with its own area information requirements and support for decision making, but they also share common information needs in the context of library as a whole. Thus, the design and development of an integrated library information system relating to total library activities is the best choice. The recent development in information technology provides us capabilities for the development of integrated or unified library management system for all library functions.

Today, we can design and develop an *integrated or unified* library management system that incorporates nearly all library functions and provides information to library members and staff according to their needs. While developing such an integrated information technology based library management system, at the outset we may not implement all the library applications, but the basic structure can so designed that in due course of time all the library functional systems can be implemented.

An integrated or unified library management system can be seen as comprising of a set of library functional or transaction processing systems designed to provide bibliographic information and services to library members and to support the operational, managerial, and decision-making information needs of library staff. The types of system we are concerned with include a computer (hardware and software) as one of its components.

5.2 Structure of the Library Information for Management System

An **information technology based library information for management system** consists of people (who use and manage the data — system personnel, database administrators, end users and so on), procedures, programs, databases (comprising of data, metadata and digital collection/library), internet and world wide web technologies, communication media and computers that are dynamically linked to achieve the goal of information management. By ***information management,*** we imply the task of gathering data about say a function, organising or processing the data into reliable and accurate information and creating metadata and presenting or distributing it in a useable form among the end users. Today information technology based library information for management systems also store or have access to widely spread collections of digital documents and other information bearing objects (IBOs) in electronic form, generally referred to as digital library or digital collection. They provide an organised and structured access to information contents of digital items in a distributed environment and assist users in searching, evaluating and utilizing resources irrespective of their format.

The scope of the library information for management system varies from library to library. One can develop integrated or comprehensive computerised library information for management system incorporating near total library activities; functions, or a stand-alone computerised transaction-processing system for each of the major functional activity of a library system. Very often it is considered that the stand-alone library transaction-processing system, such as, a *book acquisition system, serial acquisition and control system, bibliographical information system* (online-catalogue), *bibliographic items circulation system, financial control system*, and *personnel management system, digitised sources of information handling system*[1], are self-reliant systems. This actually is not the correct view. Every stand-alone transaction-processing system of a library system is dependent upon and related to other transaction-processing systems of the library system, as the whole in one way or other.

A comprehensive or integrated computerised library management system is basically a configuration of four intertwined subsystems:

i. Library Transactions Processing Systems or Functional Subsystems

ii. ***Specialised Information Systems For Management*** consisting of Structured Information System (also called Management Information System), Decision Support System, and Expert System

iii. ***Bibliographic Information System***, and

iv. ***Digitised Information Resources Handling System.***

The *computerised bibliographical information system* of a library system supports information needs of *library users*, by providing information relating to the bibliographic items and their contents. The computerised library transactions processing systems support work practices and information needs of *library staff* concerning their work. The *digitised information resources handling system* of a library system may contain full-text documents in electronic form in addition to other types of digitised information sources and facilitates their storage and access to the library users electronically. The *specialised information systems for management* support the decision-making functions of the senior library managers.

Thus, we can say that a computer-based library information system is a complex of digitised and non-digitised information resources, staff, functional subsystems, library techniques[2], equipment, computer hardware and software, and other resources.

It serves as a library transactions processing system, bibliographic information system, and information system for management and provides:

a. Access to digitised sources of information, in general, and digitised and non-digitised sources of information available in the holdings of the library, in particular, to the library users.

b. Bibliographic information about the holdings of a library and their status, to the library members.

c. Information required by library staff and management to carry out their day-to-day library activities.

d. Information that supports managerial and decision making functions of different levels of library managers, particularly is useful to them for tactical (or short run) planning and for strategic (or a long term) planning.

One can structure a *computerised library information or management system* in many ways however broadly it can be viewed as constituting of the following three broad subsystems:

1. Library Technical Operations Management Subsystem, which can be further divided into:

   * **Bibliographic Items Acquisition Subsystem** encompasses the activities, transactions and information relating to selection, ordering, receipts and inventories of digitised and non-digitised bibliographic items as well as store data relating to these activities.

   * **Bibliographic Items Processing Subsystem,** involving activities and transactions relating classification and cataloguing of bibliographic items, creating their catalogues (bibliographic database or online catalogues), and release of processed documents for the use of library

users, as well as store data relating these activities.

- **Bibliographic Information System** (Online catalogue), which stores, updates and makes accessible bibliographic information about the holdings of the library to the library users.
- **Reference Services Subsystem,** which is concerned with keeping documentation of the essential activities or transactions carried out by library staff relating to satisfying the information needs of the library users. It is concerned with keeping record of the queries of library members and action taken relating to search efforts and delivery of information. The operations involve, (i) searching from printed and online information sources and collecting the general information required by library readers, (ii) identifying the bibliographic items of interest of library users and providing information about them to library users, and (iii) obtaining bibliographic items or their reprints on interlibrary loan for the use of the readers and maintain the record of transaction. It may also provide Selective Dissemination of Information (SDI) service.
- **Circulation and Reservation Subsystem**, which encompasses lending, recall and reservation of bibliographic items to the library users and maintaining the record of transactions.
- **Digitised Information Sources Storing and Access Subsystem**, involving electronic storage and access of digitised items by the users and maintaining the record of transactions.

2. **Library Administrative Management Subsystem**, which consists of:

- **Finance, Account and Budgeting Subsystem,** concerned with keeping records of transactions relating to financial resources of the library system and store data about the library funds.

* ***Personnel Administration Subsystem***, concerned with keeping records about the transactions relating to human resources of the library - selection, appointments, salary, retirements, and other activities connected with the employees of the library system.
* ***Equipment and Materials Acquisition and Control Subsystems***, concerned with keeping records about the equipment and other materials acquired by the library system.

3. **Library Planning, Management and Control Subsystem,** concerned with collecting, processing and providing information to senior library mangers for overall, planning, management and control of the library system. The stored data and processed information produced by the system help the senior library managers to review and improve library policies, rules, methods, techniques, and procedures. The supervision, control and development of the library system as a whole or its subsystems, is facilitated by the *information system for management and control*. To carryout the activities of each functional or transaction processing subsystem of the library the staff get data, facts and information from the feedback system of the respective transaction systems, which is intermeshed with the functional subsystem. The relevant data of each library functional processing systems is consolidated and processed and made available to the senior library staff in decision making and taking appropriate actions to regulate the activities of the library system as a whole and its functional subsystems by the planning, management and control subsystem of the library information system.

The library planning, management and control subsystem of the library information management system is often composed of three subsystems or modules

* ***Library Structured Decision Support System (LSDS)***, which helps library management by producing

structured, summarised reports on regular or recurring basis for overall operational.

* ***Library Decision Support System (DSS)*** is an interactive computer-based facility that supports decisions of the library management for control and strategic planning.
* ***Library Expert Systems (ES)***. A library expert system (ES) makes the knowledge of experts available to library managers in situations where they require expert knowledge or support of knowledgeable people or professionals engaged in design, development and application in a well-defined area.

In the Figure D-4, we illustrate the hierarchical division of a library information management system into levelled sets of subsystems.

Computerised Library information management systems can be structured in different ways, varying from highly centralised to a decentralised structure. Generally, the structure of a library information system should correspond to the library structure. As such, it is inappropriate for a computerised information system of a small school or public library to be completely decentralised. Similarly, it shall be completely unfitting if the computer-based information system of a very large public library or university library system with many semiautonomous (i.e. loosely integrated) units, departments or branches are completely centralised. A distributed system is best suited for such a large library system.

Centralised System

Broadly speaking a **centralised library information or management system** is one in which a working group (the staff and library members) handles all information processing at a single computer site sharing hardware, software, and storage. This means a working group or library having a standalone computer(s) or a centralised computer connected to several terminals and maintains, possibly, a single central database, to share information or to produce outputs. The configurations of various hardware devices (computers,

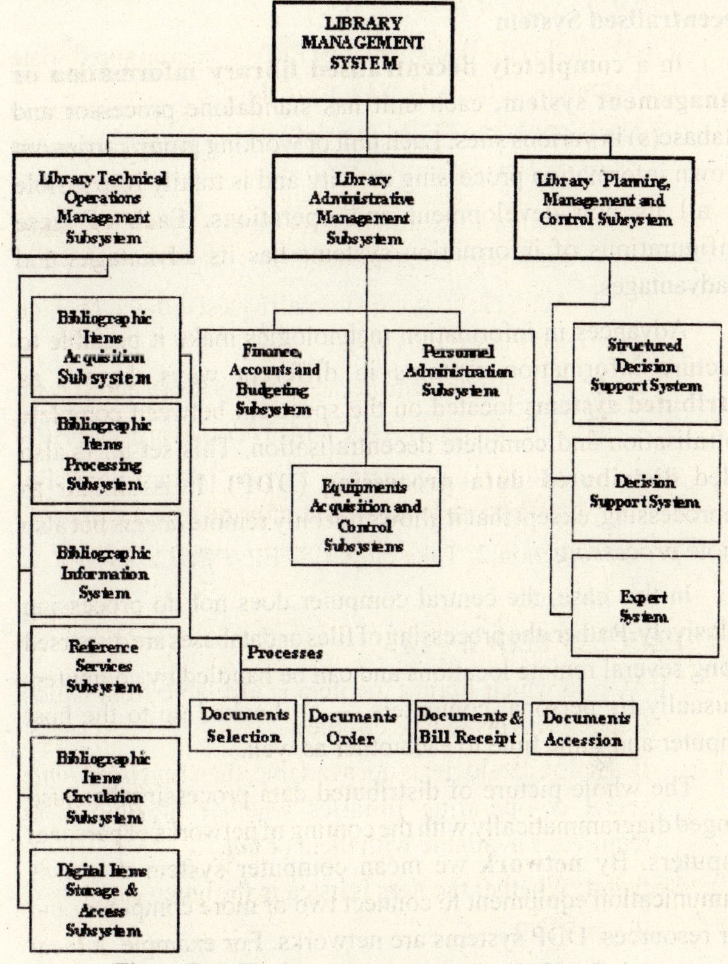

Figure D-4: The hierarchical structure of a library Information or Management System

printers, modem, etc.,) are so designed as to allow the users (members of a working group) to share access to various computer hardware facilities. For example, the end users (library members) access the processed data or information through **teleprocessing systems** — terminals connected to the central computer via communication lines. The teleprocessing system permits users to have access to the central computer from their terminals in other buildings and even other cities. However, although access to the computer system is decentralised, all processing is centralised — that is, performed by one computer.

Decentralised System

In a **completely decentralised library information or management system,** each unit has standalone processor and database(s) in various sites. Each unit or working group carries out its own information processing activity and is totally responsible for all its non development and operations. Each of these configurations of information systems has its advantages and disadvantages.

Advances in information technologies make it possible to structure information systems in different ways, known as **distributed systems** located on the spectrum between complete centralisation and complete decentralisation. This set up is also called **distributed data processing (DDP).** It is similar to teleprocessing, except that it allows not only remote *access* but also remote *processing*.

In this case, the central computer does not do processing exclusively. Rather, the processing of files or databases are dispersed among several remote locations and can be handled by computers — usually by personal computers — all hooked up to the host computer and same time to each other as well.

The whole picture of distributed data processing has also changed diagrammatically with the coming of networks of personal computers. By **network** we mean computer system that uses communication equipment to connect two or more computers and their resources. DDP systems are networks. For example, a **local area network (LAN)** that is a multi-user computer system composed of multiple, independent computers and other devices connected with each other by way of some communication lines, supports hardware sharing, E-mail and data processing. Since, in *LAN type* configuration each computer possesses intelligence; considerable processing can be conducted independently of file server and other computers. A working group or a user in one of the micros can run an application based on a local database, search and retrieve information from a central database residing in the central file server. This configuration has an advantage that users have more independence and more control over their own local processing. Its disadvantage, however, is that processing on several computers can quickly become uncoordinated and chaotic.

Distributed System

A **distributed library information or management system** is one where the authority over one or more activities relating to management and control of a library information or management system has been distributed — that is, delegated.

The two areas of management and control of a library information and management system activities that are distributed or delegated are: (i) execution activities, and (ii) control activities [*cf.*, **Bachman**, 4; **Ahituv**, 1].

Execution activity involves (a) *development exercises* — system analysis, system design, application programming, system documentation, staff and library user training, application development, and (b) *operations* - hardware operations, data entry, processing and outputs. Systems analysts, programmers, database administrators carry out the development exercises, and operators and users carry out operational activities.

The *control activities* involve control and regulation of the information system services, budgets, and personnel, scheduling tasks, security and so on.

The common definition of a distributed system is the spread of hardware and data to multiple sites around the library units, interconnected by a communication network. This definition is deficient and must be associated with the distribution of above listed activities appropriately while structuring a distributed information system of an information organisation or a library system. There are several criteria that help in deciding the degree of distribution and must be planned according to the organisational conditions or set up. Some principal alternative structures are mentioned below:

Distributed processing with a central database: In this case, some processing takes place on the local microcomputers (for instance data entry and validation at different locations or units — in the acquisition section, the circulation desk, and the reference desk, and so on) but without support of a local database. This type of structure is best suited for a library housed in one building under the control of a chief librarian.

Hierarchical system with local databases: In this case, processing is done locally and a local database is updated from local transactions instantaneously and periodically from the central database. Summary of data is sent to the central computer for global processing and central database processing. This type of structure is best suited for a library system having partly or completely autonomous units or branches spread in different buildings or locations. In such a set up, a global database for bibliographic items located in different service units may be maintained in a central computer system housed in the main library. Local databases of bibliographic items located in the respective local units need to be maintained for local acquisition and/or circulation control, and providing information services to users. A duplicate copy of a global bibliographic database or a union catalogue can also be kept in the local computer system. Similarly local databases can be maintained for library members and staff associated with each branch and their accumulated, aggregated, or global databases can be maintained in the central library.

Besides having local computer systems and local bibliographic, library membership, and personnel databases, the local users can access other local databases for low probability events (e.g. verifying whether the particular book recommended for purchase by a user in one unit is on order or not in another unit or to find out the status of a bill forwarded for payment to the central financial unit, and so forth).

Fully Distributed Network

In a fully distributed network environment the library information or management system is composed of multiple autonomous processes and partitioned databases that have equal control status. This is a non-hierarchical structure without central control and no single computer playing a central role. It allows sharing of resources (primarily programs and data) among network sites by using telecommunications.

A library may assign the responsibility of development and control of a library management system to a **system unit,** to be managed by a **system manager** or **database administrator**, who directly reports to the chief librarian. The system manager or database administrator may also be made responsible for managing the central or distributed library management system.

6 COMPUTER BASED LIBRARY INFORMATION OR MANAGEMENT SYSTEMS DESIGN AND DEVELOPMENT PROCESS

The library management initiates the computer based library information or management system development or re-engineering project, when necessary or get the opportunity to implement information technology based library systems in place manual systems or re-engineer the existing ones when resources, new or better becomes available. The responsibility to carry out the project is assigned to the systems analysts or team of experts, whose job is to study the needs of the library system and determine how best the manual functional systems of the library can be converted into information technology based systems.

The design and development of the computer-based library information or management systems is an on going process involving a set of activities, tools and techniques and constitutes of four phases, namely: (i) ***Planning phase, (ii) analysis phase, (iii) design phase,*** and (iv***) system construction and implementation p*****hase.** The detailed description of the various phases of the design and development process is given below.

Note: *Systems analysts uses various tools and techniques during the various phases of the computer based systems design and development process. The brief description of these tools and techniques is given in an earlier chapter followed by detailed description in later chapters*

Phase 1: Planning

The systems design or re-engineering projects start with an **initial investigation** or **feasibility study:**

* To determine the exact nature of the project - that is, what the problem is and what to do about it?
* Establishing the scope of the project: What the new or the re-engineered system is supposed to do and not do?
* Specifying the system objectives — what the system needs to do?

During this phase, the systems analyst or designer is concerned with gathering facts about the system and analysing those facts. The purpose of gathering and analysing data is twofold — (1) to understand the system, may be or may not be computerised and, (2) as a by-product of the understanding, to establish the system requirements. The systems analyst tries to establish system improvement or reengineering objectives and translate those into functional requirements in the form of description of activities and services a computer based system must provide.

It also involves groundwork necessary to decide if the systems project should be pursued or not. The net result is a rough plan on how to go on with the project. The general scope and objectives of the computerised library information or management system, related application and its database design are also laid down.

The planning process consists of defining the need for developing or designing new computerised information or management system and applications for a library; identifying the people who are likely to use it or be affected by it, establishing their needs and describing in general terms what the system will do to meet the defined needs. And also to find out whether it is to develop the system technically and organisationally. The analyst tries to identify and specify explicitly the financial, equipment, software and hardware, personnel requirements and the constraints affecting the proposed system.

The end-result of planning phase is a written statement, informing management the results of the study and the recommendation about the general purpose, functions and scope of the proposed system. It also specifies the financial and staff requirements. This report about the technical feasibility of the contemplated system is submitted to the management to help them to examine and take decision about the proposed implementation plan for installing the computerised system and make it operational. Once the management approves the proposed plan, then the systems analyst takes further steps, as discussed below, to implement the plan.

Phase 2: Systems Analysis Phase

Systems analysis is the process of studying an existing system, in detail, to find out how it works and how it meets the needs of its users. Systems analysis lays the groundwork for improvement or to re-engineer the system or to design a new system. The study involves a detailed investigation of the system. The systems analyst (or the study team) identifies the mission and objectives of the system, what currently the system is accomplishing, who are involved in doing the work, and the complexity of the processes. This also includes finding out, what type of information the system is processing; from where data comes from, how it is processed, where it goes; and who uses it. In addition, one must study and critically examine the way the management control is exercised in the system to suggest the measures that may be taken to improve it, if necessary.

The analysts or study team, also conduct a survey to identify the exact needs of the **sponsor** and **users** of the system. The ***sponsor*** is the organisation, management, or librarian directing the systems analyst to carry out the project or contracting to have the work done. The ***users*** are people who ultimately use the system — usually employees and library members. A related goal is to establish the new system requirements.

The systems analyst interacts with the librarian, and with the present and potential users of the proposed system to find out their present and future requirements. He/she also collects and lists all other vital information needed for the development of the system.

The system analyst then evaluates the results of the study to identity the system's responsiveness to current and future needs and objectives. If any deficiencies are found, these are explicitly recognised and evaluated to decide whether or not the system needs modification. If so, what alternative or new design needs to be developed and implemented.

The study will also include detailed analysis of procedures and processes of the library system. Processes are the work or actions performed by people, departments, or computers on incoming items or data flows to produce outgoing items or data flows. In evaluating the system and the processes, it is necessary to ascertain their operating costs. Subsequently these cost estimates serve as benchmarks to compare with those of the proposed system alternatives identified during systems design phase. The cost estimates also help to find out in which areas and what manner the cost is to be reduced. Systems analysts conduct the functional analysis of the library functional systems in terms of activities or processes and information or data flow between them.

At the end a comprehensive report, which includes a summary of the problems or deficiencies and drawbacks found in the current system (manual or computerised). Description of the requirements of the new system and recommendations on what the course of action to be taken are given. The proposal must include description about the

* Objectives of the new system.
* Entity types and their attributes whose record need to be created.
* Data elements and their possible contents that may comprise constituent elements of various entity types records

* Estimates costs of the required hardware, software and other equipment.
* Staff requirements.
* Preliminary time and cost estimate including system installation cost and continuing cost for the development and implementation of the system

The final report should be factual, and should cover broadly on following aspects:

* Project Definition: Nature, Scope, and objectives.
* Identified objectives of the new system
* General description of proposed alternative solutions that should include: (i) account of the conceptual schema of their respective databases; (ii) specifications of their output, input, processing, control, and backup mechanism; (iii) kind of hardware and software required, and recommendation regarding the best solution to be implemented supported by a report on its operational, technical and economic feasibility.
* Information about the type of hardware, software and other equipment required and their estimated cost.
* Staff requirements.
* Estimated cost of installing the recommended system and making it operational, supported by a costs and benefits analysis. The cost includes development cost (those required to construct the system) and operating cost (cost of day-to-day running of the system).
* Schedule or time chart for completing the project.
* Summary of findings.

If the management decides to pursue the project, the next phase is taken up.

Phase 3: Systems Design

The **system design** is the phase in which the new system is planned. This phase is composed of two stages. During first stage a **prototype** or **working model** of the proposed system is created followed by **detailed design** of the system, in which the analyst determines the exact design specifications. A prototype is the first limited version of a system, developed quickly. While developing a prototype, select or essential features of the system are considered and not all the details. The prototype allows the systems designer to verify that the system satisfies the requirements of the management. The idea is that one can get a general idea of how the system might look like and then major aspects of the system are considered while developing detailed design. Prototyping reveals essential design requirements. One can use software packages, now available for fast prototype development.

Detailed Design Specifications

Once a prototype of the proposed system is developed and tested, the system analyst or designer can develop detailed design specifications of the system. During this stage, one considers or judges every facet of the system in detail. Using the set of software known as **CASE - Computer-aided software engineering**—tools we can develop systems directly without prototyping them. The CASE tools provide an automatic means of designing and changing systems. However, it is an evolving technology and one may not get very satisfactory results all the time.

For detailed design specification, it is essential that, at the outset, the designer or system analyst makes clear specifications of the objectives, principal operations (i.e., an integrated set of activities) or functions of the proposed system. The system is factored into component subsystems, functions and tasks and depicts the structure using a decomposition diagram. Document the interactions between subsystems, functions, and tasks using logical data flow diagrams, decision tables and other appropriate analysis and diagramming techniques.

For example, the functions of a library information or management system may be:

* To create, maintain and process the records (a) of *orders* placed with vendors, (b) of *vendors*, with whom orders are placed or likely to be placed, (c) of *documents*, whose orders have been placed or likely to be placed (d) of *bills*, sent by suppliers or vendors (e) of *acquired documents* or added to the collection the library (f) of *members* enrolled (g) of *bibliographic items*, issued on loan to or due from library members, and so on.
* To keep and handle the data about the transactions or necessary actions to be taken or taken — such as, to keep records about: the date when the supply of a document is expected — (Supply Due Date); or the date the document on loan must be returned by a user (Item's Return or Due Date); or the date of supply of an item is expected (Expected Date of Supply), and so forth.
* To provide bibliographic information about the information sources available in the library.
* To process, maintain and provide data, required by library managers for effective, planning, management and control of the system or to generate reports needed by the management.

The designers of the system must make decisions after carefully analysing and describing the functions and processes of the system, keeping in view, the present and future needs of users, hardware and software requirements, and about matters such as:

* What groups of the real world *entities* - objects, things, persons, events, or locations possibly represent the system?
* What are the relevant *attributes* (elementary properties) of the *entity types*, with which we are concerned?
* What are the relevant *relationships* between entity types, which link them in a given context? For example, ***Written-by*** is a relationship that establishes association or link between the Entity types **WORK** and **AUTHOR**. Reciprocally ***Author-of*** is a relationship, which establishes association or link between the entity types **AUTHOR** and **WORK**.

* What is/are the bona fide source or sources for collecting data? (That is, the authoritative sources of information from where the value of the attributes or date elements of an Entity type may be gathered). For example, we provide data about attributes or data elements of a monograph — which is an individual Entity type - as found on the title page of the book and its overflow pages; and,
* In what manner the values of the attributes of the **Entity-types** are to be entered, rendered or recorded while creating database records? For example, we may enter bibliographic data while creating bibliographic records in a manner that it is possible to display bibliographic information of a document in the form prescribed by the Classified Catalogue Code and/ or AACR-II code, and/or any other bibliographic standard.

By **Entity Type** (also called *Object type*, *Object set*, or *Entity set*), we mean a collection of similar objects, things, persons, events, or locations about which information or data is to be collected and recorded for use.

By relevant attributes and relationships we mean only those attributes and relationships one must consider or select that are pertinent or whose values are essential to identify, describe, or specify an entity, in a given context. For example, an Entity-type MONOGRAPH possesses the attributes — *title proper*, *parallel title*, *volume*, *format*, *date of origin*, *edition*, *price*, *cost*, etc. It can also possess properties, based on its relationships with other entities such as, *Published-by*, *Written-by*, *Supplied-by*, *Belonged-to* (or *Property-of*), *Loaned-to* and so on. However, the attribute *cost* and the relationships — *Supplied-by, Loaned-to* are *not significant enough* or *relevant* for selection, in case we are designing a bibliographic information system or an on-line catalogue of a library system. As the data values of these characteristics of monographs have no utility to identify or describe a monograph, in the given context. However, the data values of these characteristics are pertinent in case we are designing a monograph acquisition or book order system for a library. In the same way, we must consider and define the attributes of other entity types, whose records need to be created keeping in view the objectives and functions of a library information or management system or the related databases.

The result of this study will be a list of Entity types (also called Object-types), their Attributes and the Relationships among them. The values of both attributes and relationships specify facts, information or data about entities. Therefore, the term data element is often used to represent attributes and relationship values.

During the detailed design phase the following facets of the system are also considered:

* Output requirements.
* Input requirements.
* Design of the database structure: (i) at conceptual level and (ii) at actual implementation level, as per requirements of a DBMS.
* Systems processing.
* Systems control and backup set up.

Description of Output Requirements

For the description of the output the following aspects are to be considered:

1. The types of *reports* required by users.
2. The *contents* of the output — what data is needed for the reports?
3. The *medium* of the output — paper, microfilm, computer screen and so forth, and;
4. The *formats* of output — in what forms the output will be printed, displayed on the screen, or produced in any other medium.

Description of Input Requirements

Once the desired output is decided, the type of input required to produce it is considered. This requires specification of *contents* of the input — the data elements (fields) of input and the design of the data entry *forms*, to organise the data before it is entered into the computer.

NOTE: ***Description*** *and listing of desired outputs first, helps to identify and specify input easily.*

7 DATABASE DESIGN

7.1 Introduction

Computer-based information systems and their databases are developed using **database management system (DBMS)**, which is composed of a set of programs that create, modify, store, manage, protect, and provide access to the database and enable the end users to retrieve information in a variety of ways.

A **database** is collections of logically related data, data records or a set of related data files about something, say about an enterprise, people, objects, events or a certain problem area. The data records or related data files are stored with minimum redundancy in a computer system. The data is organised or structured in such a flexible manner that multiple applications or the functional systems can share the entire data, and the end users get the information out of it very quickly. Basically, a database has the following attributes:

A database represents some aspect of a *real world*, sometimes called, mini world, or the universe of discourse. It may be *an institution, an organisation*, an *area of study, or a field of investigation or research*, whose database is to be constructed. The *mini world* or *the universe,* whose database is created, consists of specific entities and relationships that exist between them. By specific entities, we mean those entities that must be considered or are important in the context of an enterprise or area of study or investigation for which the database is being created.

* A database is designed and built for a specific purpose - for the use of intended groups of users and some applications in which these users are interested.
* A database is just one of the components of a computerised information or management system of an organisation, such as a library.

* A database may be generated and maintained manually or by machine. It can be of different sizes and varying complexity.

* A computerised database is created and maintained by a DBMS. A DBMS is a general-purpose software (a group of programs) that helps to organise and process data in a way that allows fast and easy access to information, such as **CDS/ISIS or WINISIS** [*cf.*, **UNESCO,** 2003] Oracle, Sybase etc.

  Some benefits of DBMS software are:

a. Different users can share the data in the database and thus their information needs and other requirements are fulfilled. Creating separate data file for each function of a system is unnecessary. In a database, data is usually stored in one place. This reduces the amount of duplicate data (redundancy) in the system.

b. A common and controlled approach is used for adding or inserting new data and deleting, correcting, modifying and retrieving existing data records or portion of it within a database, and

c. Users and applications that access data need not be aware of the detailed storage structure of the data on a computer storage device. Thus, the data are stored in a way that they are independent of one or more applications that use the data.

A database can also be seen as a collection of interrelated, largely similar data or data records in a set of linked or integrated files designed to facilitate the retrieval of information, which may be processed by one or more application programs. Further, the files of the database are organised and administered in such a flexible way that these can be adapted to new, unforeseen tasks.

Data becomes the central resource in a database environment. Library information systems, functional systems or applications are built around this central resource to give the end-users flexible access to data. The end users of information systems or applications use the DBMS, to process transactions, maintain the data, access the data and generate scheduled reports, etc.

7.2 Categories of Databases

Broadly, we can place databases into two major categories namely: i. **Databases of Primary Sources of Information** (also called source databases), and ii. **Databases of Secondary Sources of Information** (also called reference databases).

A Source Database provides information in electronic form or are databases of electronic documents, containing primary information also in electronic form. Source databases can be grouped according to their contents. For example:

* *Full-text databases*, which contain the full text of bibliographic items (knowledge sources) in electronic forms.
* *Numeric databases*, which contain numerical data of various kinds.

A Reference Database leads the users to the sources of information: a document, person or organisation. They can be divided into three categories:

* *Commercial bibliographical databases*, the databases of indexing or abstracting services, booksellers and publishers, which include citations or bibliographic references to monographs and articles published in serials, and sometimes abstracts of literature.
* *Library bibliographic resources database*, which provide bibliographic information about the bibliographic documents available in a given library or about bibliographic holdings of a group of libraries.
* *Referral databases*, which are databases of electronic reference sources that contain general information such as the name, address, specialisation, products, services etc., of persons, institutions, business enterprises, geographical entities, information systems, and so on [**Chowdhury**, 13, P. 14].

8 DATABASE DESIGN APPROACH

8.1 Introduction

The purpose of database design is to describe the conceptual schema, a high level description of the structure of the database. The basic intention being to describe the data contents of the information system or its database rather than storage structures that are required to store and retrieve data from a computer storage device. The conceptual schema forms a basis to create a *logical schema, design*, or *model*, which is a description of the structure of database that can be handled by a DBMS. In other words a conceptual schema is converted into *logical schema.* A *logical schema* further forms the basis to create a physical design of a database, which is a description of the implementation of the database and adapted to a specific DBMS.

The starting point for the design of a database is an abstract and general description of entity types and their data types to be stored in the database. The description of data structures i.e., establishing the logical relationships between records that comprise the database is first achieved by separation of the logical definition of data in a database from the physical implementation of data (i.e., storage of data in storage devices), and secondly, by providing application data independence. By application data independence we mean separation of overall or global logical data definition of the data and its subsets or subschema. Subschemas are the views of different users concerning their applications.

Logical schema or data definition of data is the expression of the user or programmer's view of data or the way they think about data. It is depicted as a data model. The data model may reveal little about exactly where each item of data is stored. A DBMS and operating system work together to convert the logical view of data into physical view of data. The physical view is stated in terms of specific locations in a storage device plus internal techniques used to store and find the data; that is, exactly what the machine does to store, find and retrieve the data from a storage device.

The designing of an efficient and effective database structure has led to the identification of three distinct planes or levels of data abstraction and description. These three-levels of design are: the conceptual schema level, the internal level or physical level, and the external or users view level. The Standards and Planning Committee of the American National and Standard Committee on Computers and Management Processing first proposed this three-level architecture [*cf.*, **ANSI/SPARC Report**, 3].

The essence of the proposal made by the group was to divide the database structure in such a way that its three distinct layers or aspects could be described at different levels of abstraction, with clearly defined interfaces between them. The merits of this three-level architecture have long been recognised and most *DBMSs* support, to some extent, the three separate organisations or views of a database namely:

i The ***Conceptual level view*** : A global organisation of the database — an overall logical description of the database called conceptual schema or model of the database. The **conceptual schema** describes the structure of the database as a whole for a community of end users. From a conceptual schema, one can derive multiple external organisation or sub-schema keeping in view the need of each user group. There may be several external schema each relating to different or possibly intersecting subsets of the data defined in the conceptual schema. A high-level data model or an implementation-independent logical data model can be used to describe the database structure at this level. Conceptual designing process starts from the specification of requirements and results in conceptual schema of the database. A conceptual model is a tool for representing the reality and described through linguistic and graphical representations.

ii The ***Internal level view*** : A physical organisation — a layout of physical representation of data on a storage device, called internal schema or model, a layout of storing of data on a storage device. It is concerned with the indices, pointers, chains, and other means of locating physical records and techniques used for inserting new records and deleting records. Internal schema uses physical data model to describe the complete details of data storage and access paths for the database.

iii The ***External level view*** : An external organisation of the database that includes many outlines called external sub-schema, or user views. External schema describes specific parts or portions of the database to be organised, retrieved, and displayed in distinctive patterns or configurations, keeping in view the interest or needs of various user groups. External schema hides the rest of the database, which is of no interest to a user group. A high-level data model or an implementation model can be used, to describe an external schema.

The term **logical** refers to the way the end users view data and **physical** refers to the way the data are physically stored in a computer storage device. A DBMS allows us to implement a database schema or an implementation model of a DBMS, into a physical level model or internal schema. The physical level or internal schema, that is, physical organisation and layout of the database or files on a storage device, also called internal view or schema is the concern of the **database system programmers**. The physical schema defines physical records, files, access methods, file organisation, indices, blocking, pointers, and physical attributes. This aspect of the database is not the concern of most systems analysts and end-users.

The development and implementation of a logical database design using a DBMS consists of two phases:

* **Conceptual Database Design Phase**, involving development of a **conceptual schema** (also called **implementation-independent logical model**) of a database, including external sub-schema using high-level data models, and,
* **Implementation-dependent Logical Database Design Phase**, involving design of a logical data model, representing the conceptual schema, which may be mapped onto actual

implementation, or structuring of a database physically, using a DBMS. At this stage, the system designer transforms the conceptual database design into an implementation model or a physical model of DBMS. This logical structure design, database schema or implementation model of the DBMS is also called the ***record format*** of a database, necessary for the creation of individual database records, within the framework of the DBMS software used. Once a database schema is ready and implemented, the database is actually constructed, tested and made operational using the DBMS.

Conceptual Schema Design

A conceptual schema or model is an application-independent and electronic storage-independent description of data of an organisation, and is used to define the database content and structure at global level. *The conceptual level design relates to the representation of or overall descriptions of that part of the 'real-world' that the database is about.* That is, to begin the design, we must identify and describe the objects or entities (or Entity-type), their Attributes, about which data is to be included in the database and Relationships between them. Using Entity-relationship diagram technique, we can design the conceptual schema or logical model of a database. For example, if we intend to develop a computerised database for all the ' BIBLIOGRAPHIC DOCUMENTS' available in a library, then the part of the real-world with which we are concerned is — All BIBLIOGRAPHIC DOCUMENTS; available in the library, or later purchased or acquired from PUBLISHERS, SUPPLIERS or from other sources, processed and are made available in the library or given on loan for definite periods to the LIBRARY MEMBERS [*cf.*, **Kashyap,** 1996; 1982; 1993; 1999].

Similarly, the part of real world that an online library catalogue is about *all types of bibliographic items commonly collected by libraries*; namely, monographs - simple and composites, serials, and independent contributions or work forming part of monographs and serials. Using a high-level conceptual data modelling approach, we can create a conceptual schema or model of a database. The conceptual schema (also called the conceptual or logical view of a database) is the precise description of the data requirements of users. It specifies what data are to be collected on each entity type and constitutes as a guide in the production of individual records that compose the database.

A conceptual schema is changed into implementation level logical model with the help of the data-definition language (DDL), which in turn is mapped into physical representation or physical level schema (also, called internal schema) by the routines or programs of the DBMS used. Conceptual schema is also converted into logical subsets of the data in the database (usually called sub-schema or external schema). A sub-schema is the way a particular application or user views the data from the database. There may be many users and applications using the same data. Therefore, many sub-schemas can exist.

A system analyst, or database administrator, designs the structure of the data in terms of record types, field types, relationships, which exists between record types. The analyst or the database administrative then uses data definition language (DDL) to physically establish those record types, fields and relationships or to design a database structure of a DBMS.

A conceptual schema or model (also called metadata) can be defined using *Entity-Relationship approach to data modelling and analysis* and displayed by means of the graphical notation known as *Entity-Relationship Diagrams (E-R diagrams)* [*cf.*, **Chen**, 1976; 1983].

Data modelling is a technique for establishing, organising and documentation of information system data. Data modelling first gained recognition in **Dr. Peter Chen's** article *Entity-Relationship Model: towards a Unified View of Data* (1976). Since then, data modelling or database modelling has become the standard approach in information systems development that is in the design of database systems. The Entity-Relationship [E-R] modelling technique is used to specify a conceptual or universal data model, sometimes called conceptual or logical design of an enterprise database. The conceptual model is converted into a logical model and the logical model into a physical model (also called implementation *model* or *technical model*).

The conceptual or logical models depict the data requirement of end users of information systems. They are implementation independent; whereas physical models are implementation dependent and reflect technology requirements. Different DBMSs have different database structures for representing data. For example, in relational databases the fundamental structures for representing data are what we call *relational tables*. Thus, a physical model or implementation model of a relational database system will reflect the preferences and limitations of the chosen DBMS, such as **Microsoft Access** or **Oracle**.

The E-R approach is an analytical technique, used for identifying and describing the entities associated with an enterprise/organisation/problem area or about which an enterprise, organisation or person wishes to store information. This database modelling approach is based on the following fundamental concepts for presenting the conceptual model of an enterprise database:

* **Entities**, which represent the object set (mini world) with which one is concerned. The things about which one wants to collect and keep *facts, data* or *information.*
* **Entity type or class**, which represent a set of distinguishable real-world objects or things (mini world) with common properties and about which an organisation or a person wishes to store *facts, data* or *information.*
* **Attributes**, which represent the properties of these objects. An attribute is the data element/item that describes the property of an entity or a relationship.
* **Relationships**, which represent the associations or connections among entities. Examples of typical relationships are '**works-in**', '**member-of**', '**places-orders**' or any verb that connects entities. The entities acquire certain descriptive elements or properties due to their association, connections

or relationships with other entities. Relationships between entities are either optional or mandatory, may be one-to-one, one-to-many, or many-to-many.

We may point out here that another data modelling approach, named the ***object-oriented analysis and modelling approach,*** is also popular. There is some similarity between the concepts or terms used in both of these data modelling approaches. *Object modelling* is a technique for identifying objects within the systems environment and the relationships between them. According to the object modelling technique:

> "An **object** is something that is or is capable of being seen, touched, or otherwise sensed, and about which users store data and behaviour.
>
> **Attributes** are the data that represent characteristics of interest about an object.
>
> ***Behaviour*** *refers to those things that the object can do and the correspondence functions that can act on the object's data (or attributes). In object-oriented circles, an object's behaviour is commonly referred to as a method, operation or service"* [**Whitten**, et al, *2001*. pp. 646-672].

We can also apply the postulates and principles of S.R. Ranganathan's 'Theory of Knowledge Classification' in designing a conceptual schema or model for specialised databases [*cf.*, **Neelameghan**, 1991; 1992]. There is also, similarity between the *Entity-Relationship Data Modelling* Concepts stated by Peter Chen, and others *and S.R. Ranganathan's Postulation based analytico-synthetic approach to knowledge classification.* Both the theoretical approaches are concerned with the organisation of knowledge, information or data, and apply almost similar theoretical principles, concepts, and techniques for the design and development of a framework for the organisation of knowledge, information, or data, in their respective domains (*cf.*, **Kashyap**, 2003).

Ranganathan's *postulations-based approach to subject classification*, also known as *analytico-synthetic approach to subject classification*, is based on a set of postulates, principles, canons, and the principle of facet analysis and synthesis, as enunciated in his classical work ***Prolegomena to Library Classification*** (**Ranganathan,** 1937; 1957a; 1957b; 1967) and further elaborated, extended and interpreted by him in his latter writings. One can apply this approach for:

* Designing a faceted scheme for library classification.
* Classing and organising bibliographic documents possessed by libraries in a helpful classified order or in APUPA PATTERN, as S.R. Ranganathan named the sequence.
* Developing subject indexing systems such as, POPSI.
* Formulating specific subject headings and developing thesauri and so forth.
* Organising records of the bibliographic items as library catalogues, which enable the library users to search and identify the bibliographic items of their interest through various access points (Kashyap, 1983).

According to S.R. Ranganathan, "library classification is the classification of subjects or knowledge classification" (**S.R. Ranganathan**. 1967, P. 94), and a *subject* is an organised or systematised body of ideas, facts, data, information or knowledge concerning *some thing/things* or an *exposition of theoretical construct(s)* embodied in a bibliographic item. The content of a bibliographic item is the product of intellectual, transintellectual, creative activity or the imagination of man recorded in an intelligible, coherent and communicable form. The focus of study and description in a work or document can be about a ***conceptual*** (*abstract*) or ***concrete*** (*physical*) ***entity/entities, their properties*** and ***mutual relations***. The postulates, principles and cannons for classification are concerned with developing a framework for a scheme for subject classification and subject indexing system for organisation and identification or retrieval of documents, respectively. The techniques and tools developed by S.R. Ranaganathan can only used for organisation information about entity types documents and their contents, but also about other abstract or physical entity/entities, their attributes and mutual bearings.

Library classification and indexing systems based on the theory of knowledge classification of S.R. Ranganathan or his facet analysis and synthesis approach are formal devices, which have been used very effectively for organising bibliographical documents in helpful sequence and to indicate their subject matter with the purpose of identifying the documents on specific subjects and related subjects available in a library. Facet analysis and synthesis approach of S.R. Ranganathan (also called concept based indexing approach) can also be effectively used to organise and search the large volume of information being generated on the Internet or on the World Wide Web (or the WWW).

Use of faceted classifications is becoming increasingly common on the World Wide Web, especially on commercial web sites (*cf.*, **Adkisson**, 2003; **Denton**, 2003). The advantages of using facet analysis to organise and search WWW resources is well demonstrated by **Ellis** and **Vaconceos** (1999). They also point out that ''if S.R. Ranganathan were alive today he would be aware of the potential of his ideas for searching and organising WWW materials. Indeed, the genius of S.R. Ranganathan is attested to by the very portability of his ideas across time, technology and culture, simply because they address the very foundation of effective information storage and retrieval. Perhaps, in this respect, contemporary WWW developers may find themselves having more in common, or have more time for, S.R. Ranganathan, than the current generation of IR researchers appear to have, despite their borrowing IR research results in the form of search algorithms embedded in the various search engines".

The application entity-relationship approach is limited to the domain of data analysis and modelling, a technique for documenting, organising and representing enterprise data. Whereas, S.R. Ranganathan's analytico-synthetic approach to *knowledge classification* is applied to create and handle very complex database systems and efficient data retrieval systems relating to the entire knowledge for the use of very diverse users and specialists in diverse fields. It enables us to identify entities, their attributes and relationships with other entities associated with any domain of study. We differentiate and classify these entities into subtypes and supertypes easily, because of his Canons for Characteristics, Canons for Succession of Characteristics, Canon of Exhaustiveness, and Canon of Exclusiveness.

"It can be stated that Ranganathan's ideas address the very foundation of knowledge classification, organisation and representation and that we should devote more time to ponder over the profoundness of his ideas. What was considered decades ago as a "paradigm shift" in library classification theory could surely emerge as a potential "paradigm set" in knowledge representation. Such is the power of Ranganathan's idea that they have transcended all barriers of space, time, technology, and culture" (**Binwal and Lalhmachhuana**, 2001).

Process Model Design

A **process model** shows in diagrammatic form the flow of data in an information system. The process model is a picture of the flow of data and the processing that is performed on the data. One can draw a process model using the data flow diagramming technique and a data flow diagram depicts system boundaries, sources and sinks, the process that manipulates data. The dataflow models support the concepts of process, dataflow, data store, and interface.

A ***dataflow*** is an exchange of data or information between processes. A *data store* is a repository of data or information. An *interface* is a user of the information system who may be the originator and/or the receiver of information. According to data flow diagramming convention, **data flows** (that is, ***packets*** of data) represent inputs or outputs, such as bibliographic items, invoice, forms, letters, computer-to-computer data transmission, phone calls and other conversations. All data flows must begin and/or end at a process, because a data flow either starts a process or results from a process.

A ***process*** means the actions performed on incoming data flows to produce outgoing data flows. A data process adds to, modifies, or deletes data.

A ***data store*** is a repository of data or a logical file until a process needs it. The physical data stores are tapes, disks, file folders or boxes (In or out file boxes or trays) and so forth. In contrast logical data stores represent entities, objects and events about which we need to store data.

An ***interface*** is an entity that produces a data flow, or is a *source* of data origin outside the computer system. An *interface* is also an entity that absorbs data flow or is a destination of data. The entities (or agents, also called sources and sinks) are: people (e.g., library members), offices, departments, organisational units, and other agencies such as booksellers, research organisations, libraries with which the system interacts.

Entities can be external and internal. External and internal entities (also called agents) define the systems boundaries. Entities are external if they are not part of a system or organisation. Examples of external entities are booksellers, publishers, government agencies and other libraries associated with a library system. The examples of internal entities are employees, enrolled members, acquired documents, library units, equipment and so forth. The entities or agents are also called the sources (of data - the net input to the system) or destinations (of information - the net output to the system).

In the earlier illustrative example — vendors, documents, bills, library members and so on are some [or agents (external and internal entities] of the proposed system.

Phase 4: System Implementation and Maintenance Phase

This phase is a final phase of a computerised systems design and development life cycle and involves the following activities:

* System conversion and installation
* Training: To prepare the users of the new system
* Maintenance

System Conversion or Installation

This activity involves phased or parallel conversion from old system to start on the new one depending upon the situation.

If you are converting from manual systems to computer-based systems for the first time then an important consideration is to acquire and install a computer and all the peripheral equipment, including system software, utilities, word processing software, database system, and furniture.

To install equipment you need site preparation, including air conditioning and humidity control. This requires site planning in terms of availability of space, accessibility and cleanliness and making the space available to install the equipment. For site planning one needs to know the exact dimensions and weight of new equipment to fit it through doors and locate it in various parts of a building. In addition, one must know the ways and means to protect the hardware and software and other equipment from damage from dirt, water leakage and fire. One needs to consider electric capacity, cabling, electric connections, flooring and ease of access for repair of computer and related equipment.

Every DBMS has its own database structure to store information. To implement a computer-based management system, using a DBMS software one must define the logical database schema for implementation with the help of the implementation program of the DBMS. The logical database schema for implementation is the picture or a map of the records to be physically implemented, and it must correspond with the database structure of the DBMS software used. The defined implementation level logical data base schema or model is then entered into DBMS; that is, the implementation level database schema is physically transformed into a database structure that conforms to the features of the particular DBMS used.

After converting the implementation level database schema into a physical database structure of the DBMS being used, the experimental database is created to test the implemented database structure to ensure that the system is working as expected. If its working is satisfactory, it can be scaled to perform and made operational. The working of the system is monitored, from time to time, to keep it at optimum level of working efficiency.

It may be relevant to point out that in order to develop computerised library systems and services and implement a database schema with the help of a DBMS, what we require is:

1. A comprehensive view of Library systems including their objectives, functions, processes, activities, and functional subsystems and the various entities associated with a system.
2. Knowledge about the capabilities and limitations of the DBMS software used to create a given library database system.
3. Proficiency in the use and application of the data-definition and data-manipulation languages of the DBMS, including its indexing and search techniques and converting the conceptual scheme into logical structure or data schema within the framework of the DBMS.

In addition, one must:

a. Identify and describe the actual entity types (objects about which information is to be collected for use) and selecting relevant or appropriate attributes or data elements of the given entity types that may comprise the database record structure.

b. Provide unique identifiers and names to the attributes (data elements and fields), that is, assign unique codes to each data element and field. These unique codes, also called content designators, consist of field tags, indicators, and sub-field codes and serve as means of identifying data elements or values of fields in a machine-readable record.

c. Specify a set of rules or guidelines:

   i to delineate the sources for collecting information about the attributes of Entity types, that is, the appropriate sources from where the values of the attributes of each Entity type is to be collected for description.

   ii to specify the domain of attributes (or data elements,

which define the valid values of an attribute (or data element) and guide decision in case there are exceptions.

iii to describe the data values of the attributes of the Entity types that form inputs to the system; that is, to outline how the given piece of information about an entity is to be entered in a record and represented in outputs. These rules are necessary for the uniform consistent description of the contents of the data elements (fields and subfields) comprising the database records and constitute the input and output of the system.

iv to generate access points (elements for searching the database records) depending upon the information retrieval system indexing techniques.

d. Precisely stipulate the formats of required outputs or reports, with the aid data-manipulation language or formatting language of the DBMS.

e. Conceive and design one or more screen layouts or electronic worksheets, for creating and/or updating records of the database.

f. Define the criteria for extracting relevant data from the master file records of the database to create the search terms dictionary (inverted file), which helps to build an effective and efficient information retrieval system with the help of the DBMS software Search Language or with help of mechanism provided by the DBMS to search and retrieve information from the database.

g. Formulate appropriate search expressions, using the DBMS Search Language, for the retrieval of relevant data or information.

Training of Staff and Library Users

Once the information system becomes operational, in the next phase the users — library staff and library members must be given hands-on training to learn to use the system. Two types of training exercises are to be proposed, one for the library staff and other for the library members. The exercises must be prepared in the manner that they simulate tasks, which the two different groups of system users will be required to do. Other important tools in training are the *staff manuals* and the general manuals prepared for library members or end-users.

Maintenance

The system maintenance process is an ongoing activity. It involves effective control, backup set up, and continuous monitoring and necessary adjustments as and when required. Maintenance task includes improving or upgrading the computer system — hardware and software, database organisation, and services being provided to the library users with the installed information systems.

References and Reading List

1. Ahituv, Niv; others. *Principles of Management Systems*. Ed 4. Wm C Brown Communication, Dubuque, IA, 1994.
2. Adkisson, Heidi P. Use of faceted classification. http://www.miskatonic.org/library/ (accessed, 2 November 2003).
3. Bachman, C. W. Data Structure Diagrams. *Database*. v. 1, 2; 1969; p. 4-10.
4. Binwal, Jagdish Chandra; Lalhmachhuana. Knowledge representation: Concept. Techniques and the Analytico-Synthetic Paradigm. *Knowledge Organisation*. v. 28, 1; 2001; p. 5-16.
5. Chowdhury, C. G. *Introduction to Modern Management Retrieval System*. Library Association, London, 1999.
6. Denton, William. How to Make a Faceted Classification and Put It On the Web. Nov. 2003. http://www.miskatonic.org/library/facet-web-howto.html (accessed, 2 November 2003).
7. Kashyap, M. M. Common Communication Format for On-Line Ordering: A Proposal for Implementation to Book Trade and Libraries: Paper presented to the 15th Annual Convention and Conference of Society for Management Science, Bangalore, 18-20 Jan 1996. **In** MALWAD (N M), *ed. Digital libraries: Dynamic storehouse of digitised management*. 1996, p. 76-89.
8. –. 1982. Data Processing and Computer Application in Libraries. *Journal of Library and Management Science*. v. 7, 1; 1982; p. 62-83.
9. –. 1993. *Database System: Design and Development*. New Delhi, Sterling Publishers.

10. –. 1991. Database Technology: Basic Concepts and Terminology. *Library Herald.* 30, 1; 1991; p.1-19.

11. –. 2001. Likeness between Ranganathan's Postulates based Approach to Knowledge classification and Entity Relationship Data Modelling Approach. Knowledge Organisation. v. 30, 1; 2003; p. 1-19.

12. Neelameghan, A. Concept Categorization and Knowledge Organisation in Specialized Databases: A Case Study. *International Classification.* v. 18; 1991; p. 92-97.

13. –. 1992. Application of Ranganathan's General Theory of Knowledge Classification in Designing Specialized Databases. *Libri.* v. 4, 3; 1992; p. 202-226.

14. Ranganathan, S. R. *Prolegomena to Library Classification.* Madras: Madras Library Association, 1937.

15. –. Library Classification a Discipline. **In** *International Conference on Classification for Information Retrieval (Dorking)* (1957). Proceedings. p. 3-14.

16. –. *Prolegomena to Library Classification.* 2nd ed. London: The Library Association, 1957.

17. –. *Prolegomena to Library Classification*, by S. R. Ranganathan and assisted by M. A. Gopinath. 3rd ed. Bangalore: Sarda Ranganathan Endowment for Library Science, 1967.

18. Whitten, Jeffrey L., at al. *Systems Analysis and Design Methods*, by Jeffrey L. Whitten, Lonnie D. Bentley, and Kevin C. Dittman. Ed 5. Tata McGraw-Hill, New Delhi, 2000, p. 646-672.

19. Unesco, Division of Software Development and Applications, Office of Management Programmes and Services. *Mini-Micro CDS/ISIS 2.3: Reference manual & CDS/ISIS Pascal manual.* UNESCO, Paris, 1989.

FOOT NOTES

So Called Attachment not found

E
Design of a Prototype of a Library Subsystem: A Case Study

1 INTRODUCTION

Library managers require well-defined objectives, policies, methods, procedures, and controls to ensure that the system functions properly. The existing system, manual or computerised, should be thoroughly studied to re-engineer it or design and set up an entirely new system in order. The absence of well-defined objectives, policies, methods, procedures, and controls in many library systems makes the task of designing or re-engineering systems very arduous. For this purpose, that is, to make their work practices or functional activities transparent, we need to analyse them or decompose them into smaller subsystems and their elements.

The work practices are the methods used by people to do work, with or without the aid of computers and other equipment. Methods define the sequence of events that produce outputs from the inputs. Specifically, a method is a way of doing something. A procedure is step-by-step instructions (or an algorithm) for doing a task, or a set of detailed directions to carry out work.

An operating library system is always in a flux due to the oft-occurring changes in the environmental conditions and constraints. An operating system or a task subsystem is shaped by specialised knowledge and skills required to run the system efficiently, using the appropriate type of machinery and equipment, and providing a proper layout of the available facilities. Analysing and decomposing the functional areas, processes, procedures or operations of the library system into series of logical decisions and actions can provide a greater level of detail of a library subsystem. This detailed analysis enables clearly identify and describe the inputs, step-by-step process (structured operations), and to produce outputs.

The result of the analysis can be used to answer such questions — who does what? When they do, what they are supposed to do? How it will be done? In addition, the analysis of library procedures is necessary, both, for programming, and developing computer-based system and logical database design.

Library systems analysis techniques help to study library systems and methods, and to examine in depth the aims and problems of the library systems and their activities. The result of the study aid in the design and implementation of new systems and procedures that will correct to overcome the problems of the library systems. It enables the library staff to make more efficient use of the resources available, and achieve library systems' objective efficiently and effectively.

Systems analysis and design study of a system is a highly conceptual process. It is during systems analysis that

* We learn about the existing library system, come to understand its problems, specify its requirements,
* Define objectives and priorities for its improvement.
* Identify and evaluate alternative solutions or designs and choosing the one that is most suitable for implementation.

It requires a detailed examination of the available alternatives about their relative capabilities, performance, cost, and other characteristics. Quality of the design selected for implementation very much depends upon a good systems analysis.

Analysis of a library system requires the use of several models, which can be developed using certain structure techniques and diagramming methods. For example, organisation charts depict managerial responsibilities and line of command, decision tables give a tabular view of the decision logic in a procedure or program, flowcharts depict and clarify the relationship between various activities, data flow diagrams show the overall data flow through a system and draw the basic procedural components and the data that pass among them. Selection of the appropriate model depends upon, what one is trying to describe and using the appropriate system modelling technique or method.

A library functional or task system consists of a group of logically interrelated activities, operations, functions, processes, methods, procedures and elementary tasks. These elements of a library system define the sequence of events that produce outputs from their requisite inputs. Each process or procedure, within a functional area, entails performance of certain processing steps involving decisions and actions by the staff or computer or by both.

Analysis and design of the library system can start at the highest functional areas, task systems or subsystems and proceed into detailed description of its functions, processes and procedures. A higher level functional or task system is decomposed into lower level activities, operations, processes; these are decomposed further into detailed procedures or work methods involving certain decisions and actions. This approach is called *top- down approach* for conducting analysis and description of a system.

The term **functional subsystems** or simply **subsystem** refers to a major functional area or units in a library system. For example, document acquisition, document organising, document circulation and control, services, library management and administration and planning, personnel management, financial management and control activity, and so forth. These functional areas or task systems comprise a group of processes and procedures that together support some goal, function or one aspect of running the system.

The term **activity** is often used as a generic term meaning function, operation, process, or procedure of a system.

The term **function** refers to major areas of activity in a library or and enterprise. A hierarchy chart as a tree structure is the common way to show the major functional areas of an enterprise and the way in which these are constituted of other simpler functions. This break up of whole into its parts is known as top-down decomposition. An organisation chart decomposes an enterprise into its component units or bodies. The functional area chart is usually different from an organisation chart. It represents the basic functional subsystem or major activities carried out in a system as whole, whatever physical units or department may exist or not. A library may have separate units or departments to look after each major activity or sets of activities; still its logical functional areas exist or can be envisaged as distinct from the physical or organisational units.

A **process** is a specific activity, uniquely definable, which has to be carried out in a library functional or task system. In each functional or task system there are many processes. For example, book selection process, pre-order process, order process, supplies receiving and checking process, and so on are the specific activities or operations carried out in an acquisition subsystem (a functional area of a library system).

The term process also refers to an activity without describing the mechanisms by which it is accomplished. A process involves a series of actions carried out to achieve a particular result or to accomplish a task or to complete an activity. For example, we may use different methods or procedures to carry out document circulation activity in a library. We can use either ***Newark*** or ***Brown*** book issue and return method, for circulation of documents in a library. We can use either of the procedures to perform the document circulation function, as either of the techniques serves the same purpose.

The term **procedure** refers to a specific way in which work may be done, or a specific method of doing an activity, a task or a process. Specifically, a procedure is a step-by-step instruction (or an algorithm) for doing a task, or some step-by-step direction for the accomplishment of the process or method. Further, procedures put policies into action. The term procedure also refers to step-by-step directions in accomplishing a unit of work, involving *decisions* and *actions*.

Decision is an act of finding the appropriate course of action required to complete a task or function, or to solve a problem. A person (a decision-maker) selects a course of action out of all perceived or available alternatives, based on some criteria, policies, rules or directions. **Action** is the chosen step or the sequence of steps to be taken as a result of the decision-making process.

All the procedures that are repetitive and routine in nature have well-defined parameters. Decision situations falling in this category are simple and can be understood by the straightforward application of decision-making process. Such decisions are called *structured* or *programmed decisions*. A well defined decision-logic can be worked out for handling them so that they do not have to be treated *de novo* each time they occur. To carry out the repetitive or structured decisions their decision-logic can be clearly defined as, ***structured English narrative***, ***decision tables***, or ***logical flowcharts***. This enables the staff to carry out such decisions easily and effectively on routine and automatic basis.

Following this brief introduction, in the next part of this Chapter, outlines a prototype design of *inter-library document borrowing subsystem* of a library system, to illustrate the pattern in which an end result of system analysis and design process is generally presented. This illustrative design is described using certain system and process modelling techniques, and communication tools.

2 INTERLIBRARY DOCUMENTS BORROWING SUBSYSTEM: AN ILLUSTRATIVE PROTOTYPE DESIGN

2.1 Introduction

It may be mentioned that an interlibrary borrowing activity is not an inborn or integral constituent of a library system. This activity came into practice as a means to overcome certain inherent ***constraints*** that come in the way of fully accomplishing the ***library's mission***, namely: ***'Every Reader His Book.'*** The major constraint being the gap that generally exists between the financial need of a library and funds that can be or are made available. Consequently, a library cannot get all the published documents, which may be of use or required by library members presently or with the passage of time. Thus, certain bibliographic items required by the library members, at a given point in time, may not be available in library holdings. The other possible reason could be that though the funds may be available, but the documents required by the library could not be purchased or added to the collection for one reason or other. The possible reasons could be:

1. The documents may be out of print or not available in the market.
2. The items may be manuscripts, restricted documents not for sale.

To overcome these limitations, at the start, libraries began borrowing documents, informally, from other libraries and in return lending the documents not available in their stock and which their respective members needed.

Note: *These days, due to the introduction of photocopying technology and other means of reproduction the libraries can get out of print and rare publications reproduced and add them to their collection for use. However, still in certain cases it may not be possible to get photocopies and we have to resort to interlibrary loan.*

In due course of time, to carry out these activities, formally, libraries incorporated the following **operational objective** in their setting:

* "To establish a co-operative alliance with other library systems to obtain and reciprocally lend bibliographic items on interlibrary loan, which may not be available and urgently required by library members of the receptive libraries, for their study and research".

The addition of this objective make it obligatory on the part of the library's management to enter into agreement with other libraries, for co-operative ventures, to borrow and give on loan those documents, which may not be available and needed by the members of the respective libraries. Moreover, this objective led to implementation of following **action plan*** by the libraries:

* Entering into agreements with other libraries to borrow and lend documents and setting up functional unit or units assigned with the responsibility of
    i. Obtaining documents on interlibrary loan from co-operating library systems that are not available in the library and requisitioned by the library members.
    ii. Reciprocally lending documents to the co-operating libraries.

The reference desk or the circulation unit of a library is generally assigned the interlibrary loan borrowing function, whereas the circulation unit of a library system handles interlibrary lending job. Together these functional activities are referred to as Interlibrary Loan Activity or System.

After this brief introduction, we will explore the cause of emergence of Interlibrary Loan System and other co-operative activities of venture introduced by the library systems.

2.2 Emergence of Interlibrary Loan Subsystem

As spelled out in the previous section, the establishment of interlibrary loan subsystem as a constituent of the library system is the result of the step taken to overcome environmental constraints in the way of achieving the library's mission. The conceivable reasons of its growth or addition as a component of the library system, at certain stage of library development are:

* One of the Missions of the library system is: 'Every Reader His Book.'
* Certain traditional constraints come in the way of library system in the accomplishment of the above mission, fully. The *traditional constraints* being:
* Availability of finite or limited financial resources.
* Certain bibliographic items, required by the readers, could not be purchased cr added in the collection, for one reason or other — may be they are/were out of print or not available in the market, or may be the items are/were rare manuscripts, secrete or restricted documents not for sale.

Because of the above constraints, at times, a library cannot buy or add to its collection certain published or unpublished bibliographic items, required by members. To overcome the above constraints, libraries informally introduced the practice of borrowing bibliographic items on interlibrary loan from other libraries. This way, up to certain extent, libraries overcame the limitations faced in fulfilling the library's mission. In due course, libraries incorporated *new operational objectives* and *programmes of action* in their framework, as described below:

* **New Operational Objective**

To established co-operative activities with other library system for obtaining on inter-library loan such bibliographic items, not available in the library collections and are urgently needed by the library members, and the following *programme of action* was accepted and implemented to accomplish the above objective.

* **Programme of Action**

Setting up of administrative and operational units to:

i. establish liaison with other library system,

ii. obtain bibliographic items which are not available in the library and needed or demanded by the library members for their research and study on interlibrary loan from the co-operating library systems, and

iii. lend on interlibrary loan the bibliography items to the co-operating libraries.

This was the beginning of the formal co-operation among libraries. Encouraged by the results of this co-operative venture, libraries started co-operating in other areas of interest and in due course of time established many other co-operative activities, generally known as ***resource sharing activities***.

2.3 Recent Trends in Interlibrary Co-operation

Some of the co-operative activities, in which modern library systems are involved, are

* Computer Networks.

* On-line Union Catalogues.
* Interlibrary Loan.
* Shared Acquisition.
* Standardisation.
* Uniformity in the use of classification, cataloguing and indexing techniques in the creation of computerised bibliographic databases.
* Use of a common communication format for exchange of data.
* Online access of bibliographic data as well as digital collection of cooperating libraries through internet.

Some of the **programmes** implemented to carry out these activities, are:

* Establishment of computer networks and resource sharing programs with other dynamic library systems.
* Developing library standards and achieving uniformity in the use of classification, cataloguing, and indexing techniques.
* Formulation and use of common communication formats and application level protocols.
* Establishing protocols for using or adopting uniform or compatible technology for searching and access of digital documents and bibliographic data via internet

The introduction of these new functional activities in library systems is the result of growth, differentiation, ideal seeking and dynamic behaviour of the library. An open system remains dynamic, only if it has dynamic management. We do find library systems that hardly serve the needs of their users through active or effective interlibrary loan system, or through other co-operative activities, though these library systems may be members of a library network involved in resource sharing. The reason is always passive or indifferent disposition of its management or staff, or both, towards these co-operative ventures. Thus, failure or success of a library system depends upon its watchful and dynamic manager.

In the following sections, as an example, a detailed outline of the scope, structure, goal, objectives, policies and activities of a prototype Interlibrary Borrowing Subsystem of a library is given. The description of the elements of the prototype Interlibrary Borrowing Subsystem is based on the situations that exist in a library before the full-scale introduction of computer and related management technology. The redesign of this subsystem; in the case the activities of library systems are fully computerised and become part of a city, national, or global library network, particularly in Indian context will be necessary.

2.4 Scope and Structure of Interlibrary Borrowing Subsystem

As explained earlier, the establishment of an Interlibrary Loan Borrowing and Lending Subsystem as constituents of a library system is the result of the steps taken by the library management to over come environmental constraints coming in the way of achieving the library mission namely: ***'Every Reader His Book'***. Thus, when we consider Interlibrary Documents Borrowing System as a constituent of a library system, we also visualise its counterpart subsystem, namely, Interlibrary Documents Lending Systems. Both these functional systems constitute subsets of Interlibrary Co-operation System. In the total library system framework, where these subsystems fit, are shown in the following diagram (Figure Chapter E-1) of interlibrary co-operative activities with in a library system.

The Goal, Objectives, Policies of the Subsystem

As explained earlier the basic purpose in the establishment of interlibrary Borrowing Subsystem, as a constituent of a library system, is to carry the activities to fulfil the objective:

To establish liaison with other libraries with a purpose to obtain, on interlibrary loan, original bibliographic items or their reproductions (i.e., photocopies). Normally, the library should obtain those items on interlibrary loan, which are not available in the holdings of the library system and for which urgent demand is made by a library member for reference, study or research. {This limited objective has been laid down to overcome the constraints faced by

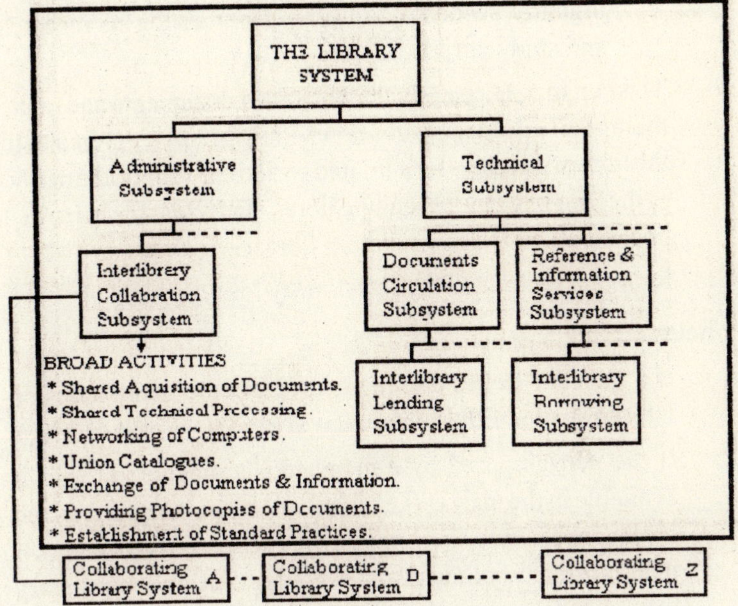

Figure E-1: Group of interrelated subsystems involved for the performance

the library system in accomplishing its mission — **Every Reader His Document**, fully or in absolute sense.}

* **Goal of the Subsystem**

To make available, by locating and obtaining on interlibrary loan such documents: (a) which are urgently required by the library members for their study and research, and (b) which are neither available in the library holdings nor can be easily acquired by the library either by purchase or other means, such as exchange or gift.

* **Objectives or Functions of the Subsystem**

1. To search and obtain on interlibrary loan or get photocopies of the documents from other libraries:
   * which are either out of print, rare, or cannot be immediately added to its stock (i.e. purchased or obtained through exchange or as gift, even if the items are in print) by the library for one reason or other, and

* urgently needed by a library member for his research and study purposes.

2 To keep in safe custody the borrowed documents and make them available for consultation within the library premises to the library members for a limited period based upon the period of the loan fixed by the lending library and return the borrowed documents to the co-operating libraries in time.

3. Maintain records of the interlibrary loan transactions.

Policies

1. If a member makes a request to obtain too many items on interlibrary loan, then obtain few at a time (say, two or three).
2. If the item required by a member is a monograph, and is available in the market (i.e., it is in print) and can be obtained in reasonable time, then, normally, one should buy, or get the item as gift or by other means. Avoid getting it on interlibrary loan.
3. The Reference unit is expected to make formal request to the Acquisition Unit, to purchase or get the item in print for the member immediately. The Acquisition Unit is expected to take immediate steps to find and get the monograph. If it is felt that the item cannot be obtained within a month then the Acquisition Unit must intimate the Reference Desk to this effect. In such cases, the Reference Desk should take steps to get the monograph on interlibrary loan simultaneously. The member is to be informed about the action taken by the Acquisition Unit.
4. The Reference Unit must follow up the case. If there is an extraordinary delay in the acquisition or processing of the item, then remind the acquisition and processing system to speed up the action. Intimate the member when the item is processed and released for use.
5. If the item required by a member is an article published in a periodical publication or a contribution in a monograph then, normally, can be made its photocopy in place of whole volume

of the host document. Subject to the condition that the lending library can make available photocopy of the item.

6. When a bibliographic item obtained on an interlibrary loan is very rare document, out-of-print and important, we should get its photocopy made for future use. In this connection, one must take care that all Copyright formalities are completed, if required.

7. Items obtained on an interlibrary loan should not be issued out of the library. The specific instructions given by the lending library for its use and return must be adhered to.

8. Cost for getting the items through post or otherwise is to be normally met by the borrowing library.

9. For exceptions or any problems, library staff is advised to go to the immediate in-charge, or to the librarian or his/her nominee and act according to the advice or instructions of the person concerned.

Subsystem's Work Method—Input/Output and Operations of the Subsystem

The following sections describe in detail, the input and the procedure to be followed to convert a library member's request for obtaining a document on interlibrary loan, into the output of the system.

Input/Output

The input/output of the system results in the performance of the task. An output of a system or subsystem frequently becomes an input of another. Handling of the each input, as it progresses through the system, results in multiple records of the same input/output. Input is turned into output, and the output into input, may be many times, as it goes through transformation on the basis various actions taken by the library staff or computer process until the final output is produced. The primary input starts the system. A formal request made by a library member to obtain a bibliographic item on interlibrary loan, normally forms an initial or primary input to the interlibrary borrowing system.

The form of the input /output of a system have bearing on the efficiency and economy of operations. We propose an Interlibrary Loan Request Card (ILLR Card) consisting of a set of columns as shown in Figure Chapter E-2a and E-2b to constitute as an initial input to the system. A library user's request for obtaining a document on an interlibrary loan is to be submitted by completing the Interlibrary Loan Card or Form at the Reference Desk of the library. He is supposed to provide necessary bibliographic data about the document required by the user on interlibrary loan. Request made by a member in any other way or means, say through telephone, must be converted into an initial input of the system by filling the required data on a ILL Card/Form, by the staff member receiving or handling the request. Library staff while taking further action on the request is also required to fill the other columns of the card or form, at the various stages of work or as and when necessary steps are taken by them to process the request.

INTERLIBRARY LOAN CARD (CARD SIZE 5" × 3")

Front of Card

Interlibrary Loan Request Form

Author:

Title, etc.:

Member's Name:

Membership No:

Address:

Have you checked the catalogue? Yes/No

Date of Request/Receipt:

Checked Library records On: By:

Result: On Order/Under Processing/Not Available/in Print/Out of Print.

Call No:

Member Informed on: By:

Action — Feed Back to Member:

Figure E-2a: Format of Interlibrary Loan Request Card

Back of the Card

Verified from Union Catalogue/Inquiry made		
fromlibraries on	:	
byName of Libraries	:	
Availability Status	:	
Reminder Date(s)	:	
Lending Library	:	
Date of Request	:	
Received on:		To be Returned On:
Renewal Requested On	:	NO:
Returned on	:	
Expenditure In	:	
Expenditure Out	:	
NOTE:		

Figure E-2b: Format of Interlibrary Loan Request (ILLR) Card

3 INTER-LIBRARY BORROWING PROCEDURE

3.1 Introduction

It is not easy to explain a procedure or process of a system logically. Statement of a procedure in plain English or in any other natural language tends to be excessive in scope or confusing. Conditional instructions in a procedure show whether certain steps are to be performed or not to be performed. A conditional statement implies, under what condition a given step or steps may be taken. In case a condition or situation is not satisfied or exits then what alternative step or steps need to be taken? To express or write a conditional statement properly is very often difficult. Combinations of many conditions further complicate the problem. To overcome these difficulties certain techniques and tools have been developed by experts for documenting the details of processes and procedures unambiguously. Some of the important tools are: **Structured English, Logical Flowcharts** and **Decision Tables**. However, to express the details of processes or procedures logically with these tools, one should first specify the broad steps of the procedure in a natural language, like English. Later, it becomes easy to elaborate the procedure with the help of these tools of precise communication.

Functional units handle the most basic activities of an organisation. Each activity, operation or transaction triggers one or more actions. For instance, a library member's request, for obtaining a bibliographic item on interlibrary loan from some other library, may require

* Checking and completing the bibliographic details of the item
* Verifying or cross checking from the library catalogue whether the item is actually available or not in the library.

Further, staff working in the unit needs the details of activities or process involved and certain facts or indicators to carry out their daily work effectively and efficiently. They need such pointers, indicators or facts that tell them when specific actions need to be taken today or are pending. The supervisory staff needs to know about the actions taken or the transactions carried out or not carried out in the system by the staff. All these facts are called *operational data*.

The information about: What is to be done? When is it to be done? What does someone require? Who requires it? When is it required? What happened? When did it happen? What was involved? Who was involved? How much money was involved? Moreover, other similar facts are required to do a task or accomplish work. These facts or pointers to the actions are recorded manually (hand written), mechanically (type written), magnetically (i.e., ATM), or electronically (using a key and screen) on an electronic worksheet or form.

It is essential that data or information for taking future actions need to be captured processed and made available to staff to carry out the activities of functional systems, effectively and efficiently.

Virtually any type of operational information and management information can be processed from this data. **Operational information** is used daily and routinely and allows the functional unit clerical staff to carry on their daily tasks. Unlike operational information, **supervisory staff or managers use management information** as the need to make decision arises. It supports the process of decision-making at all levels and types of management functions.

The operational data of a functional system must be captured and converted into information. This is the task of a transaction processing system (which handles data about day to day transactions carried out in a functional system) and is an integral part of a functional unit. It also handles the workload of a library information system for management. Information systems simultaneously produce operational and management information. Such information systems are made operational using computers. The production of operational information electronically is, in fact, no more than a take over of the processes of traditional manual systems by computer from human. However, management information derived from computer-based information systems constitutes a new component or factor in the field of library activities.

Thus, the step-by-step description of procedures involves explanation of what steps need to be taken to accomplish a task, when certain actions need to be taken, what facts need to be recorded for transactions and actions performed by the staff manually or electronically.

3.2 Step-by-Step Description of Interlibrary Borrowing Procedure

1. Receive interlibrary loan request card from the member and record the date of its receipt on the card.
2. Check, whether the library member has entered the required information in the columns of the card. If not, then the member should be requested to enter the information in the empty columns.
3. Crosscheck the library records, to ensure that the item is neither available in the stock, nor on order, nor under technical processing.

4. Verify, complete and correct the bibliographical details of the item, if necessary. Also, check whether the item is in print. (Note: In case, some difference is found in the data about the item (and its host document, if any), as provided by the member with those given in the bibliographic source. Then, it will be necessary to intimate the member about this fact. Further action(s) to be taken depends on the member's reply)

5. In case the item requisitioned by the member is in print and can be purchased or obtained by other means, then forward a request to Acquisition Unit/Section to get the item. Inform the user about this action and advise him/her to contact Acquisition Unit in future. Otherwise, take next steps:

   a. Locate in which library the document is available from Union Catalogues.

   b. Record the name of libraries in coded form on the card in which the item is available. Alternatively,

   c. Inquire from select libraries whether the item is available with them.

   d. Record the name of libraries from which the inquiry is made in coded form on the card. Note down the number and date of the inquiry letter and the mode of sending the inquiry letter — by messenger, post, fax, telephone and likes. File the card in follow action tray, behind the Reply Expected date Guide Card. Send a reminder, if no reply is received from a library by the expected date of the reply. Follow up with a reminder, if necessary.

   e. When a reply is received from a library, note down whether the item is in its stock or not, in the appropriate column below the name of the library concerned.

   f. Forward a letter requesting one of the libraries, through a messenger (in case of a local library), by post, or by any other mode of communication, to send the item on interlibrary loan. The loan request may be made for a specific period. Record the letter number and mode of communication followed, in the appropriate columns of the ILLR card.

6. When the item is received, note down on the ILLR Card: the date of receipt and the postal or other expenditure incurred for getting the item, for statistical purposes. Also, record the approximate date when the item should be returned, so that it is returned in time and is received back by the lending library on the date of return (or due date) fixed by it. File the card in the DOCUMENTS TO BE RETURNED TRAY, behind the DESPATCH ACTION START DATE GUIDE CARD. Fix the date of return of item keeping in view when the necessary action to return the document to the lending library must begin, so that the lending library receives the item on or before the last date fixed by it for return of the book.

7. Inform the member that the document has been obtained and is available for consultation up to a certain time. Record on the ILLR card, the number, date and mode of sending the communication.

8. When a member makes a request for the retention of the document obtained on interlibrary loan, beyond the date of return fixed by the lending library and if it is felt the member's request is reasonable, the lending library may be requested to extend the loan period. Record the data about the actions taken on the appropriate columns of ILLR card. The member and consequently the library must make request to the lending library for the extension of loan period, much before the date of return of the document, fixed by the lending library.

9. Give the document to the reader for consultation within library premises, as and when the reader demands it. Issue the document on a reader's ticket and keep its record in safe custody until the item is returned. Take the item back from the user on the same day, check it for misuse and keep it in safe custody.

10. Keep check on the date when a document is to be returned by way of checking the ILLR cards kept behind the DESPATCH ACTION START DATE GUIDE CARD on daily basis.
11. Pack and return the borrowed item, in time, to the lending-library system by registered post or through messenger locally. Note down the expenditure incurred on the card.
12. After the acknowledgement letter is received from the lending library for the receipt of the item, file the interlibrary loan card in dead cards tray for future reference.

If you go through the above broad sequential description of the procedure, you will observe that we need to further elaborate these specifications to make them more clear-cut. For example, while reading the steps, certain questions arise, such as:

* From where should one check and complete the bibliographical details of an item? What is the appropriate bibliographical source?
* What sources are available to check or complete the essential bibliographical details of the item, in the library?
* To identify the item unequivocally, what information or data about the item is essential?
* What course of actions is to be taken when a particular condition is satisfied or not satisfied?

To give correct answers to these questions one needs to know the process being followed in a library to execute that task or function.

Note: *A professionally trained librarian normally has the idea how one can accomplish a particular library task, but he/she needs to know the detail information about the way library work is performed in the particular library. There are always variations in the processes of each library. As such, the details of procedures must be available to the staff, at the initial stages. For this purpose, written staff manuals serve as effective tools of communication, direction, and control.*

We also find that an activity, task or function may be performed in different work situations or cases. For example, we verify and provide certain necessary bibliographical details of a bibliographic item during following situations:

a) While selecting a bibliographic item.

b) While ordering an item.

c) While cataloguing an item.

d) While preparing a bibliography or list of items for a reader.

e) While an item is requisitioned or demanded by a reader, and so on.

The generic process for identification and description of bibliographic items will be the same in the above cases. However, in actual practice, certain variations do exist in the bibliographic data of different types of items. The variations in the required data multiply from situation to situation and depend upon the environment of a library.

Preparing details of a procedure or its modules (also called processes, that is, a group of steps or instructions to be followed to perform a complete unitary function or activity) is a difficult task. Nevertheless, once the details are prepared, it is easy to modify them. As an end product, a manual of procedure is created, which serves as an instruction tool for the staff. It enables them to refer to it, as need be and perform library tasks efficiently and effectively, in all similar situations.

3.3 Limitation in the Specification of Procedures in Ordinary Language

Specification of procedures in detail, in ordinary language, is a tedious job and creates several problems. Very often, statements of procedure written in ordinary English are confusing or excessive in scope. The statement of conditional instructions, particularly combination of many conditions in clear terms is rather difficult. For example, each broad step of the procedure, stated above, involves a series of situations or conditions where one has to decide what appropriate action or series of actions should be taken in a particular situation.

Very often, we find it rather difficult to identify and describe the decision situations and the actions to be followed logically, in each situation, in natural language. Structured systems analysis technique provides us some common tools for documenting a procedure or process methodically with ease and clarity. These tools and methods are: *structured English, a decision table, a logical flowchart, a data-flow diagram*, etc. These tools or methods help us to describe processes and procedures, as well as structured steps unambiguously. We will discuss these tools and methods in detail in subsequent Chapter.

The Illustrative examples of the above stated system's procedures are later described in structured statements based on the convention of the Structured English, and using other systems modelling tools.

Our aim is not to prepare the detailed procedure of an Interlibrary Loan Borrowing System. The purpose is only to show, how a process or procedure can be specified logically and meaningfully using the relevant tools and techniques. These tools and techniques are often used to develop computer library applications and programs, and produce manuals for the use library staff for the execution of these applications, programs and procedures.

3.4 Description of the of Interlibrary Borrowing Procedure Modules (Sub Processes) In Structured English

INPUT: Inter-library Loan Request Card

PROCESS BLOCK — 1

FOR ALL Interlibrary Loan Requests take the following steps:

PROCESS BLOCK —1.1

RECEIVE Inter-library Loan Request Card (ILLR card) from the Member.

CHECK whether the required information has been provided by the member against the following columns of ILLR card or slip: (a) Author; (b) Title of the bibliographic item, and so forth, including the reference to the host document, if it is an article published in a serial or part/section/Chapter of a monograph; his/her — (c) Name; (d) Address, (e) Membership No; and, (f) Date of Request.

IF data provided on the ILLR card is incomplete THEN

Ask the member to fill the respective columns

ELSE or OTHERWISE

Collect the form

Take the NEXT STEP: *PROCESS — 1.2*

ENDIF;

PROCESS BLOCK — 1.2

VERIFY or CONFIRM from the Library Catalogue that the ITEM or the HOST DOCUMENT (in case the bibliographic item that is required by a member is an article published in serial or part of a monograph) is not available in the library.

IF the ITEM or the HOST DOCUMENT is listed in the catalogue

THEN

Note down its Call No on ILLR card

Locate and collect the item from stacks

Whether located? Yes/no.

IF Yes (i.e., the ITEM is located) THEN

Collect the item, inform and/or issue the item to the member

IF No (or ELSE)

VERIFY from the circulation record, whether the item is on loan.

The item is on loan? — Yes or No

IF on loan (i.e., Yes) THEN

Reserve the item and inform the reader.

ELSE (i.e., not on loan)

Try to trace the item for some time. If not found, then treat it as lost or misplaced and try to get it on interlibrary loan

ENDIF;

ELSE — that is, it is not listed in the catalogue

Take NEXT STEP: *PROCESS 1.3*

ENDIF;

PROCESS BLOCK — 1.3

CONFIRM from the acquisition record (file) that the item is noton order, if necessary, subsequently from the processing record (file) that the item is not under processing.

IF the ITEM is on order THEN

Note down its Order No on ILLR card

Inform the member about the status of the item, and make it available to member immediately after it is released for circulation.

ELSE IF the item and its invoice are received and the item is being accessioned THEN

Note down this fact on the ILLR card

Inform the member about the status of the item and make it available to member, immediately after it is released for circulation.

ELSE IF (that is, the item is being processed) THEN

Note down its accession number

Inform the member about the status of the item and make the item available immediately after it is released for circulation

ELSE

Take NEXT STEP — *PROCESS — 2*

ENDIF;

PROCESS BLOCK — 2

FOR ALL Bibliographic Items Requisitioned by a Member

PROCESS BLOCK — 2.1

VERIFY and COMPLETE bibliographic details of the item from the relevant bibliographic sources.

IF the ITEM is not traced and identified from any bibliographic source — may be data provided the member is incorrect THEN

Note the fact on the ILL Card.

Report the fact to the member.

ELSE IF, that is, the document is identified AND it is found that the information or data about the item given by the member is incomplete and/or partially incorrect THEN

Complete and/or correct the bibliographic information of the Item Take NEXT STEP — ***PROCESS 2.2***

ELSE, that is, the document is identified AND the information or data provided by the member is complete and correct THEN

Take NEXT STEP — ***PROCESS 2.2***

END IF;

PROCESS BLOCK — 2.2

VERIFY from an appropriate bibliographic source whether the ITEM is in print or out of print

IF the DOCUMENT is in print THEN

Record this fact on the ILLR Card

Take NEXT STEP — ***PROCESS 3***

ELSE, that is, the DOCUMENT is not in print

Record the fact on the ILLR card — 'Out of print'

Take NEXT STEP — ***PROCESS — 4***

END IF;

PROCESS BLOCK — 3

FOR EACH MONOGRAPH for which request is made by a MEMBER to obtain it on interlibrary loan AND the MONOGRAPH is found to be is in print.

IF MONOGRAPH is in print (and the item is neither in stock, nor on order, nor under processing)

THEN

Request the Acquisition Unit to purchase the item, or get it through exchange or gift.

Note this fact on the ILLR card.

Inform the member that the item is in print and efforts are being made to purchase or get it through other means.

Record the date of intimation to the member on the ILL card.

File the ILLR card in the follow-up-action tray behind the next follow up date guide card.

Take appropriate follow up action after required wait time (e.g., Check with the Order Unit whether the item has been acquired and processed).

When the requisite monograph is added to the library collection after processing keep it for the member and inform him/her to collect it for use

END IF;

PROCESS BLOCK — 4

FOR EACH ITEM for which request is made by a member to obtain it on interlibrary loan and the item is neither in stock, nor on order, nor under processing, nor in print. LOCATE in which library the item is available from a union catalogue. Otherwise, check with select libraries, whether the item is available with them or not. The inquiries can be done either through post or using any other mode of communication.

IF the required UNION CATALOGUE is available THEN

Locate the information from the union catalogue.

IF the ITEM is listed in the union catalogue THEN

Record on ILLR card the name (s) of the library/libraries in which it is available.

Select one library and forward formal request to the library, to send the item on interlibrary loan.

Note down the date and number of the letter on ILLR card.

File the ILLR card in the tray, behind the reply expected -date-guide-card.

IF the ITEM is not received from the library till wait time THEN

Send reminders until the ITEM is received.

ELSE IF the ITEM is received from the library THEN

Take NEXT STEP: ***PROCESS — 5***

END IF;

ELSE IF the required UNION CATALOGUE is not available THEN

Make inquiry from various libraries on phone, by post or by any other communication mode.

Note down the date and number of the query letter on ILLR card.

File the ILLR card in the tray, behind the reply-expected date-guide-card.

IF the REPLY about the query is not received from a library till wait time THEN

Send reminders until the REPLY is received.

ELSE IF the ITEM is received from the library THEN

Take NEXT STEP: ***PROCESS — 5***

END IF;

ELSE IF the REPLY is received from the library and is in the affirmative (i.e. the item is available) THEN

Record the name(s) of library/libraries on ILLR card.

Select first or any one library, and forward a formal request to the selected library, to send the item on interlibrary loan

Note down the date and number of the letter on ILLR card

File the ILLR card in the tray, behind the reply expected date guide card.

IF the ITEM is not received from the library till wait time THEN

Send reminders UNTIL the ITEM is received.

ELSE IF the ITEM is received from the library THEN

Take NEXT STEP: **PROCESS — 5**

END IF;

ELSE the REPLY is received and is negative (i.e. the item is not available) THEN

Record the fact on ILLR card and Stop.

END IF;

END IF;

PROCESS BLOCK — 5

FOR EACH ITEM that is received from a lending library on interlibrary loan

RETRIEVE the ILLR Card

Note down the date of receipt, the postal or other expenditure incurred for getting the item.

Record the approximate date when the process of returning back the item should start, so that it is despatched in time to lending library and is received back by the library on or before the date of return (or the due date), fixed by it.

Send a letter of acknowledgement to the lending library.

Notify the member that the document has been obtained and is available for consultation up to certain time.

Record on the ILLR card, the number, date and mode of sending communication.

FILE the card in the Documents to Be Returned Tray, behind that Despatch Action Start Date

Guide Card, which acts as **pointer to the date** fixed to start action for returning the document to the lending library, so that it reaches to its destination on or before the last date fixed by the lending library for its receipt.

Keep the document in safe custody.

PROCESS BLOCK — 6

FOR EACH ITEM received on interlibrary loan and kept in safe custody for use of the library member

PROCESS BLOCK — 6.1

IF the member requests the document obtained for him on interlibrary loan for consultation THEN

RETRIEVE the ILLR Card and the document

Prepare a temporary book card of the document

Take the reader's ticket and issue the document to him for use in the library

Keep the reader's ticket coupled with book card and file it in the tray

END IF;

WHEN the reader returns the document; check its condition.

IF the condition is okay THEN

Return the ticket to the member after removing the book card from the ticket.

Destroy the book card.

Keep the document in safe custody.

ELSE act appropriately

END IF;

PROCESS BLOCK — 6.2

IF a MEMBER makes a request for extension of date of loan of the document fixed by the lending library AND the borrowing library decides to make formal request for getting the loan period extended THEN

RETRIEVE the ILLR card

Write a letter to the lending library to extend the loan period Despatch the letter

Record the number and date of the letter, and the extended period of loan of the item on the appropriate columns of ILLR card

File the ILLR card in the tray, behind the reply expected date guide card

END IF;

PROCESS BLOCK — 6.3

KEEP CHECK on the documents to be returned by way of examining the Despatch Action Start Date Guide Card regularly

IF an ILLR card or a set of cards are found behind the guide card on a date when the document or documents obtained on interlibrary loan is are to be despatched THEN

Retrieve the document and its ILLR card.

Fill in the forwarding memo form or

Prepare letter.

Pack the document along with forwarding letter or memo form for despatch.

Despatch the packed document by registered post or through messenger locally.

Note down, number and data of forwarding letter, and the expenditure incurred on sending the document on the card.

File card in the tray containing records of the documents to be returned, behind the date guide card, with the date when a letter is expected to be received from the lending library, confirming the receipt of the item returned.

File the copy of forwarding letter or memo in the related file.

END IF;

3.5 Graphical Representation of Interlibrary Borrowing Procedure Using Logical Flowcharts and Decision Tables

The procedures based on existing policies can be graphically depicted as decision situations and course of actions to be taken with the help of **Flowcharts** and **Decision Tables**. These are alternative and complementary tools to the **Structured English**, is used to provide a logical description of a process, which can also be helpful to draw a logical flow chart of a process or procedure. Traditionally flowcharts have been used to represent decision-making logic graphically. However, decision-tables are preferable than flowcharts, because, they offer a more compact view of the decision logic than that provided by the flowcharts.

In the following sections, we will give logical descriptions of select **Interlibrary Loan Borrowing Procedures or Processes** in slightly different form than given earlier. Subsequently, we will represent the logic of the processes in the form of a **Decision Tables** and **Logical Flowcharts**. It may be observed, for purpose of drawing the flowcharts, the logical description of the processes given here is partially changed, from the one given earlier in Structured English.

3.6 Logical Description of Select Processes of Interlibrary Borrowing Procedure For Purpose of Drawing Flowcharts and Decision Tables

Introduction

When a document is **requisitioned for use** or **recommended for purchase** by a library member, we first verify whether the document is available in the library or not, by searching the library catalogue(s). In case the item is not listed in the library catalogue(s) then we also check the document acquisition (selection, order, and receipt) files, the document-processing file, the binding file, etc. Once, we are sure that the item is not available in the library, then, before taking further action, we try to verify and/or complete the bibliographical details of the item from standard bibliographic information sources. It is possible that the bibliographic data provided by the member about an item or items may be incomplete or incorrect. As such, it is advisable to confirm the bibliographical detail from a standard bibliographic source. It may be library catalogue or any other reference source.

The process of finding or confirming whether a document is available in the library or not, establishing the present state, whereabouts, or simply status of the available document and/or completing the bibliographic details of a document are carried out under the following circumstances in a library:

a) When a library user recommends a document for purchase.

b) While ordering a document for the library.

c) To prepare a bibliography on the request of a library member.

d) To search and make available a bibliographic item requisitioned by a library member from library holdings or getting it on interlibrary loan from another library.

The description of the above and other processes blocks in Structured English, followed by the flowcharts (Figure Chapter E-3.1 to E-5.5) displaying the sequence in which the various process blocks of the interlibrary loan borrowing procedure are to be executed, and the control logic that governs their execution is given below. This is followed by an alternative description of a process of interlibrary loan procedure followed by a system Flowchart showing how a computer operator may execute a computer process.

It may be pointed out that the steps involved in a procedure or process remain reasonably the same, whether one performs a procedure or process manually or using a computer. However, there may be change in the sequence of execution of steps and the control logic that govern their execution in a computerised system vis-a-vis or manual system. To highlight this fact the alternative descriptions of a few select processes (sub-procedures) of the complete interlibrary procedures are given in the following section.

3.7 Description of the Select Processes in Structured English

PROCESS BLOCK — 2.1

VERIFY and COMPLETE bibliographic details of the item from any relevant bibliographic source or database.

Decision: Is the item listed?

IF the ITEM is traced and identified from a bibliographic source

AND the information or data provided by the member is incomplete and/or partially incorrect THEN

Action 1: Complete and/or correct it.

Action 2: Take NEXT STEP: ***PROCESS — 2.2***

ELSE IF, that is, the document is not traced or identified THEN

Note down this fact on the ILLR card / database record.

Inform the member about the fact, indicating may be the data provided or recorded by him is possibly incomplete or incorrect.

Note down the date of intimation to the member on the

ILL card or ILL record.

END IF;

PROCESS BLOCK — 2.2

FIND whether the document is IN PRINT from an appropriate bibliographic information source/database.

Decision: Is the ITEM in print?

IF Yes THEN

Action 1: Record the fact 'In print' on the Request card/ slip/ database record.

Action 2: Forward a formal request to the acquisition section for purchase.

Action 3: Inform the member about the action taken.

ELSE IF, that is, the DOCUMENT is not in print THEN

Action 1: Record the fact on request card/slip/ database record — 'Out of print'.

Action 2: Take NEXT STEP: ***PROCESS — 4***

END IF;

PROCESS BLOCK — 4

TRACE in which library the item is available from Union Catalogues (printed or on-line).

IF a union catalogue is not available, then find from some select co-operating libraries whether the document required is available with them or not.

Decision: Whether the item is listed in the union catalogue?

IF yes THEN

Action 1: Note the information in which libraries the item is available on the ILL card/database record.

Action 2: Select one library for getting the item on interlibrary loan, if many have the item.

Action 3: Compose a letter, making request to the library to supply the book on interlibrary loan.

Action 4: Get the letter signed from the person authorised to sign.

Action 5: Forward the letter by post, by hand or via email to the library.

Decision: Is it local library?

IF Yes THEN

Action 1: Send a messenger with the letter to collect the item from the library.

Action 2: Record the name of the lending library, letter number and date of forwarding on the ILLR card or database record

IF No THEN

Decision: Is the library online or has internet facility?

IF Yes THEN

Action 1: Send the request by email.

Action 2: Record the name of the lending library, letter no and date of forwarding on the ILLR card / database record

END IF;

ELSE

Action 1: Send the letter by post.

Action 2: Record the name of the lending library, letter no, and date of forwarding on the ILLR card/ database record

Action 3: Intimate the user about the action taken by post, email etc.

Action 4: Record the letter number date on the ILLR card/ database record.

Action 5: File the ILLR card, behind the expected reply date guides card, in the tray.

Action 6: File the office copy of the letter in the corresponding file.

END IF:

IF No (i.e., Entry is not found or a relevant bibliographic reference source is not available THEN

Action 1: Make written inquiry from some select libraries in the city, region, country or abroad. Send faxes, email or make a phone call.

Action 2: Record the name of the libraries, letter number and date, and possible date of receiving the reply from a library in the appropriate columns of the ILLR card

Action 3: File the ILLR card, behind the expected reply date guide card, in the tray. Decision: The reply is received in time?

IF Yes THEN

Action 1: Record the information on the card.

Action 2: Take NEXT STEP

IF No THEN

Action 1: SEND and REPEAT Reminder UNTIL a reply is received.

END IF;

END IF;

END;

3.8 Logical Flowcharts Showing Graphically Interlibrary Borrowing Procedure

In this section, the logical flowcharts (Figure Chapter E-3.1 to E-3.5) that show are given the processes of the Interlibrary Borrowing Procedure described in the earlier section.

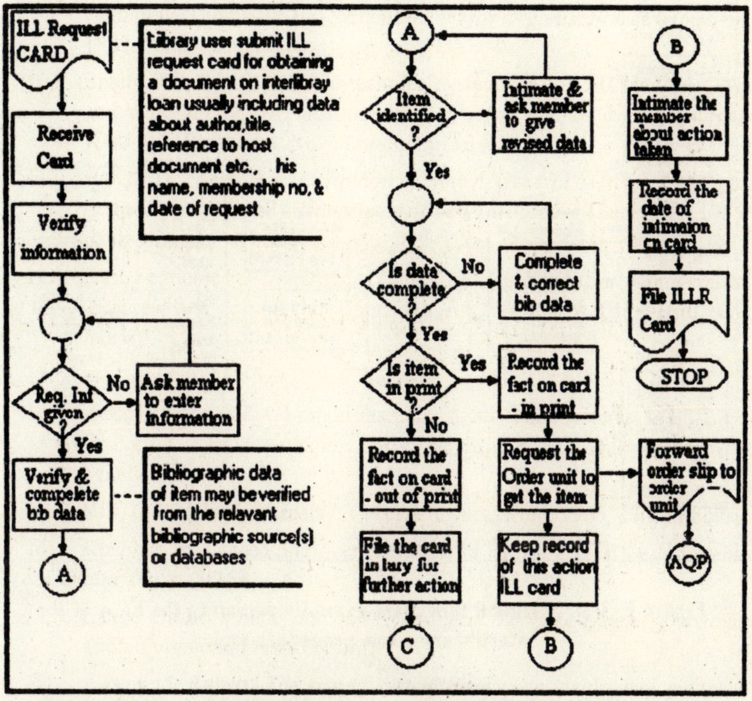

ILL Request CARD

Library user submit ILL request card for obtaining a document on interlibray loan usually including data about author,title, reference to host document etc., his name, membership no. & date of request

Receive Card

Verify information

Req. Inf given ?

No

Ask member to enter information

Yes

Verify & compelete bib data

Bibliographic data of item may be verified from the relavant bibliographic source(s) or databases

A

A

Item identified ?

Intimate & ask member to give revised data

Yes

Is data complete ?

No

Complete & correct bib data

Yes

Is item in print ?

Yes

Record the fact on card - in print

No

Record the fact on card - out of print

File the card in tary for further action

C

Request the Order unit to get the item

Forward order slip to order unit

AQP

Keep record of this action ILL card

B

B

Intimate the member about action taken

Record the date of intimaion on card

File ILLR Card

STOP

Figure E-3.1: A logical flowchart partially depicting the flow of the interlibrary Loan procedure logic.

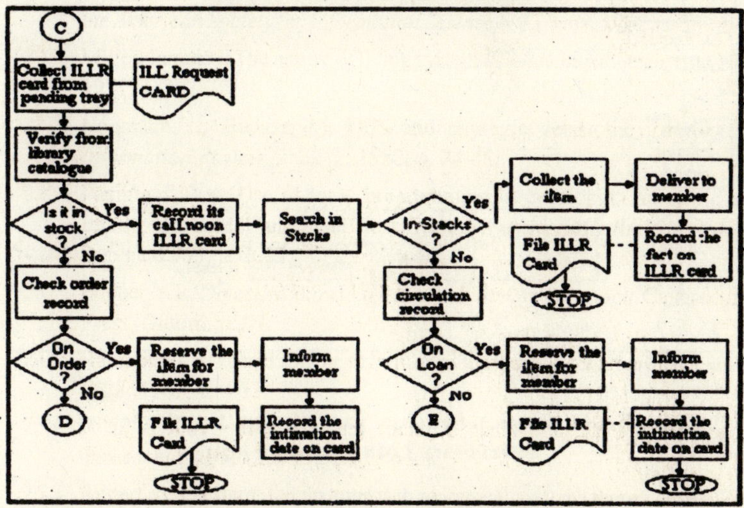

Figure E-3.2: A logical flowchart partially depicting the Flow of the interlibrary Loan procedure logic

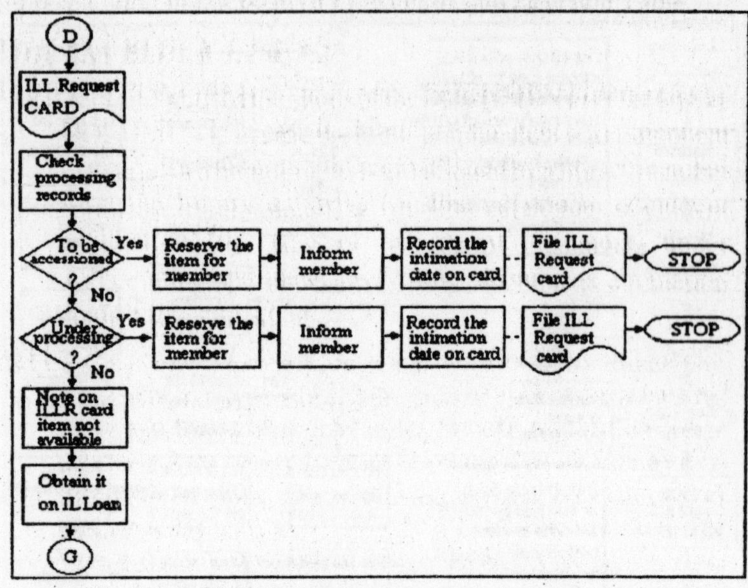

Figure E-3.3: A logical flowchart partially depicting the Flow of the interlibrary Loan procedure logic

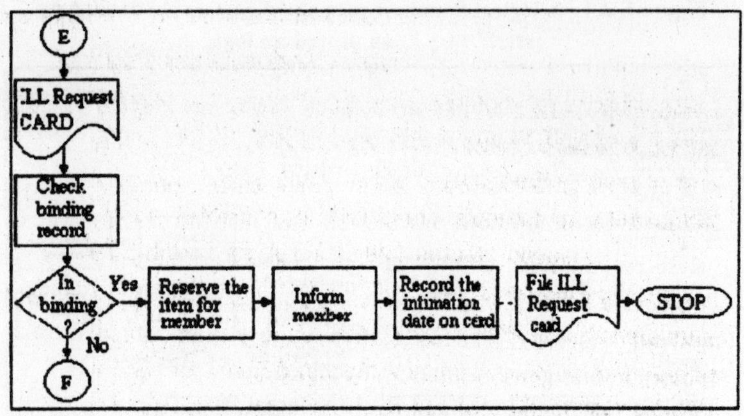

Figure E-3.4: A logical flowchart partially depicting the flow of the Interlibrary Loan procedure logic

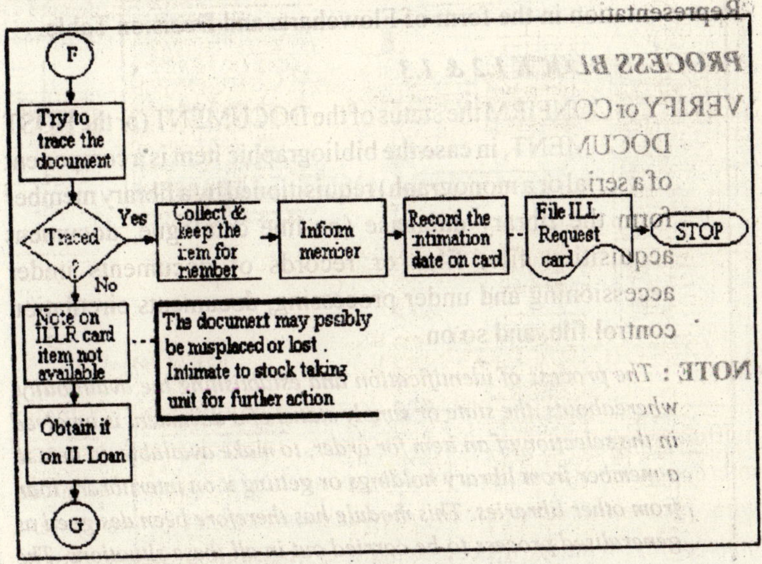

Figure E-3.5: A logical flowchart partially depicting the Flow of the Interlibrary Loan procedure logic

A **flowchart** presents a visual map of a process, procedure or program. A computer programmer draws a flowchart, and then draws a flowchart and then prepares or writes a program based on a flowchart. Both the flowchart and program listing are parts of program documentation.

A flowchart that represents *the flow of logic in a procedure or program* is called a **logical flowchart**, and a flowchart that shows *the flow of data through computer system* is called **a system flowchart**.

In a flowchart 'arrow' is used to represent the direction of the process, procedure or program flow and 'boxes' and other shapes to display actions. We will use ANSI flowchart symbols introduced earlier. Templates of ANSI symbols are available in office supply stores and are helpful in drawing flowcharts by hand. They are also found in most popular flowcharting and word processing software.

An Alternative Description of Select Processes of the Interlibrary Loan Procedure in Structured English and their

Representation in the form of Flowcharts and Decision Table.

PROCESS BLOCK 1.2 & 1.3

VERIFY or CONFIRM the status of the DOCUMENT (or the HOST DOCUMENT, in case the bibliographic item is a component of a serial or a monograph) requisitioned by a library member form the library database (on-line catalogue, document acquisition file, files or records of documents under accessioning and under processing, documents circulation control file, and so on.

NOTE : *The process of identification and establishing the availability, whereabouts, the state or simply status of a document is involved in the selection of an item for order, to make available an item to a member from library holdings or getting it on interlibrary loan from other libraries. This module has therefore been designed as generalised process to be carried out in all these situations. The sequence in which statements or process blocks are executed and the control logic that governs their execution has been described keeping in view an integrated computerised database system for all library activities.*

IF the RECORD of the ITEM exists in the library database or files THEN

SELECT the appropriate case:

CASE 1: WHEN the status field of the ITEM's RECORD shows that the Item is ON LOAN THEN Reserve the Item for the Member. Make entry in the corresponding field to this effect. Inform and advise the member to contact the Circulation Desk for further inquiry. Stop.

CASE 2: WHEN the status field of the ITEM's RECORD shows that the Item is under BINDING THEN Reserve the Item for the Member. Make entry in the corresponding field to this effect. Inform the member to contact the Binding Section for the item

CASE 3: WHEN the status field of the ITEM's RECORD shows that the Item is on ORDER THEN Reserve the Item for the Member. Make entry in the corresponding field to this effect. Inform the MEMBER that the item is on order and shall be made available immediately after acquisition and processing

CASE 4: WHEN the status field of the ITEM's RECORD shows that the Item is UNDER PROCESS THEN Reserve the Item for the Member. Make entry in the corresponding field to this effect. Inform the MEMBER that the item is under processing and shall be made available immediately after processing.

CASE 5: WHEN the ITEM in stock and none of the above conditions exist (the item is likely to be in the stack or reading room) THEN Record it's Call Number. Trace the ITEM from the stacks and the reading rooms.

IF found THEN

Collect the item.

Keep in safe custody at Reference Desk.

Inform the member to collect the item from the Reference Desk.

ELSE (e.g., Not Found)

Treat the item as lost and not available.

Record the fact in its record (i.e., on status field).

Inform the member accordingly.

ENDIF;

ENDSELECT;

ELSE, that is, the RECORD of the ITEM does not exist in the library database THEN

Note on ILLR card the information Status: Not available.

Take NEXT STEP — Verify whether the item is in print or out of print.

3.9 Logical Flowcharts: Which Show the Flow of Logic in the Interlibrary Processes

In the following section, the logical flowcharts (Figures

Chapter E-4.1 to E-4.2) that portray the processes of the Interlibrary Borrowing Procedure described in the previous section are presented.

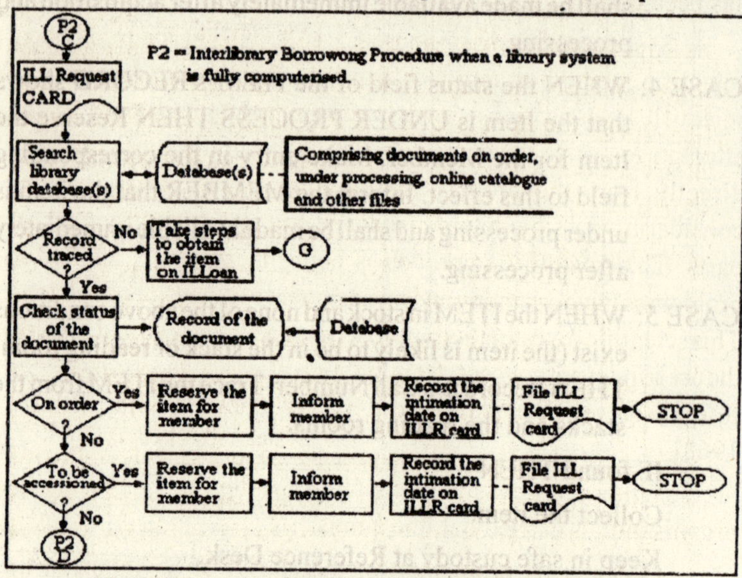

Figure E-4.1: A logical flowchart partially depicting the Flow of the procedure logic

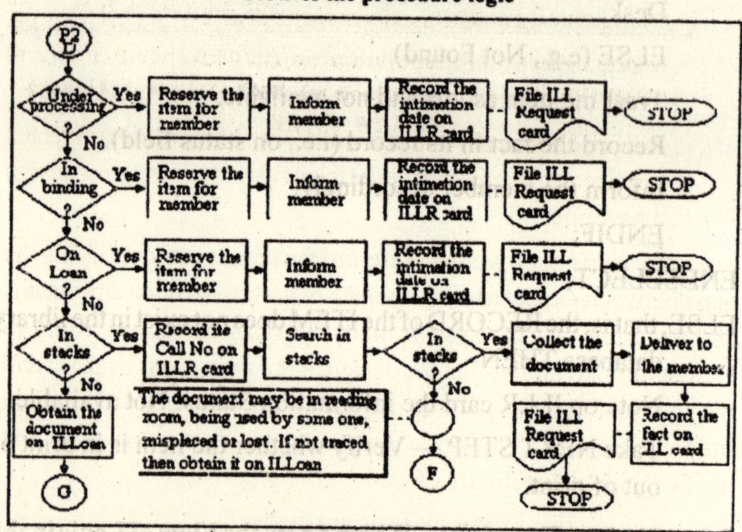

Figure E-4.2: A logical flowchart partially depicting the Flow of the procedure logic.

3.10 Description of Interlibrary Loan Procedure Logic In Decision Table Format

The description of a procedure is often based on the policies of an organisation. Therefore, the policy statements or guidelines for taking appropriate actions for getting an item on interlibrary are enumerated below. Later the decision table is drawn, showing interlibrary loan procedure logic, based on the given policies or guidelines.

Policy Statements

If the item required by a member on interlibrary loan is:

* a monograph in print then we should normally purchase the item instead of getting it on interlibrary loan.
* an article published in a periodical publication; or a contribution in a monograph then obtain its photocopy, instead of borrowing whole volume or the host document, subject to the condition that the lending library can make available a photocopy of the item.
* a manuscript or a rare copy of a published monograph, and a lending library does not lend it, then get its photocopy, in case the lending library agrees or can manage to provide the photocopy.

3.11 Representation of Interlibrary Borrowing Procedure as Decision Table

Based on the policies stated above, the decision logic involved in Interlibrary Borrowing Procedure is represented as Decision Table in Figure Chapter E-5. The table is organised according to the logic that "If this condition exists or is met, then do this".

Decision tables are useful in cases that involve a series of interrelated decisions; their use helps us to ensure that no alternatives are overlooked. Programmers can code part of a program right from a decision table.

TABLE: 1 Process Name: Interlibrary Loan	1	2	3	4	5	6	7
C1 The document required by member is a monograph	Y	Y	Y	N	N	N	N
C2 The item is a contribution forming part of a monograph	N	N	N	Y	Y	N	N
C3 The item is an article forming part of a serial	N	N	N	N	N	Y	Y
C4 The monograph is in print	Y	N	N	-	-	-	-
C5 The lending library can provide photocopies	-	Y	N	Y	N	Y	N
A1 Get it on interlibray loan			X		X		X
A2 Obtain its photocopy		X		X		X	
A3 Request Acquisition Unit to purchase the item	X						

Figure E-5: Decision Table for Borrowing a Bibliographic Item on Interlibrary Loan

F

Systems Modelling Tools and Techniques

1 INTRODUCTION

Systems analysis and design is a method for understanding and modelling complex systems. The essence of this method is fourfold. We:

1. Divide complex systems into simple subsystems.
2. Analyse, delineate and design the interfaces that exist between the subsystems.
3. Recognise and define the goals and objects of a system and its subsystems, and
4. Analyse, specify and design the processes that go on within the systems.

The result of systems analysis can be used to answer such questions: Who does what, and when they do? How it is done, and should be done? More to design or re-engineer systems, develop computer programs and create logical database designs.

A systems analyst constantly deals with unstructured problems. Through systematic analysis, one can impose structure on an unstructured problem. If you structure some thing, you arrange it in an organised pattern. A system, process, activity, etc., which is properly structured, is neatly organised, and therefore efficient and can be easily understood by people. One way to structure a problem or a system is to use models. A model is a physical, narrative, mathematical, or graphic representation of something. One can build or construct Models for existing systems - to better understand those systems and for systems design or describing methods and procedures.

Systems analysts make use of different types of structured techniques to model, design or structure complex systems, activities and procedures, or to develop programs. In the following sections of this chapter and in later chapters, we will describe some structured techniques used for analysis and data modelling. Most of these techniques also serve as diagramming and documentation tools. These tools and techniques enable a systems analyst to think, analyse, design and depict systems.

The structured techniques we will discuss are ***structured English, data flow diagram, flowcharts, decision tables, entity-relationship diagrams***, and ***bubble charts***. Except the structured English other techniques are diagramming or graphical techniques. The diagrams that a systems analyst uses in analysing, designing, structuring a system or program, aid him to clear thinking; act as a communication tool to interchange ideas between the end users and other colleagues of the system or program development team. When systems are set up or modified, clear diagrams are an essential aid in implementation.

Process modelling techniques, namely, flowcharts and data flow diagrams serve as valuable tools for depicting present procedures and data flow through a system or program, in graphic forms, during the system analysis phase. These techniques can also be used in the systems design and implementation phase to ease communication between the system analyst and the users. (**Note:** A process model is a picture of sequences of a process or flow of a procedure).

A decision table or decision logic table is an alternative model for a function or process and provides a graphic view of decision making involved in a process. It shows the alternative actions to be taken under particular conditions.

Entity-relationship diagrams are the basis of high-level data models and illustrate the ways in which database structures are drawn. To computerise the activities of a library system, the date items (elements) it uses must be defined, catalogued, and organised. A data element by itself is not of much use. It becomes useful and interesting when it is associated with another data element (or attribute). Bubble charts provide a way of drawing and understanding the association among data elements. This understanding is necessary to create records that are clearly structured.

2 STRUCTURED ENGLISH

Structured English is a blend of English language with the syntax of structured programming, used to define procedural logic. **Structured programming** is an approach to computer programming that emphasises breaking a program into logical sections. Structured programming uses a limited number of control structures for controlling the flow of logic in a program. Similarly, to describe the procedural logic the structured English also uses the following four basic types of constructs:

* Sequence structure.
* Condition structure.
* Case structure.
* Repetition structure.

When we write a procedure in English, many ambiguities may occur. To overcome this limitation of English language certain restrictions are placed on the use of English within Structured English. The procedures or programs are written in such a way that users can understand them easily. They are hierarchically structured and indentations are used to show logical hierarchy. To make the structure clear the following keywords are used: IF, THEN, ELSE, ENDIF, REPEAT WHILE, REPEAT UNTIL, ENDREPEAT, EXIT. The Key words: AND, OR, GT (*greater than*), LT (*less than*), GE (*greater than equal to*), LE (*less than or equal to*) are used for logic.

2.1 Description of the Four Constructs of Structured English

Sequence Structure

The **sequence construct** (also called ***sequence control***

structure) is the most straightforward structure. One statement simply follows another in a top-to-bottom sequence,executed sequentially. Each statement in a sequence construct is placed on a separate line. If the statement requires more than one line then continuation lines are indented. The last statement is punctuated by semicolon (;). The sequence construct may be constituted of a single statement or group of statements (also called compound statement) and may be preceded by a title. The end of sequence structure may be suggested with the word EXIT possibly followed by the sequence title. The *syntax of the SEQUENCE Construct* followed by the *flowchart* (Figure Chapter E-1) showing how it is executed.

Condition Structure

The condition constructs are used to specify logical decisions. The condition structure (also called decision construct or selection control structure) of structured English allows you to place branching instructions within a sequence of instructions and its format is: *If a certain condition is true (satisfied or applies), then a given action will be taken; if not, a different action may be specified.* This construct has two forms IF-THEN-ELSE and IF-THEN.

The IF-THEN-ELSE construct allows us to select one of the two alternative statements, by evaluating specified Boolean condition and works as follows:

IF - a certain condition *applies* or is *true*, THEN a given action or actions will be taken IF NOT (ELSE or OTHERWISE), i.e., the condition is *false* a different action or actions may be taken.

IF-THEN is a special case of IF-THEN-ELSE, and less complicated. Its format is:

IF the condition is *true*, THEN do **something** However, if the condition is *false* or *not satisfied*, then do **nothing**.

An example of a SEQUENCE construct
BILL RECEIPT PROCESS FOR ALL DOCUMENTS' BILLS RECEIVED IN ACQUISITION UNIT Receive an invoice Record the date of receipt on the invoice Keep the invoice in the file or tray for further action END; EXIT BILL RECEIPT PROCESS.

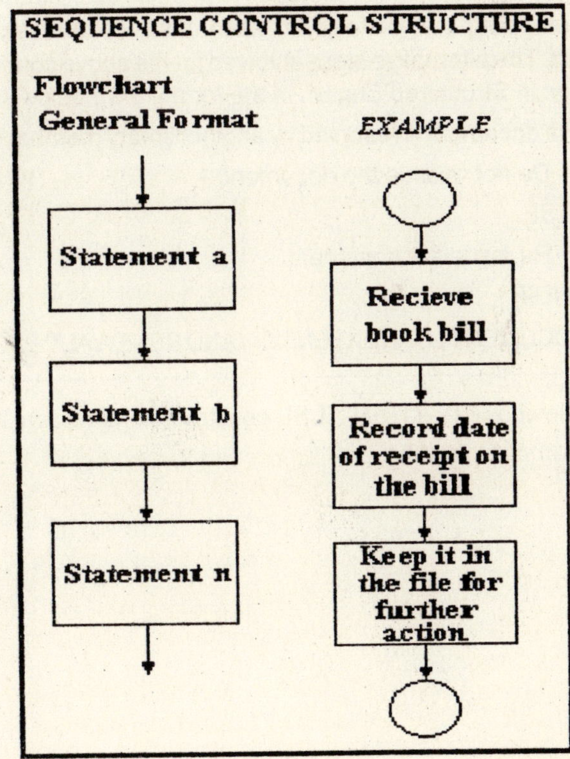

Figure F-1: Sequential Construct Execution FLOWCHART

The syntax of the IF-THEN-ELSE structure and IF-THEN structure is given below, followed by the flowcharts (Figure Chapter F-2 & F-3) showing how they are executed:

An example of IF-THEN-ELSE CONSTRUCT

```
DOCUMENT LOAN EXTENSION AND RENEWAL PROCESS
    FOR ALL documents loan renewal requests
        Scrutinise library circulation record (file)
        (A decision spot or situation)
(Note: The above step requires checking the condition - whether
the bibliographic item for which extension or renewal of a loan is
requested by the user is reserved for another user or not? The
condition being true or false, in each case, certain steps are
involved. The alternative steps involved for the above condition is
specified in Structured English in the form shown below.)
    IF a document is reserved by another library member THEN
        Do not reissue the document.
    ELSE
        Re-issue the document.
    ENDIF;
EXIT DOCUMENT LOAN EXTENSION AND RENEWAL PROCESS;
```

The above IF-THEN-ELSE construct is represented below in the form of flow chart.

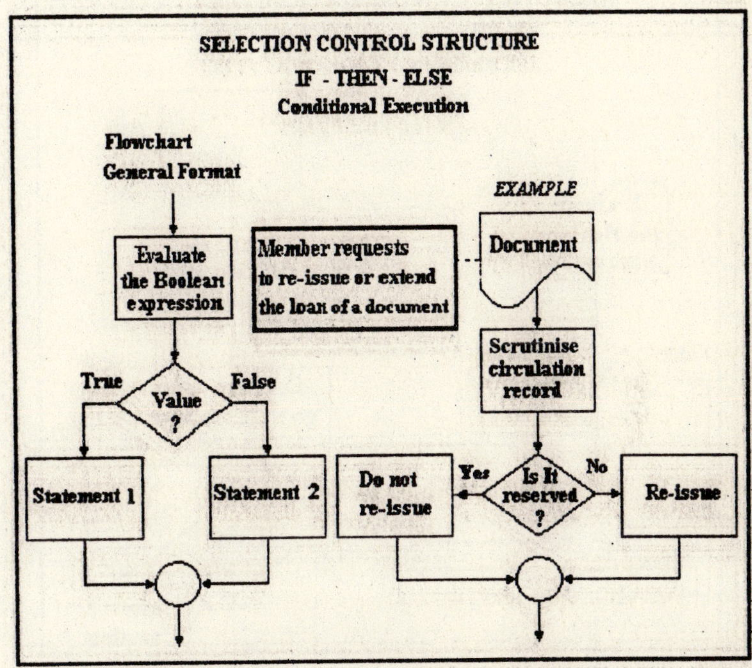

Figure F-2: IF-THEN-ELSE construct execution flowchart

An example of the IF-THEN construct

VALIDATE BIBLIOGRAPHIC DETAILS OF A DOCUMENT:
COMPARE Bibliographic details of a DOCUMENT with those given in a BIBLIOGRAPHIC INFORMATION SOURCE or DATABASE
IF errors THEN
Correct and complete details
ENDIF;
EXIT VALIDATE BIBLIOGRAPHIC DETAILS OF A DOCUMENT;

The above IF-THEN construct is represented below in the form of a flow chart.

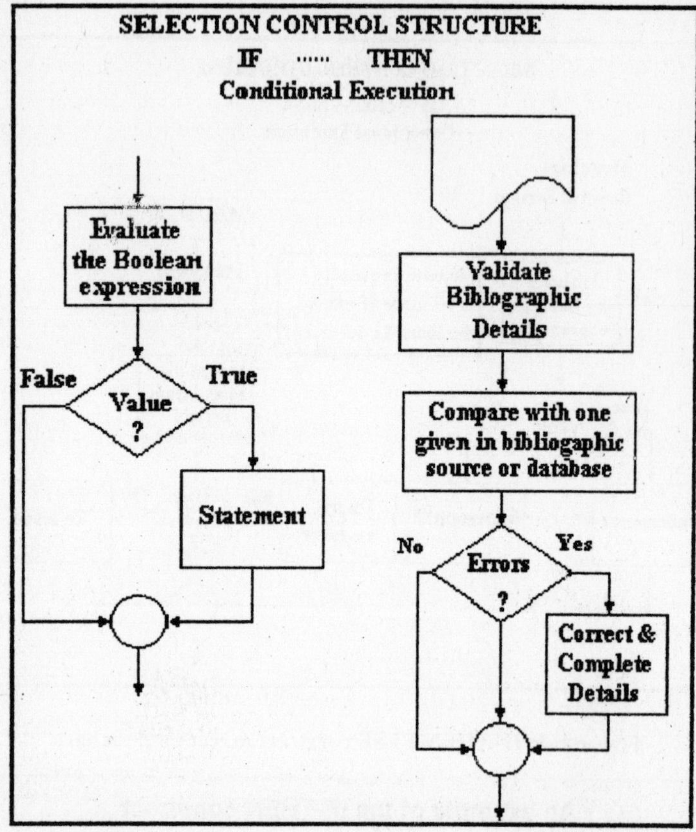

Figure F-3: The IF-THEN construct execution flowchart

Case Structure

Attimes, one of several mutually exclusive conditions applies. The case structure shows what action (action set) is taken for each possible case and allows you to select one condition or case for execution out of a set of alternative conditions or cases. Thus, we can say that a case structure comprises a set of mutually exclusive conditions and shows what action or a set of actions is to be taken in each case. During the execution of the case structure, you or program selects only one possible statement for execution; the remaining statements are skipped.

This structure has the form: SELECT CASE 1 WHEN .... CASE 2 WHEN .... CASE 3 WHEN .... and so on. When the case clause ends, it is useful to write ENDSELECT. Sometimes the words IF .... ELSEIF .... ELSEIF .... ELSE are used for representing mutually exclusive conditions.

The syntax of the CASE structure followed by the flowchart (Figure Chapter F-4) showing how it is executed.

An example of a CASE Construct

```
Find out THE STATUS OF MONOGRAPH REQUISITIONED BY A MEMBER
SEARCH LIBRARY FILES or DATABASE - Acquisition file, processing file, on-line catalogue,
    circulation file, binding file.
    IF the record of the ITEM is found THEN
        CHECK its STATUS AND
        SELECT the appropriate case:
    CASE 1: WHEN Status = `On Order' THEN
        Reserve the Item for the Member. Enter `Date of Reservation' and 'Membership No' in the
            database record in the corresponding field.
        Record the STATUS VALUE & date of reservation' on the REQUISITION SLIP.
        Issue the message to the member: "The item is on order and shall be made available after
            acquisition and processing"
    CASE 2: WHEN the Status = `Under processing' THEN
        Reserve the Item for the Member. Enter `Date of Reservation' and 'Membership No' in the
            database record.
        Enter status value & the date of reservation on the REQUISITION SLIP.
        Issue the message: "The item is under processing and shall be made available soon after
            processing"
    CASE 3: WHEN the Status = `On Loan', that is, the item is issued on loan THEN
        Reserve the Item for the Member.
        Enter `Date of Reservation' and 'Membership No' in the database record.
        Enter the status value, call number & the date of reservation on the REQUISITION SLIP.
        Issue the message: `The item is on loan. We have reserved the item for you. Contact the
            Circulation Desk for further inquiry'.
    CASE 4: WHEN the Status = `Sent for binding' THEN
        Reserve the Item for the Member. Enter `Date of Reservation' and 'Membership No' in the
            database record.
        Enter the status value, call number & the date of reservation on the REQUISITION SLIP.
        Issue the message: `The item has been sent for binding. We have reserved the item for you.
            Contact the Binding Unit for further inquiry'.
    CASE 5: WHEN the status = `In Stacks' THEN
        Note down its Call Number
        Trace the ITEM from the stacks and reading rooms
            IF found THEN
          Collect       the item.
                Keep in safe custody at Reference Desk
                Inform the member to collect the item from the Reference Desk.
            ELSE (i.e. Not Found)
                Treat the item as not available (may be misplaced or lost).
                Record the fact on the database record and on the Requisition Slip
          Inform        the member accordingly.
          ENDIF;
        ENDSELECT;
    ELSE (No record of the bibliographic item is found in any file) THEN
        Note down on Requisition Slip: ` The item is not available'
        Take Next Step.
EXIT FIND STATUS;
```

The above stated CASE construct is represented below in the form of flow chart.

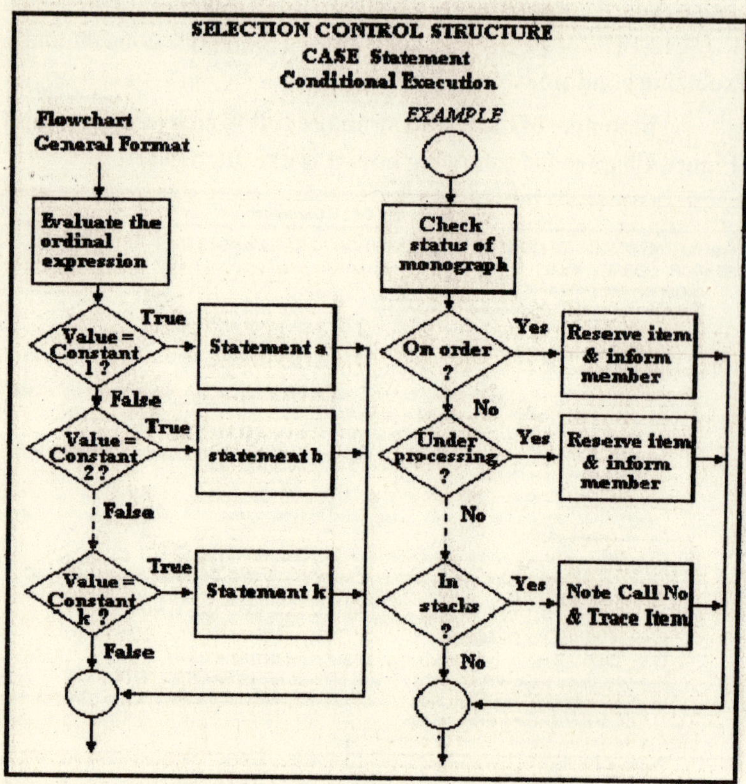

Figure F-4: The CASE construct execution flow chart

Repetition or Iteration Structure

There are times when a given set of operations is executed repetitively or we perform certain steps repeatedly. The condition that terminates this repetition (also called a looping mechanism) is given either at the beginning of all loop statements or at the end of all loop statements. If you put the loop-ending decision at the beginning of the loop statements then it is called REPEAT WHILE Control structure. If you position the loop-ending decision at the end of loop statements then it is called REPEAT UNTIL control structure. The position of decision point constitutes the difference between REPEAT WHILE and REPEAT UNTIL repetition control structures. These structures are outlined below:

Repeat While Structure

REPEAT WHILE: the operations are repeated while a specified condition applies or is true. The condition is tested before the execution of the operations (that is, at the beginning of a loop. Sometimes the word DOWHILE or LOOPWHILE is used for this looping structure.

The general form for conditional execution controlled by REPEAT WHILE structure is

```
WHILE < Boolean Expression > DO
< Statement 1 >
------------------
------------------
<Statement n >
END;
```

The <Boolean Expression> is an expression that can be checked to see if it is true or false. If it is true then the <statement> (or a group of statements), following DO is executed. The cycle is then repeated as the <Boolean Expression> is again evaluated and decision is made to execute the <statement> following <Boolean Expression>. The process continues until the <Boolean Expression> is false; when execution proceeds to the step following the <statement> governed by Repeat WHILE loop.

The syntax of the REPEAT WHILE structure followed by the flowchart (Figure Chapter F-5) showing how it is executed.

An example of a REPEAT WHILE control structure

```
Counter = 20
    REPEAT WHILE counter is greater than Zero
    Compute Overdue Charges
        Subtract 1 from counter
    ENDREPEAT;
```

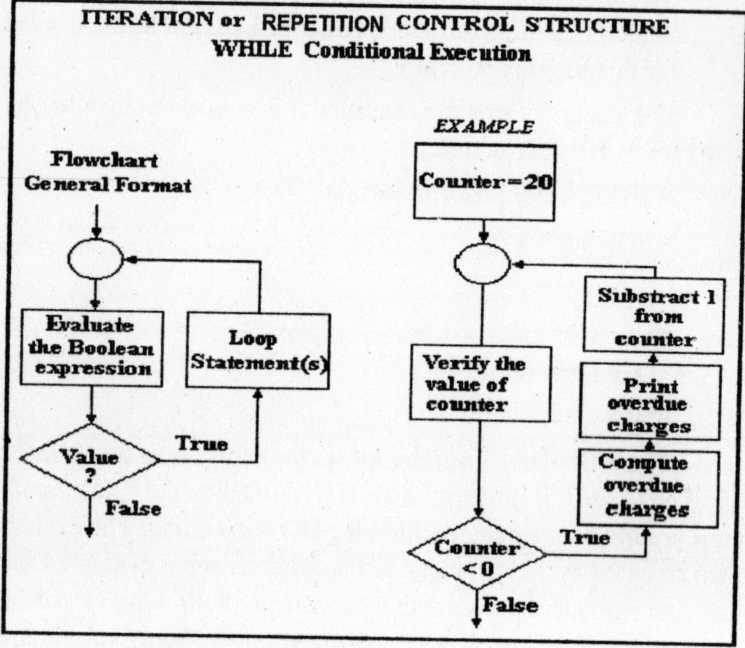

Figure F-5: The REPEAT WHILE construct execution flowchart

Repeat Until Structure

REPEAT UNTIL: The operations are repeated until a specified condition exists or is true. The condition is tested after the execution of operations, (that is, at the end of a loop. The REPEAT UNTIL loop, guarantees the loop statements are executed at least once, because the loop statements are executed before you make a test whether to get out of the loop. Sometimes the word DO UNTIL or LOOP UNTIL is used for this looping structure.

The general form for conditional execution controlled by REPEAT WHILE structure is:

REPEAT

< Statement 1 >

< Statement n >

UNTIL < Boolean Expression >;

The REPEAT UNTIL construct is similar to REPEAT WHILE construct, except that a loop statement (or a group of statements) is (are) first executed and then the specified <Boolean Expression> is evaluated. The cycle is repeated UNTIL the <Boolean Expression> becomes true. The difference in this construct from the REPEAT WHILE construct is that the loop statement(s) is/are always performed at least once before the <Boolean Expression> is checked. As long as the <Boolean Expression> is false the statement is repeatedly executed.

The syntax of the REPEAT UNTIL structure followed by the flowchart (Figure Chapter F-6) showing how it is executed.

An example of a REPEAT UNTIL control structure

```
Counter      = 1
REPEAT
 Compute          overdue charges
 Add          1 to counter
    UNTIL Counter = 20
```

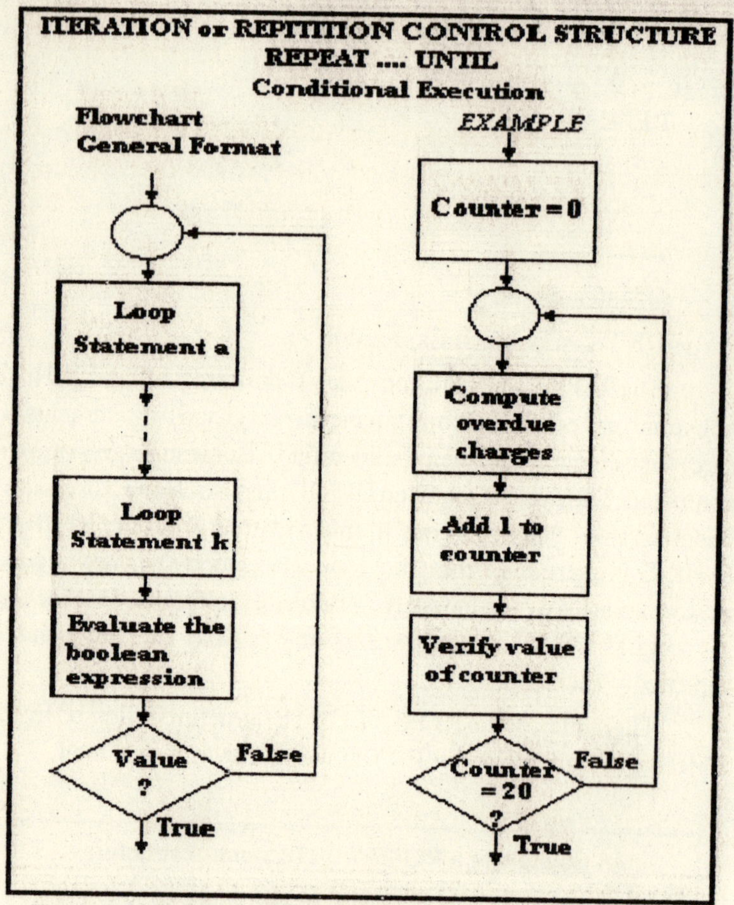

Figure F-6: REPEAT UNTIL Construct Execution FLOWCHART

3 DIAGRAMMING TECHNIQUES

3.1 Introduction

A systems analyst like an architect needs different techniques and tools to conceive, design and physically build systems. One category of tools that many system analysts use is the diagramming technique that enables them to represent diagrammatically the various features of the designed systems and processes. Using diagramming techniques, can be built models for existing systems and processes can be built. These help in better understanding the systems and processes, and design or redesigned target systems and processes. Clear diagrams also help to review the designed systems, programs or processes.

Essentially, diagramming techniques help in documentation and communication of ideas effectively. The manuals or reports developed using diagrams serve as means in establishing precise communication among members of the system development team, between them and end users of the system. Use and application of diagramming techniques also help them in clear thinking and ultimately play an essential role in designing complex systems and processes.

Systems analysts often use diagramming techniques to analyse and design complex systems, and to depict their structure, activities — functions, processes or procedures, flow of data among process, and data structures graphically. Some of the diagramming techniques used by systems analysts are:

* Decomposition diagrams.
* Flowcharts.
* Data flow diagrams.
* Bubble Chart.
* Entity-relationship diagrams.
* Decision tree and tables.
* Decomposition Diagrams

The diagrams often used to depict simple hierarchy or hierarchical structures, are known as tree diagrams. In a tree diagram a high level system, unit, activity or process of a system is decomposed into lower-level subsystems, units, activities, and processes showing more details. This top-down structuring or decomposition makes the complex organisations or activities easier to comprehend. It is also much easier to describe complex systems, functions, processes, activities and procedures in decomposition diagrams than in text. There are various ways to draw a tree structure. A common way of drawing a tree structure is shown in the following figures. (Figure Chapter F-7 & F-8):

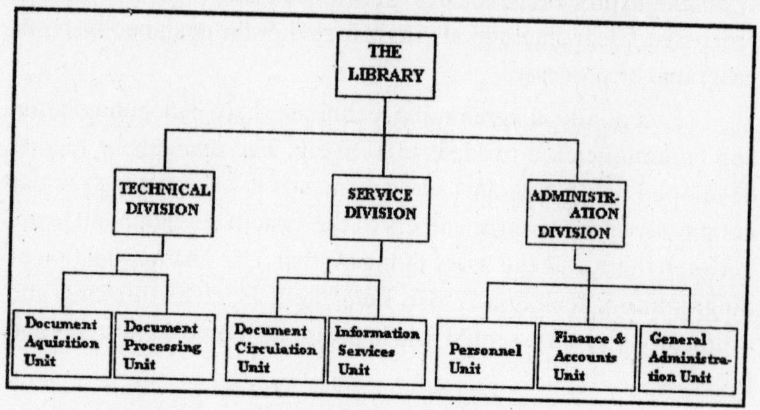

Figure F-7: Representation of organisation structure of a library as a tree diagram

We can also draw a left-to-right tree as shown in the following Figure Chapter F-8:

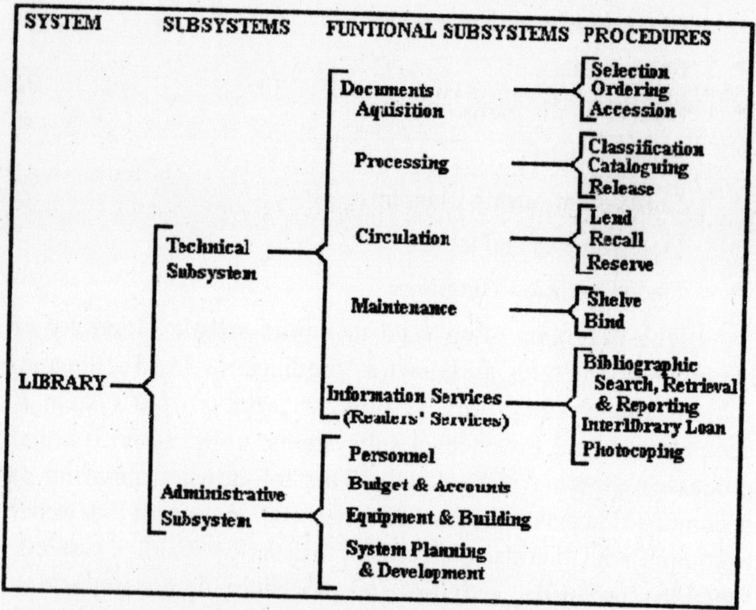

Figure F-8: Left-to-right tree structure diagram with brackets.

4 DATA FLOW DIAGRAM (DFD)

4.1 Introduction

All information systems process data to produce information and maintain stored data. A data flow diagram (DFD) illustrates processes of a system and the flow of data among these processes. It is primarily a systems analysis tool to draw a picture or model of the basic functional subsystems or procedural components of a library system and the data that pass among them. Thus, a DFD shows the flow of data and work through a system.

Analysts draw two types of system's process model implementation independent models (usually called *logical models*) and physical models. Logical processing modelling defines input, processing and output requirements independent of their implementation. A physical model shows not only what a system is or does, but also how it is physically devised. We need process models to set up processes and to develop computer programs. A process model is a picture of the flow of data or document through a system and the processing performed on that data. For this reason, process models are also frequently called data flow models.

A **data flow diagram** (DFD) is the tool used to depict the data flow model diagrammatically. It shows the overall data flow through a system and the work performed by the system. A data flow diagram depicts:

* System boundaries.
* Processes, which manipulate data and data flow among them. Processes transform inputs into outputs. The inputs for any given process must contain all the data necessary to produce the outputs.
* Data Stores and Data Flows.

Data flow diagrams can be used both in the analysis phase and design phase, and facilitate communication between the system analyst and the users of the system.

Elements of a Data Flow Diagram

The DFD is built from four basic elements:

* The *data flows* (also called *vectors* and represented by directional arrows),
* The *processes* (represented by circles, or bubbles),
* The *data stores* or *files* (represented by an open-ended box), and
* The *terminators—sources and sinks* (Also called entities or external agents and represented by a square).

With the four symbols, representing these elements, we can model data processing for any information system.

There are two types of sets of symbols available to draw data flow diagrams (both are equivalent). These sets of symbols are known as:

* Gane-Sarson symbol set, and
* *Yourdon symbol* set. We mix the symbols of both the sets while drawing data flow diagrams.
* The Gane-Sarson notation is more popular, however, the symbol set, that is found convenient may be used.

Data Flows (or Vectors)

The *data flows* are packets of data that form inputs to and output from processes, such as letters, memos, forms, bibliographic records, reports, computer to computer transmission, files, databases, phone calls and other conversations. A logical data flow represents the minimum, essential data needed by the process that receive the data flow. Sometimes data flows are single data item such as a membership number or call number of a book. Others are composite such as book requisition slip containing bibliographic data about a book, required for its proper identification.

The data flow diagram records the flow of data through functional systems or a set of processes and the data flows show how the processes are connected. The *data flow* either initiate a process or result from a process; that is, all data flows must begin and/or end at a process. Permissible directions of data flows are:

1. From a source to process (i.e. a data flow begins from a source and ends at a process).
2. From a data store to process (i.e. a data flow begins from a data store ends at a process).
3. From a process to source (i.e. a data flow begins from a process and ends at a source).
4. From a process to a data store (i.e., a data flow begins from a process and ends at a data store).

A **vector** represents a Data flow. ***Vectors*** are simply **arrows,** lines with directional notation, which show direction of a data flow. A data flow is identified by name, and the name is written alongside its corresponding arrow or vector. A vector must come out from a process symbol or go to a process symbol. For example, the flow of data aggregation or packet (i.e., data flow) called BOOK ORDER (an order for a bibliographic item or items) is shown in the following Figure Chapter F-9:

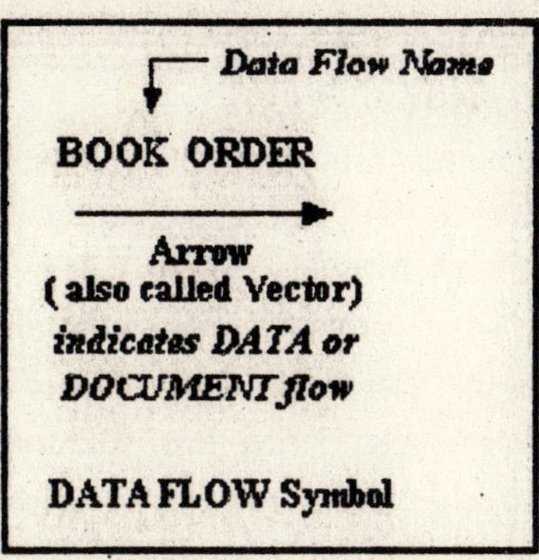

Figure F-9: The Data Flow symbol used in data flow diagrams

All data flows are labelled or named noun clauses. The data elements that comprise or make up data flows are normally documented separately from the DFD (data flow diagrams) in a **data dictionary**. The data dictionary contains definition of all data in the DFD. It also includes physical management about the data, such as data storage devices and data access methods.

The medium of a data flow is never shown in the DFDs. For example the data flow, MEMBER'S QUERY, MEMBER'S ENROLMENT REQUEST, or BOOK PURCHASE REQUEST could be in electronic form, it could be provided verbally over the telephone, or in writing on a query form, on a membership enrolment form, on a book purchase form, respectively, or in some other manner.

Processes

A process transforms the incoming data flows into outgoing data flows. Processes are activities performed by people or computers, or by both at different locations. Basically, a process is a procedural component in the system. It is an activity, uniquely definable, which can be accomplished completely in a finite time.

In a data flow diagram, a process symbol represents work or actions performed on incoming data flows to produce outgoing data flows. The types of actions taken on the data are comparing, checking, authorising, filling and so forth. Processes are shown in rectangles with a rounded corner, or are represented by circles or bubbles in DFDs. Each process is given a name and number for easy reference, and the number assigned to a process does not represent the sequence of processes.

In a DFD the name or number of the process is written inside the box or circle, as shown in Figure Chapter F-10. The process name consists of an imperative verb followed by an object and the first letter of each word of a process name is capitalised. For example, the name of a process is: *Check Monograph Availability*. Examples of other acceptable process names are: Receive Query, Answer Query, Process Order, Search Item, Retrieve Item, Report Result and so forth.

Normally a data flow begins and/or ends at a process. Often there are multiple data flows in to and out of a process, as shown in the following diagram (Figure Chapter F-11):

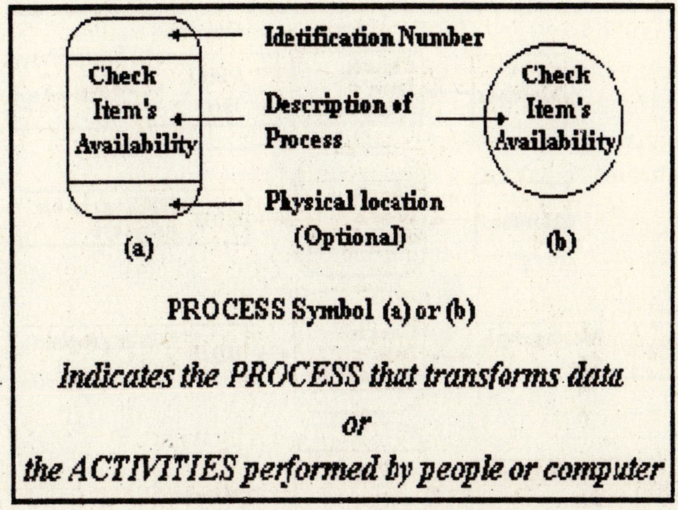

Figure F-10: Process symbols used on data flow diagrams

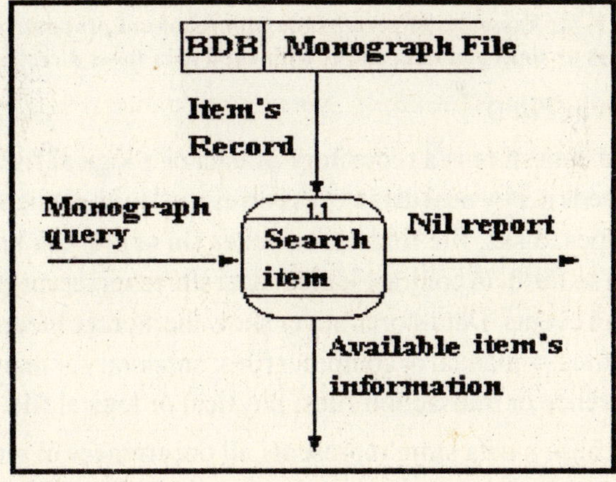

Figure F-11: An example of multiple data flows in and out of a process

The data flow shows how the processes are connected with *sources or sinks* and *data stores*. The permissible connections with valid data flow directions are shown in the following diagram. (Figure Chapter F-12):

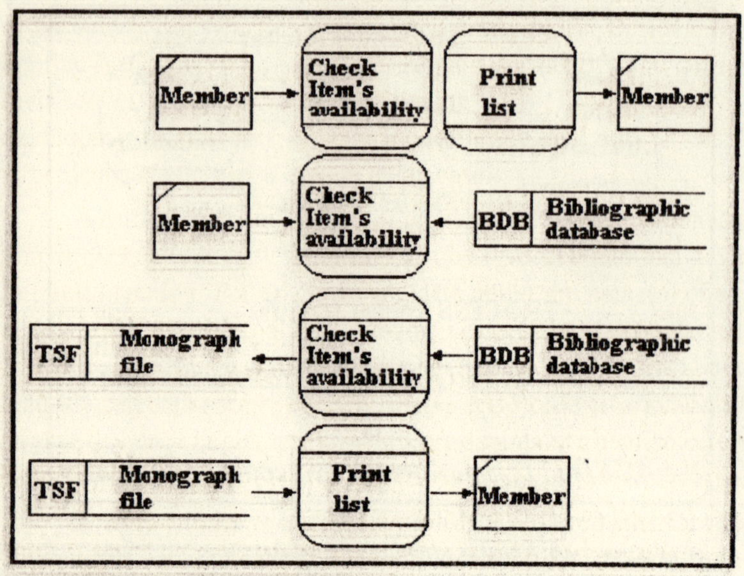

Figure F-12: Examples of permissible connections of processes with sources or sinks and data stores with valid data flows directions

Data Stores (Files)

The data store is a repository of data or a logical file until a process needs it. Physical data stores correspond to implementations such as tapes, disks, file folders, or boxes (In or Out file boxes or trays) and so forth. In contrast logical data stores represent entities, objects and events. Data stores never show the storage medium but only data files—manual or computer files; temporary or permanent files; reference or transaction files; physical or logical file.

Because a data store represents all occurrences of an entity type, its name is always written in plural, such as MEMBERS FILE, VENDORS FILE, ORDERS FILE, and SERIALS CATALOGUE. It is drawn on the DFD as a pair of parallel lines, sometimes closed at the end. The name of the data store is written between the lines, as shown in Figure Chapter F-13 below:

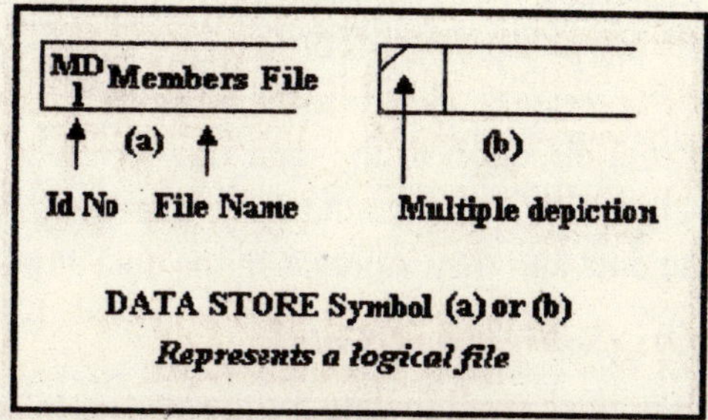

Figure F-13: The Data Store symbols used on data flow diagrams

The data store is connected to a process by a data flow. The direction of the data flow arrow from a data store to a process means those data are being read from the data store into the process and the process uses that data. The direction of the data flow arrow to data store means that the processes manipulate the data and produce new data, then store it in the data store.

In the example below (Figure Chapter F-14), A LIBRARY MEMBER (*source*) makes a query about a bibliographic item or items, information (a list of item(s) or a nil report) is produced by SEARCH *procedure* and written out to AVAILABLE ITEMS FILE and output is printed by PRINT RESULT *procedure*, to be delivered to the MEMBER (*sink*).

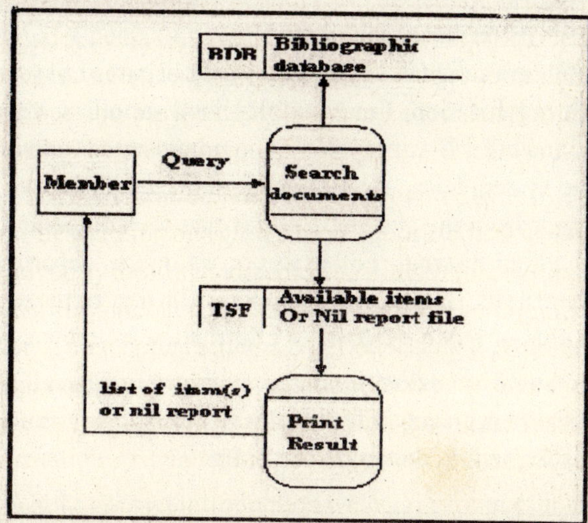

Figure F-14: The directions of data flow arrow from data store

Figure Chapter F-14: The direction of the ***data flow arrow*** from a data store to a process means the data are being read from the data store (i.e., ***Documents' File***) into the process (Namely: ***Search Item***). Further, the direction of the data flow arrow to data store (***Available Items File***) means that the process produces or manipulates the data and then stores it in the data store.

The Terminators (Sources and Sinks)

The *terminators* provide data for the system to process and display the origin of data used by the system. They also exhibit the ultimate destination of data produced by the system. Briefly, they show the origin of data called **a *source*** and the ultimate recipient of data called ***a sink***.

The terminators are the external or internal entities (or agents), which define the boundary of the system. These entities are called **sources** (of data) or **destinations** (of information—**sinks**). A *source* is an entity that produces a data flow, or is a source of data origin outside the computer system. A *sink* is an entity that absorbs data flow or destination of data. They provide the net input to, and receive the net output from, the system. Examples of entities or agents are: people (e.g., library members), office, departments, organisational units, and other agencies such as booksellers, research organisations, libraries with which the system interacts.

Entities are called external if they are not part of a system or information organisation. For example, book suppliers, vendors, publishers, and other library systems and organisations outside the scope of the system being modelled but may provide inputs to or receive output from the system. Entities that are component of a system are called internal. For example, an office, departments, organisational units, staff, library members, who may be the sources of systems data or receive output or information from the system.

A rectangle box a double square, as shown in Figure Chapter F-15, are used to represent a terminator or entity. The name of an entity is written within rectangle or square.

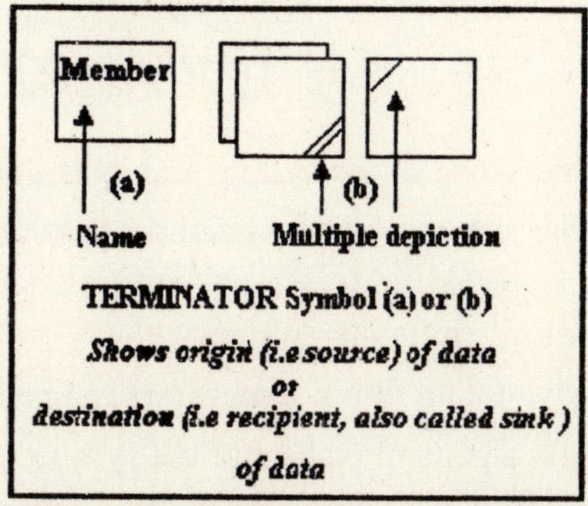

Figure F-15: Symbols used for Terminals (Sources or Sinks) on data flow diagrams

The data flow diagrams initially used by **DeMacrow** [1], **Yourdon and others** [7, 8] and subsequently adopted slightly differently by **Gane and Sarson** [2] are shown in the following diagram (Figure Chapter F-16):

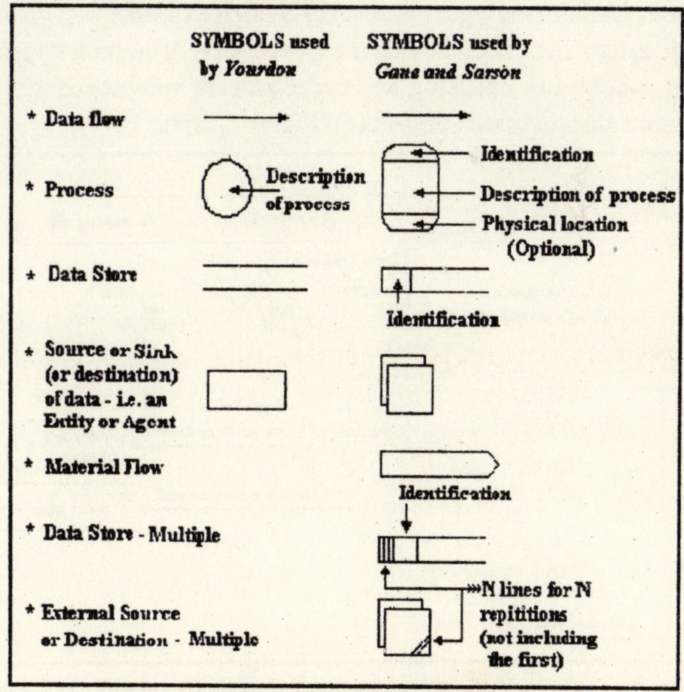

Figure F-16: Symbols used on data flow diagrams

Process of Developing Data Flow Diagrams

The broad steps involved in developing data flow diagrams are given below:

* Define the scope of the system and its boundary.
* Define the sources (of data) and destinations (of outputs). That is, internal and external entities, such as, people, organisations, and other systems.
* Make lists of data flows, data stores and processes.
* First, draw a general picture of the system. Then draw first level data flow diagrams. Check for completeness.
* Subsequently, draw lower levels' data flow diagrams or modules, until all the essential components are covered and can be understood.

Data flow diagrams are developed progressively from the general to the specific — Top level to lower levels, giving ever more details. Understanding at one level of detail is exploded into greater detail at the next level. (Provides a top-level view of the bibliographic item availability checking and order placing sub-procedures of document acquisition subsystem) (Figure Chapter F-17):

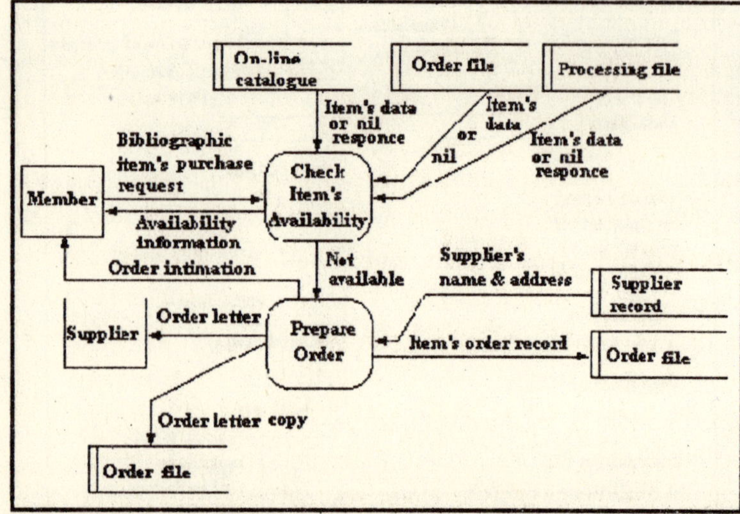

Figure F-17 : A top-level view of the item's availability checking and order placing sub-procedures of document acquisition subsystem.

5 FLOW CHARTS

5.1 Introduction

Flowcharts are one of the earliest forms of graphic representation of procedures, showing the decision that need to be made and action that must be taken to complete a task. **Goldstine** and **von Neumann** [4] are considered brain behind developing flowcharting technique. Although with passage of time, the flowcharting conventions have changed from what they advocated, however, the fundamental principles and rationale remain much the same. Today we use flowcharts to analyse a problem or system, to design or implement a solution, and provide documentation for training use and operating personnel. Essentially a flowchart is a pictorial representation of a step-by-step solution of a problem or description of a procedure or program. It consists of arrows representing the direction the program takes and boxes and other symbols representing actions. Through the use of standardised flowchart symbols one can represent both manual and machine systems. Generally, two types of flowcharts are drawn

* Program flowcharts
* System flowcharts

5.2 Program or Process Flowchart

A **program flowchart** (also called a ***process flowchart*** or ***logical flowchart***) shows in diagrammatic form the sequence in which a procedure, process or program is implemented or completed and the control logic that governs their execution. These flowcharts are used for two purposes. First, as a tool to plan detailed and complicated process or program logic. Second, as a process or program documentation or communication tool. Illustrative examples of process flowcharts, describing the processes of the library monograph acquisition and processing system are given in Figures Chapter F-18 to 26 below:

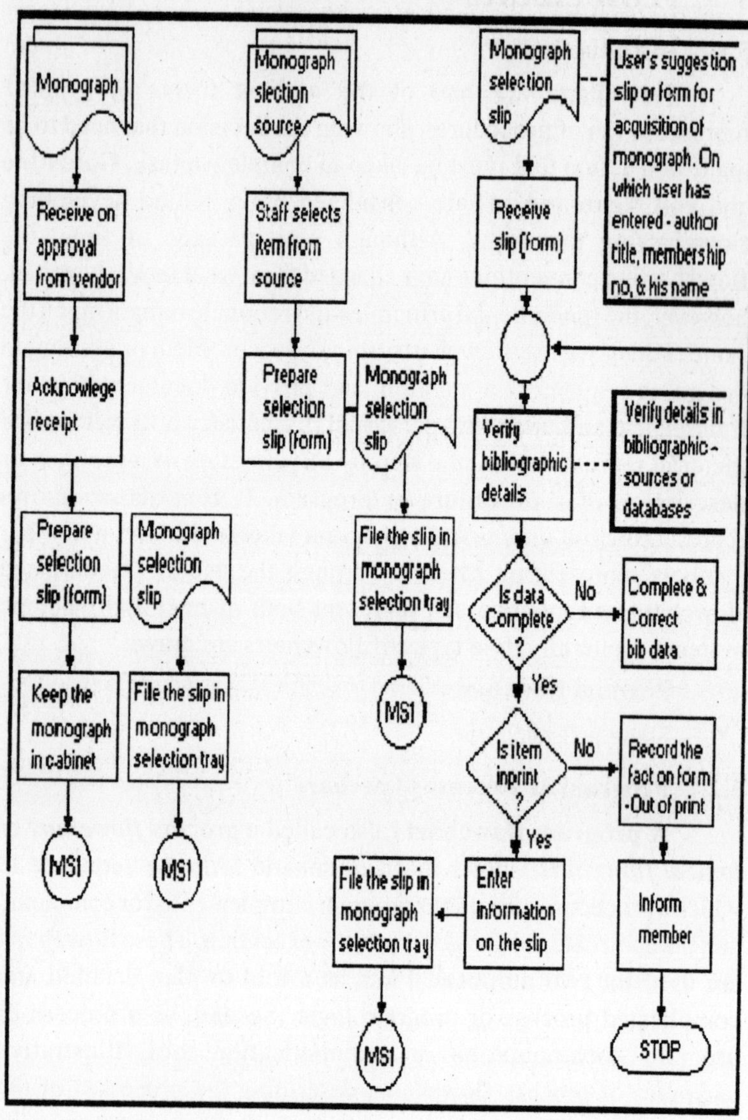

Figure F-18: Monograph selection process flowchart-1

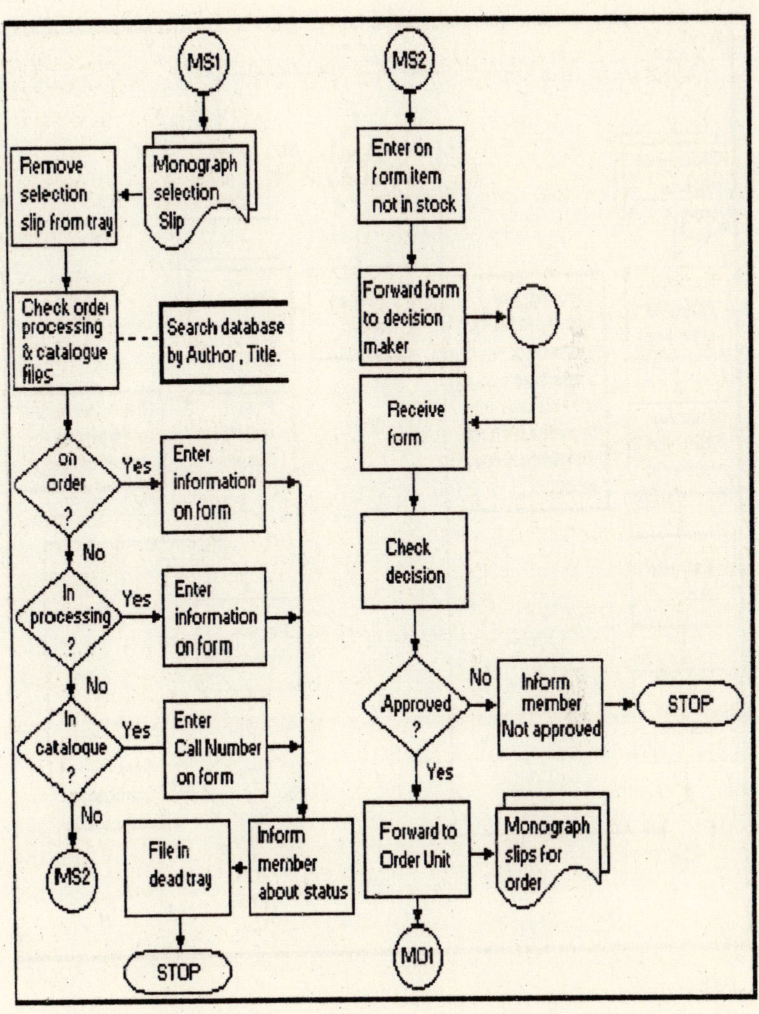

Figure F-19: Monograph selection process flowchart-2

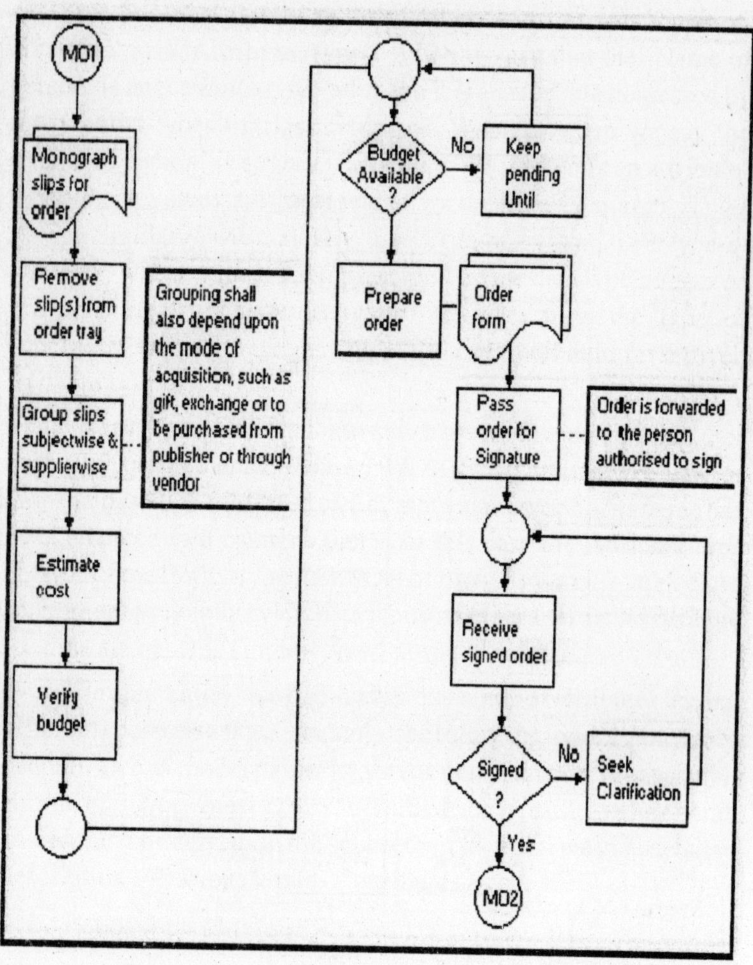

Figure F-20: Monograph order process flowchart-1

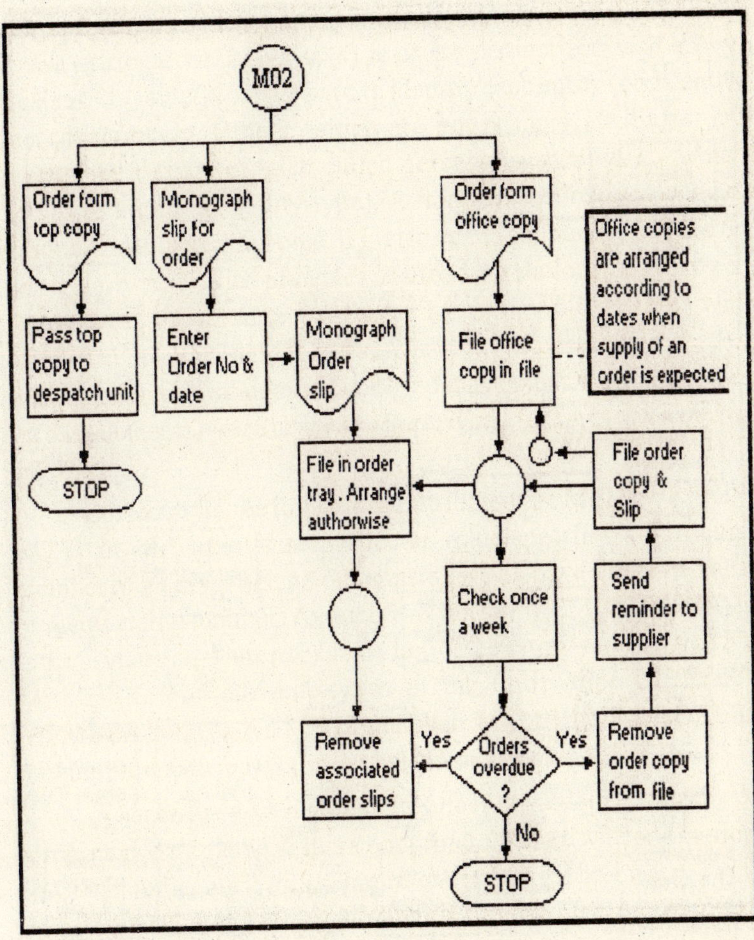

Figure F-21: Monograph order process flowchart-2

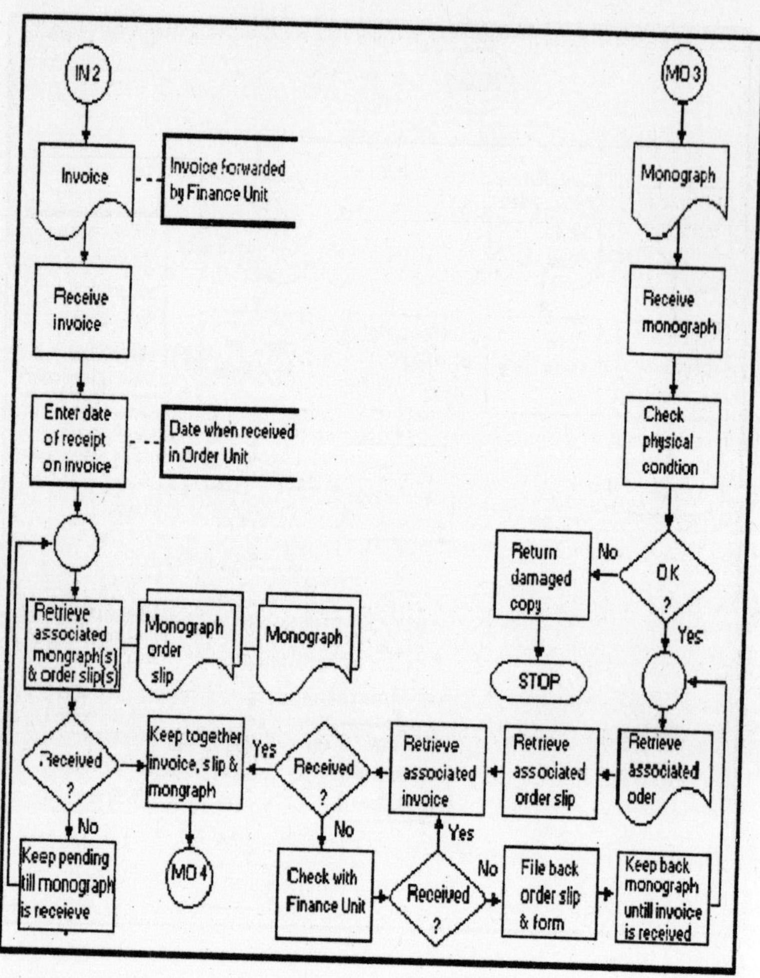

Figure F-22: Monograph order supply receipt process flowchart

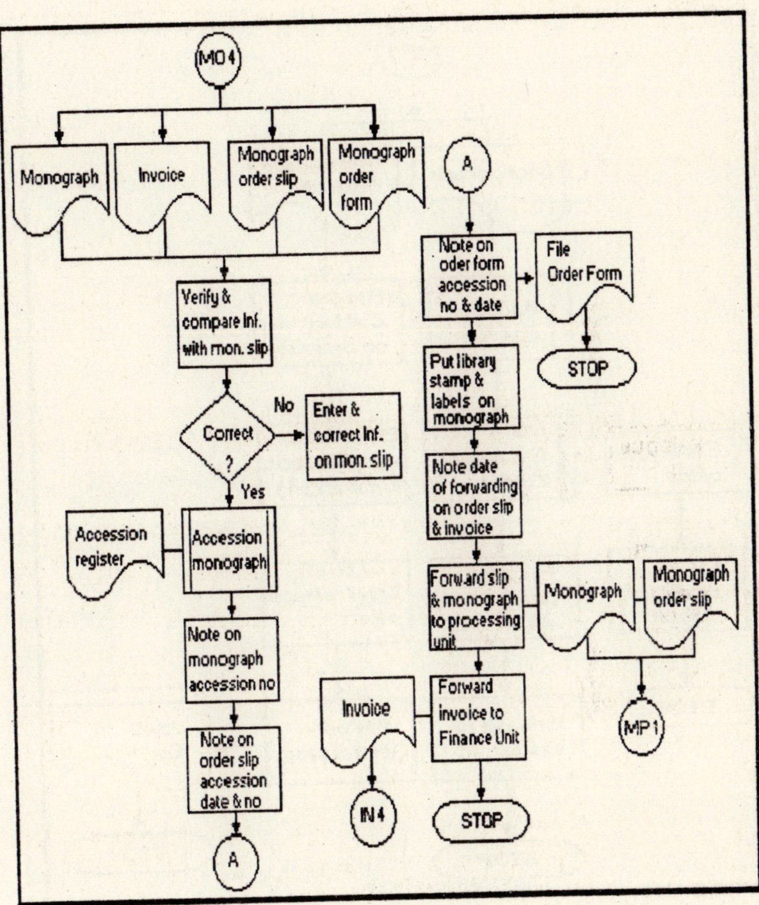

Figure F-23: Monograph accession process flowchart

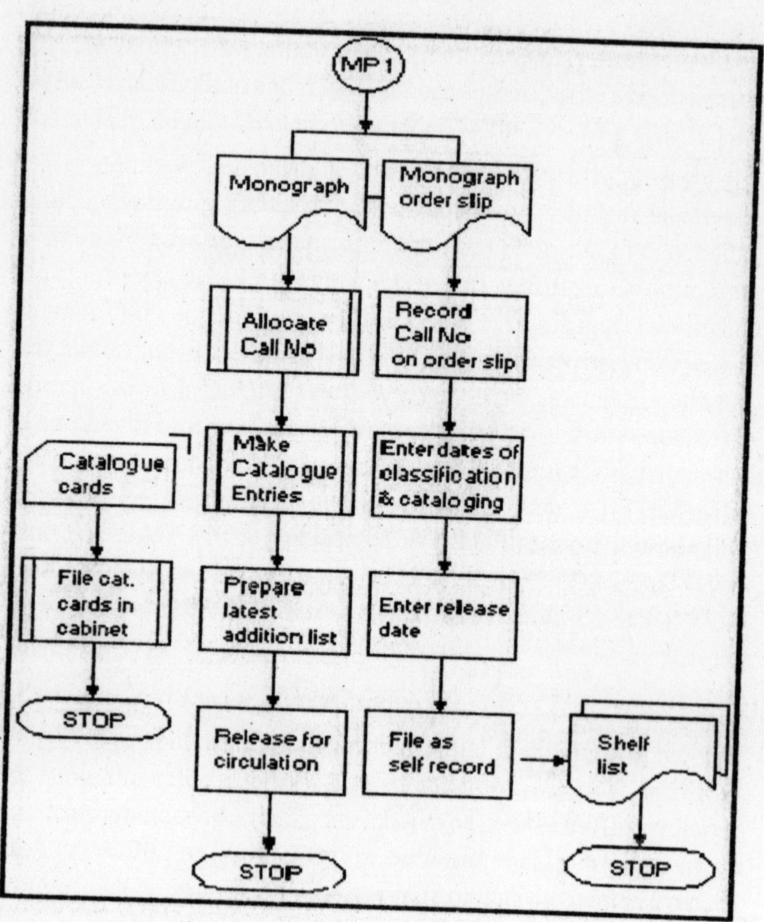

Figure F-24: Monograph classification and cataloguing process flowchart

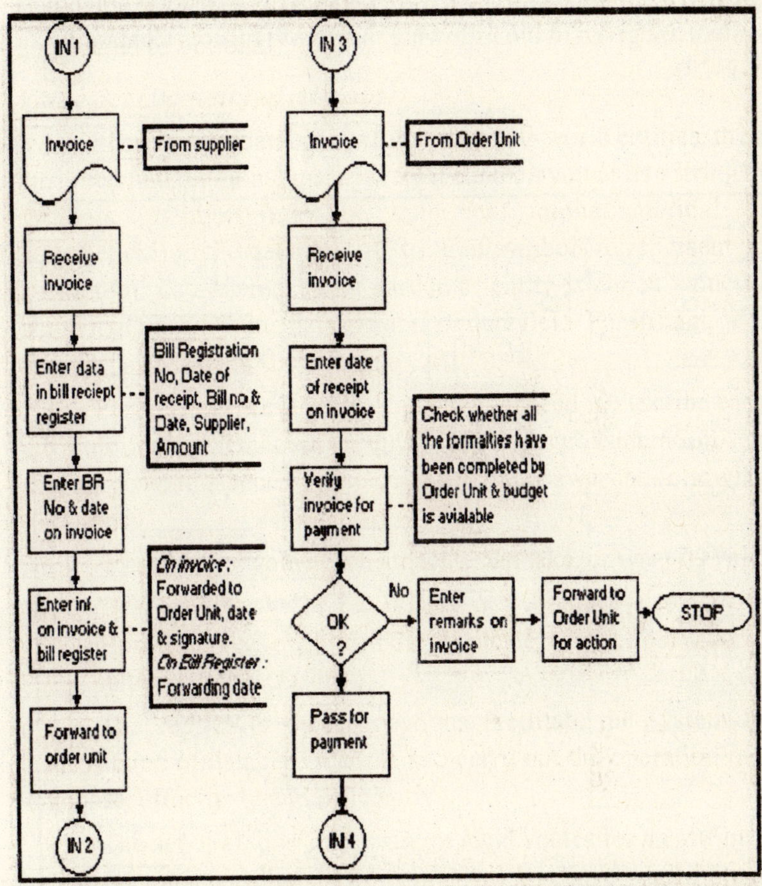

Figure F-25: Invoice receipt and payment process flowchart

5.3 System Flowcharts

A system flowchart shows in a diagrammatic form the basic input, output, and processing components for a computer system or program. Usually input and outputs are represented as physical files. The system flowcharts basically serve as operations documentation, showing the computer operator how to execute the system. Illustrative examples of system flowcharts, describing the steps involved to create database records, inverted file and backup file of a database using CDS/ISISI database information processes system are given in the following diagrams (Figures Chapter F-26 & F-27).

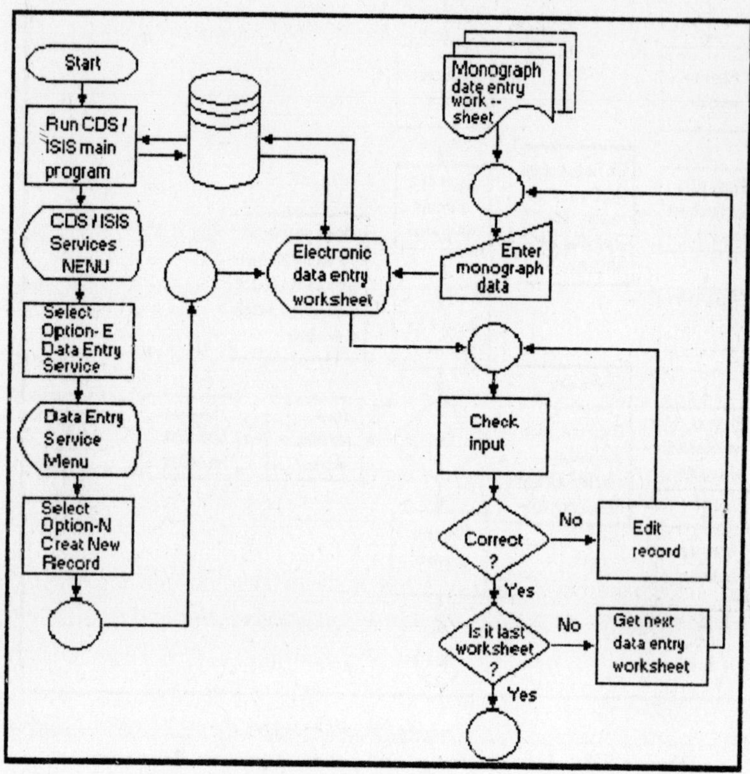

Figure F-26: System flowchart showing CDS/ISIS data entry process

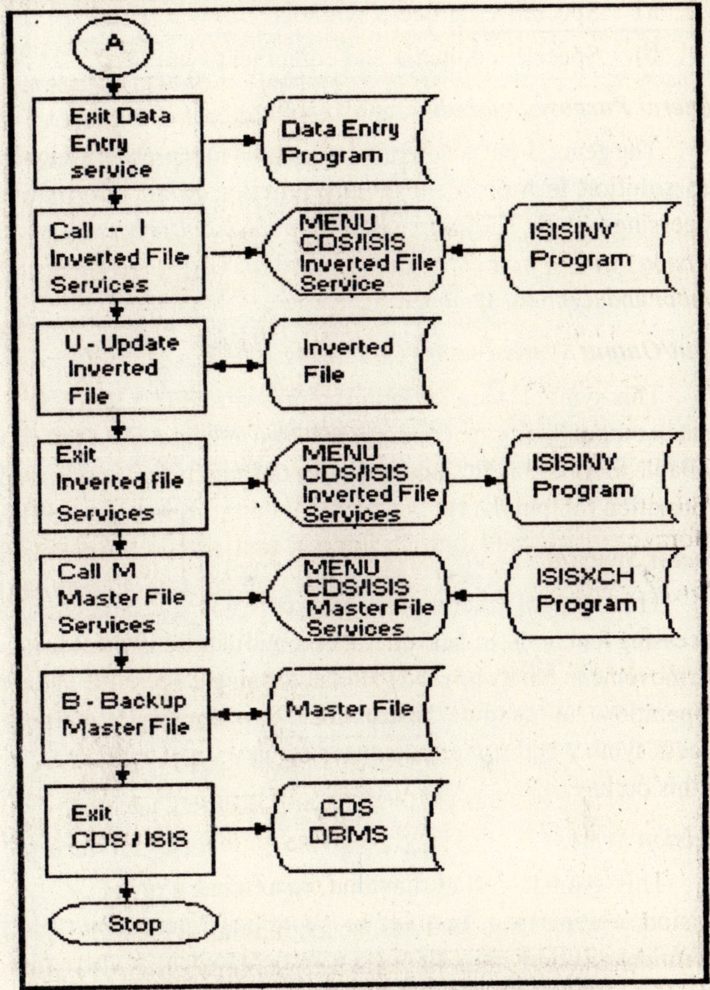

Figure F-27: System flowchart showing CDS/ISIS inverted file and back file up date processes

5.4 Flowchart Symbols

The various symbols used in the preparation of flowcharts are divided in two categories, namely:

1. General purpose symbols and
2. Special purpose symbols consisting of two subsets, namely:

a) Specialised process symbols.

b) Specialised media and equipment symbols.

General Purpose Symbols

The general-purpose symbols are used to represent a step-by step solution to a problem or any function in an information processing system. These are: *Input/output symbol, process symbol, decision symbol, flow line symbol, annotation symbol, connector symbol* and *terminal symbol.*

Input/Output Symbol

This symbol (parallelogram) represents an input or output function or operation. It also indicates all of the data available for processing (input data); or the recording of processed information (output data).

Process Symbol

This symbol (rectangle) represents any processing functions, logical operations, and data transformation or data movement. It may be used to indicate a single operation or a set of operations, or computer instructions. This is a general-purpose process symbol and some specialised symbols may be substituted for this outline.

Decision Symbol

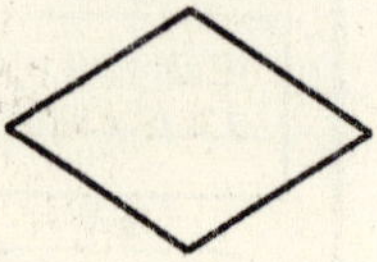

This symbol, called diamond, represents decision, comparison, testing, or switching operations which determine, select or show among a variety of logical or alternative paths (sequence of operations) which path needs to be followed, or an action or series of actions need to be taken when the stated condition is true (i.e., satisfied) or not true (i.e., not satisfied). The entry into the decision symbol is normally shown from the top. Exits may be made from the bottom (normal) or either sides.

Standardised symbols are used to identify or show the path to be followed for a given condition to be True or False. Some of these are illustrated below:

Condition	Path Identification
Condition exists or satisfied	Y or Yes
Condition not exists or satisfied	N or NO
Equal	= or EQ
Unequal	≠ or NE
Negative	- or NEG
Greater than	> or GR or GT
Greater than or Equal to	≤ or GR/E or GE,
Less than	< or L or LT
Less than or Equal to	≥ or LT/ET
High	Hi
Low	Lo
Zero	0 or Z

On-Page Connector

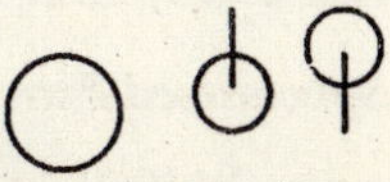

The connector symbol (small circle) is used to maintain a flow of continuity on the flowchart. An on-page connector is used to illustrate a physical break due to an awkward line requirement.

Off-Page Connector

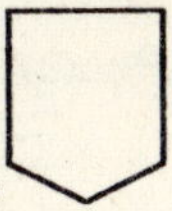

This symbol is used as off-page connector to illustrate a physical break in the flowchart due to paper limitation.

Terminal: Start or Stop Program Symbol

The terminal symbol (slim rectangle with half-circle ends) is used to indicate the initial stating point or stop of a program. It is used to show exits from a logical path, delay, interrupt, pause, halt and return from an interrupted process, and the like.

Flow Line Symbols

A flow line symbol is used to link other symbols. It shows the sequence of actions, executable operation or direction of flow. The normal flow direction is represented by lines drawn between symbols, from top to bottom and left to right. Open arrowheads can be placed on the flowlines to ensure an understanding of the flow of direction on the chart, particularly when the flow does not follow the normal direction (left to right and top to bottom). Flowlines may cross when they have no logical interrelation. Two or more incoming flowlines may join with one outgoing flow line. Open arrowheads may be placed near the junction points to illustrate flowlines entering and leaving a point.

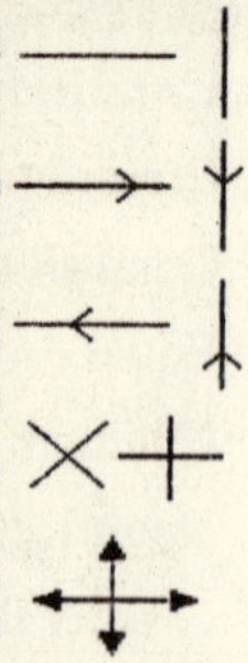

Annotation Symbol

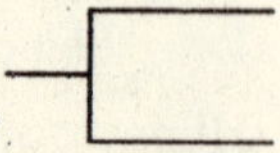

The annotation symbol (*rectangle with right side open*) is used to add descriptive comments or explanatory notes to a chart. This symbol is connected to any other symbol by a broken line at the point where the comment is most meaningful.

Specialised Process Symbols

Specialised process symbols are used to provide greater clarity to a flowchart by identifying specific type of processing operations in lieu of the basic process symbol. These symbols are shown below.

Predefined Process Symbol

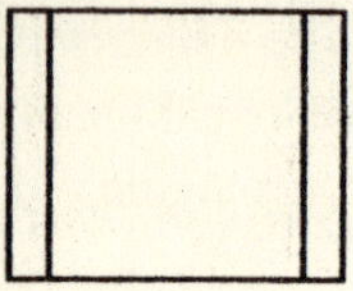

This symbol (*rectangle with bars at left and right ends*) represents linkage to a process, subroutine, sub program, or one or more operations that are not specified in detail on the flowchart, but elsewhere may be in a different flowchart or a staff manual.

Preparation Symbol

The preparation symbol represents operations on the program itself. They are usually control, initialisation, clean up, setting an internal switch, or increasing or decreasing an index register.

Auxiliary Operation Symbol

This symbol (*square*) represents any offline operation performed on equipment that is not under direct control of the central processing unit and which operates at its own speed or a speed determined by some thing other than the human operator. The symbol may be used to indicate auxiliary operations, such as punched card sorting, or punched card collating on unit-record equipment.

Manual Operation Symbol

This trapezoidal shaped symbol represents any offline input or output producing process, which has the speed of a human operator. For example, entering data offline by means of keyboard as in key-to-magnetic disk, and key-to-magnetic tape, or filing a file in a file cabinet drawer.

Merge Symbol

This symbol (*equilateral triangle*) represents online or offline operations that create one set of items from two or more sets, having same sort sequence.

Extract Symbol

The extract symbol represents online or offline operations that generate two sets of items from one set and in the same sort sequence as that of the original set.

Sort Symbol

This symbol is used to indicate online or offline sorting of a set of items into some sequence.

Collation Symbol

The collation symbol shows a combination of merge and extract operations. Two or more sets of items may be created from two or more other sets. This symbol may be used for online or offline operations.

Specialised Media and Equipment Symbols

Manual Input Symbol

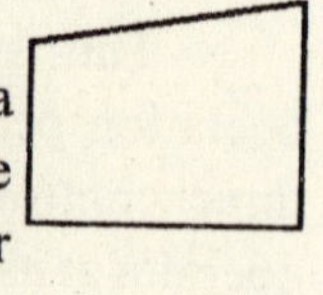

This symbol shows manual insertion of data into information processing systeḿ via an online device, such as online keyboard, light pen, tag reader and the like.

Document Symbol

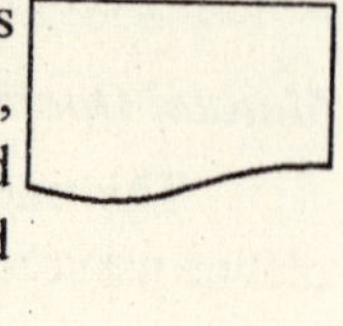

This symbol represents data or information as hard copy input or output of any type. For example, printed, hand written, typed, or optical mark read documents; or plotter outputs (i.e., graphs produced by a plotter).

Display Symbol

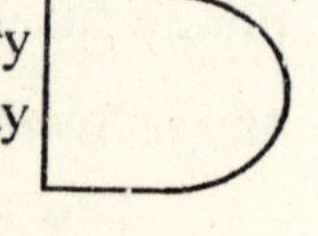

This symbol represents a display of transitory data or information on a media such as CRT display units, video devices, consoles, and like.

Punched Card Symbol

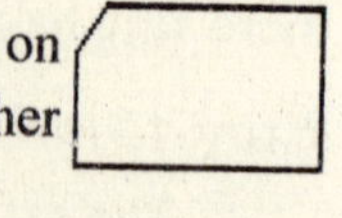

This symbol represents inputs or output data on punch cards of any style, size or shape. Two further punched-cards symbols are described below.

Card Deck Symbol

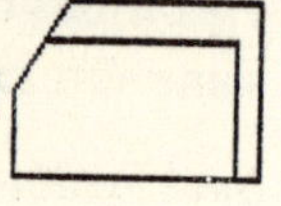

This symbol represents a collection of punched cards

Card File Symbol

This symbol represents a file of related punched cards.

Punched Tap Symbol

This symbol represents data in the medium of any punched continuous material, such as paper tape, punched plastic tape, and punched metal tape and the like.

Magnetic Tape Symbol (Sequential Access Storage)

This symbol (a circle with a horizontal rightwards pointing line, tangent to the bottom) represents input/ output data on a magnetic tape.

Magnetic Disk Symbol

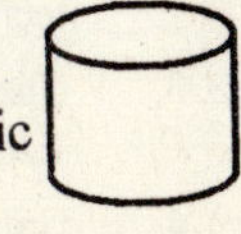

This symbol represents data stored on a magnetic disk device.

Magnetic Drum Symbol

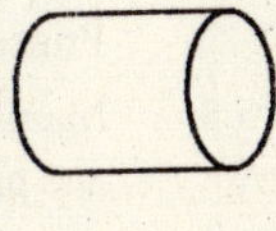

This symbol represents data stored on a magnetic drum device. Or Direct Access Storage

Core Symbol

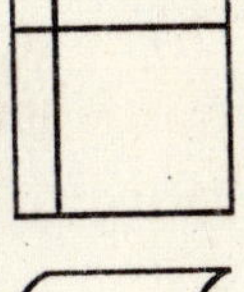

This symbol represents input or output data stored on a magnetic core or a high speed-device linked to the primary storage unit (Internal Storage) to augment storage capability.

Online Storage Symbol

Off-line Office Storage Symbol

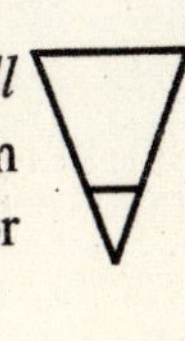

This storage symbol (*equilateral triangle with a small bar*) represents any data offline regardless of the medium and equipment used. In common practice, it is used for manually maintained data files.

Communication Links

These symbols (zigzag flow lines) represent communication link that is, the automatic transmission of information or data from one location to another, from one medium or equipment to another. The normal direction of flow for the communication is left to right and top to bottom. An open arrowhead may be used in conjunction with the flow line to improve charting clarity, particularly when the direction of flow does not follow the normal path and to indicate a bi-directional flow.

References and Reading List

1. DeMacro, Tom. *Structured analysis and system specification*. Prentice Hall, Englewood Cliffs, NJ. 1978.
2. Gane, Chris; Sarson, Trish. Structured system analysis: Tools and techniques. Prentice Hall, Englewood Cliffs, NJ. 1979.
3. Chapin, Ned. Flowcharting with the ANSI standards: a tutorial. *Computing survey*. v.2(2); 1970; p. 119-43.
4. Goldstine, H. H.; Von Neumann, John. Planning and coding problems for and an electronic computing instrument. V.3, 1947 & 1948, Van Nostrand, Princeton.
5. Martin, James; McClure, Carma. Diagramming techniques for analysis and programming. Prentice Hall, Englewood Cliffs, New Jersy. 1985.
6. Yourdon, Edward; Constantine, L. Structured design. Yourdon Press, New York. 1978.
7. Yourdon, Edward. Modern structured analysis. Yourdon Press, New York. 1989.

G
Data Collection Techniques

1 INTRODUCTION

The exercise to solve organisational problems is called systems research. Systems research is a formal and systematic activity in which systems approach and scientific methods are applied to investigate a specific problem. It involves a series of well thought-out and carefully executed activities. The first step in organisational or systems research is to know the problem areas in the organisation and to identify the problem that needs to be rectified. Once the problem is clearly defined, then we take steps to gather facts or data about the problem through *observation, experiment*, and *testimony,* then analyse the collected facts or data and draw logical conclusion from it or stipulate the factors associated with the problem. In the next step, efforts are made to find a workable solution to solve the problem and to take necessary corrective actions by implementing the solution. [*cf*., **Kashyap**, 5].

Most organisational research or systems studies are conducted in the natural environment of the organisational setting, with a least amount of interference in the normal work of the organisation. A study conducted in this manner in any particular organisation is usually called survey research. The term *survey research* is very often used as an umbrella term (i.e. As more general and more encompassing term) to cover the investigations often described or referred to as: *Exploratory survey or study, descriptive study, analytical study, evaluation study, opinion survey, field study, users survey, motivational research, field survey, sampling survey* and so forth.

The survey investigation involves the description, assessment, interpretation, and evaluation of processes, products, systems, or any phenomenon. The unique characteristics of survey research are that systematic collection of facts or data from the population (universe) or samples of population is carried out using one or more data collection methods. The standard data gathering methods are: i. **Interviews,** ii. **Questionnaires** (personally administered and mail questionnaires), iii. **Observations** (direct or participatory), iv. **Sampling**, and v. **Other sources of data that are not people**, such as: (a) *documentary records* (i.e., published and unpublished documents and other records kept in organisations, and (b) other type of *unobtrusive data sources* and indicators (e.g., citations of documents in works, the wear and tear of documents in a library, documents circulation records could be good indicators of their usage, or their popularity or both.

Almost all the data collection methods have some built in biases associated with them. As such, collecting data through multi-methods and from multi-sources lends rigour to research. While conducting systems study, one may use all these methods to collect facts about a system or different aspects of a system. However, some may be found appropriate and others not. The following sections, examine the first four data-collection methods in detail.

2 INTERVIEWING

One method of collecting data is to interview the respondents — library staff and users to obtain data or information on their interest to the systems analyst. Interviews can be — *structured or unstructured* (also called *formal* or *informal*, *inflexible* or *flexible*, *controlled* or *uncontrolled*), and may be conducted either face to face or by telephone.

The interviewer conducts a **structured interview** when he knows exactly what information is needed. The questions to be asked from the respondents are worked out or structured in advance, in which the questions, their wording, and sequences are fixed. The interviewer refers to this list while conducting the interview, usually sticks to these questions, and asks no more. Identical questions are put to each respondent. This is done to make sure that when variations occur among the replies of respondents, they can be attributed to the actual variation in their perceptions of the situations not due to external reasons.

The structured questions can be paraphrased or reworded by the interviewer, if it is found that a respondent has not exactly understood the question. While rewording, the aim of the question is not changed. An example of such questions, prepared for asking questions from library members based on a structured interview is given in the **Table 1** below:

Table 1

QUESTIONNAIRE

Note: We would like to know to what extent you are satisfied with the feedback (in the form of bibliographic lists) and response you get, on the requests made by you to the reference desk for getting bibliographic lists, on the topics of your interest. To help us, please answer the following questions by circling the number on the scale against each question that reflects your opinion.

LIST OF QUESTIONS

		Very Little				Very Much
1.	To what extent the lists contain relevant or pertinent items — the one, which are useful to you and answer your specific information or study requirements?	1	2	3	4	5
2.	To what extent the lists contain irrelevant or non-pertinent items — the one that are not useful to you?	1	2	3	4	5
3.	How much delay is generally there in getting the lists, after you make a request?	1	2	3	4	5

In the unstructured or **informal** approach no set questions are asked. That is, the interviewer does not enter with well-planed sequence of questions that he will be asking the respondent. Here the answer to one question may lead to another question. The object of the informal interview is to uncover some preliminary facts and formulate a good idea of what needs further in-depth investigation.

An unstructured interview may include questions prepared in advance, but the interviewer may deviate from the line of questioning and pursue with other questions if they seem appropriate. It is advisable to ask broad, open-ended questions during the informal interview. The system analyst may ask, say a staff member, like this:

> ***Tell me something about your unit in terms of work, staff, services and whatever else you think is relevant to your unit?***

Alternatively, the question may be more specific, such as:

> ***Tell me if you are encountering any problem or bottlenecks in providing efficient reprographic service to the library members?***

If the respondent says that every thing is fine, and he is not facing any problem, the interview may possibly end. In case, the respondent points out some problems or bottlenecks, a further question may be:

> ***Can you suggest some remedial measures to remove the bottlenecks?***

Very often, the main aim of the informal interview is to explore the factors or causes of a problem, which may be obscure or unknown, but central to the broad problem area. During this process it might become evident that the problem identified is only the symptom or the cause of a more serious or deep-rooted problem. Then one can solicit further information with the help of a structured interview, to identify and establish the critical problem.

The unstructured interview is more productive but demands greater skill of an interviewer than structured interview method. Using unstructured approach one can *dig deep.* Thus, this approach can be very useful and practical in complex cases. In structured interviewing the personal biases of the respondents are likely to creep in. Therefore, we can say that the structured interview method is less demanding, but also less reliable, particularly in certain complex situations.

When sufficient data or information has been collected, with the help of a structured and /or an unstructured interview, it may enable us to understand and describe the important factors or causes of the problem area. Then, the collected information is analysed and the data tabulated. This helps us to identify the exact problem, describe the nature of a problem in precise terms, and find ways and means or solutions to resolve the problem.

2.1 Tips to Develop Proficiency in Interviewing

To develop proficiency in interviewing, the analyst must learn the techniques of good interviewing and posses some essential social manners to be an effective interviewer. He should be friendly, pleasant to talk to, tactful and business-like. One should not be over-aggressive or too friendly. The manner of speaking should be natural and should put the respondent at ease.

To obtain honest information from the respondents, the analyst should be able to establish rapport and trust with the interviewees. The respondent, particularly the employees of the organisation, must be assured that their identity will not be revealed. The analyst must make the respondents comfortable enough to give information and truthful answers, without fear of adverse consequences. An analyst can motivate respondents to give honest opinions or truthful answers by explaining them that their contributions will help, and that they may stand to gain from such surveys. For example, the quality of services given to the library members will improve, and so also the quality of work environment and job opportunities in the organisation for the employees.

Besides, he should be completely objective and honest in his work. While conducting the unstructured interviews, the interviewer should ***correctly and faithfully record the answers***. One may record the interview on a tap or a video tap, if the respondent has no objection. However, the tape or videotape interviews may sometimes bias the respondents' answers; because they may be uncomfortable knowing that the interview is not completely anonymous.

3 QUESTIONNAIRE METHOD

A questionnaire is a predetermined written set of questions to which respondents record their answers. Unlike interviews, questionnaires can be used to get information from large groups. Administering questionnaires to many individuals is less expensive and less time consuming than interviewing. They allow people to respond without revealing their identity, so that they can respond without any reservation or impediment, consequently, truthfully and fearlessly. One can *administer* the questionnaires **personally** or through **mail,** to the potential respondents.

3.1 Personally Administered Questionnaires

When the survey is confined to local area and the questionnaires can be distributed at the workplace, personally administering the questionnaires is the best way to collect data. The main advantage is that the analyst can distribute and collect all the completed responses within a short period. In this case the response is also higher compared to the questionnaires sent by post.

3.2 Mail Questionnaires

This is the most useful method of distributing questionnaires and getting response from a geographically scattered population. One can forward the questionnaires to the respondents by post or email, which they can complete at their convenience and return them in due course of time. One advantage of this method is that it is cheap. Its limitation is getting an adequate response. Nevertheless, providing the respondents with self-addressed stamped return envelops and sending follow up letters can increase the rate of response.

3.3 Questionnaire Design Criteria

The following criteria may be kept in mind while constructing a questionnaire:

1. The ***language and wording*** of the individual questions in the questionnaire should be simple and clear. The choice of words would depend on the educational and cultural background of

respondents. One must use familiar, commonplace or well-known terms. Short questions are preferred to long ones [*cf.*, **Oppenheim**, 11].

2. The sequence of questions in the questionnaire should be logical such that the respondent is lead from questions of a general nature to those that are more specific. For example, the respondents (staff members) may be first asked questions of global nature - say about whole organisation. Then ask more specific, detailed, critical questions regarding the specific unit, job, or procedure.

3. The questions must be sensible, specific and comprehensible. Irksome, ticklish and embarrassing questions should be avoided.

4. In a questionnaire inclusion of ***double-barrelled questions, ambiguous questions, leading questions, loaded questions,*** **and** ***soliciting distant recall*** must also be avoided. The detailed explanation these types of questions is given below:

* ***Double-Barrelled Question***

A double-barrelled question is a question that lends itself to different possible answers to its subparts. For example, the question: **Do *you think that the library has good textbook collection and you use it well?*** It may be observed that this question can bring **'Yes'** response to the first part (i.e. The library has good textbook collection) and a **'No'** response to the latter part for the question for various reasons - may be the particular respondent is a teacher who has his own collection of textbooks on his subjects of studies and is not using the documents kept in the textbook collection of the library. The first part of the question is also somewhat **ambiguously** worded, as the respondent may not be sure whether the question refers to the total collection concerning all the courses of study or to the textbooks belonging to his subject or subjects of interest. Thus, responses to ambiguous questions have built-in bias, as different respondents might interpret such questions differently. The result would be a mixed bag of ambiguous responses that do not accurately reflect the actual feelings of the respondents. Consequently, we will get misleading results from the study.

* ***Leading question***

A leading question is one that leads the respondent to give the responses that the analyst or the researcher would like to elicit or draw out. We should not ask the question in such a way that might prompt the respondent to give an answer that he or she might think is what we want to hear. An example of such a question might be: '***Don't you think that the information centre must provide explicit directions to the employees in the form of job description, work manual, and a broad outline of these responsibilities and duties to get best results from the employees?***' By asking such questions, we are signalling the respondent to say 'Yes'. Hardly, any body will say 'No'. Another way of asking this question to get better response would be to put the question in the form: '***To what extent do you agree that the explicit directions provided by the management in the form of job description, work manual, and broad outlines of responsibilities and duties make the employee show their best on a job.***' In this case, some respondents may strongly agree, some may be in the middle of scale, and so on, the reason being showing best results by an employee depends upon many other variables or factors. If those factors are also included in the questionnaire then each respondent will give different weightage to each listed factor, depending upon his or her point of view. With the result the finding of the study will be more accurate and scientific.

Let us consider another example. For instance, you ask the leading question: '**d*on't you think that a professional librarian must become member of at least one professional association at national level***? 'In this case, if the respondent is a professional librarian, he is likely to say '**Yes**'. If you further ask from the respondent: '***whether the respondent is a member of any professional association***? '. Then this follow up question is likely to put the respondent in an ***embarrassing*** situation, particularly if the respondent is a professional librarian and has given the answer in affirmative (i.e. '**Yes**''), to the first question. Alternatively, you can frame the questions in such a manner that questions are neither loaded nor embarrassing. For example, putting questions in the form: 1. ***Are you member of any library association at national and/ or state level***? **If so, give the name of such associations**. 2. ***To what extent you agree that a professional librarian should become member of at least one national level library association***. Please show to what extent you favour or oppose the issue by circling one of the following statements: **(a) Strongly agree, (b) Neither for nor against the issue, (c) Strongly against the issue**. 3. *Please, also, briefly state the reasons you responded the way you did.*'

* ***Loaded Question***

A loaded question is one that is phrased in an emotionally charged manner. An example of such a question is: 'To what extent you think computerisation of library services implies possibility of losing the job or elimination of certain posts and leading to displacement, or removal of certain category of employees from their job by the management'? The issue of computerisation creates many doubts or misgivings in the mind of employees. Therefore, asking a question such as the above would elicit highly biased emotional responses. If the purpose of the question is to find out whether staff members are in favour or against computerisation of library service and for what reasons, the following two questions would probably elicit less biased and desired responses:

QUESTIONS

1. What are your views on computerisation of library services? Show to what extent to which you favour or oppose the issue by circling the number on the scale, given in the opposite column, which reflects your opinion	***Strongly in favour of*** ***Neither for nor against*** ***Strongly against*** 1 2 3 4 5
2. Please briefly state, in the opposite column, the reasons you responded the way you did.	

* ***Recall-dependent question***

A recall-dependent question requires respondents or interviewees to recall experiences from the past that may be vague or hazy in their memory. Answers to such questions are likely to be not absolutely factual, therefore undependable. For example, if an employee who has had worked twenty years in a library is asked to state about the dates of his posting in various units or the dates of his promotions during the total span of his service, he may not be able to give correct answers and is likely to be way off in giving the correct dates. A better source for obtaining the information would be his service record.

5. The questions can be structured in an open-ended format or as closed questions. **Open-ended questions** allow respondents to answer them more freely. An example of an open-ended question is asking the respondent to state why he feels that the indexing technique used by the library be changed to one he is suggesting. A **closed question**, in contrast, is structured by giving a set of fixed alternative choices. Such questions help the respondent to decide in making a choice among the alternatives provided. However, care should be taken that the alternatives are mutually exclusive and collectively exhaustive.

6. The questionnaire should not be too long. **Lengthy questionnaire** will *tax the respondent* and he may become indifferent in answering the questions or not answer at all. Moreover, the questions must be framed so that all the questions taken as whole provides information about the basic issue. Organising the questions logically and in appropriate groupings with relevant notes and/or instructions will help the respondents to answer the question without difficulty.

3.4 Scales for Questionnaire Items

Introduction

The aim of the analyst in systems study is to collect facts about a system or service, objectively and precisely. These facts are not collected, considered or seen in isolation from one another, but one attempts to identify the nature and exact relationships among these facts to interpret and find the probable causes or explanation of the problem, limitation, drawbacks that exist in the system or the service under study. For this purpose questionnaire method is a handy and effective data collection device. However, to get facts to find out the extent or magnitude of some thing (say, the extent of technical skill possessed by the library staff) from people, or to determine the quality or quantity of something with precision, scales of measurement are required.

A **scale** is a tool, or yardstick by which entities, attributes, phenomena, events, systems, services, are distinguished on the variables of interest in the study. **Variables** are general characteristics, attributes, features or traits of an entity that we measure and the change in either amplitude and/or intensity of a variable is shown as differing or varying value on the scale. Variables are of two types: dependent variable and independent variable. A **dependent variable** is the property or response that is measured. An **independent variable** is the presumed cause of the dependent variable. Thus, independent variables affect the depended variables, or the independent variables are determinants of dependent variables.

In a questionnaire a set of questions are so constructed that the entities or their attributes being measured, or facts about entities, events or phenomena being collected can be systematically assigned scores or values on corresponding scales. The assignment of such scores on the scales is related to the range of values an entity or an attribute of an entity is likely to possess. A respondent tick marks a value on the scale, which according to his/her judgement is possessed by a system, service or an entity under study.

There are four basic types of scales: **nominal, ordinal, interval,** and **ratio**. These scales are actually four levels of hierarchy of measurement procedures, the lowest being the ***nominal scale measurement*** and the highest being the ***ratio scale measurement***. This is why some researchers use the expression ***levels of measurement*** in place of *scales **of measurement***.

Nominal Scale

This is most basic scale of measurement. It consists of forming purposeful and associated (i.e. having logical relationships) set of classes or categories of entities, facts or data, on the basis of some distinguishing factor (s), that is, any characteristic(s), feature(s), trait(s), or *variable(s)* possessed by the entities or data. Nominal scale allows a respondent to assign entities to some categories or groups Each category and its members are represented by some symbol or numeral as way of differentiating two or more classes of entities and keeping track of them. For example, on the basis of the variable ***gender***, we can group individuals (say users or library staff) into two categories: Male and female by assigning the numeral 1 or symbol 'M' to males and numeral 2 or symbol 'F' to females; or as Librarian, Deputy librarian, Assistant Librarian, Clerk. Peon, Administrative Officer and so on, by assigning numerals 1, 2, 3, 4, 5, 6 and so on, to each category.

As a rule, nominal measurement is achieved, when a set of entities (under consideration or observation) can be assigned to a set of classes that are

1. **Collectively exhaustive;** that is, they would include all the entities or data in the set. In other words, there is no other

category into which an entity under consideration would fall

2. **Mutually exclusive or non-overlapping;** that is, in no case an entity or data of the set under consideration should belong to more than one category; and

3. A distinct symbol or label can represent each class or category.

At nominal level of measurement one either uses the numerals as labels or type numbers, or words or letters for the same purpose. Further, two kinds of numeral assignments are possible:

Type-1: Assigning unique ***numerals*** **or** ***symbols*** to runners taking part in a race for the identification of individuals. Here, the numbers assigned to runners serve as their name or labels, and

Type-2: The '**numbering**' of classes, categories, or sets where each number of a class, a category, or a set is assigned the same numeral or symbol

Actually, the first is a special case of the second type of assignment, considering when we label runners we are dealing with unit classes of one member each. The only statistics relevant to nominal scales *Type 1* is number of cases. For example, a cricket team consists of eleven members, which is equal to the numerals assigned to the players. But when the classes containing several individuals have been formed, as in *Type - 2* assignment, we can determine (a) number of cases in a given set, and (b) the most numerous class (the modal). In addition, under certain conditions we can test, by the contingency methods, hypothesis regarding the distribution of cases among the classes.

Mathematically, the basic characteristic of the nominal level measurement is that the entities or data placed in a given category are equal to each other in regard to a given characteristic or characteristics. The relation equivalence between objects expressed by the sign: = (i.e. equal to) has the logical properties being reflective, symmetrical, and transitive. **Reflexivity** means that every entity in a category is identical to itself or alike. For example, A=A in a given category. In a **symmetrical relation,** if A stands in a certain position by B, then B stands in the same position in regard to A (i.e., if A = B, then B = A). For example, if A is placed in the same category as B, then B is placed in the same category as A. In a **transitive relation**, if A stands in a similar position by C, then A also stands in that position by C (i.e., If A = B and B = C then A = C). These three logical properties are operative among objects or symbols in a nominal scale.

Thus, nominal scales categorise individuals or objects into mutually exclusive and collectively exhaustive groups. We are able to decide whether a given person, object, fact or datum belongs to a given class or it does not. Therefore, through nominal scaling the basic empirical operations possible are (i) determination of equivalence, or (ii) non-equivalence between objects or data. Nominal scaling is only concerned with discriminating and comparing entities or data whether the type of trait or characteristics possessed by them or not, rather on the degree to which a trait is possessed.

Nominal measurement is the least sophisticated and considered the weakest level of measurement. It is basic to all the higher levels of measurements. Further, an operation determining the equivalence or non-equivalence among entities or data is not merely the first step in measurement, but it is more than that. Classification of data or taxonomy very often leads us to discoveries. For instance, the chemical table of basic elements arranged in a systematic manner predicted the discovery of certain unknown elements; some properties of these elements were predicted by their position in the Periodic Table.

An example of nominal measurement in the scaling of organisational role of the staff in a library is given below. Table 2 contains an illustration of the questionnaire distributed to a set of respondents (employees).

Table 2

Questionnaire Items Please *circle* the code numbers representing the appropriate response for the following items.	
1. Your Job Status Job Level	Code
Professional	A
Semi Professional	B
Non-professional	C
1.1. Your Designation (*Job Title*)	
Assistant Librarian	A1
Deputy Librarian	A2
Documentation Officer	A3
Library System Analyst	A4
Senior Professional Assistant	A5
Professional Assistant	A6

In **Table 3,** below, each respondent is mapped onto one of the job title code or label. Based on this tabulation, what we will find out is the ***sameness*** or ***equivalence*** between the respondents (i.e., the library staff) placed in a particular category:

Table 3

STAFF SET	JOB TITLE SET	LABEL SET
Arun Kumar		
C D Varma	Assistan Librarian	A1
K L Gupta		
K L Rao	Deputy Librarian	A2
Kusam Lata	Documentation Officer	A3
Pushpa Rani		
Ram Kumar	Library Systems Analyst	A4
Rattan Lal	Senior Professional Assistant	A5
Stanam Singh		
Sarup Singh	Professional Assistant	A6

The result of tabulation indicating number of staff in each category, and the total number of respondents is given in Table 4 below:

Table 4

Tabulation 1: Respondents - Professional Staff	
A1 - Assistant Librarian	= 2
A2 - Deputy librarian	= 1
A3 - Documentation Officer	= 1
A4 - Systems Analyst	= 1
A5 - Senior Professional Assistant	= 1
A6 - Professional Assistant	= 3
Total	**= 9**

Ordinal Scale

In ordinal scaling one can not only categorise the entities, variables, or data but also rank-order the categories in some meaningful way, as to denote qualitative differences among various categories.

The entities belonging to each category are ranked by the degree to which a particular attribute is possessed by the entities. Thus, through scale of measurement we seek to decide the rank order or inequality of objects to which numbers or labels are assigned. A typical example is: **A is *greater than* or *better than* or *more useful than* B, B is *greater than* or *better than* or *more useful than* C** and so on. Such relations are designated by the symbol > (which means (***greater than***) or symbol < (which mean ***less than***), both denote qualitative difference between entities, variables or a particular attribute of the entities.

The relation of higher or lower order (> *or* < ***relation***) has the logical properties irreflexive, asymmetrical and transitive. *Irreflexivity* is a logical property in which it is not true for any A that A > A. ***Asymmetrical*** means that if A > B then B is not > A. ***Transitivity*** means that if A > B and B > C then A > C. So, if a variable quality in library staff such as ***efficiency*** is measured on ordinal scale, one can infer that a staff member A is *more efficient* than a staff member B, and if B is ***more efficient*** than C, then A is

more efficient than C, and the relation is maintained concerning all the individuals in the group.

Ordinal scales allow slightly more refined measurement than do the nominal scales. Because, they do allow, for each entity measured, to find out whether the entity has more (i.e. >) of the quality in question than any other entity, or the same (i.e. =) amount, or less (i.e. <). For instance, it is easier to identify and label willing workers in contrast to unwilling workers, rather than making comparison among workers in the exact degree (or quantity) to which the trait is possessed. An ordinal scale does not reflect *how much*, in absolute sense, the quality or the property is possessed by entities, or how far apart are the entities on the basis of the value of the attribute or the property possessed by them.

With any variable for which the categories or the entities are to be ordered according to some preferences the ordinal scale may be used. The preferences would be ranked 1, 2, and so on. For example one may ask the respondents (Supervisors, Heads of Sections) to show their preferences for placement in the different library units and show their ranked choice. Professional assistants, by ranking them on the basis the importance they attach to their *quality of work* or *efficiency level.* Such a question might take the following form (*see* Table 5):

Table 5

Rank the following professional assistants in terms of how efficient they are in your judgement. You should rank the *extraordinary efficient* as 1; *very efficient* 2; *considerably efficient* as 3; *little efficient* as 4; *very little efficient* as 5.

STAFF SET	RANK VALUE
1. Devi Lal (DL)	3
2. Dalpat Ram (DR)	2
3. Hukam Singh (HS)	4
4. Karam Chand Gupta (KCG)	2
5. Mohan Lal Sharma (MLS)	3
6. Pushpa Rani (PR)	2
7. Rattan Lal (RL)	4
8. Sarla Devi (SD)	3
9. Sarup Singh (SS)	5
10. Usha Rani (UR)	1

An individual staff member is then mapped onto his or her efficiency level, as judged by peers or senior officers. The ranking of individuals according to their derived ranked value is shown in the following Table 6:

Table 6

Ranking of Individual according to their Rank

Staff	Rank Value
UR	Ist
DR, KCG and PR	2nd
DL, MLS and SD	3rd
HS and RL	4th
SS	5th

In the above table data indicate that in efficiency level, **UR > DR, KCG** and **PR > DL, MLS,** and **SD > HS** and **RL > SS**. Thus, we find that *Usha Rani* (UR) is **more efficient** than *Dalpat Ram* (DR), *Karam Chand Gupta* (KCG), and *Pushpa Rani* (PR). Whose, **efficiency level *is equal*** among themselves but ***higher than Devi*** *Lal* (DL), *Mohan Lal Sharma* (MLS) and *Sarla Devi* (SD), and so on. The numbers assigned to the ranked staff are called rank values or ordinal numbers. It is important to stress that assigned numbers show rank-order and nothing more. The numbers do not suggest that the difference or interval between them is equal, nor do they show absolute quantities. It cannot be assumed that the numbers are equally spaced; the quality they represent is also equally spaced.

For instance, member UR is ranked I and group members DR, KCG PR are ranked II, two other group members DL, MLS, SD and HS, RL are ranked III and IV, respectively. One cannot infer the difference between the two pairs is equal by the increase in the degree of efficiency; it can be more or less.

It may be observed that the ordinal scale not only supply the differences in the items or categories them, but also provides additional information about how respondents distinguish among these items by rank ordering them. Note, however, that the ordinal scale does not suggest magnitude of the differences among the ranked categories.

An advantage of the ordinal scale over the nominal scale is that one can calculate *percentiles*. Other statistical operations that can be applied are *median, quartiles, rank order, correlation,* and *sign test*.

Interval Scale

In interval scale the entities or variables not only are ordered or ranked by some measured attribute but the distance or difference between neighbouring ranks is also reflected. The distance or difference is a **constant element** between each successive interval and rank. The interval scale is a form of measurement that is **quantitative in** the ordinary sense and introduces an arithmetical element in the measurement of variables or the attributes of the entities. The nominal and ordinal scales qualitatively distinguish the groups of entities by categorising them into mutually exclusive and collectively exhaustive sets (nominal scale), and establishing the relative position or preferences among these categories (ordinal scale). The interval scale measures the magnitude of the difference between the categories or entities. For example, with interval scale, it is not only possible to say that A is taller than B and B is taller than C, but also that A is 4 centimetres taller than B, and B is three centimetres taller than C.

Very few interval scales have been developed in the area of social sciences. The same is also true in the field of library and management sciences. We can achieve interval measurement of attributes of library elements such as (a) interest, attitude, personalities and motivation of the library staff, (b) reading interests of library users, and (c) recall, relevancy or usefulness of document types to readers. For such studies, we can design numerical rating scales beginning from an arbitrary zero point representing the total absence of the attribute or quality measured and increasing the value in successive equal units on the scale up to the desired limit.

However, we may point out that it is an arduous job to create a measure or scale that exactly and precisely represents equal successive units representing an increase in equal quantity in all cases.

Let us consider the following example of 11 points rating scale for measuring relevancy of a document or set of documents to a reader or a set of readers.

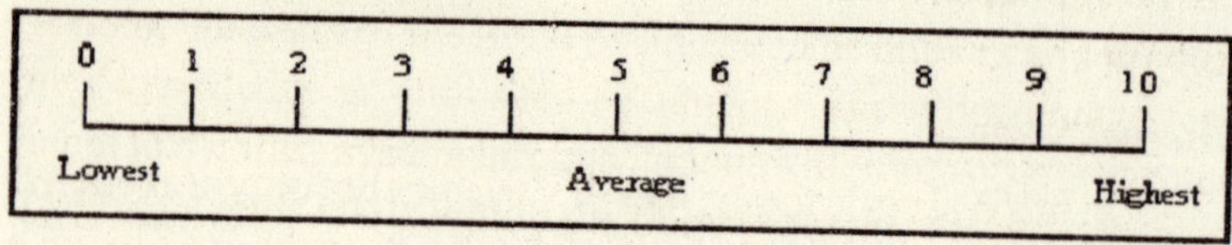

Figure G-1: 11-point scale

In the above scale there is a logical zero point, indicating an absence of relevancy and the scale moves from zero to 10 point, meaning maximum relevancy in equal **apparent units** of 1 (one). It looks as if it could logically and scientifically define the proposition that each of the eleven point intervals (between 0 to 1, 1 to 2, 2 to 3, and so on) represents exactly the same increment in relevancy. Of course, to do this, we have to define precisely the concept of relevancy and describe meaningful stages or grades of relevancy that are equidistant and of equal magnitude and then attempt to develop a scale, starting from the point where the value of relevance is nil to the stages of maximum or highest relevancy. If it is not done, then this scale, despite the intervals appearing equal remains only an ordinal scale. An illustration of the process of creating an interval scale on the lines discussed above is given in the following sections.

Suppose we define that the relevant document (serving the need of the readers) is one that is cited by scholars in their works or taken on loan by readers. Then, among the documents that are found relevant based on citation count taken from a source document or set of documents, say from the published works or thesis of research scholars who are members of a given library, or taking count of the loan record of documents, we can find out or measure their degree of usefulness on a numerical interval scale, as shown below, in which each successive point on the scale indicate 10% rise in citation/loan frequency (*Note*: It may be pointed out that if a document is cited even once in another document, or taken on loan once, this *fact* itself is indicative of some relevance or usefulness of the cited document, but not in an absolute sense, and there are limitations in this assumption).

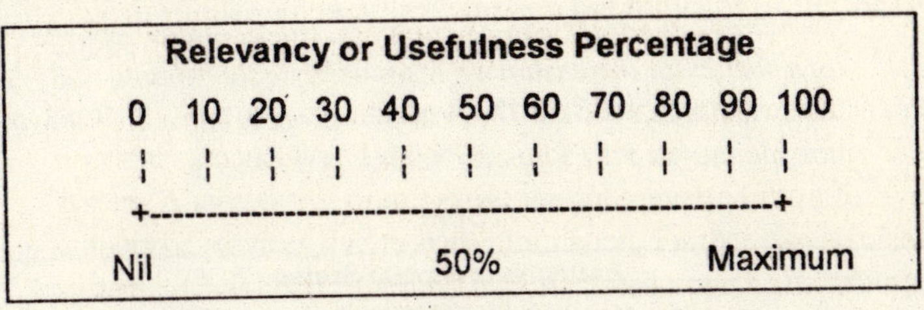

Figure G-2: An example of an Interval Scale

The interval scale, which connotes differences, order, and equality between points on the scale, is also known as '**equal appearing**' or '**Likert-type**' interval scale [*cf*., **Fishbein,** ***ed***,]. The scale could start at an arbitrary number 1 and have as many points on the scale as we consider necessary. Thus, there can be a 5-point, a 6-point, a 7-point, a 9-point or an 11-point interval scale. Studies, however, indicate that the reliability of results does not improve statistically if one uses any higher point scale beyond 5-point scale [**Elmore & Beggs**, 1]. That is responses on an 11-point scale do not contribute any more to the accuracy, precision, or quality of information than on a 5-point, 7-point, or 9-point scale.

We give some examples of Likert-type scales in the Tables 7 and 8. The example of scales given in the tables are so constructed that the respondent may discern the 5 points on a continuum representing: '***extremely significant, important***, ***effective, strong***' dimension (or *quality*) of the variable (or attribute) at one end of scale to '***extremely insignificant, unimportant***, ineffective or ***week***' dimension *or quality* of the variable, at the other end of the scale, with '***neutral, average***, or ***moderate*** (i.e., **neither significant, important, effective** or **week,** *nor* **insignificant, unimportant, ineffective** or **very week / strong)** *dimension* (or ***quality***) of the **variable** (or ***attribute***) signifying the *midpoint on the scale*. The 5 points are spaced such that the distance (indicating increase or decrease in quality) between, say, 1 and 2 points on the scale, would be considered by the respondents, as of the same magnitude as the distance between 4 and 5, or 3 and 4, or 2 and 3.

Note: *One can design scales for questionnaire items either in unipolar format or bipolar format. The bipolar scale contains opposite ends of a particular dimension while unipolar scale contains one end of a particular dimension. The examples given in Table 7 & 8 illustrate the bipolar and the unipolar scales, respectively.*

Table 7

Examples of Bipolar Scales					
		VARIABLE/ATTRIBUTE			
		Efficiency:			
	Extraordinary Efficient	Very Efficient	Average	Very Inefficient	Extraordinary Inefficient
Rank Value	1	2	3	4	5
		Quality of Work:			
	Excellent	Above Average	Below Average / Average	Average	Poor
Rank Value	1	2	3	4	5
	Constantly Superior	Sometimes Superior	Average	Often Unsatisfactory	Constantly Unsatisfactory
Rank Value	1	2	3	4	5
		Errors:			
	Almost Never Makes Error		Errors Often Made		Frequently Makes Errors
Rank Value	1	2	3	4	5

Table 8

Example of Unipolar Scale					
		How much stress do you feel on the job?			
	Very Little		Moderate		Very Much
Rank Value	1	2	3	4	5

As an interval scale has an arbitrary zero point - not an absolute or natural zero point - indicating absence or non-existence of the characteristic or variable being measured on the scale. This arbitrariness of the zero point is apparent, when one compares the Celsius scale with the Fahrenheit scale. In Celsius scale, the zero point corresponds to the point at which water freezes; whereas, in the Fahrenheit scale the zero point is well below the freezing point of water. The zero point on both the scales is a matter of convention and convenience; and a value on one scale can be transformed into a value on the other scale by the equation of form Y = a + b. Algebraically, this is expressed as follows:

> If X is the measurement on one interval scale then Y = a + b will be the measurement on another interval scale, identified by specific constant values of 'a' and 'b'.

Thus, one can convert Fahrenheit temperatures into corresponding Celsius temperatures and vice a versa by use of the following equations:

$$C = \frac{5}{9}(F - 32)$$

and

$$F = \frac{9}{5}(C) + 31$$

Making use of the above interval scales of measuring temperature, we cannot say that a body at 100°F is *twice as hot* as 50°F, or 40°C is 20°C. However, we can say that 50°F = 10°C and that 100°F = 38°C approximately.

Ratio Scale

Ratio scales are the most sophisticated of all the four measurement scales. A ratio-scale has all the properties of nominal, ordinal, and interval scale and in addition it overcomes the arbitrariness of the zero or origin point given to the interval scale, in that it has absolute or unique zero point (not an arbitrary zero or origin point. The weight balance, scales of length, and temperature measured in Kelvin scale are good example of ratio-scale. They have an absolute zero origin, which allows us to calculate the ratio of difference between the weight, length, and temperature of two or more individual objects.

For instance, a given body at 40° Celsius cannot be said to

possess 4 times heat or kinetic energy than 10° Celsius. On the other hand, if the temperature of the body is measured on the Kelvin Scale, which is true measure of kinetic energy of heat associated with the random motions of molecules of substances, we can say that a body possesses 4 times the kinetic energy of heat, or the motion of molecules is 4 times as rapid at 40° Kelvin as at 10° Kelvin. We know that heat is internal or kinetic energy that a particle, a substance, or a body possesses because its molecules are in motion and the 0° (zero degree) *Kelvin* is a point on the Kelvin scale at which matter ceases to agitate. In other words, at 0° K/A, molecules of all bodies are completely at rest. It may be pointed out that 0° Kelvin = - 273.18°C, or -459.72°F, the absolute lowest temperature (i.e. absolute zero), which can ever be achieved.

On the ratio-scale a numerical value can be transformed into another unit of ratio-scale by multiplying each value by a constant. Expressed algebraically:

> If X is the measured value of a given variable in some unit, then Y = aX would be measured value on another scale, where the value of 'a' is constant and 'a' units of second kind (X) make one unit of the first kind (Y)

Thus, length of an object in inches (in) can be converted to corresponding length in centimetres (cm) by using the equation Y = aX, as illustrated below:

We know 100 in. = 254 cm

To convert the value of a variable in inches into centimetres (cm) or in centimetres into inches, the equations can be stated in the following terms:

1. Let X be the value of a variable in centimetres is known (say length of an object) then this value can be converted into inches using the following equation:

$$Y = \frac{254}{100}X = \frac{254}{100}xX = 254xX = \frac{10000}{3937}xX$$

$$\text{That is, inch} = 2.54 \text{ cm or } \frac{10000}{3937}cm$$

2. If the value of a variable is known in inches then this value can be converted into centimetres by the following equation

$$X = \frac{100}{254} xY = \frac{100}{254} = .3937xY = \frac{3937}{10000}$$

$$\text{That is,1cm} = .3937 \text{ of an inch or } \frac{3937}{10000} \text{ inch}$$

It may be noted that "foremost among the ratio scales is the scale of number itself - number in empirical sense - the scale we use when we count such things as eggs, pennies, or apple. This scale or numerosity of aggregates is so basic and common that it is not ordinarily mentioned in discussions of measurement" [*cf.*, **Stevens** - 14, P 28]. In measures of numerousness obtained by counting entities, facts, data, not only natural Zero exists (i.e. non-existence of value, fact, or data) but also we can speak meaningfully of ratio of frequencies. This can be illustrated by the data shown below (*see* Table 9). These data are obtained by counting the number of times a staff member has been absent from work during a given year, from an attendance register. (Here, we are measuring the variable ***absenteeism*** among employees by increment of one and can conceptualise an ***employee*** being absent nil or zero time. The analysis of data shows that Usha Rani has been absent ***Zero*** times (it shows that the scale has a true zero point) and other data provides us ratio of frequencies).

Table 9

Mapping of Staff into the Sets of Absence Frequencies

STAFF SET	ABSENCE FREQUENCY SET
1. Usha Rani	0
2. Dalpat Ram & Devi Lal	1
3. Karam Chand Gupta Mohan Lal Shrama & Sarla Devi	3
4. Hukam Sing & Ratan Lal	5
5. Sarup Singh	6

4 METHODS FOR TESTING RELIABILITY AND VALIDITY OF A MEASURING INSTRUMENT

4.1 Introduction

The quality of investigation largely depends upon the precision and effectiveness of the measuring technique, process, and the instrument of measurement. The basic requirements in any meaningful measurement are an exact formulation of the research problem and providing precise definition of entities, attributes, factors or variables that are important in a given problem situation. That is, one must know very clearly what is being measured.

Objects that can be physically measured by some calibrated instrument pose no measurement problem. For example length and breath of a book can be easily measured with a measuring scale. Similarly certain facts about people can be easily obtained by asking simple straightforward questions such as:

* How many persons are working in the unit?
* How long have you been working in this unit?
* What is your job title?

However, when we want to collect facts about human feelings, attitudes, and perceptions the measurement of these factors becomes difficult.

Operationally defining a concept, particularly an abstract concept, so that it becomes measurable is important. For example, to measure or collect data about the usefulness or effectiveness of any bibliographic service, one must explicitly define, what is meant by usefulness or effectiveness of the bibliographic service. Conceptualise, what could be the indicators or observable attribute of its usefulness or effectiveness. One must ask whether the extent of coverage and the time taken between submission of a request by the user and his/her receipt of search results, or providing a user with bibliographic description of some or all (i.e. maximum possible) documents relating to a particular subject (subject search) and of providing him/her with correct citation for a specific document or documents when only an incomplete or inaccurate bibliographic description of it is available" [*cf.* **Orr**, 12] are the valid indicators or measures of evaluating the effectiveness of the service.

The other requirement in a meaningful measurement is the use of a valid and reliable measuring device, on which largely depends the goodness and integrity of the collected data. A measuring instrument must produce information that is reliable and valid. Thus, validity and reliability are the two very important properties of all sound measures. We must, therefore, ensure that only after the reliability and validity of a measuring device, whether newly constructed or adapted, is established that it is put to use.

4.2 Reliability of a Measure

The **reliability** of a measure is the degree to which the results of measurement are free of error. To be absolutely reliable, a measuring instrument must yield error free, consistent and stable results under repeated observations or measurements. Thus, a measuring instrument is considered reliable if its results remain consistently similar when the measurement of a given object, attribute, or variable is taken by different observers, at different points in time and/or places, under same or similar conditions.

The ability of a measure to maintain stability over time, despite uncontrollable testing conditions and state of the respondents themselves, shows robustness and low vulnerability to changes in situations. The stability of a measuring instrument can be assessed by ***test-re-test method*** and ***parallel-form method***. Consistency can be tested through ***split-half method*** and ***inter item consistency reliability testing method***.

Recently, **Cronbach** ***and others*** [3] have revised the traditional concept of reliability by introducing the notion of *generalizability* [Clesser, 4].

4.3 Validity of a Measure

The **validity** of a measure is defined as the degree to which a measuring device actually measures, what it is intended to measure. Validation of a measure provides us the information on how well it fulfils its functions. The validity of a measure is considered high if it provides the data or information that we exactly need.

Validation always requires logical assessment and empirical investigation of an instrument. Whether it is newly developed or is adaptation of an earlier one. One must gather some sort of evidence to validate even an existing scale or test or any data collection tool, because a measure does not possess universal validity. It may be valid for use in one situation but not in another situation. **Cronbach** [2] points out that "a test (i.e., a measure) that helps in making one decision may have no value at all for another. This means that we cannot ask the general question `is this test valid'? The question to ask is "how valid is the test for the decision (or measurement) I wish to make".

Several types of validation procedures are used to test the goodness of measures. Various writers use different terms to denote these validity tests. For sake of clarity, we group these under three categories: *logical validity, empirical validity*, and *other types of validity*. Logical validity may be tested through *content validity* and *construct validity*. Empirical validity encompasses *criterion-related validity* (both predictive and concurrent validity) and *congruent validity* (both convergent and discriminate validity). Other types of validity include *face validity* and *factorial validity*.

Thus, the goodness of a measure is established through different kinds of validity and reliability tests stated above. In order for research to be scientific, we need to use well-validated and reliable measures. A number of measures have been developed in the area of organisation research. These instruments may be used by citing the source, or if need be, develop new one on the lines suggested by experts [*cf.* **Kashyap**, 7].

4.4 Observation Method

Observation is a classical data collection method of scientific inquiry. Through interviews and questionnaires we elicit information or facts, indirectly, from people. Observation is direct method of collecting data, by observing phenomena, events, people etc. in their natural setting or work environments and recording their occurrences, activities, or behaviours. As an analyst and observer, you go to into the organisation and can gather field observational data as a non-participant observer or as a participant observer.

As a **participant observer** you joint the work team or become part of the unit to collect first hand information about the working of the unit. For example, if an analyst wants to collect data about the working condition of a circulation system of a library, he gets himself associates with the unit as member, by design with the contrivance of the management. In this way, the staff working in the unit considers him as part of the team and not as an outsider how has joined to observe the working of the unit on the behest of management. In this situation other employees and one can collect unbiased data or facts.

The analyst can also collect data without becoming integral part of the working team or unit as non-participant observer. As a **non-participant observer** the analyst sits in a corner and merely observes the activities and records them on the paper.

Observational studies could be either structured or unstructured. In a structured approach the analyst observes predetermine set of categories of activities or phenomena. Whereas, in an unstructured observational approach, an analyst has no definite ideas of the particular aspects to be focussed on in the observation, but records particularly everything that is observed.

Observational studies are time-consuming, as the observer must be physically present at the workplace or participate in the activities of the unit for prolonged periods.

5 SAMPLING

5.1 Introduction

The purpose of **sampling** is to obtain data on a subset of some population or the universe to make inference about the population (i.e. the whole set) based on the data from the sample (i.e. the subset). Population (also called ***a universe***) refers to the entire group of people, events or things of interest that the investigator wishes to investigate. A ***sample*** comprises some *elements* (also called *members* or *subjects*) carefully selected from the population or population frame.

In practice the population is usually an ideal rather than reality, because it in not completely available, it is hard to be bounded or circumscribed, it is mobile or constantly changing, or it is inaccessible or imperfect. Therefore, a '*frame*' is used to stand for population. The **population frame** is a *listing* of all the elements in the population from which the sample is to be drawn. Listings (also called *listing units*) are used to identify and select into sampling units from *lists*. For example, a list of library members on roll at a particular point in time could be the population frame, if their views on library services are to be collected. The payroll of a library could be a population frame, if data about their work experiences is to be collected. One chooses particular sample elements of the universe, such that the chosen elements or the subset is considered typical or representative of the whole. By studying the sample the investigator can draw inferences about the population, that is the whole set.

The population is defined jointly with the elements or basic units that comprise and define the population. The population is defined in terms of (1) *contents*, (2) *units*, (3) *extent*, and (4) *time*. For example, in the design of a survey regarding the *requirements* or *expectations* of library members of a university library system, we may specify: (1) all students, teachers, and administrative staff, (2) enrolled or working in various colleges, departments or units (3) in the University of Delhi (4) in 2003. Often one redefines the desired population to obtain particular *survey population*. For example, the above population might be redefined as: (1) all teachers, research scholars, and post graduate students, (2) enrolled and working in various colleges or departments (3) located in the main Delhi University Campus (4) on October 1, 2003.

A survey may yield information about several diverse populations. Different *contents* may be covered by the same survey. Different *units* may be formed from same data. Members' data may be presented referring to their subject specialisation, or research interest etc. Different *entities* may be considered as subclasses for which survey results may be prepared and presented. Different *times* may be represented in a survey when information is obtained or available for two or more periods.

5.2 Survey Approach and Sample Design

The overall design of a survey begins with the general problem statement that requires solution and includes the following aspects which taken as a whole may be called the statistical survey approach.

1. Define the appropriate statistical population and its frame. Specify the extent and contents of the survey population
2. Quantify the problem in pertinent survey population parameters
3. Decide what information or data is required to solve the problem. The type and amount of the quality of data required, including the extent (percentage) of error to be tolerated.
4. Decide the methods of data collection, measurement and processing. If sample data is to be used, then its sample **design** must be decided. Sample design includes (1) a sample selection process, that is, the rules and operations or methods to be used by which some members of the population are included in the sample; and (2) an estimation process, the size of the sample necessary to generalise the findings from the sample data to the total population.
5. The methods of analysis to be followed for making correct inferences from the data collected.
6. Estimates of resources—financial, personnel, facilities, and time required

5.3 Sample Survey Terminology

An important sample survey research decision to be made is about sampling design or technique to use. We define below some terms used in this section.

Population

A population is the collection of objects or entities (abstract or physical) about which we would like to learn or find something, or collect information.

The Target Population

The target population is the population about which we need information.

The Survey Population

The survey population is the population about which we can obtain information. The survey population (also called study population) may differ somewhat from the target population. Strictly speaking, only the survey population is represented in the sample. Survey population is difficult to define exactly, and it is easier to define the target population.

Element

An element is a single member of the population.

Sample

A sample comprises some members selected from the population and provides statistical inference to the survey population. A single member of the sample is called a **subject**.

Sampling Unit

A sampling unit is a potential member of the sample. Sampling units contain the elements, and they are used for selecting elements into the sample. In element sampling, a sampling unit contains only one element; but in cluster sampling the sampling unit called *cluster* may contain several elements. For example, a sample of faculty members of a library may be obtained from the sample of departments and/or the sample of colleges. The same survey may use different kinds of sampling units, and in multistage sampling a hierarchy of sampling units or cluster is used so that elements belong to uniquely to the sampling unit at each stage. To improve the selection the population is divided into **strata**. The aggregate of strata comprises the population. [*cf.*, **Kish**, 10]

5.4 Survey Sampling

Survey sampling deals with the method for selecting and observing a part (sample) of the population to make inference about the whole population. It is a process of selecting a reasonable number of items from the population so that by studying the sample, and understanding the characteristics of the sample subjects, we can generalise the properties of the population. Sample statistics - such as, central tendencies, dispersions, etc., are used as estimates of the population parameters. The *sample statistic* or *sample value* is an *estimate* computed from the number of elements in the sample.

The reasons for choosing a sample rather than collecting data from the entire population are obvious. It is impossible to collect data from, or to test, or to examine every element of a large population. Even it is possible, it would be prohibitive in terms of time, cost and human resources required to collect data. Thus, a sample survey has certain advantages over complete census survey, such as - economy, speed and timeliness, quality and accuracy. On the other hand, a complete census survey possesses special advantages in some situations, particularly if the population is small: (a) data for small units can be obtained easily, (b) public compliance and response is easier to secure, to collect data, and (c) people also easily accept the results obtained from complete data.

No single sample is an exact replica of the population from which it is drawn. We must choose the sample in a scientific way, so that we can be reasonably sure that the sample statistics will be as close to the population parameters as possible.

Almost every characteristic, quality, or attribute of the population is generally **normally distributed**. An attribute, such as, height or weight is such that most people will be clustered around the mean and there will be people at the extremes who are either very tall or very short, very heavy or very light, and so on. This feature is also called **normality of distributions** in a population. Thus, if we have to estimate the population characteristics reasonably precisely from the characteristics represented in a sample, the sample has to be chosen such that the distribution of the characteristics of interest follows the same type of normal distribution in the sample as it does in the population. The more representative is the sample of the population, the more generalisable will be the findings of the study. Generalisability is one of the distinctive features of scientific investigation.

5.5 Types of Sampling Design

There are two types of sampling design: probability and non-probability sampling. In **probability sampling**, the elements in the population have some known chance or probability of being selected as sample subjects. In **non-probability sampling**, the elements in the population do not have a known or predetermined chance of being in selected sample. Probability sampling plans lead us to greater generalisability than non-probability sampling designs. Non-probability sampling plans are useful for obtaining certain type of information or data quickly and relatively inexpensively. When time available for the survey is short, non-probability sampling is often used.

Probability Sampling

Probability sampling can either be **simple random sampling** (also called *unrestricted probability sampling*) or **complex probability sampling** (also called *restricted probability sampling*).

A sample is known as **random sample**, if the sample is selected in such a manner, that: (a) every member of the population is available for inclusion, (b) every member of the population has an equal opportunity to be included in the sample and (c) every sub-sample of a given size, lower than that of the population has an equal probability of being selected.

Probability sampling requires that actual selections of units into the sample be made by a mechanical procedure. The mechanical selection of a sample is achieved by properly selecting a set of numbers from a good table of random numbers to identify a set of numbers on a list of sampling units; from the selected listing, units identification is made to a set of physical units that comprise the actual sample [*c.f.*, **Kendal and Smith**, 7; **Kendall and Stuart**, 8].

Unrestricted (or simple) random sampling is the primary sample selection process, and various unrestricted (or complex) probability-sampling designs are their modifications. More information can be gained for a given sample size using some unrestricted (or complex) probability sampling process. Simple random sample and few major common complex probability sampling approaches namely: systematic sampling, stratified random sampling, cluster sampling, two phased (or double) sampling are explained in the following sections.

Unrestricted (Or Simple) Random

In simple random sampling (SRS) design, as already mentioned every element in the population has a *known* and equal chance of being selected as an element of the sample. This sampling design has the least bias and offers the most generalisability. However, this sampling process could become cumbersome and expensive in certain situations. For these and other reasons other probability sampling designs are often chosen instead.

Systematic Sampling

Systematic sampling process involves selection of a random starting point between 1 and n on the list. After this, every kth item on the list is chosen for inclusion in the sample. Suppose we want a sample of 21 libraries out of 115 government libraries in a particular state, and let us say the random number 5 is chosen as the starting point. Then we could sample every fifth library starting from numbered 5, 10, 15, and so on, until 21 libraries are sampled, for the sampling from the listing. Systematic sampling procedure is often used jointly with stratification and cluster sampling.

In systematic sampling there is a possibility of systematic bias creeping into the sample. In the above example, for instance, let us say every 5th library happens to be a relatively small government department library compared to others in the list. That is, every 5th library may not be representative of the population surveyed. The result of the survey may thus become biased. It is, therefore, desirable that we consider carefully and make sure that the systematic sampling is appropriate for the study, before making a decision to use it.

Stratified Sampling

Stratified random sampling is a two-stage sampling process. In the first stage, one divides the population into sub-populations, called *strata*, using one or more criteria that serve as a basis for assigning population elements to mutually exclusive categories or groups that are relevant, appropriate, and meaningful to the study, followed by random selection of subjects from each stratum

Suppose we are interested in studying Job Satisfaction level of employees in a library. We may assign each staff member to one of three mutually exclusive categories: (i) professional staff (ii) paraprofessional staff, and (iii) Non-professional staff. It may be interesting to find out whether there are significant differences in the job satisfaction levels of employees belonging to these three different categories, and/or whether there is significant difference in the kind of environment or opportunities the staff members in each category seek. This kind of stratification would give the library management a better idea of the kind of changes, if any, need to be made to increase job satisfaction level of staff, in each category.

This sampling design is more efficient than the simple random sampling, because from a stratified random sampling for the same sample size, we get more representations from each important section of population and obtain more valuable and differentiated information about each group or stratum.

Cluster Sampling

Cluster sampling involves selection of groups of heterogeneous elements of a population, as selection units. Library committees of college libraries or university libraries; University library members (teachers, research scholars, postgraduate students) from various constituent colleges or departments, provide good examples of clusters. The library committees, or library members belonging to various constituent colleges or departments, usually consist of faculty members and students drawn from various disciplines, having different requirements, attitudes and orientations. For this reason there is likely to be more heterogeneity among the members within each group, and more homogeneity among the various committees or library member groups.

The cluster sampling design can be of two types: (1) single-stage cluster sampling design and (2) multistage sampling design. *Single-stage cluster sampling* involves the division of population into convenient clusters, randomly choosing the required numbers of clusters as sample units or subjects, and investigating all the elements in each randomly chosen clusters. Cluster sampling can also be done in several stages, called *multistage cluster sampling*. Multistage sampling consists of sub-sampling of clusters extended to two more than two stages. It consists of a hierarchy of different types of sample units. Each first-stage unit being divided into second stage units and so on. A frame is required at each stage for the units that have been selected at that stage.

In other words, multistage cluster sampling involves a probability sampling of the primary sampling units; from each of these primary units, a probability sample of the secondary sampling unit is then drawn; in turn, a third level of probability sampling is done from each of these secondary units, and so on, until we reach the final stage of a breakdown for the sample units, when we will sample every member in those units.

Two-Phase (or Double) Sampling

A sampling design is called two-phased sampling when we use a sample in a study to collect some preliminary information of interest, and later a sub-sample of this primary sample is used to examine the matter in more detail. For example, through a structured interview of library staff we may identify a sub-group of the respondents having more insight in the library problems. Then, these respondents may be interviewed again with additional questions to seek more information. In this case, this study would be considered having been conducted using a two-phased sampling procedure.

Non-probability Sampling

One can make inferences about populations from arbitrary or informal samples to form the basis of research in many fields. An arbitrary, haphazard, accidental, or fortuitous sample forms the bases of non-probability sampling designs. Thus, in a non-probability sampling design the elements of the population under study do not have any probability attached to their being selected as sample subjects. We will discuss next the non-probability sampling designs, which fit into the broad categories of convenience and purposive sampling.

Convenience Sampling

Convenience (also called incidental or accidental sampling) is a term used to describe sampling of a non-random nature in which the researcher collects data from one or more units of population simply because they are conveniently available to provide or to obtain the desired information or data. For example, it is convenient to obtain the views of library members by interviewing them as they walk in or out of a library, during different hours of the day, with the purpose of deciding to bring change in opening and closing times of a library.

Purposive Sampling

The rationale underlying purposive sampling is that instead of obtaining information from those who are most conveniently available, to obtain information from specific targets and pick "typical" units or groups - those judged to be near average of the characteristic(s) under consideration, or "representative" units, or portions, which reflect variation in the characteristics and hence tend to be spread through the frame, or specific type of persons or groups who will be able to provide the desired information, either they are the only one who can provide desired information or because they conform to some criteria set by the researcher. Judgement Sampling and Quota Sampling are two major types of purposive sampling designs.

Judgement Sampling

Judgement sampling involves the choice of subjects who are in best position to provide information needed - persons who can provide first hand information, or have practical experience and expected to have expert knowledge. The judgement sampling design is generally used when limited number of respondents or units can provide data or information sought.

Quota Sampling

Quota sampling is a form of purposive sampling in which a predetermine portion or numbers of elements from each of the distinguishable subset of some population are sampled. This form of sampling is widely used in opinion surveys. For instance, we are interested in discovering the jobs, which the professional library staff in a library values. Alternatively, find facts about the work attitude of professional library staff. It may be premised that variable such as age and sex are valuable correlates of values. Rather getting a random sample of professional staff, if we decide to interview at least fifty persons in each of four categories '**Young Male**'; '**Young Female**' (both up to the age of 35 years); '**Old Male**'; '**Old Female** ' (both beyond the age of 35 years) among the professional library staff. Then we must interview the fifty subjects in each group, until data have been obtained from each group according to established quota.

References and Reading List

1. Elmore, P. E.; Beggs, D. L. Salient concepts and commitment to extreme judgement in response pattern of teachers. *Education.* v. 95 (4); 175; p. 325-34.
2. Cronbach, Lee J. Essentials of psychological testing. Ed 3. 1970. Harper & Row. p. 121-22.
3. –; et al. Theory of generalisabilty: A liberalisation of reliability theory. *British Journal of Statistical Theory.* v. 16; 1963; p. 137-63.
4. Clesser, Goldin C.; at al. Generalizability of scores influenced by multiple score variance. *Phyhometrika.* v. 30; 1963; p. 395-418.
5. Kashyap, M. M. The basic features of the scientific method. *Library Herald.* v. 23; 1984/85; p. 61-73.

6. –. Measurement theory and its application in library systems study and research. *Journal of Library and Information Science*. v. 9; 1984; p. 16-35.

7. –. Methods of testing reliability and validity of a measuring device developed for behavioural research in libraries. *ILA Bulletin*. v. 22; 1986; p. 1-18.

8. Kendall, M. G.; Smith, Babigton. *Tables of Random Sampling Numbers*. Cambridge University Press, Cambridge, 1954.

9. –; Stuart, A. *The Advance Theory of Statistics*. Griffin and Co, London, v. 2; 1958.

10. Kish, Leslie. *Survey Sampling*. (Wiley Classics Library Edition, 1995). John Wiley, New York, 1965.

11. Oppenheim, A. N. *Questionnaire Design and Attitude Measurement*. Basic Book, New York, 1966.

12. Orr, R. H. Measuring goodness of library service: a general framework for considering qualitative measures. *Journal of documentation*. v. 29, 3; 1973; p. 235-67.

13. Sekaran, Uma. Research Methods for Managers: A Skill-building Approach. John Wiley, New York, 1984.

14. Stevens, S. S. Mathematics, measurement and psychophysics. **In** Stevens, S. S., Ed. *Handbook of Experimental Psychology*. John Wiley, New York, 1958, p. 28.

H
Entity-Relationship Diagrams

1 INTRODUCTION

Entity-Relationship Diagrams (E-RDs) are data modelling tools used for graphically depicting an information system's data. All information systems capture and store data about various entities (regardless of whether computers are used or not). Any entity represents a real world object or concept, such as monograph, serial, library member or library job. E-RDs show the Entity-types - *persons*, *objects*, *events*, *places*, *organisations* and other systems with which the system interacts or are involved in running the enterprise and the relationships among these Entity-types.

Entities are described by their properties, called *attributes* and the *relationships* among them. E-R diagrams show *data at rest*; that is, data being stored or to be stored in the proposed system, independently of how that data will eventually be processed or used. E-RDs complement data flow diagrams or flow charts, which show data in motion.

Systems analysts use this tool to develop implementation-independent data models, which allow them to communicate with end-users in non-technical language. The implementation-independent models are usually called ***conceptual***, ***logical*** or ***essential*** **models**.

A data model contains metadata that is, data about data. There are a number of data models proposed and are essential for design and development of a database of an information system. They provide realistic support for logical (implementation-independent) organisation and physically (implementation-dependent) structuring of the data useful to an enterprise. The data modelling process involves identifying and defining unambiguously the components of an enterprise, which are associated entity-types. Besides, the entities associated with an enterprise we also identify and define their *attributes* and *relationships* among them. These help us in developing frameworks or data model for logical and physical structuring of enterprise data in a database.

A **database** is a collection of related data. By **data**, we mean known facts about something that can be recorded and that have implicit meaning. For example, the data about the name(s) of an author or authors, title, publisher's name, cost, etc., of a book selected for acquisition, and recorded on a book selection slip, are data about data of a selected book. Similarly, these facts stored on a computer storage device as an electronic record, are data about a book selected for acquisition.

A **data model** is a statement of data requirements for the database and its applications. One can construct, data models, from the general to the specific using top-town approach or from specific to the general type, using bottom-up approach. Alternatively, both approaches can be used.

In **top-down modelling** , we identify the entities associated with the system and important to the users. The essential attributes or data elements of the entities are decided, and the relationships among the entities are specified. The results are shown as E-R diagrams. The **bottom-up data modelling** technique proceeds from the specific to the general, or the bottom, up. With this technique we obtain specific examples from the library staff and the library clientele about their needs. We start with collection of forms, manuals and reports currently used in the library and analyse these documents to list the data elements contained in them. The data elements are then organised in groups, each group being associated with an entity-type. Relationships among them entity types are also identified and documented in E-R diagrams.

In any data model it is important to distinguish between the *description of the database* and the *database* itself. The description of a database is called **database schema**, model, (or ***metadata***). The database schema is specified during database design and is not expected to change frequently. Most data models have certain conventions for diagrammatically displaying the schema.

We can categorise data models based on the types of concepts they provide to describe the database structure. *Conceptual* or high-level data models provide concepts that are close to the way end-users perceive data. Whereas, low-level or *physical data models* provide concepts that describe the details of how data is stored in the computer storage device. Concepts provided by low-level data models are generally meant for computer specialists, not for typical end-users. Between these two extremes is a class of implementation (or representational) data models, which provide concepts that may be understood by end-users but that is not far removed from the way data are organised within computer storage devices. Implementation data models are the ones used most frequently in current commercial database management systems (DBMSs), and they include the three most widely used data models: **Relational, Network**, and **Hierarchical**. [**Kashyap,** 1994. Chapters F and G]

Using a high-level conceptual data modelling approach, we can create a conceptual schema or model for a database. The conceptual schema (also called the conceptual or logical view of a database) is a concise description of the data requirement of users. It describes the various Entity-types, their Attributes and the Relationship between them.

The ***conceptual schema*** may be regarded as an overall logical database description or a global model representation of a database as conceived by the library database administrator or systems analyst and is entirely independent of physical storage organisation of a database. A conceptual schema is defined using E-R model concepts and displayed by graphical notation known as E-R diagrams. A database conceptual schema is specified during database design of an information system and is not expected to change frequently.

After this brief introduction we will introduce the E-R model concepts, that is, the basic constructs for depicting data on an E-R chart. We will also describe the diagramming conventions and the symbolic notations used to draw E-R diagrams.

2 BASIC CONSTRUCTS OF ENTITY RELATIONSHIP DIAGRAMS

2.1 Introduction

The E-R diagrams as a data-modelling tool was introduced by **Peter Chen** [2, 3] in 1976. Since then, many modifications to the E-R model have been suggested. This popular graphical technique originated in the area of database design and evolved into a systems analysis technique. Systems analysts use this technique to identify, analyse, and model or graphically represent the data to be stored in the designed or proposed information system. The drawn E-R chart or a data model depicts entities, attributes and their relationships, about which we need to store data in the target information system. Once an E-R diagram is developed, the systems analyst can use it to develop detailed data structure diagrams.

An E-R diagram illustrates the data to be stored in an information system, which constitutes a database of the system. The data to be stored in a database pertains to an entity or a set of entities, objects, phenomena, transactions, processes or events in the "**real world**", sometimes called the **mini-world** or the **Universe of Discourse (UoD)**. The data associated with any entity are essentially the Values of its Attributes or Attribute set and its Relationships with other entities. (Relationships are also attributes that an entity acquires that is, relationships with other entity types). This diagramming technique is based on the following fundamental concepts, namely:

* ***Entities***, which represent the object set of interest. The things about which one wants to store data or facts.
* ***Attributes***, which represent the intrinsic properties of these objects and relationships between them.
* ***Relationships***, which represent the association among entities. Relationships add special ***attributes*** or ***properties*** to the

associated entities, which represent connections between entities and meaningful dependencies between them.

2.2 Entity

An **entity** represents a real world object or concept, such as, a person, place, thing, transaction, an event or a concept (i.e. any being or existence - real or abstract) about which facts or descriptive information is to be recorded or stored; and, which is capable of independent existence and can be distinctly identified. For example, the book entitled **Database Systems: Design and Development,** belonging to a library and assigned ***accession number 0212546*** is an entity, since it is uniquely identified as a particular book of a given library. Similarly **Dr. S R Ranganathan** ***born in 1892*** is an entity, being a particular person in the universe.

2.3 Entity-Type

Essentially, when we use such terms as - Book, Library Member, Library, Author, Subject, Invoice, etc., to represent an entity, it means that there exist **Entity-types** - Book, Library Member, Library, etc., and there may be many instances or ***entity-occurrences*** of these types of entities.

The concept of Entity-type is very relevant for drawing E-R diagrams or developing logical data models, and to specify distinct real-world items in an application or all things about which data may be stored in an information system, such as:

* People, (e.g. library members, staff, suppliers or vendors)
* Things, (e.g. documents, furniture, equipment)
* Transactions, (e.g. book orders, invoices)
* Events, (e.g. appointments, retirements, conferences)
* Locations, (e.g. India, Delhi)

An Entity-type is a named class of entities that has the same set of Attribute-types and Relationship-types (also called Associations-types) with other Entity-types. A name and its Attributes as shown in the following table (Figure Chapter H-1) describe each Entity-type in a database:

ENTITY TYPE	KEY ATTRIBUTE	COMPOSITE ATTRIBUTES	SIMPLE ATTRIBUTE
Library Member	Membership # (No)	Name, Address	Phone No

Figure H-1: Entity-type and its Attributes

An entity instance is one specific case of Entity-type. For example, the book entitled DATABASE SYSTEMS: DESIGN AND DEVELOPMENT is an instance of the Entity-type MONOGRAPH. There can be many instances of an Entity-type. A collection of instances or a group of individual entities of a particular Entity-type is called an **entity set**, which is also referred to as the ***extension of the Entity-type***. For example, a collection of monographs in a library is an *entity set* and constitutes extension of the Entity-type monograph.

A database of an information system includes a collection of data records about various Entity-types, and each database may hold any numbers of records of entities of the same type or various types. An entity record typically contains data values related to one instance or specific occurrence of some real world Entity-type. A particular monograph or its record would be an instance or entity-occurrence of the Entity-type monograph. An entity-occurrence or its record occurrence in a database is represented by the set of values of certain Attributes of that entity.

While creating a database of a particular library we can define the following Entity-types, associated with the library system:

* **LIBRARY MEMBER:** The set of all the enrolled members of the library.
* **EMPLOYEE:** The set of all the persons who work in or employed by, a library.
* **DOCUMENT:** The sets of all the pieces of bibliographic items needed to be obtained, ordered, and are available in the library. (This Entity-type can be divided into two subtypes for example, MONOGRAPH and SERIAL.

* **BIBLIOGRAPHIC ITEM ON LOAN:** The set of all bibliographic items borrowed by a user or other libraries on interlibrary loan. Alternatively we can say, the set of all the bibliographic items on loan to the library members or other libraries.
* **ORDER:** The sets of all orders placed with suppliers.

Entity-type need not be disjoint (i.e., may include subsets). For example, we may say that a library collection is constituted of the Entity-type - BIBLIOGRAPHIC DOCUMENT, instead of MONOGRAPH and SERIAL, entity-types. However, sometimes it is necessary to divide Entity-types into Entity-subtypes. For example, we find both the entities subtypes MONOGRAPH and SERIAL have some distinct attributes and associations with other Entity-types of a library system. So, in a given situation, the Entity-type BIBLIOGRAPHIC DOCUMENT may have to be divided into Entity-subtypes MONOGRAPH and SERIAL. In case, we store essentially the same information about the Entity-types MONOGRAPH and SERIAL, we need not consider them Entity-subtypes and regard these two categories or subsets merely ***Attribute Values*** of the Entity-type BIBLIOGRAPHIC DOCUMENT or DOCUMENT.

The description of an Entity-type in an E-RD normally includes the following:

a The set of **attribute-*types*** that describe various properties of each Entity-type;

b A ***key attribute*** for each Entity-type, whose values can be used to identify each entity uniquely; and

c Specification of unique ***Identifiers*** - names, symbols, or tags of the chosen attributes and their characteristics.

2.4 Weak Entity-Types

Some Entity-types may not have ***Key Attributes*** of their own; such Entity-types are called ***weak entity-types***. Entities belonging to this category are identified by relating to specific entities belonging to other Entity-types, in combination with the values of their attributes. We call the other Entity-types the identifying owners. We call the relationship type that relates a weak entity to its owner the ***identifying relationship of the weak Entity-type***. Consider the relationship between the Entity-types FAMILY MEMBER and EMPLOYEE. Two or more dependents of two or more distinct employees may have same NAME (or may have same values for their attribute-types — Dependents Name, Relationship, and Date-of-birth). They can be identified or recognised as some distinct persons, only after identifying the employee entity with which each is related and what is the relationship between them. Here each employee entity is said to own the dependent entities related to it. However, not every existence dependency results in a weak entity. For example, a MEMBERSHIP-IDENTITY CARD entity cannot exit unless it is related to a MEMBER (PERSON) entity. However, each ID Card has its own unique key or identifier, namely: ID CA whose values are represented by the data type *integer or character string*. (The term 'type-of–attribute' mean the 'type' of data (also referred to as *data type*) the field will hold for a given attribute type). RD-NO and, hence, is not a weak entity.

2.5 Attribute

Each entity has particular properties, called **Attributes.** An ***attribute*** whose values are represented by the data type *integer or character string*. (The term 'type-of–attribute' mean the 'type' of data (also referred to as *data type*) the field will hold for a given attribute type). or ***attribute-type*** is the quantity-like or quality-like property of an Entity or Entity-type. The specific value of an Attribute provides us a particular fact, data, or piece of information about that entity or Entity-type.

In a database an Entity-type or an entity is meaningfully described in terms of its properties called as its Attributes (Attribute-types) and by its Relationships (Relationship-types) with other entities (Entity-types). For example, an entity (or Entity-type) MONOGRAPH may be described by the Attributes: Title, Written-by, Price, Physical format, Subject, Language in which written and so on. The entity LIBRARY MEMBER may be assigned attributes.

namely: Membership Number, Name, Residence Address, Residence Phone and so on.

A particular entity has a **value** for each of its Attributes. The values of the Attributes become major part of the data stored in the database. A database usually contains data of groups of entities that are similar. The most elemental piece of data is called a **data element**. It is also called a ***data item*** or a ***data field*** (or simply field). To computerise the activities of a library system one must identify, define and organised the Entity-types, their Attributes (or data elements) and Relationships among them.

An ***attribute*** is thus a characteristic, a piece of information or data about an entity, or about its relationship(s) with another entity or entities. *Title*, for instance, is an Attribute of an entity (Entity-type) MONOGRAPH, and so is *written-by, published-by, cost,* etc. (Note: AUTHOR and PUBLISHER are not the Attributes of a MONOGRAPH or a DOCUMENT, as we generally regard, but they are the entities (Entity-type) that have relationships with the entity (Entity-type) MONOGRAPH, the relationship being AUTHOR-OF and PUBLISHER-OF (which these entity-types have with) the Entity-type MONOGRAPH, respectively. Similarly an Entity-type MONOGRAPH has a relationship WRITTEN-BY with the entity (or Entity-type) AUTHOR and PUBLISHED-BY with the entity (or Entity-type) PUBLISHER. In simple terms, the relationships PUBLISHED-BY, WRITTEN-BY, constitute the Attributes of the Entity-type MONOGRAPH. Hence, it is not correct to designate these attributes by the terms AUTHOR and PUBLISHER, respectively.

2.6 Properties of Attributes

Attributes of Entity-types have certain properties of their own and when an attribute is defined the characteristics of each of its property must be specified. For example, the value of the property of an attribute (or a data element) may be represented in the form of an integer, a real number, a character string, and a Boolean value or in any other way. This property of an attribute is known as '***Type***

of Data Value an Attribute has. Thus, when we use the term '***Type-of-Attribute***'; we mean the *way data value of an attribute is represented*. These aspects need to be specified, while defining a database. We must clearly distinguish between the terms 'Type-of-Attribute' and 'Attribute -type'. When we say that the 'Name of person' is an *attribute-type*, we mean it is an attribute possessed by many entity-types of class 'Human'. Whereas when we say the 'Name of person' is a *type-of attribute*, we mean it is an attribute-type whose values are represented by the data type a *character string*. Similarly we may say that 'Age-of-Person' is a *type-of attribute,* whose values are represented by the data type *integer or character string*. (The term 'type-of–attribute' mean the 'type' of data (also referred to as *data type*) the field will hold for a given attribute type).

At times a given attribute may have more than on value. For example, a particular PERSON or PLACE may be known by two or more names, or is conferred two or more names, or his/its name has been changed two or more times. In this case the Attribute-type NAME of the Entity-type PERSON or PLACE is multi-valued. As such, logic requires that we must specify whether a particular attribute (or data element) is single-valued or multi-valued.

To summarise, we list the various kinds of attributes having different characteristics. Generally, the following kinds of attributes occur in an E-R model **primary** versus **nonprime** (or **secondary**); **simple** versus **composite**; **single-valued** versus **multi-valued**; and, **stored** versus **derived**. In the succeeding sections, we give detailed description of various kinds of attributes.

2.7 Kinds of Attributes

Primary, Nonprime, Secondary and Concatenated Attributes

As stated earlier, each entity-type we may be concerned with in a given situation, has a set of attributes associated with it. The associated or chosen attributes are the characteristics of the entity-type that describe the particular entities of that type. Although, all attributes describe an entity-type, only one or some attributes uniquely identify or distinguish one entity occurrence from all others of the same type comprising an entity set. Such an attribute or attribute group is called ***Primary Attribute***, ***Key Attribute*** or simply ***a Primary key.*** In other words, we can say that a **primary attribute** is that attribute whose value(s) is or are distinct for each entity. Besides, its value(s) can be used to identify each entity (or an entity record) uniquely. Others, which are not primary attributes, are **nonprime attributes** (also called ***descriptive attributes*** - which add meaning to the Entity-type). A ***nonprime attribute*** does not uniquely identify entity-type. It is also called supportive **attribute**, particularly that which indicates or supports relationships between Entity-types. **Nonprime attributes** have One-to-One links with other attributes. One value of a **non-secondary** attribute is associated with one value of other attributes (or data elements). All attributes (or data elements) are either ***primary attributes*** (or ***keys***) or ***nonprime attributes***.

For example, we find that the attribute-type MEMBERSHIP-NO is an attribute whose particular value specifies a particular member of a library and no other member will have the same value or membership number. As such, we can say MEMBERSHIP-NO is the primary attribute or primary key of the Entity-type LIBRARY MEMBER. The attribute-types of the Entity-type LIBRARY MEMBER such as NAME of member, MEMBER'S ADDRESS are nonprime attributes (or data element types).

A **secondary attribute** or **key** does not uniquely identify an attribute or data element. It is a nonprime attribute with one or more links with other attributes. That is, one value of a secondary key is associated with one or more values of another attribute or data element.

Under certain conditions an Entity-type can only be uniquely identified with the help of combined values of more than one Attribute, when this occurs, then these Attributes are given the name **concatenated attributes** or simply ***concatenate key*** or ***entity identifier***. For example, we can uniquely identify a particular volume (a single item or document) belonging to a library by the concatenation of three attributes CLASS-NO, BOOK-NO, COLLECTION-NO of an Entity-type document. As such we can say, here, the attributes CLASS-NO+BOOK-NO+COLLECTION-NO together constitute the entity identifier.

Simple and Composite Attributes

Attributes that are not divisible are called **simple** or **atomic attributes. A composite attribute** (or **composite data element**) is an attribute (or data element) formed from or consists of simple attributes (or simple data elements). The smaller subparts of a composite attribute are more basic elements each having independent meaning of its own. For example, one can further subdivide the attribute **ADDRESS** of an entity into the subparts namely: **Building; Street Address; Locality; Village, Town or City; Taluk/Tehsil, District, Region or State; Country; Postal Code**. The value of a **composite attribute** is the concatenation of the values of its constituent **simple or atomic attributes**. The term **composite attribute** corresponds to a **grouped data element, a grouped-field** or a **combined field** in a record.

We can treat an attribute either as composite attribute or as simple attribute, in given situations. For example, we can treat the attribute name-of-person as simple attribute as a whole. We can also, consider it as composite attribute by breaking it into two parts - Entry element and Other part of the name, or into three parts or components - Forename (i.e., first name), Middle name, and Surname (i.e. last name). In other words, an attribute consisting of simple or atomic attributes; or one that is defined as consisting of atomic attributes is called Composite Attribute. Whereas, a Simple Attribute is one that consists of a single atomic attribute (or data element) or more than one atomic attributes or atomic data elements, but these are treated as a whole. We need to specify whether a given attribute is a Simple Attribute (or is to be treated as Simple Attribute), or a Composite Attribute (or is to be treated as Composite Attribute). Composite attribute is sometimes called Aggregated Attribute.

Derived and Stored Attributes

Sometimes values of two (or more) attributes are related and the value of one is derived by processing or calculated from the value(s) of other attribute(s). For example, by adding the COST of individual items listed on the bill we can derive TOTAL-AMOUNT. The AGE and DATE-OF-BIRTH attributes of a person are related and the AGE of a person can be determined by subtracting from the value of that person's DATE-OF-BIRTH the value of PRESENT-DATE. In these cases the Attributes - TOTAL-AMOUNT and AGE are ***derived attributes*** and are derivable from COST Attribute, and BIRTH DATE and PRESENT (or CURRENT) DATE attributes respectively, called ***stored attributes***. In case of *derived attributes* we may or may not store them in a database. They may be processed whenever data is retrieved based on physical or implementation level decision. The logical representation of data includes such attributes without saying whether or not the data are stored.

Single-valued and Multi-valued Attribute

Multi-valued Attribute may be defined as an ***attribute*** having one or more values. It is also called *multi-occurring attribute*. For example, a book or a document may deal with more than one SUBJECT or may be *written-by* more than one AUTHOR. Therefore, we may say that the attributes SUBJECT and WRITTEN BY of the Entity-type document are multi-occurring or multi-valued attributes. Some attributes have only a single value; such attributes are called *single-valued* (also called *single occurring*). For example, size is a single-valued attribute of a book; similarly age of a person is a single-valued attribute. A multi-valued attribute may have lower and upper bounds on the number of values for an individual Entity-type. For example, for the multi-occurring attribute for a book — Heading, the bound limit fixed for description of its values, in the classified catalogue code (CCC) of Ranganathan is between one and two. Under CCC rules, the *name of a single author* or *names of two and only two joint authors* can be used as Heading. **In addition**, if there are three or more joint authors, the name of the first mentioned author alone is to be used as Heading. However, in AACR-II cataloguing code, for representing the Heading attribute the *lower bond limit fixed* is **null** and *upper limit* is **one** value. According to AACR-II rule, if one author writes a monograph his name is included in the Heading field and if two or more authors write a book then no name is to be represented or included in the Heading field.

Multi-valued attributes and single-valued attributes are also called ***repeating group*** and ***non-repeating group***, respectively. Although repeating groups are important elements of conceptual design, most DBMS's cannot directly deal with them. By definition, a record that contains a repeating group or fields must be variable in length. In such cases, i.e., if an Entity-type table contains a repeating group, then it is split into two new Entity-type tables. Alternatively, a number of independent fields are provided, which are equal to the maximum number of distinct values a multi-occurring attribute can possess. For example, the multi-valued attributes AUTHORSHIP and SUBJECT will be represented, as if they are two or more distinct sets of attributes, in the form AUTHOR 1; AUTHOR 2; AUTHOR 3, so on and DESCRIPTOR 1, DESCRIPTOR 2, DESCRIPTOR-3 so on, respectively.

Essential and Optional Attributes

In certain situations it is not essential, meaningful or required to show the value of an attribute of an entity. We must, therefore, indicate whether a particular attribute-type is ***essential*** (also referred to as ***required*** or ***mandatory***) or ***optional***; that is, whether or not value must be supplied for the attribute or data element in a record. For example, consider the following Entity-type:

USER (***Entity-type***): [MEMBERSHIP # (***Key Attribute***), Name, Address, Phone-no (***Secondary Attributes***)].

The value of the attribute MEMBERSHIP # is always a unique value for each member so that each member record in a database can be correctly identified and described. The same is probably true for NAME. Therefore MEMBERSHIP # and NAME are ***essential attributes***, whereas the remaining secondary attributes may be treated as ***nonessential*** or ***optional*** (e.g., the attribute PHONE-NO can be considered as optional).

Value Set (Domain) of Attribute

In building a database, we examine real-world entities, their attributes and relationships, and represent their values as a string of symbols (symbols may be numerical, alphanumerical or alphabetical) in the database. A string of symbols to represent an attribute or data element of a particular entity is called value or content of the attribute, data element or data field. For instant, 'Rs. 350.00' is a value of the attribute Cost.

Further, while creating a database we need to describe each attribute or data element of the entity type under consideration. For this purpose, it is necessary to consider and answer the following questions:

1. What kind of value each attribute can take, or what its valid values are?
2. How the values of an attribute should be recorded or rendered in the database record?

The replies to these questions facilitate the systematic construction of database records and carry out the operation of a database, effectively and efficiently.

The set of all possible, valid or legal values for an attribute or data element is called the domain or value set of the attribute or the data element. As an example, the domains of the attribute COLOUR could be {black, brown, white, yellow, red, purple, etc.}; the domain of the attribute NAME could be the names of all members or employees of a library system. The domain of the Attribute EMPLOYEE-NAME would be the names of all employees of a particular organisation. If in a given context two or more attributes represent sets of facts (e.g. if the attributes EMPLOYEE-NAME and NAME both represent names of same group of people), then such attributes are said to be domain compatible. However, the value sets or domains of the attributes are not displayed in E-R diagrams.

Note: *The concepts or terms — Entity, Entity-type, Entity-set, Attribute and Value are used in connection with the design of logical data models or a conceptual schema of a database system. Whereas, the concepts or terms - Record, Record Type, Record Set, Data Element, Data Item, Data field and Field Value (or content of a field) are used in the realm of physical data modelling. Physical models show how may system is physically implemented. Thus a physical model of a data may describe the format of data, the media on which data is recorded, or how data is organised (for example as an indexed file or database record). Logical models represent an essential requirement of the system, those requirements that must be fulfilled no matter how one may set up the system physically. As such, logical models are called implementation-independent or essential models, because they model essential requirements of the system.*

2.8 Relationship

A relationship is an association between two and more Entity-types. Relationships connect entities and represent meaningful dependencies between them. In other words, a **Relationship** *represents associations or connections among the entities*. Actually in the real world an entity does not stand-alone and acquires certain attributes from its relationships with other entities, or due to *actions* performed on it by other entities or agents that bring changes in its state or conditions. A particular bibliographic item in a library, say a monograph is *written-by* an author or authors, *published-by* a publisher, *sold-by* a vendor, is *bought-by* a library, is *classified-by* a staff member, and so forth. Each of these is an example of a relationship, a logical connection between two or more entities. For example, the terms *written by* and *edited by* show relationship between the entity-types MONOGRAPH (i.e., a published work of an author) and the AUTHOR. Thus, we can say that the *name of author* or *editor* of a MONOGRAPH is the attribute acquired by an entity MONOGRAPH because of its association or link with the entity AUTHOR. The relationships exist only between entities, not between attributes of entities. Thus, ***a* relationship *can be defined as a logical connection or dependency between occurrence of one Entity-type and occurrence of another Entity-type*.** A ***relation***

occurrence is an individual entity's connection with other entity or entities concerning a specific relationship.

Entity relationships are described by:

* Their ***Dependencies*** on each other and
* The ***Extent*** of the relationship

Entity **Dependencies** are of two types:

* **Existence Dependency** — that is, one entity type is unable to exit in the database unless some others do not exit or are also present. For example, the entity Order cannot exist without Item(s) ordered and Supplier, to whom the order is placed for the supply of items also exit.
* **Identification Dependency** that is:
    * An entity cannot be uniquely identified by its own attributes, and
    * Identification is possible only through the relationship it has to some other associated entity or entities. For example, in a large group two persons may have same names. Thus, one can only identify a person uniquely within a large group, either by his name and name of a parent, or by his name and institution, subgroup, or unit with which he may be associated.

Extent of Dependency includes:

* The direction of the relationship, and
* The type of association between them.

Both the extents are represented graphically in an ER-diagram by line and arrow or by a line and a crow's foot, which show mutual dependence.

2.9 Degree or Types of Relationships

All relationships or associations are described by words or symbols that indicate the number of occurrences of one entity that can exit for a single occurrence of the related entity, and vice a versa. In general, there are three ***Types of Relationships***

(Associations) or ***Degree of Relationships (Associations)*** that exist between entities:

* ONE-to-ONE (1:1) relationship.
* ONE-to-MANY (1: M) relationship.
* MANY-to-MANY (M: M or N: M) relationships.

These three degrees of relationships or associations) are also called the relationship ***cardinality***. The term **cardinality** refers to how many of one entity is associated with another. The cardinality ratio specifies the number of relationship instances that an entity can participate in. In the following section we shall describe these relationship types.

The ONE-to-ONE (1:1) Relationship

By ONE-to-ONE relationship, we mean that for one instance or occurrence of an **Entity-type A**, there can exit only one related instance or occurrence of the **Entity-type B**, and vice versa. It also implies that entity set A and entity set B are connected in such a way that the maximum branching factor of the relationship is 1 (one) in both directions. For example, the relationship MANAGED-BY or MANAGES between the Entity-types LIBRARY and CHIEF-LIBRARIAN is One-to-One relationship. That is, a LIBRARY is managed by a ***single*** CHIEF-LIBRARIAN or a ***single*** CHIEF-LIBRARIAN manages a LIBRARY. Another example of this relationship type is between a LIBRARY AND INFORMATION SCIENCE DEPARTMENT and HEAD-of-the DEPARTMENT. We can assume that there can be at the most ***one*** HEAD or DIRECTOR of a LIBRARY AND INFORMATION SCIENCE DEPARTMENT or one HEAD or DIRECTOR administers a LIBRARY AND INFORMATION SCIENCE DEPARTMENT.

A ONE-to-ONE relationship can be completely *symmetrical* or *unsymmetrical*. **Unsymmetrical association** implies, if there exists an entity A, there may or may not exist corresponding entity B, or for ONE occurrence of A there is ZERO or ONE occurrence of B. (The unsymmetrical association is represented d*iagrammatically* in Figure Chapter H-2 (b)). In contrast of this relationship is the one that may be completely **symmetrical**. That is, if an entity of type B exists, then exactly one corresponding entity of type A exits. Alternatively either we can say, what is true for A is also true for B or for one occurrence of A, there is always one and only one Occurrence of B. We illustrated these associations diagrammatically in the Figure Chapter H-2 (a).

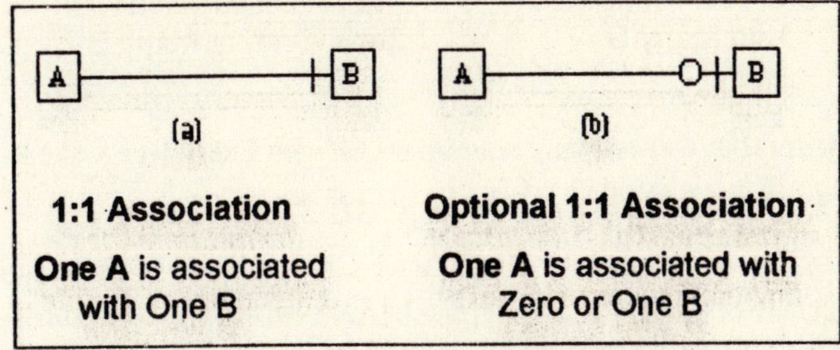

Figure H-2: ONE-to-ONE Association

The ONE-to-MANY (1: M) Relationships

By One-to-Many relationships we mean that one or more than one instances of an Entity-type B can be associated with Entity-type A. On the other hand, for each existing entity of type B, there exists exactly ONE entity of type A. For example, the relationship between the Entity-types PUBLISHER and MONOGRAPH is ONE-to-MANY (also written as 1 to M or 1: M or 1: N relationship). We assume here that a PUBLISHER may publish many MONOGRAPHS but a given MONOGRAPH is PUBLISHED-BY by one publisher only. Alternatively, we can also say that for each existing entity, say of type A, there may exist NONE or ONE or MANY related entities of type B. Moreover, for one occurrence of an entity of type B there can exit ZERO or ONE occurrences of A. For example, a borrower or library member may not borrow any book on loan. Alternatively, he may borrow ONE or More books on loan. That is, a member may have NONE, ONE or MORE books standing on loan against his name at a given point in time. Whereas a book can be borrowed by ONE library member or NONE. We diagrammatically represented then one-to-many relationship in the Figure Chapter H-3 below:

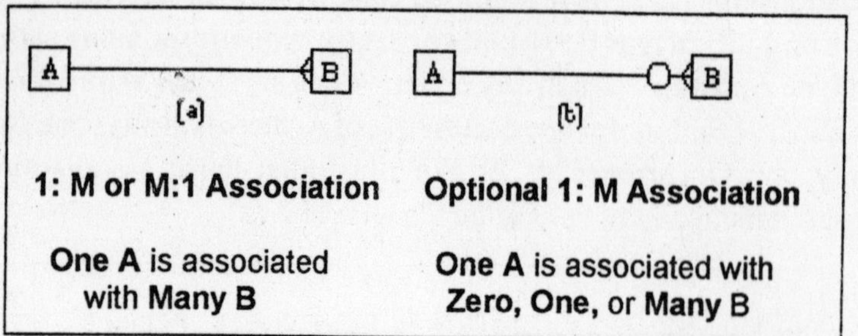

Figure H-3: One-to-Many associations between Entity-type A and B

The MANY-to-MANY (M: M or N: M) Relationships

The relationship RELEVANCE between Entity-types DOCUMENT and USER is of type MANY-to-MANY (also written as M to M, M:M or N:M relationship). A document may be USEFUL-TO or RELEVANT-TO many readers, at the same time a reader may be interested in MANY documents, or may find MANY documents RELEVANT or USEFUL for his study. In this relationship entities are connected in such a way that the maximum branching factor is M in one search direction of the relationship and M in the other. That is, for one occurrence of the entity A there can be many occurrences of the second entity B and for the occurrence of the second entity B there can exist many occurrences of the first entity. Optionally, for each ONE occurrence of A, there may exits ZERO, ONE, or MANY occurrences of B. The relationship is also symmetric, that is, for one occurrence of B, there may exist ZERO, ONE, or MORE occurrences of A. Many-to-Many relationships can be diagrammatically represented as shown in the following Figure Chapter H-4:

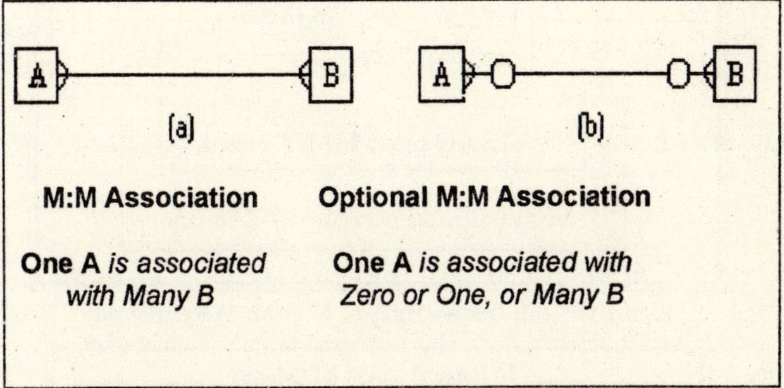

Figure H-4: Many-to-Many associations between an Entity-type A and B

2.10 Notation Used on E-R Charts

Different authors have used variety of symbolic notations to draw E-R Diagrams. ***Peter Chen's notation*** [2, 3] was the earliest notation. This was replaced by ***Bachman notation*** [1], followed by ***arrow notation*** and ***crow's-foot notation***. The following diagrams (Figure Chapter H-5 (a), Figure Chapter H-5 (b) and Figure Chapter H-5 (c)) show the equivalencies and differences among these notations:

Peter Chen's Entity Relationship (E-R) Diagrams

Entities are normally described by nouns and represented by rectangles. Relationships are normally described by verbs and represented by diamond shaped boxes.

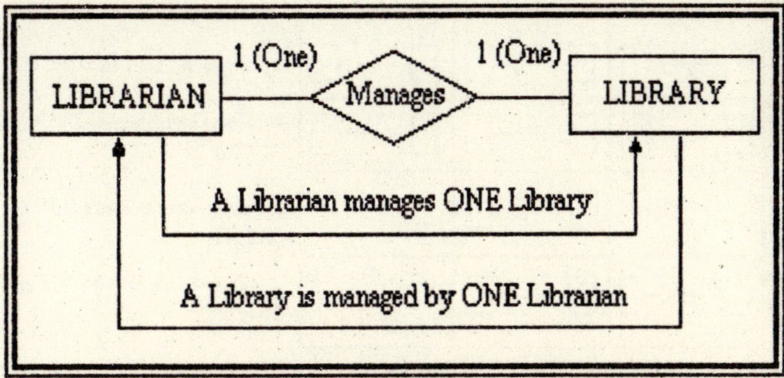

Figure H-5 (a): One-to-One (1:1) Relationship

Figure H-5 (b): One-to-Many (1:M or M: 1) Relationship

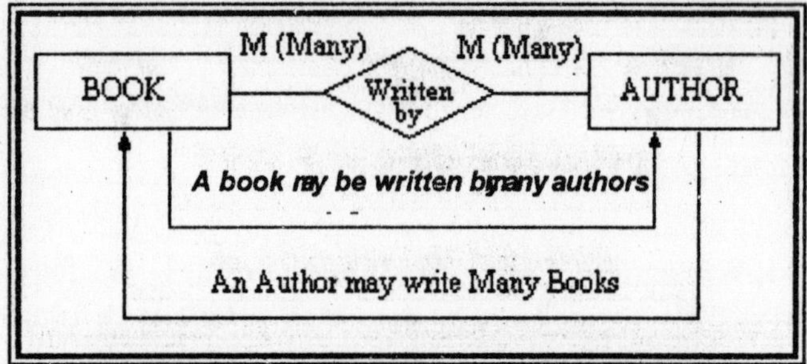

Figure H-5 (c): Many-to-Many (M: M) Relationship

The following diagram (Figure Chapter H-6) shows the equivalence in the other three notations, used for drawing entity diagrams, namely: ***Crow's foot notation, Arrow notation,*** and ***Bachman notation***.

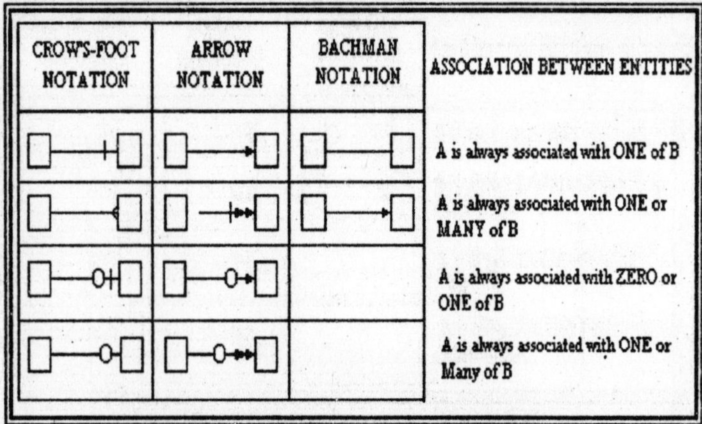

CROW'S-FOOT NOTATION	ARROW NOTATION	BACHMAN NOTATION	ASSOCIATION BETWEEN ENTITIES
			A is always associated with ONE of B
			A is always associated with ONE or MANY of B
			A is always associated with ZERO or ONE of B
			A is always associated with ONE or Many of B

Figure H–6: Tabular Representation of Differing Notation Used On an E-R Diagram

To achieve consistency in drawing E-R diagrams (often called *entity charts*) we must follow a set of standard practices and symbols. A set of standard E-R diagramming symbols and conventions are described in the following sections. [**Martin**, 4; **Martin** and **McCulre**, 5]

2.11 Standard E-R Diagramming Symbols and Conventions

Symbols Palette

The various symbols used to draw E-R charts are shown in the following diagram (Figures Chapter H-7):

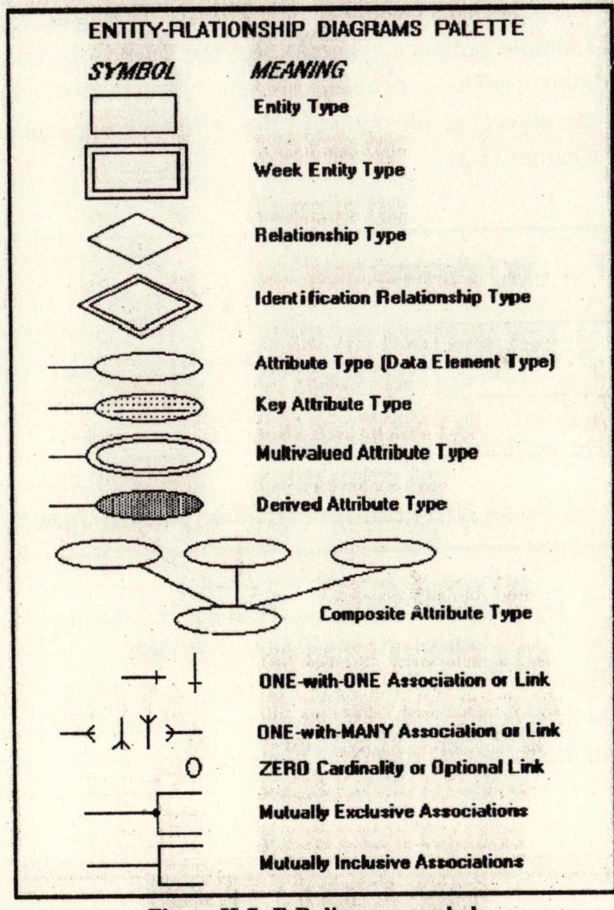

Figure H-7: E-R diagram symbols

2.12 Entity Chart Sketching Style and Conventions

The entity chart sketching style practices and conventions are described below:

a. An E-R diagram represents Entity-types and links or associations between them.

b. A rectangular box represents an Entity-type. Lines or links that represent association between Entity-types interconnect the Entity-type boxes. A link can have a maximum and minimum value of cardinality (i.e., how many values of entity B can be associated with A or *vice versa*).

c. The link between Entity-types should be thought of as forming a simple sentence. The entity at the start of the link is the subject of the sentence and the entity that the link goes to, is the object, as illustrated in the following diagram (Figure Chapter H-8):

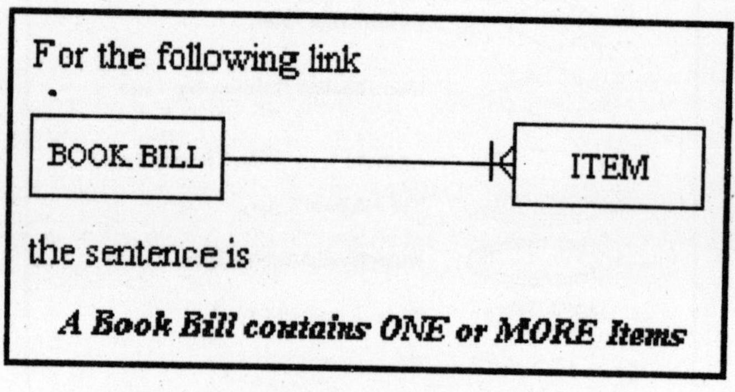

Figure H-8: An illustration of E-R diagram showing Entity-types and links between them

d. Between two entities there can be an association or links in both directions. We could draw this with two links as shown in the following diagram (Figure Chapter F-9):

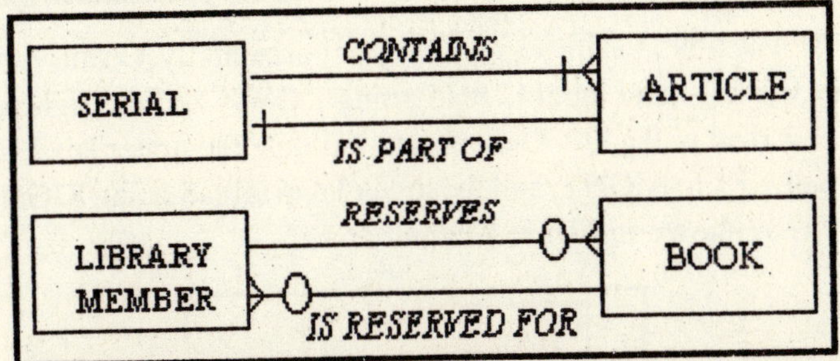

Figure H-9: An illustration of E-R diagram showing associations between two entities in both directions

Ordinarily, however, the information about both directions is combined on one bi-directional link, as shown in Figure Chapter H-10 below:

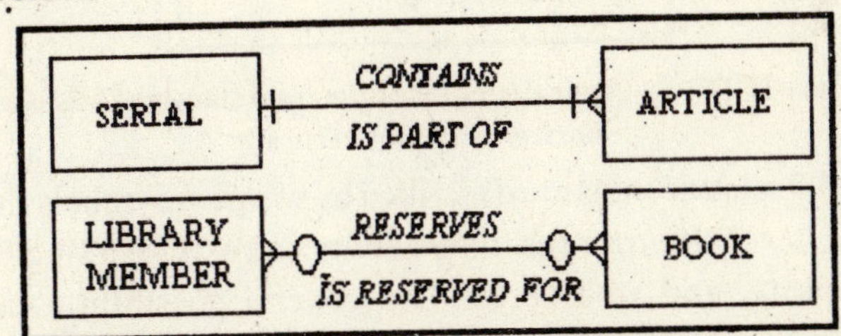

Figure H-10: An illustration of E-R diagram showing bi-directional links between two entities

Thus there are two sentences associated with a bi-directional link, as shown in Figure Chapter H-11 below:

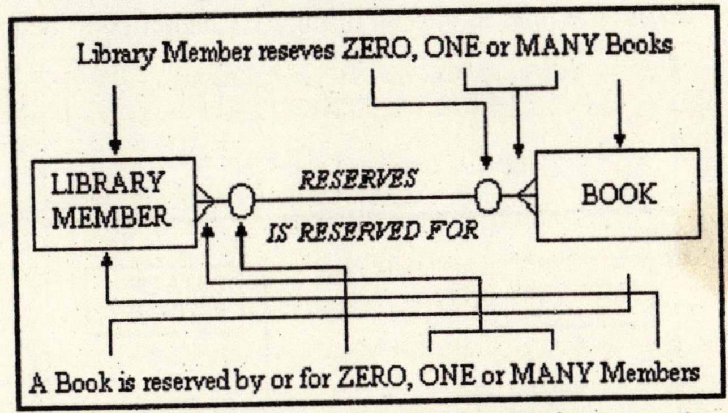

Figure H-11: An illustration of E-R diagram showing two sentences associated with *one bi-directional link*. The label on the top of a link is read from left to right, whereas, on the bottom of the link going right to left.

The links are drawn vertically or horizontally. On the vertical links the left-hand label is read going DOWN and the right-hand label is read going UP. On a horizontal link, the upper label is red going LEFT to RIGHT, and the lower label is read going RIGHT to LEFT, as shown in Figure Chapter H-12:

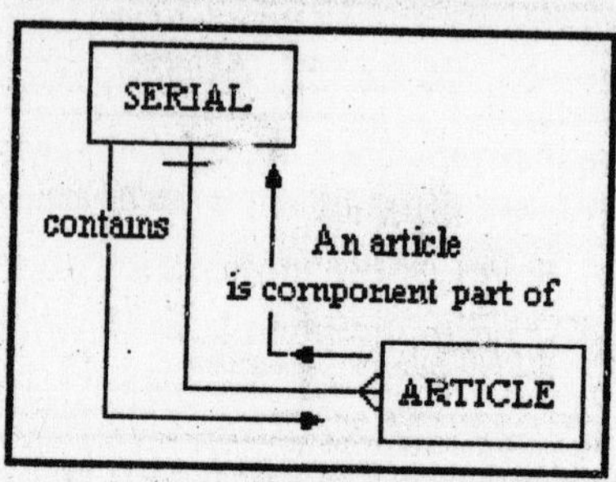

Figure H-12: An illustration of E-R diagram showing *links drawn horizontally and vertically*

All relationships are described by words or symbols showing the number of occurrences of one entity can exit for a single of the other entity, and vice versa. The general possibilities are the following:

1. **ONE-to-ONE Relationship (1:1):** For one occurrence of the first entity A there can exist only one related entity B and vice versa. A one-to-one association is drawn with a bar across the link, as shown in Figure Chapter H-13 below:

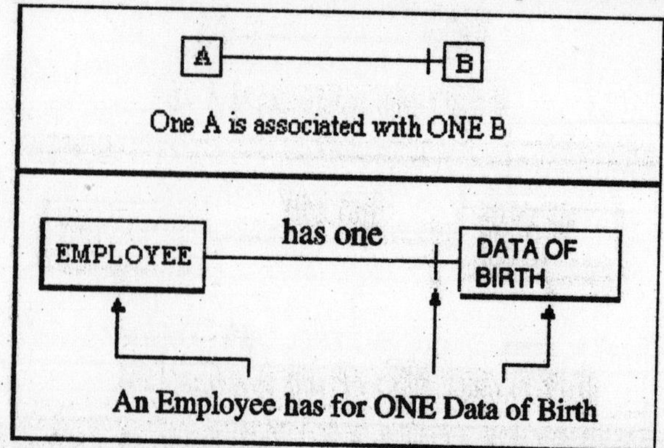

Figure H-13: An illustration of E-R diagram showing *One-to-One Relationship between entities.*

2. **ONE-to-MANY Relationships (1: M or M: 1) :** For one occurrence of the first entity A there can exit many related occurrences of the second entity B1, B2, B3 and so on. It does not matter, which is the first and which is the second. A one-to-many association is drawn with a crow's-foot, as illustrated in Figure Chapter H-14 below:

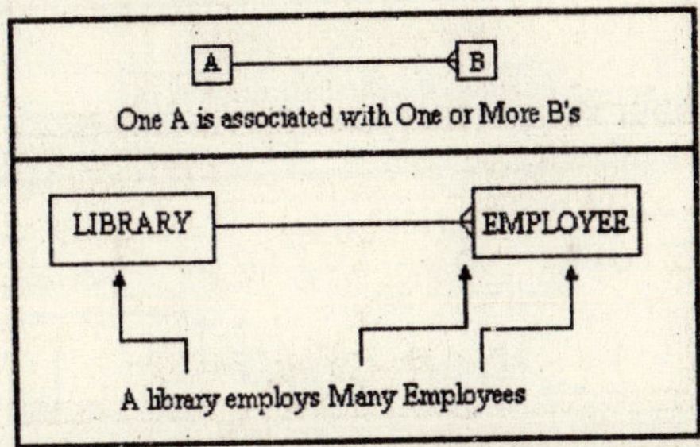

Figure H-14: An illustration of E-R diagram showing *One-to-Many Associations between entities*

3. **MANY-to-MANY Relationships (M:M or N:M) :** For one occurrence of the first entity there can exist many related occurrences of the second entity; and, for one occurrence of second entity there can exist many occurrences of the first entity. Many-to-Many relationships or associations are drawn as illustrated in Figure Chapter H-15 below:

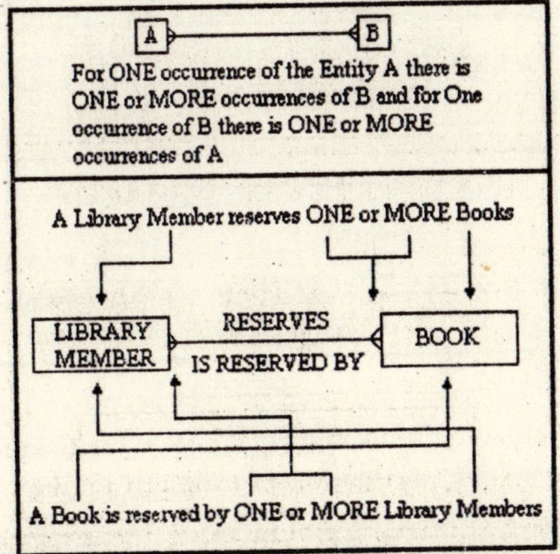

Figure H-15: An illustration of E-R diagram showing *Many-to-Many Relationship between entities*

4. **Zero Cardinality :** An Entity-type may be associated with a ZERO of another Entity-type. It means that the following conditions and the zero cardinality are represented by a small circle 'O', drawn on the link before the One or Many indicator (bar or crow's-foot), as shown in the following diagrams (Figure Chapter H-16 (a) and Figure Chapter H-16 (b)):

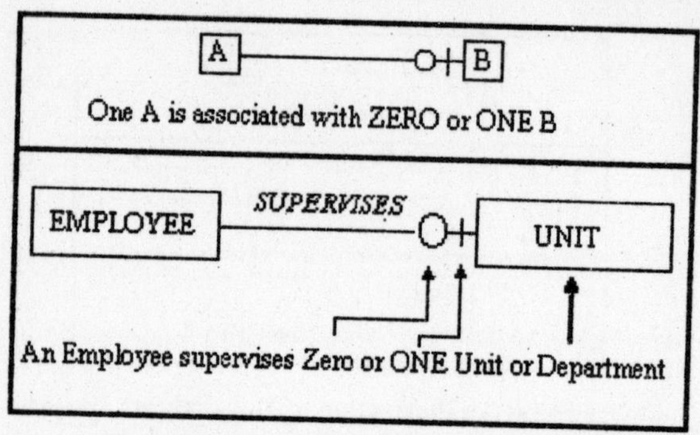

Figure H-16 (a): An illustration of One-to-One Relationship with optional link. Includes the cardinality symbol 'O'

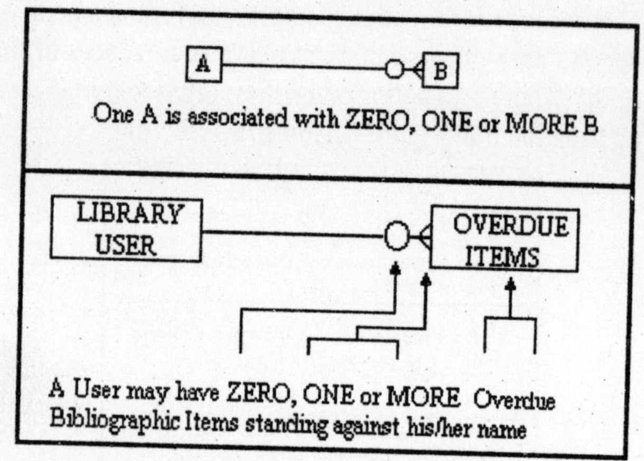

Figure H-16 (b): An illustration of One-to-Many Relationship with optional link. Includes the cardinality symbol ' O '

Mutually Exclusive Associations: Some linked associations are mutually exclusive; that is, an Entity-type A can be associated with either B or C, but not with both. We draw this association with the line branching at a dot, as shown in the diagram (Figure Chapter H-17) below:

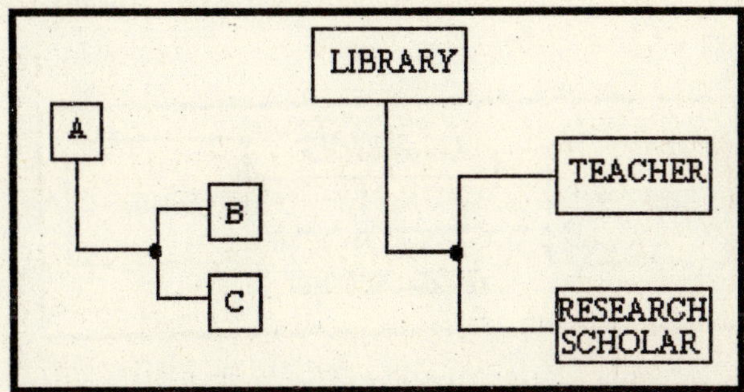

Figure H-17: An illustration of E-R diagram showing mutually exclusive associations between entities — Associations branching from a dot are mutually exclusive. Only one of them can exit for any one occurrence.

Mutually Inclusive Associations: Some linked associations are mutually inclusive; that is, if Entity-type A is associated with B, it must also be associated with C. We draw this association with the line branching (without a dot), as shown in diagram (Figure Chapter H-18) below:

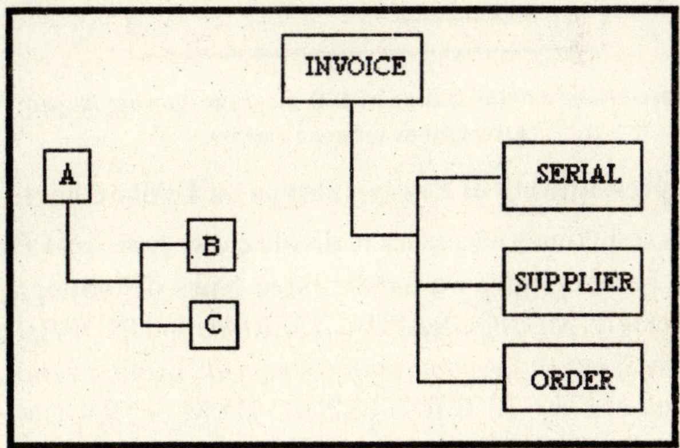

Figure H-18: An illustration of E-R diagram showing mutually inclusive associations between entities. Associations connected by a branch are mutually inclusive. All must exit together for anyone occurrence

Subset Associations : Two associations may exist between the same Entity-type and one association may be a subset of other. In this case, the associations are linked with an S around the subset association, as illustrated in the following diagram (Figure Chapter H-19):

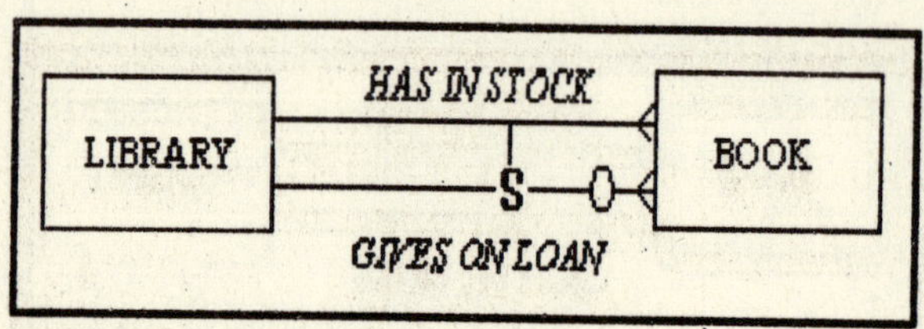

Figure H-19: An illustration of E-R diagram showing two associations between the same entities and one is a subset of the other.

Looped Associations : Some times an occurrence of an Entity-type of a given type is associated with one more occurrence of same type. We show such associations in the form of a loop, as illustrated in the following diagram (Figure Chapter H-20):

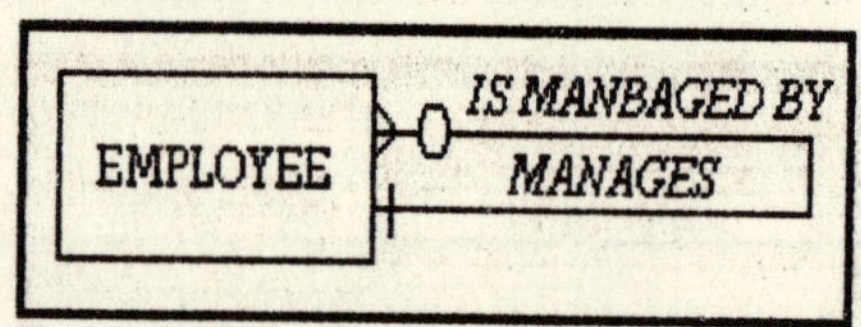

Figure H-20: An illustration of E-R diagram showing looped associations between entities.

2.13 Representation of Entity-subtype on Entity Chart

It is sometimes necessary to divide entity types into *Entity-subtypes*. For example, we handle three types of bibliographic entities, namely, MONOGRAPH, (2) SERIAL and INDIVIDUAL PART of the Entity-type *monograph* or a *serial*. In other words, the entity-types of class BIBLIOGRAPHIC ITEM or DOCUMENT can be visualised as consisting of the *entities-subtypes*, namely: (1) MONOGRAPH, (2) SERIAL, and INDIVIDUAL PART of the Entity-type *monograph* or a *serial*. Further, the entity-type **MONOGRAPH** can be of type **SIMPLE** or **COMPOSITE**.

Documents belonging to a SERIES may be of *subtypes*: MONOGRAPH, and SERIAL. Alternatively, we may subdivide entity-type SERIES into *sub-types*: COMPOSITE MONOGRAPH, SIMPLE MONOGRAPH and SERIAL each of these may be further subdivided into Entity-subtype INDIVIDUAL PART of a MONOGRAPH or a SERIAL (For example, an ***article*** published in a ***serial*** or a ***composite monograph***). The Entity-type EMPLOYEE might be subdivided into PROFESSIONAL, SEMI-PROFESSIONAL and NON-PROFESSIONAL employee types, or on the basis of some other characteristic(s).

We think of entity subtypes if we find that they have different associations to other entity types, and we do not store, essentially, the same data about these entity types in a database as we do for corresponding entity-types of higher order. However, if we store essentially same data about the Entity-subtypes as in the case of corresponding higher-level entity-types, then we may regard these categories as merely attributes of the corresponding higher level Entity-types.

We can draw Entity-subtypes as a division of an Entity-type box, as shown in the diagrams below (Figure Chapter H-21 (a) and H-21 (b)):

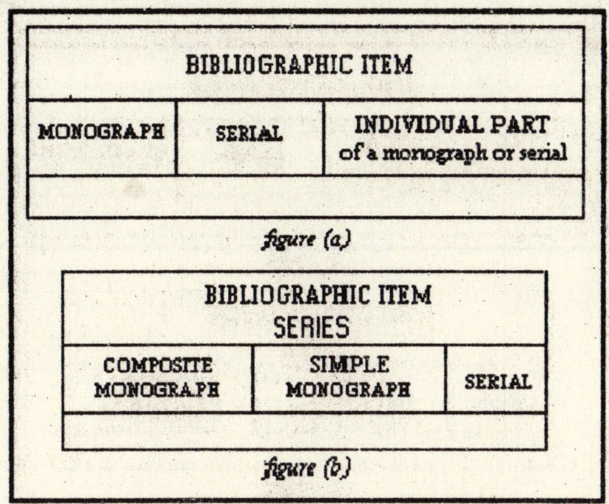

Figure H21 (a) & H21(b): The representation of an Entity-subtypes in an E-R diagram

The entity-type DOCUMENT is an entity formed by process of generalisation and is comprised of the subsets or Entity-subtypes: MONOGRAPH and SERIAL. Both of these Entity-subtypes of the Entity-type DOCUMENT have one-to-many association to the entity sub-type COMPONENT PART (i.e., individual part of a monograph or a serial). Considering that these entity-types do not possess absolutely identical attributes (that is, have some different attributes), we show the co-ordinate and subtype's hierarchy between these entity-types the following diagram (Figure Chapter H-22):

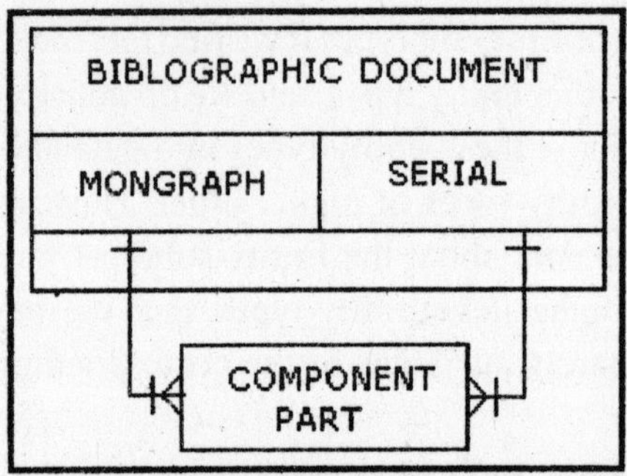

Figure H-22: The representation of hierarchies of Entity-types and their subtypes in an E-R diagram

An entity type may contain both ***mutually exclusive*** and ***not-mutually exclusive groupings***. Further, there may be more than one ***independent type of sub grouping***. We than draw multiple bands in the Entity-type box. The horizontal bands represent independent subtype groupings, as shown in the following diagram (Figure Chapter H-23):

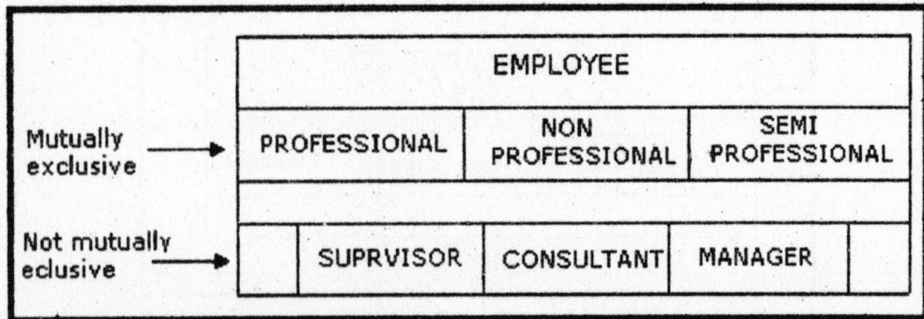

Figure H-23: The representation of mutual exclusive and mutually inclusive associations between Entity-subtypes in an E-R diagram

An *entity subtype* may itself consist of entities or may be divided into subtypes. For example, we find that the entity SERIAL is an aggregated entity formed of a set of volumes, a SERIAL VOLUME is an entity formed of a set of issues or, an ISSUE- OF-SERIAL is an aggregated entity formed of ARTITCLES. We can draw ***subtypes' hierarchies*** as shown in the following diagrams (Figure Chapter H - 24(a) to H-24(d)).

SUBTYPE GROUPINGS

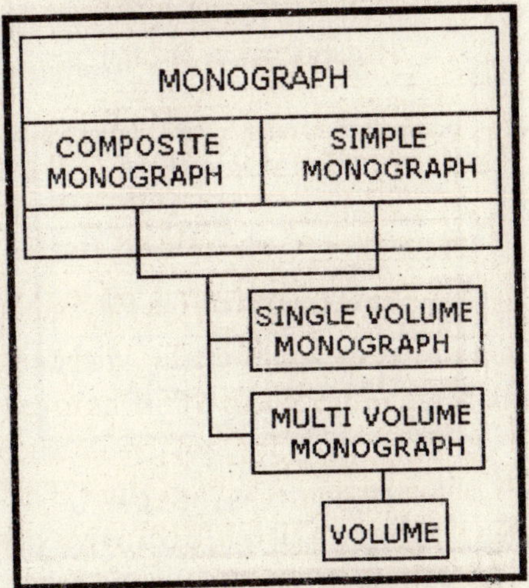

Figure Chapter H-24(a)

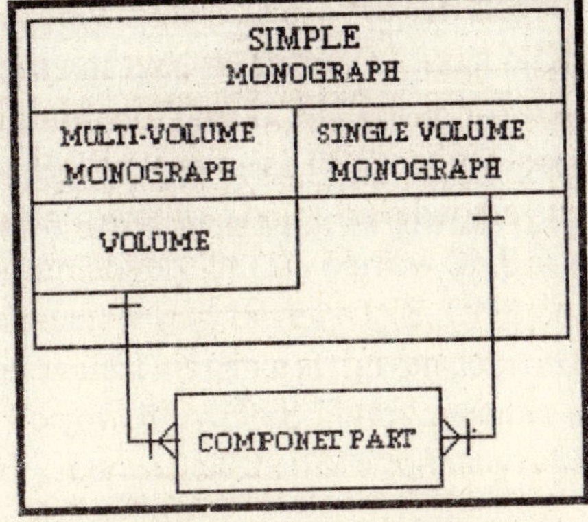

Figure Chapter H-24(b)

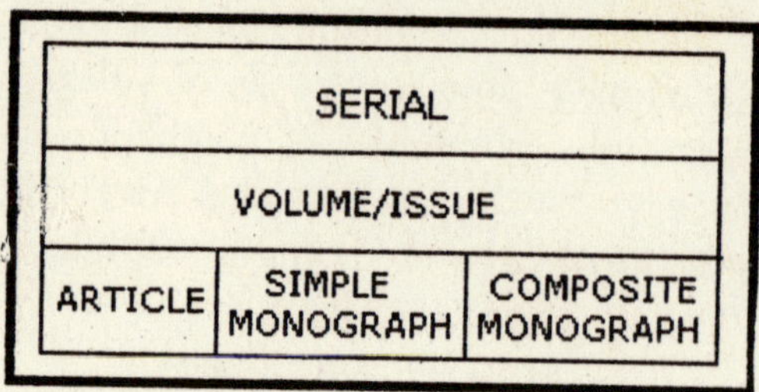

Figure Chapter H-24(c)

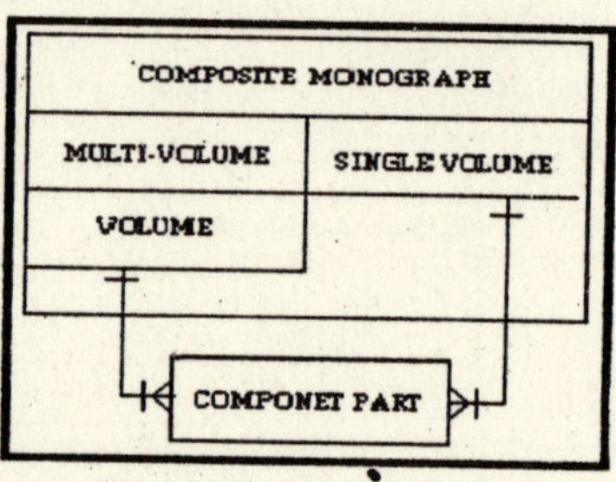

Figure Chapter H-24(d)

Figure Chapter H-24 (a to d): ***Example of Subtype Groupings***

2.14 Expanded Entity Chart

Showing the Most General Picture of a Library System

When a data model is designed, a substantial amount of information about entities, their attributes and links among them needs to be recorded. When an entity chart is expanded into a full data model, Attributes are added, and some times formula for derived Attributes is also shown, as illustrated in the following diagram (Figure Chapter H-25):

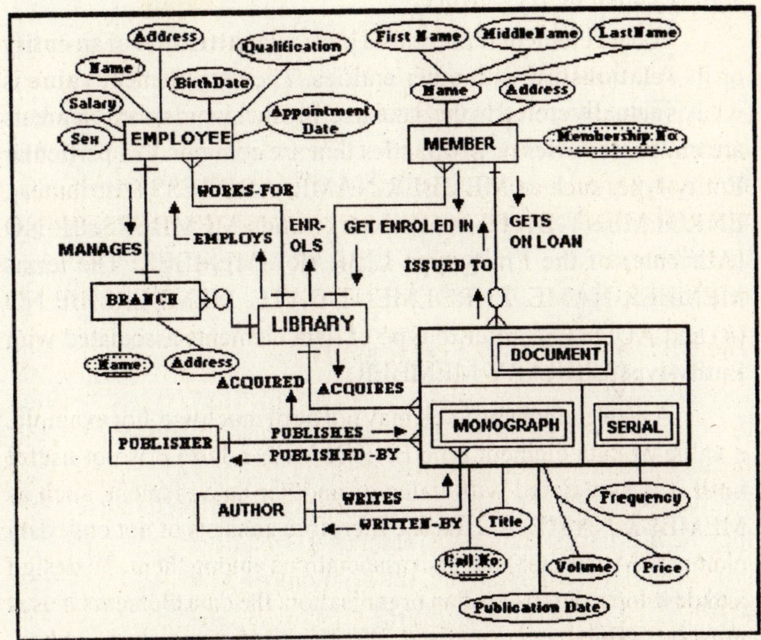

Figure H-25: An illustration of E-R diagram showing the data model or most general picture of a library system

3 BUBBLE CHARTS

3.1 Introduction

Bubble Charts provide us a way of drawing and understanding the association among data elements, data items or attributes of Entity-types. This understanding is necessary for clearly structuring database records. A database contains large amounts of data. The most elemental piece of data is called a **data element**. A data element is a smallest piece of data or unit of data into which data is divided logically containing no substructure and is explicitly or uniquely identified by a data name or tag. A data element may be stored in a field or a sub field. the container of a data element. A collection of simple/atomic data elements or sub fields, which is given a unique name and is referred to as a whole, is called **grouped data-items, grouped data elements**, or a grouped **field**. A sub field identifier identifies a sub field or simple/atomic data element (or simply called data element).

A data element represents a particular **attribute** of an **entity** or its **relationship** with other entities. The data element **value** is what is actually stored in the database. In other words, data elements are **characteristics** or **properties** that are common to a particular Entity-type, such as MEMBER-NAME, ADDRESS (Attributes), ENROLMENT-DATE (Attribute), and MEMBERSHIP-NO (Attribute) of the Entity-type LIBRARY-MEMBER. The terms MEMBER-NAME, ENROLMENT-DATE, MEMBERSHIP NO (#) and ADDRESS refer to type of data elements associated with Entity-type LIBRARY MEMBER.

A data element by itself may not be of much use. For example, a value of data element type ENROLMENT-DATE is not useful until it is associated with value of another data element, such as MEMBER-NAME. A database therefore consists of not only data elements (Attributes) but also associations among them. To design and develop a database of an organisation, the data elements it uses must be defined and organised. We also need a map showing how they are associated. This map is sometime called data model.

We create a conceptual schema of a database during the initial stage of database design and development. The conceptual schema is a concise description of the data requirement of users and includes detailed description of data elements of the real world entities, whose database we intend construct, without being concerned with storage details.

In a database, the data values of the corresponding data elements of an entity are commonly handled in-groups. As such, different software systems use different names for these groups. The group of data elements or data items is commonly called **record** - sometimes a **logical record** - to distinguish it from a **physical record**. Some software designers or application programmers use the term **segment**, some use the term **tuple** (pronounced like couple) instead of record.

A logical record typically comprises data elements or fields arranged in a predefined format or structure of an entity record, containing elementary data items or values related to the Attributes of one instance of some real world Entity-type.

We can define the term logical record as follows:

* **Definition 1:** A logical record is a collection data elements among which some logical connection exists. The data elements represent a set of properties (Attributes and Relationships) of/about the particular real word entity represented by the record and the logical connection among the data elements is maintained by their physical representation or the data structure, within the storage medium.
* **Definition 2:** A logical record can be described as a logical data structure composed of a group of related data elements that describe an information entity's Attributes and Relationships with other entities. Often, a logical database record refers to a data structure that incorporates multiple groups of data elements, fields or segments not all of them need to be read at once

3.2 Notations Used on Bubble Charts

We describe data in terms of Entity-types and Attribute-types (or data elements). Bubble charts help us to graphically represent the logical relationships between various types of attributes or data elements of an Entity-type and provide us a way of mapping and understanding the associations among the data elements that comprise a database record.

In a bubble chart each *type* of data element (normally called *data-element type)* is drawn as an **ellipse**, as shown in the following diagram (Figure Chapter H-26):

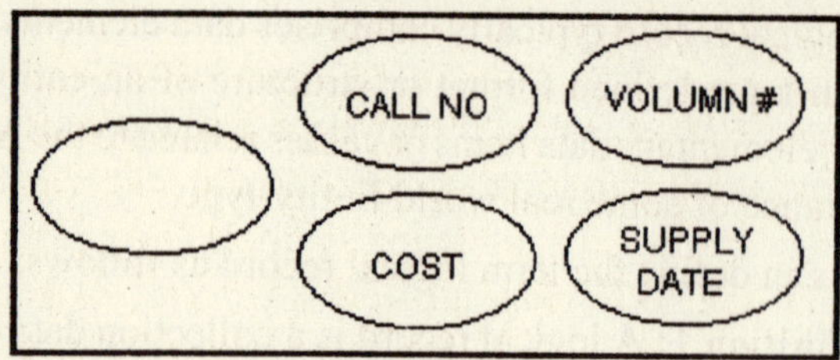

Figure H-26: The symbols used to draw data-element types on a Bubble Chart

There are two kinds of links that are drawn between data elements or attributes: a ***one-to-one association*** and ***one-to-many associations***. These associations are represented by the following link symbols, illustrated below in Figure Chapter H -27(a), Figure Chapter H-27(b) and Figure Chapter H-27 (c)):

A one-to-one association is drawn with a ***bar across the link line*** or ***single arrowhead*** at the end of the link, as illustrated below:

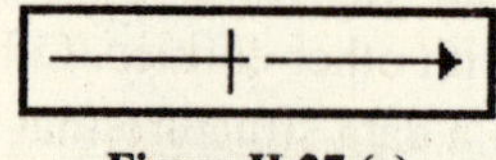

Figure H-27 (a)

An one-to-many relationship is drawn with a ***crow's foot*** or ***double arrowhead*** at the end of a link line, as illustrated below:

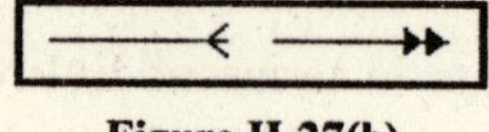

Figure H-27(b)

Where the cardinality is zero the cardinality symbol includes a small circle - "O" on the link, as illustrated below:

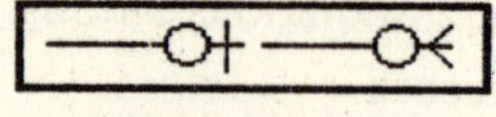

Figure H-27(c)

3.3 A Portrait of Associations

Between Attributes (or Data Elements Types) on the Bubble Charts

In a bubble chart an Attribute-type (date element or field type) is drawn as a named bubble (or an ellipse) and the various kinds of associations that exist between data elements are drawn

ONE-TO-ONE ASSOCIATION:

A *One-to-One association* between the Attribute-type (and data element type) **A** and the Attribute-type (or data element type) **B** means that for *one value of A there is one and only one value of B associated with it*. That there is one-to-one mapping from A to B. If you know the value of A, you can know the value of B. One-to-One association is drawn as a small bar across the link, as shown in the following diagram (Figure Chapter H-28):

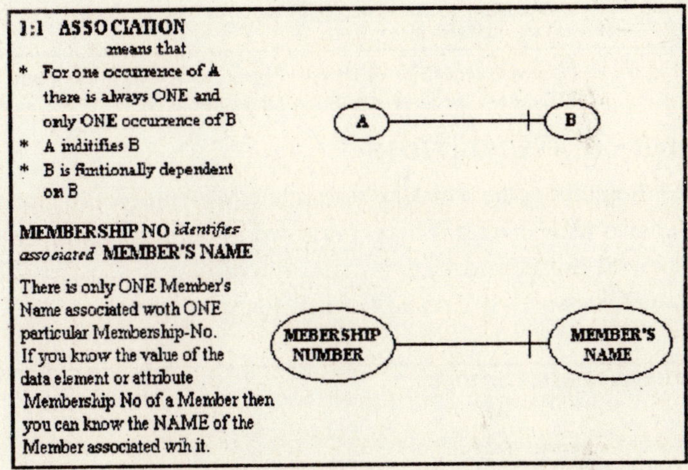

Figure H-28: Representation of One-to-One Association between Attributes (or data elements) on a bubble chart

ONE-TO-MANY ASSOCIATION

An One-*to-Many association* between Attribute-type (data element type) **A** and Attribute-type (data element type) **B** means that *one value of A has one or many values of B associated with it*. This is drawn with crow's-foot, as illustrated below (Figure Chapter H-29):

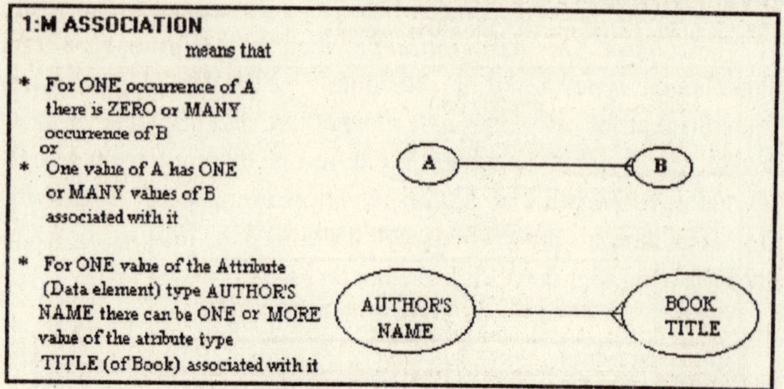

Figure H-29: Representation of One-to-Many Associations between Attributes (or data elements) on a bubble chart

OPTIONAL ASSOCIATIONS

Sometimes there may be zero or one Attribute (data element) associated with another. This is indicated by putting a *small circle* - 'O' on the link before the *One* or *Many* indicator, as shown below (Figure Chapter H-30 (a) and Figure Chapter H-30 (b)):

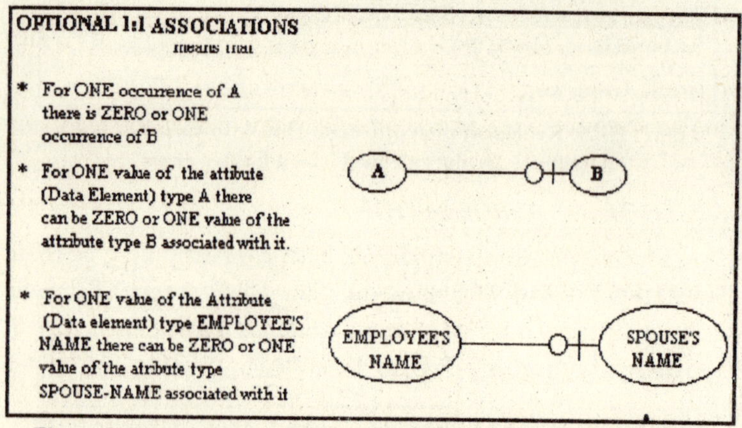

Figure H-30 (a): Representation of Optional One-to-One Association between Attributes (or data elements) on a bubble chart

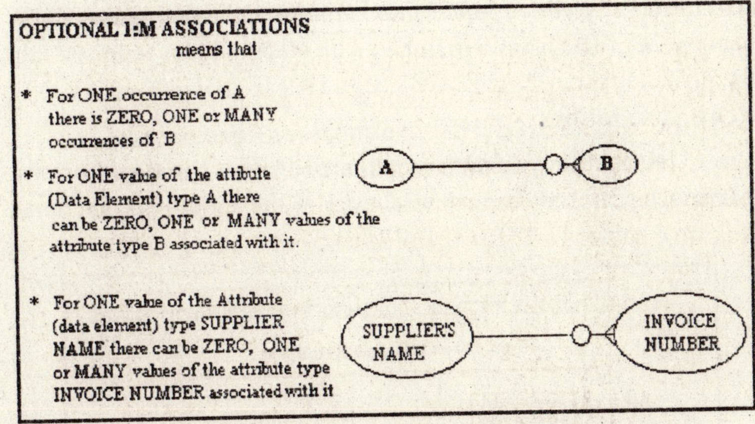

Figure H-30 (b): Representation of Optional One-to-Many Association between Attributes (or data elements) on a bubble chart

3.4 Database Record Structure Diagram

Using a bubble chart, we can represent not only an association between Attribute-type (data element types) but also structures of record types. A record comprises a group of Attributes or Data Elements. The structure of a record type LIBRARY USER is represented in the following bubble chart (Figure Chapter H-31):

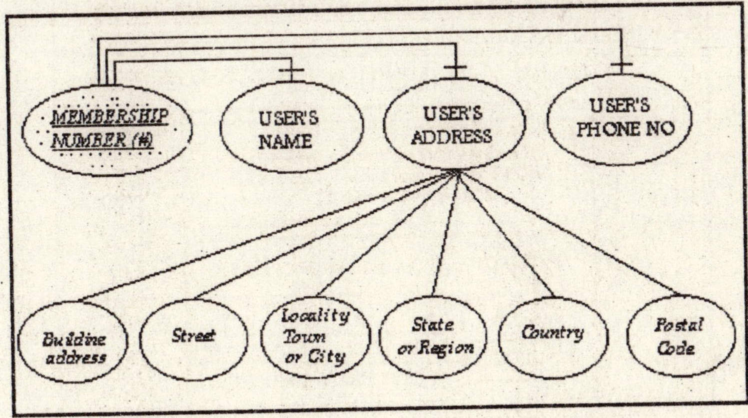

Figure H-31: Representation of Record Structure on a bubble chart

The above chart contains a bubble, representing a **Key Attribute** (also called *primary Attribute* or simply *a primary key*), namely, MEMBERSHIP #, linked with other bubbles representing the attribute-types–NAME-Of-USER, HOME ADDRESS, PHONE NO, and so forth.

The bubble chart representation of a record can also be drawn as per the different format as shown in the following diagrams (Figure Chapter H-32 (a) & H-32(b)):

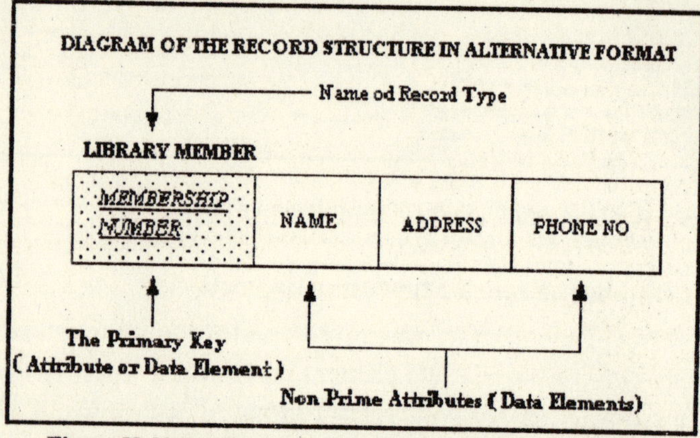

Figure H-32 (a): Drawing of record in the different format (i.e. other than bubble chart format

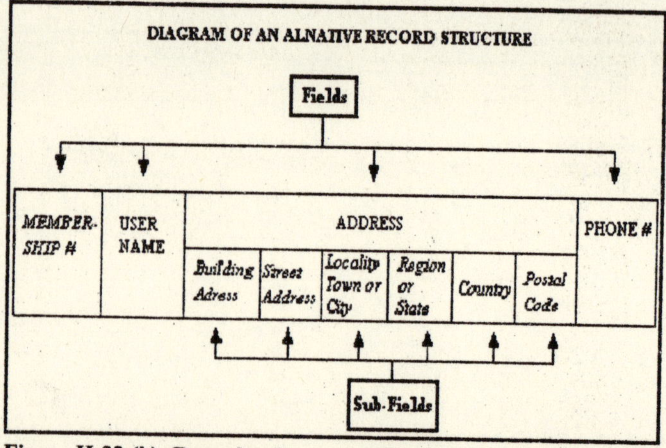

Figure H-32 (b): Record redrawn to show the decomposition of the composite attribute (data element or field) User's ADDRESS into simple attributes (sub fields)

Primary Attribute (or Data Element) and Its Representation on a Bubble

An Entity-type usually has an attribute-type whose values are distinct for each individual entity. Such an attribute-type is called a **Prime Attribute** or **Key Attribute**. The MEMBERSHIP # is a Key Attribute of the Entity-type LIBRARY MEMBER is shown in Figure Chapter H-31, as each library member is allotted a unique membership number. Some times more than one attribute together form a ***Key Attribute*** (simply called **Key**), meaning that the *combination* of the attribute-values of these attributes is unique in order to identify each individual entity. A set of attributes that possess this property are joined together and given the name **Concatenated Key**.

Functionally, a **primary attribute** (or data element) uniquely identifies other attributes comprising a record and its values can also be used to identify each record. Attributes, which are not primary attributes or keys, are referred to as **Nonprime Attributes**. All attributes (data elements), then, are either primary keys or non-primary Attributes (data elements).

A primary key has one or more one-to-one association or links with other nonprime attributes. In a bubble chart a prime key is a **bubble** with ONE or more ONE-to-ONE links going to another **bubble,** the name of the Key Attribute is **underlined** or written in **italics** inside the ellipse or bubble, as shown in the following diagram (Figure Chapter H-33):

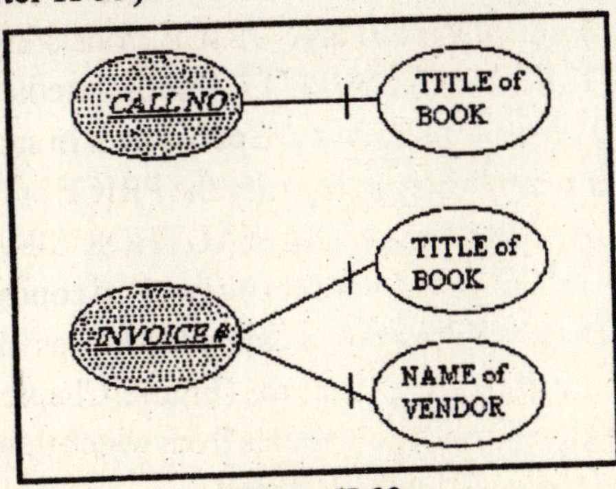

Figure H-33

Secondary Key Attribute-type and Its Representation on a Bubble Chart

A *nonprime Attribute* (data element) having association with one or more values of other attributes or data element types is called a **Secondary Key Attribute**. A secondary key does not uniquely identify another attribute or data element. In a bubble chart a *Secondary Key Attribute* (data element) is represented by a **bubble** with a one or more one-to-many links going to another **bubble**, as illustrated in the following diagram (Figure Chapter H-34):

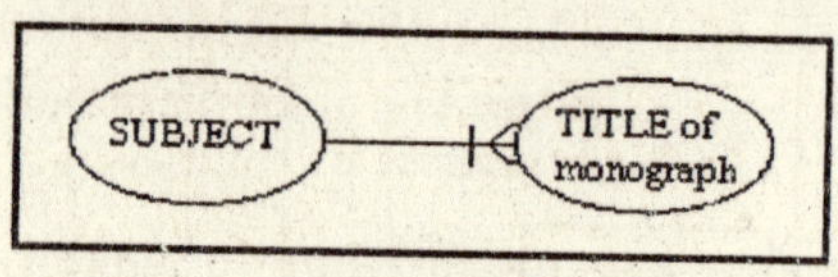

Figure H-34

Concatenated Key and Its Representation on a Bubble Chart

The primary key (also called unique identifier) that is composed of more than one data elements or attribute-types in combination is called *concatenated key*. For example, the Key Attribute TITLE is usually used to identify a book or finding the value of its attribute PRICE. However, if there are two or more books having similar titles, then in such cases, in combination of the attribute TITLE we have to use another attribute, namely the AUTHOR'S-NAME to identify the BOOK or its PRICE. In other words, we create another key to identity an Entity-type BOOK or its attribute (or date element) type PRICE, consisting of attribute-types AUTHORS-NAME and TITLE joined together. Very often, more than one editions of a book are published. In such a situation, we need to create a new key to identify the PRICE or COST of each edition of a book, which may consist of AUTHOR'S-NAME, TITLE, and EDITION join together. Such a key is called **concatenated key**. On a bubble chart we draw a concatenated key as one bubble, as illustrated in the following diagram (Figure Chapter H-35). The names of two, three, or more attributes from which the concatenated key is created are joined with "+" sign.

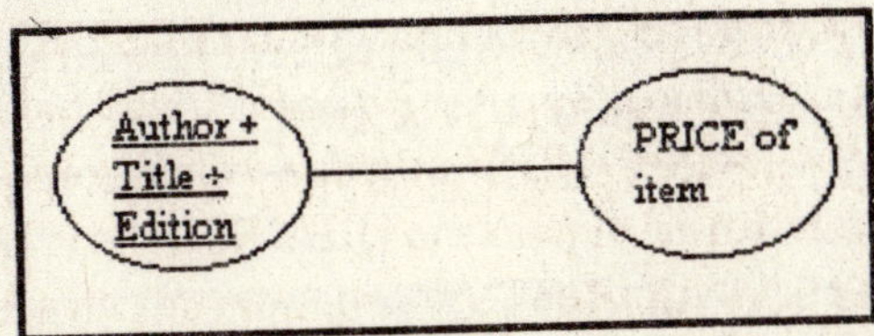

Figure H-35: A concatenated key shown on a bubble chart

Composite Attribute and Its Representation on a Bubble Chart

At times an attribute-type or data element-type is split into subparts. For example, the attribute-type ADDRESS can be subdivided into subparts (also called sub data elements or sub fields): BUILDING or APARTMENT (Name and Number); STREET (Name and/or Number); LOCALITY; VILLAGE, TOWN or CITY; REGION and/or STATE; COUNTRY; POSTAL CODE. Such an Attribute is called *Composite Attribute* Type or *Grouped Data Element* Type. Collectively the grouped attributes or grouped data elements (also called ***grouped data-item***) have a group name but do not constitute a record. Attributes, which are not divisible, are called *simple* or *atomic* attributes (data elements). If there is no need to refer to individual components of an attribute-type ADDRESS, then the whole attribute (ADDRESS) is designated as a simple attribute. The composite attribute is drawn on bubble chart and as shown in the following diagram (Figure Chapter H-36). Below the bubble chart format another alternative format is also drawn:

Derived Attribute-type and Its Representation on a Bubble Chart

The values of certain data elements or attributes are derived from the values of other data elements or attributes. For example, the AGE of a person can be determined from the value of CURRENT-DATE (today's date) and value of that person's DATE-OF-BIRTH. The TOTAL-AMOUNT of a BOOK-INVOICE may be derived by adding the COST of a single or multiple copies of a BIBLIOGRAPHIC-ITEM. Adding the COST of each copy of an ITEM can derive the value of AMOUNT of all the copies of an ITEM. A derived Attribute or a data element type may be marked on a bubble chart by shading its ellipse, as illustrated in the following diagrams (Figure Chapter H-37 & H-38):

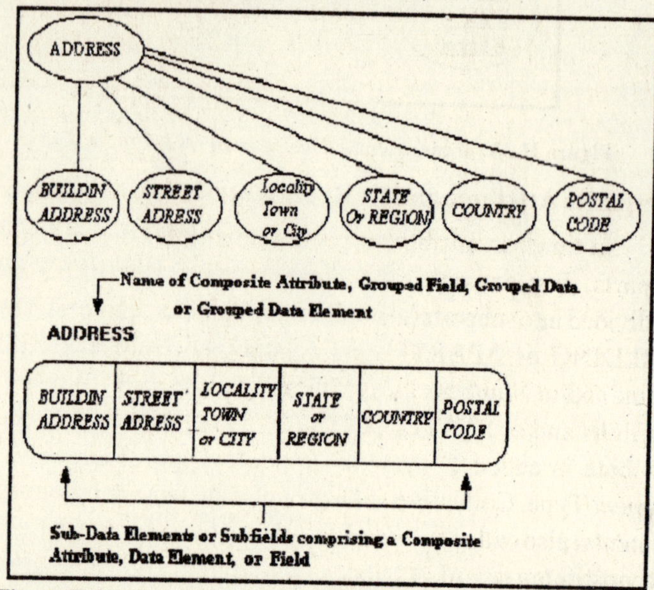

Figure H-36: Composite attribute type shown on diagrammatically

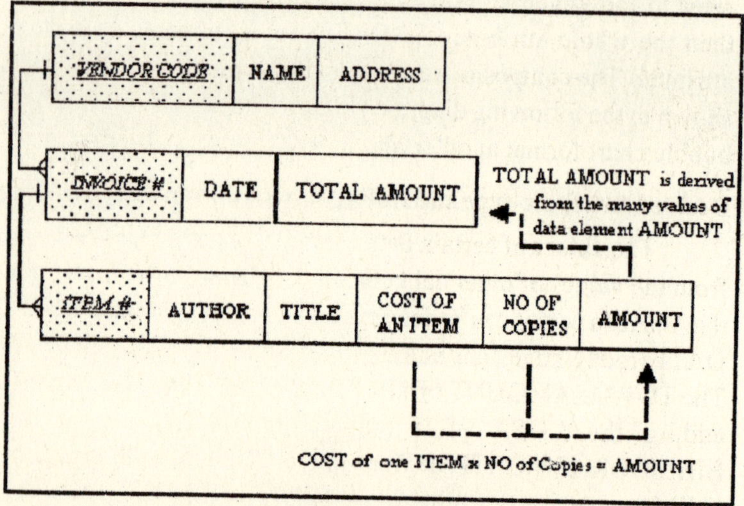

Figure H-37: Bubble chart showing a derived attribute (data element) from other attributes (data elements)

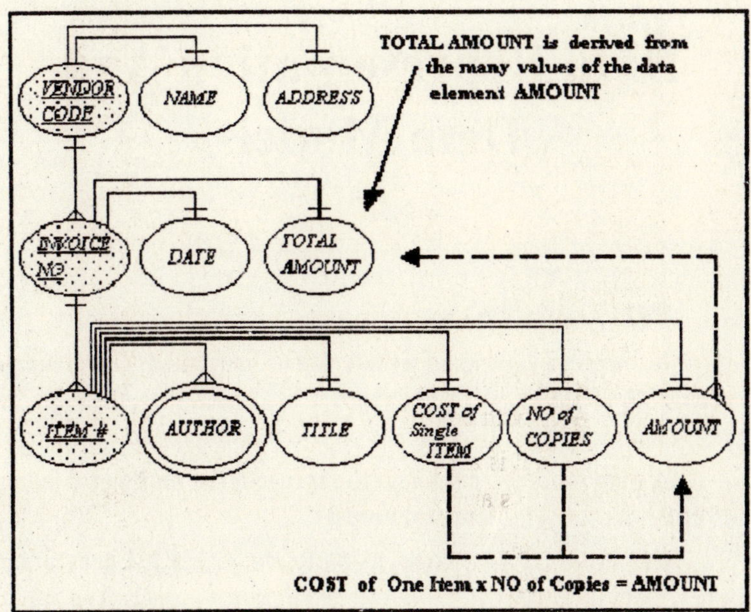

Figure H-38: Derived attribute (data element) from other attributes (data elements) shown in alternative non-bubble chart format

References and Reading List

1. Bachan, C. W. Data structure diagrams. *Database*. v. 1, 2; 1969, p. 4-10.
2. Chen, Peter Pin-sen, Ed. Entity-Relationship *approach to information modelling and analysis*. North-Holland, Amsterdam, 1983.
3. —. The Entity-Relationship model - towards a unified view of data. *ACM Transaction on database Systems*. v. 1, 1; 1976; p. 9-36.
4. Martin, James. *Strategic data-planning methodology*. Prentice-Hall Inc., Englewood Cliffs, NJ, 1982
5. —; McCulre, Carma. *Diagramming techniques for analyst and programmers*. Prentice-Hall, Englewood Cliff, NJ, 1985.

I
Data Representation And Data Models

1 INTRODUCTION

In the previous chapter we referred to data models-hierachical, network, and relational. This chapter discusses the attributes of these data models with emphasis on the relational data model.

A data model is a schema to represent the real world using information concepts and structures.

Example: User – Name, Department, Gender, Educational Level, Data of Birth

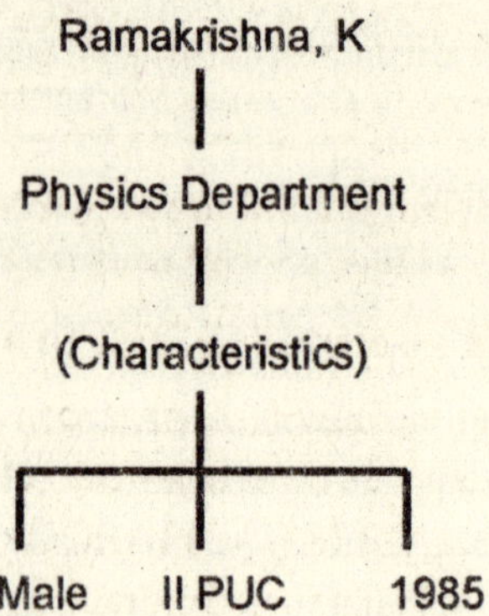

Figure I-1: Data model sample

Hierarchical, network, and relational models represent the stages in the evolution of data models with increasing capacity to represent different kinks or relationships among data entities. Neural Networks may also be included here. Database structures generally conform to one or the other, or a combination, of these data models.

2 HIERARCHICAL DATA MODEL

A succession of Parents-progeny, Genus-species, Hypernym and Hyponym (e.g. Rose is a kind of flower), Whole-part relationships (Holonym) are generally deemed to represent hierarchical relation. Structurally the hierarchical model may be shown as an upside down tree, the highest level of the tree being known as the root (paradoxically). The tree has one trunk and many branches emerging from it. Each branch may also have sub branches (Figure Chapter I-2).

The connection at which branches emerge is called a node. In the hierarchical database, nodes represent entity sets. Generally, a hierarchical model maintains one-to-one or oneto-many relationship

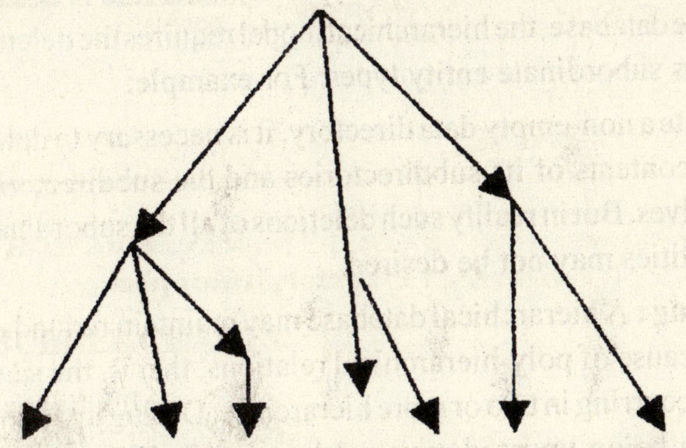

Figure I-2: Hierarchical Relation - Nodes and Branches

Example 1: **Dances**

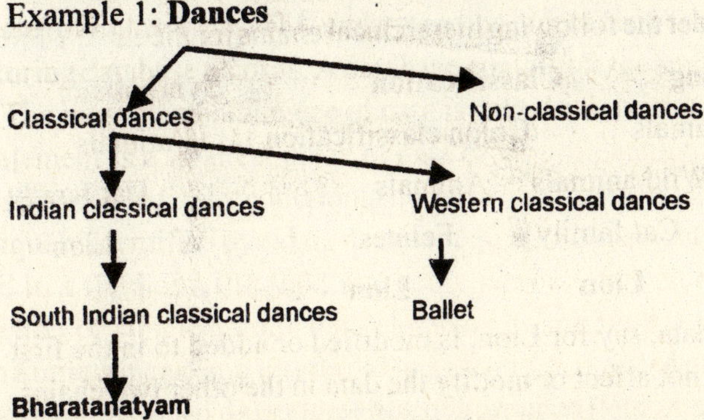

In the database conforming to the hierarchical model links between entity types are established when the data model is designed and the database created. The links provide fast retrieval response to users' queries.

2.1 Problems

Three types of problems arise with databases of the hierarchical type: they are related to the execution of Insertion, Deletion, and Updating functions.

a) **Insertion :** To add a new subordinate entity, its super-ordinate entity type must be known; otherwise it will not be maintained in the database. For instance, if we are to add the dance entity 'Mohiniattam' in the correct position (Figure Chapter I-2), we need to know the entity type to which it belongs.

b) **Deletion :** If the parent link or super-ordinate link is deleted from the database, the hierarchical model requires the deletion of all its subordinate entity types. For example:

To delete a non-empty data directory, it is necessary to delete all the contents of its subdirectories and the subdirectories themselves. But in reality such deletions of all the subordinate data entities may not be desired.

c) **Updating :** A hierarchical database may maintain redundant data because of poly-hierarchical relations, that is, the same entity occurring in two or more hierarchies. During updating, the data being updated may not be modified in all of its locations.

Consider the following hierarchical chains for the entity **Lion**

Hunting	**Classification**	**Symbolism**
Animals	Colon classification	Animals
Wild animals	Animals	Cat family
Cat family	Felines	Lion
Lion	**Lion**	

If the data, say for Lion, is modified or added to in the first chain, it may not affect or modify the data in the other two chains.

3 NETWORK DATA MODEL

A Network model is similar to the hierarchical model except that an entity is not fixed to a maximum of one super-ordinate entity. It can represent many-to-many relationship. Figure Chapter I-3 illustrates a simple network model.

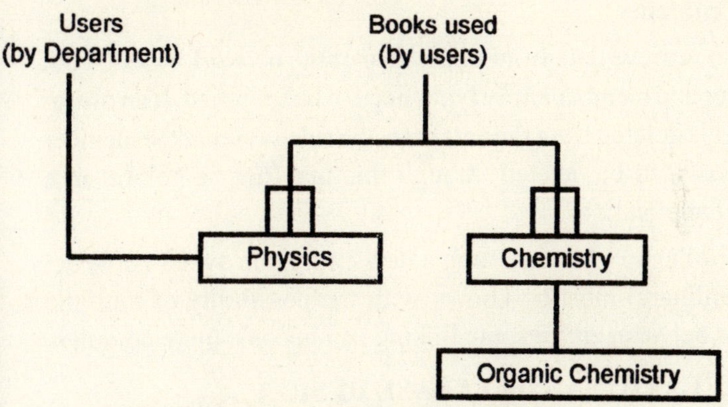

Figure I-3: Network Data Model

In Figure Chapter I-3 the fork-like link indicates multiple link / relationship possibilities. The network links can be between any of the entity types. For example, there is no restriction either to make the entity type 'users' as a subordinate entity type or to create a separate relation; simply a link is established between the entity types selected. There need not be any redundancy in data types. The data, for example relating to 'Physics', needs to be updated or modified only in one location.

The most widely used network model is the one designed by the DBTG (Database Task Group) of CODASYL (Conference on Data Systems Languages), an independent organization of vendors, researchers and government agencies that have cooperated to establish guidelines and recommendations for computer software.

Although many-to-many relationship is handled in the network model, it must be split into one-to-many relationship according to the DBTG proposal. A one-to-many mapping from one entity type to another is considered as a set. The DBTG set which consists of owner-member relationship is analogous to the Parents-Progeny relationship of the hierarchical model. As in the hierarchical model, in the network model also the relations between entity sets must be established when the data model is designed and the database created. The links / relationships also provide fast retrieval response in the network model.

3.1 Problems

To retrieve data from a database of the network model, both the owner and member entity types need to be specified. If an owner entity set is deleted from the database, the rule says that the member entity sets also be deleted, though this may not be helpful in a practical application.

Similarly, when inserting a new entity, the owner entity set (super-ordinate) must be known with the possibility of multiple relations between entities, the linking can become quite complex.

4 RELATIONAL DATABASE DESIGN

4.1 Introduction

Edgar. F. Codd first developed the relational data model in 1970. Later modified and extended by **Peter Pin-Shan Chen** [1976, 1986], **Codd** [1979, 1982], and others (*see review by* **Teorey,** *et al* [1986]; *also refer* **Maier** [1983], the relational model of data has gained recognition as a model for providing sound basis to design a relational database. Codd has also published another book, entitled: *The relational Model for Database Management – Version 2* [1990] to improve the lack of expressive power and semantic richness in the earlier proposed relational model.

It may also be pointed out that though the network and hierarchical data modelling approaches have some edge on performance of certain applications with compare to relation data modelling approach; but these models impose too many restrictions at the data modelling level, and lead to database which is difficult to maintain, modify and upgrade. For this reason, relational data model has become very popular.

The relational database design is based on the well developed '**mathematical theory of relations**' and '**normalization theory**', and is built around the concept of **normal forms**. The basic element of the relational data model is the **relation**. A **relation instance** (also called ***extension*** of the relation) is a **table** constituted of ***rows*** and ***columns***. A table contains data about a specific entity type, such as MONOGRAPH or SUPPLIER. ***Columns*** of a relation or table represent attributes of an entity type. ***Rows*** of a relation or table, technically called ***tuples*** contains values of the attributes of an individual entity instance.

The relational database schema consists of a number of relations schema or definitions. The schema of each relation is an aggregate of all defined **attributes** of an entity type, and a tuple (or row) of a relation corresponds to an entity record. The set of atomic values for a particular attribute (i.e. column in a relation) is called as **domain** of that attribute.

"The concept of **normal form** was proposed in the relational literature as a measure of freedom from the anomalies or difficulties that arise when insertion, deletion and modification are applied to relational database. The higher the normal form, the greater is the "purity' or "goodness" of the logical definition of the relational schemas." [**Batini, Ceri,** and **Navthe.** 1992. P 313].

A relationship is said to be in a particular normal form if it satisfies a certain specified conditions or constraints. For example, a relation is said to be in **first normal form relation** (1NF) if all the rows/tuples in a relation has a key or primary attribute (as an identifier) and have same set of non key attributes, and the value any attribute in a tuple/row must be single values (i.e., the attributes must not be composite and multivalved. In other words, a relation in its basic form contains just simple, single-valued attributes, one which must be its primary key. Therefore in all composite and multivalued attributes of an entity have to be converted or modelled in terms of simple single-valued attributes in a database.

In his seminal paper on the relational model, Codd [1970] has also defined two more normal forms, **second normal form** (2NF) below:

and **third normal form** (3NF). Later, third normal form was shown to have certain drawbacks or limitations and a better form was introduced called **Boyce-Codd normal form** (BCNF) [*cf.*, **Dates and Codd, 1974**). Subsequently, Fagin introduced **forth normal form** (4NF) and also **fifth normal form** (5NF), [*cf.*, **Fagin 1977, 1979**). We will discuss these normal forms later.

In general terms a relational database consists of nothing but ***'relations'*** represented as ***logical tables***. A table stands for an entity type and is comprised of a set of rows, which in turn are comprised of a set of columns (each column representing one attribute or data element of a given entity-type, and there are no repeating groups or fields). Each row of a table constitutes of a set of columns that contain values of the attributes pertaining to an entity instance. If a table constitutes of n-columns, the relation is said to be of *degree n*. The relation of degree 2 are called *binary*, degree 3 are called *ternary*, and so on. In other words, ***the degree of a relation*** is the numbers of attributes/columns in a relation. The number of rows or tuples a table may contain is called the ***cardinality*** of the relation.

4.2 Basic Characteristics of Relational Data Model

The relational database model or design consists of three parts:

* The structural part, which is concerned with definition of relations and their relationships
* The integrity part, which is concerned with keeping three types of constraints, namely: (a) Keys constraint, (b) Entity identity constraint, and (c) Referential integrity constraint

  a. **Keys Constraint** implies specification of candidate keys of each relation schema and selecting one of these as primary key, whose value must be unique for every tuple in any relation instance to ensure that each occurrence of a relation is unique. (i.e., the primary key serves as an unique identifier of a tuple /row/ record of a relation or table)

  b. **Entity identity constraint** implies that no primary key value can be null, because the primary key value is used to identify individual tuple/row/record in a relation or table; having null values in some tuples means we can not identify them.

c. **Referential integrity or reliability constraint** is concerned with two specific relations and used to maintain the consistency among tuples of those relations. The implication of this constraint is that a key of a tuple/ row in a relation or table that refers to another relation or table must refer to an existing tuple/ row in that relation or table.

* The operation part. Data manipulation is crucial part of the relational database model. The data is not only stored decisively, correctly, and safely but also retrieved, manipulated and meaningfully displayed. The basic operations involved in a relational database to manipulate data are of two types: retrieval operations and update operations.

The retrieval operations are of two types: the relation algebra operations and SQL based query statements.

The ***relation algebra operations*** are used to manipulate entire tables. For example, a relation algebra operation may be used to select tuples from individual tables and to combine related tuples from several tables for specifying a query – a retrieval request – on the database. The result of each operation is a new relation that can be further manipulated.

The relational algebra operations are of two types: (i) **Set operations** from mathematical set theory, which include UNION, INTERSECTION, DIFERENCE, and CARTESAIN PRODUCT, and (ii) **Operations developed specifically for relational database,** which are ***Select, Project*** (also called ***Projection), Join.*** The ***Select*** operation is executed by giving the value of the *primary key* to select one or more tuples or rows from the relation and to retrieve its/their data. The ***Project or Projection*** operation selects one or more columns from a table. With this operation project or projection one can extract from an existing table a subset of its columns. If one table is split into two by a project operation, such that the original table could be perfectly reconstructed (if need be) from the two tables, this process is called nonloss/lossless decomposition. The ***Join*** operation is used to combine related tuples/rows from two tables into single tuple/row.

The SQL (Structured Query Language) is a wide-ranging database language whose statements are used for data definition, query and update. However the most common use of the language is made for asking questions or stating statements for retrieving information from the database. Its statements, by convention, are written in UPPER CASE. The one basic statement is SELECT statement (This statement has no relationship with SELECT operation of relational algebra). The select statement is formed by three causes SELECT, FROM, DISTINCT, and WHERE and has following form:

SELECT *<attribute list>*	*Attribute list* is list of attributes names whose values are to be retrieved by the query.
FROM or DISTINCT *<table list>*	*Table list* is list of the relation/table names required to process the query. When one uses FROM clause duplicates tuples/records from tables are included. One can force SQL to remove the duplicates by using DFISTINCT clause.
WHERE *<condition>*	*WHERE* is a conditional search (Boolean search) expression that identifies the tuples / records to be retrieved by the query.

Example:

SELECT MemNo, NameOfMember, EnrolmentDate
FROM LIBRARY MEMBER
WHERE LIBRARY MEMBER=3

This query will retrieve following information

MemNo *(Key)*	NameOf Member	EnrolmentDate
M3	C. L. Dutta	2004-07-204.3

4.3 Rational Database Structure

A relational database has certain characteristics that distinguish it from other types of databases. As stated earlier, it consists of one or more two dimensional tables. Every table, representing a specific entity type, is made of rows and columns. Each row of a table, normally referred to as *tuple*, contains the data values that relate to the attributes of a particular instance of the entity-type represented by the table. A row or tuple containing two values of the attributes, say **name** and **address** of the entity type PERSON, is called a *pair*. A row or tuple can comprise of *N-tuple*, where N refers to the number of values.

Thus, the basic structure of relational database design is a **table,** technically referred to as **relation**. Further, a row of a table or relation may be thought of as being equivalent to database record or segment. A column may also be thought of as being equivalent to a field of a record and entire table equivalent to a logical file. In Relational model all relations are define independently; there no hierarchy, or a connection, or a link among relations or tables in the model. However relationship between relations can be established by *join (or equi-join) operation* between the attributes of different tables. In performing a *join operation,* which is algebraic operation for matching two tables having comparable, that is attributes of same domain, which are replicated in different relations. In the relational database, relationships are established at the time of retrieval. As a result, a new relationship can be established without the need to re-organize the database. However, the relationships between tables are defined at the time of designing the relational model of a database system. As an illustration a set of schemas based on the relational model are outlined in the Chart. The examples in the figures show two independent relations, LIBRARY MEMBER,

BIBLIOGRAPHIC DOCUMENT, and two relation tables LOANED BIBLIGRAPHIC ITEM and OVERDUE BIBLIOGRAPHIC ITEM. These schemas pertain to a hypothetical BIBLIGRAPHIC ITEMS CIRCULATION SYSTEM, assuming we are concerned with the two relations, at the outset.

In relational database a relationship can be of type one-to-one, one-to-many, or many-to-many. As indicated earlier, you create a relationship in a relational database by establishing an association between common attributes (i.e., columns or fields) of the tables. In other words the relationships between two or more tables are established by virtue of common data values contained in the corresponding tables, each of which allows us to identify uniquely an entity in an entity set. In most cases you define primary key, tag or identifier in each table. The primary key of a primary table is added in primary key field of other table. This key is called **foreign key**. A ***foreign key*** is the primary key of the principal table that relates it with another table and is used to establish relationship between tables by join operation.

A simple collection of sample data for each of the above defined relation schema (Table 1).

The sample data given in Table 1 of Borrower Relation schema consists of information about five borrowers. Each row/tuple/record of the table represents a particular borrower, and the attribute *MemNo* whose value uniquely identifies the individual borrower, assuming that the names of two or more members can be identical, the unique code *MemNo* is chosen as the **primary key** of the table. In the relational model the concept of **primary key** or simply **key** is similar to concept of **identifier** in ER model. A primary key of a relation enables us to identify and access each tuple or record in a set of rows/tuples (i.e., in a file). As the primary key value is used to identify individual tuple (or row) in a relation, the primary or candidate key of each relation schema must be unique and that no primary key value can be null. The remaining **non-key attributes** of the table furnish additional facts about each member. In addition, each row/tuple/record can be *searched* and sequenced by its **primary**

Relation (Entity Type)	*Primary (or Key) Attribute*	*Non-Key Attribute*	*Non-Key Attribute*	*Non-Key Attribute*	*Non-Key Attribute*	*Non-Key Attribute*	*Non-Key Attribute*
Schema 1. LIBRARY MEMBER	MemNo (Membership Number – the unique identifier attribute)	Name of Member	Address	Phone	Enrolment Date	Memship Expiry Date	
Schema 2. BIBLIO-GRAPHIC DOCU-MENT	CallNo (Class Number +Book Number) (Concatenated Identifier)	NameAuthor (Name of Principal Author)	Title	Edition	Volume	Pub Date (Publication Date)	Publisher
Schema 3. BIBLIOGR-APHIĆ ITEM -on-LOAN (Individual physical volume or copy of a biblio-graphic document)	CallNo + MemNo (Concatenated identifier)	DueDate (The date till a document can be retained by a borrower)	RetDate (The Date the item is returned)	NameAuthor (Name of Principal Author)	Title	Name Member	

Chart: Example of Relation Schemas of Library Documents Circulation System

Sample Data

Table 1: Borrower Relation Instances

Attributes Columns or Fields →	**Mem No (Key)**	**Nameof Member**	**Address**	**Phone**	**Enrolment Date**	**Membership ExpiryDate**
Row 1	M1	Amrit Lal Chadha	610 Double Story New Rajinder Nagar, New Delhi -1100060	2578 2239	2004-07-28	2006-03-21
Row 2	M2	Rajinder Kumar Chopra	5/28 New Rohtak Road, New Delhi-110005	25784321	2004-07-25	2006-03-21
Row 3	M3	C. L. Dutta	Karol Bag, New Delhi-110005	2274 3334	2004-07-20	2006-03-21
Row 4	M4	Nittan Chander	55., Gawyer Hall, University of Delhi , Delhi-10007	2292 7656	2004-07-22	2006-03-21
Row 5	M5	Joshi, S	Kishan Gang, Delhi-110007	22786556	2004-07-23	2006-03-21

key. Unlike a primary key, one or more non-key may have null values in some instances. Null value implies the data is not available. A person may have a phone and another may not have phone. In second case value of phone number is null – absence of data. Absence of data of an attribute or in a field can be for other reasons. For example, the value of an attribute may exist, but unknown or not recorded as yet; or the value is known or available but not entered by chance. In such case the value is not null but empty or left over. As far as possible, one should avoid placing attribute whose values, by and large, will be null.

The similar pattern is repeated in other sample data tables. However, in case of Table 2: Bibliographic Document Relation, the **concatenated key** – *ClassNo + BookNo* has been used as **primary key** or **access key**. This is because of the reason that in order to identify or locate specific piece of bibliographic item or volume, we need two keys *ClassNo* and *BookNo*. The alternative is to use composite attribute *Author + Title + CopyNo* as primary key. We find that the relationship between the entity types BIBLIGRAPHIC DOCUMENT and LIBRARY MEMBER is of **one-*to-many*** type, as a library member can borrow one or more bibliographic items and a bibliographic item can be loaned to only one member. Further, both the entity types have *partial participation* in the relationship, as a library member may borrow *zero, one or more* bibliographic items, and similarly a bibliographic item may be on loan or may not be on loan in given point in time (i.e., cardinality is zero or one). For this reason we define additional separate relation BIBLIOGRAPHIC ITEM-on-LOAN-to-BORROWER (see Table 3) by using the primary key Call_No of the relation BIBLIOGRAPHIC ITEM and adding primary key (MemNo) of MEMBERSHIP relation/table along certain additional required non-primary attributes.

Note both the relations BIBOGRAPHIC ITEM and BIBLIOGRAPHIC ITEM**-on-LOAN describe** bibliographic items. The table BIBLIOGRAPHIC **ITEM-on-LOAN** contains a subset of all the bibliographic items — those loaned out to library users.

Table 2: Bibliographic Document Relation Instances

Attributes Columns or Fields →	***CallNo (Concatenated Key) (Class No + Book No)***	***NameAuth***	***Title***	***Edition***	***Volume***
Row 1	C N89	Blatt, F J	Principles of Physics	Ed. 2	
Row 2	E1,5 N89	Dazelly, D H	Organic Chemistry	Ed 3	
Row 3	HV N82.1	Fluegge, S., *ed.*	Geophysics		V. 1
Row 4	E1,5 N89;1	Dazelly, D. H.	Organic Chemistry	Ed. 3	
Row 5	HV N82.2	Fluegge, S, *ed.*	Geophysics		V. 2
Row 6	HV N82.3	Fluegge, S, *ed.*	Geophysics		V. 3
Row 7	X;aa N82	Baranzini, Maur	Economic Theory		

Table 3: Bibliographic Item-On-Loan-to-Borrower Relation Instances (Representing Join Operation of Table 1 & Table 2 Primary Key (Call_No)

	Call No	***MemNo***	***DueDate***	***DateRet***
Row 1	E1,5 N78	M5	2004-07-01	2004-07-12
Row 2	HV N82.2	M1	2004-07-02	2004-07-14
Row 3	X;aa N82	M3	2004-07-03	2004-07-16
Row 4	C N89	M4	2004-07-04	2004-07-15
Row 5	E1,5 N78	M5	2004-08-01	
Row 6	HV N82.1	M1	2004-08-02	

Table 4: Overdue Bibliographic Item Relation (Representing Join Operation of Table 1, Table 2 & Table 3)

RELATION	***Concatenated Primary Key***			***Non_Prime Keys***			
OVERDUE BIBLIOGRAPHIC ITEM	Overdue Date	CallNo	MemNo	Author OfItem	Title OfItem	Name Member	Address Member

Table 5: Overdue Bibliographic Item Relation Instances Overdue List of Items

Overdue Date	*CallNo*	*Mem No*	*Author of Item*	*Title of Item*	*Name Member*	*Address Member*
2004-07-16	B3 K5	01B5	Shanti Narayan	Elementary Calculus	S. P. Kumar	Ashok Vihar, Delhi, 110009
2004-07-17	C J4	01C5	Martin, J	Text Book of Physics	Ratan Lal	Vikash Puri, Delhi, 110056
2004-07-17	D1 K5	01D5	Lazar, Peter	Civil Enginee-ring	Roshan Lal Sharma	20 Maurice Nagar Delhi, 110007

4.4 Logical Design of Relational Database System

4.4.1 Introduction

The first step in designing a set of relational database schema is to provide a **conceptual model (also called ER**-model) of a system under consideration, and then transform it into set of relations or tables applying the normalization technique. A conceptual model or design is an abstract construct, which consists of lists of entity-types, attributes of entity-types, relationships among entity-types, and constraints imposed on relationships. This conceptual model is then mapped into relational schema; it implies translation of entities, their attribute and relations defined in the conceptual model into relations or relation schema.

A set of relation definitions constitutes a relational schema. The schema of each relation is an aggregate of all defined **attributes** of an entity type, and a tuple (or row) of a relation corresponds to an entity record. The set of atomic values for a particular attribute (i.e. column in a relation) is called as **domain** of that attribute. By atomic we mean that each value must be indivisible as far relational model is concerned.

A reasonable starting point in the design of a conceptual model of a system is to define, after careful analysis, the principle activities (i.e., integrated set of operations or transactions) of the library system to be automated and the desired outputs or reports to be generated by the system. During this stage, key decisions are made concerning the overall scope of the proposed database design, its constraints and requirements on the basis of an assessment made of the present and potential requirements of the various types of users who will be assessing the database.

The identification and specification of the functional activities or operations of a library system their outputs help us in the identification of entities and events (i.e., the things that we want to keep data or records about), and to represent the associated entities in the form of particular entity-types. Further, one must list the corresponding *attributes of interest* of each entity-type (Entities possess many attributes; we may not be concerned with every attribute of an entity-type in a given context. Only those attribute are considered that represent the particular facet of an entity-type, i.e. the facet under consideration) and specify the relationships which exist among the entity-types, with a view to ultimately translate the corresponding conceptual design into a set of relations and defining their schemas or table structures, by applying the rules of normalization.

In the light above statement, we shall first provide an outline of a conceptual design of an illustrative ***Document Loan System,*** a subsystem of a library system and then define the normalised relations or tables. The outline shall comprised of a list of major operations or transactions associated with the selected system and the principle outputs to be obtained or reports to be generated by the system. Based on the listing of the major operations and required outputs of the system, the entities or entity-types, whose information is to be contained in the proposed database, the particular attributes of each entity-type representing their characteristics, and the possible relationships between different entity-types, shall be specified in the following sections.

4.4.2 Principle Transactions associated with the Bibliographic Items Loan System

A library has a set of Bibliographic Documents that are issued on loan to library members and enrols persons as members, who borrow individual items/volumes of the Bibliographic Documents. The major operations associated with the Bibliographic Item Loan Transaction System of a library can be visualized as listed below:

* Issue of individual Bibliographic Item to a library user/ member.
* Bibliographic Items are to be discharged when returned.
* Reminders are to be sent to the borrowers for the return of the respective over-due item(s) from them.
* Overdue charges, if any, are to be calculated, and collected.
* Records are to be maintained pertaining to total daily, monthly, yearly collection of overdue charges as well as of bibliographic items issue on loan.
* Maintenance of circulation data, such as: The total number of items issued daily, monthly, yearly; number of times a particular bibliographic item has been issued, and so forth.

4.4.3 Principle Reports associated with the Bibliographic Items Loan System

Some of principle outputs to be obtained or types of reports that are likely to be generated from the database system are also listed below:

1. Reminders for overdue items.
2. A report on total daily, monthly, yearly collection of overdue charges and bibliographic item issued on loan.
3. A list & number of long overdue Bibliographic Items (as and when required).
4. Reports about circulation/loan data.

4.4.4 Associated Entity-Types and Their Relationships

If we analyse each of the listed operations, transactions and outputs or reports to be obtained from the system we can identify a set of entity-types and relationships. The major entity-types in this application are the holdings of the library pertaining to the single pieces or volumes of documents and members or borrowers.

Examining the operations and expected outputs of the system we the following fact emerge: (a) A particular borrower is a member of the library; (b) he borrows or takes on loan one or more Bibliographic Item from the library, and; (c) must return it/them after use on or before a particular date failing which he must pay certain overdue charges for retaining the monograph over time. Therefore the good candidates for entity-type are:

1. LIBRARY USERS: All the enrolled library members who are entitled to borrower certain type and numbers of Bibliographic items.
2. BIBLIOGRAPHIC ITEMS: All the bibliographic items (individual volumes/pieces of documents) that can be loaned to various types of library members.
3. LOANED ITEMS: All the bibliographic items (individual volumes/pieces of documents) that are on loan, at a given point of time, to various library members. (LOANED BIBLIOGRAPHIC ITEMS constitute subset of BIBLIOGRAPHIC ITEMS.)
4. OVERDUE ITEMS: ALL the bibliographic items that are overdue items – items that are not returned and held by borrowers, even after expiry of the due-date (i.e., the date a borrower can retain

the loaned item.) - OVERDUE BIBLIOGRAPHIC ITEMS constitute subset of LOANED BIBLIOGRAPHIC ITEMS.

5. OVERDUE CHARGE: The records of the amount charged from each borrower for keeping loaned item/volume overtime.

The Most general picture of the Entities associated with the Illustrative Library Subsystem and their Relationships are shown in the following The E-R Diagram.

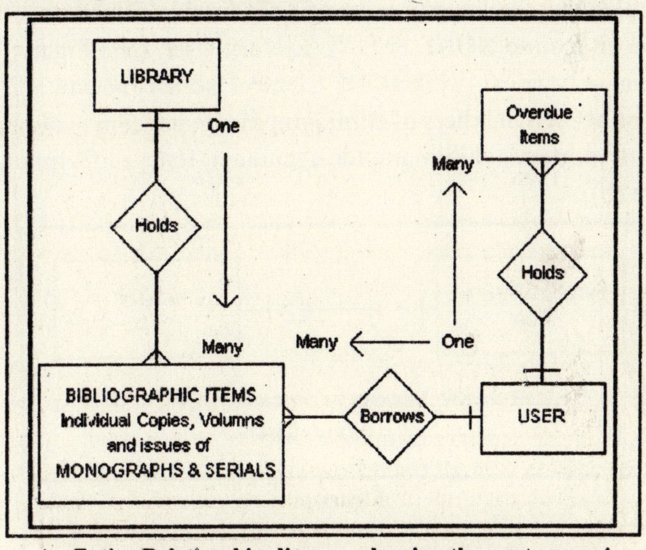

An Entity-Relationship diagram showing the most general picture of the Entities associated with the illustrative Library Subsystem and their Relationships

* **Entity Types and Associated Attributes**

Entity-Type-E-1 : BIBLIOGRAPHIC ITEM

Attributes: *<u>CallNumber</u>* (*<u>CallNo</u>*); *PrincipalAuthor (PAuthr); Title; Edition; VolumeNumber (VolNo); PublicationDate (PubDate), Publisher (Pub), PlaceOfPublication (Place), AccessionNumber (AccNo), and so forth.*

Entity-Type -E-2: BORROWER à LIBRARY USER à PERSON or ORGANISATION (BORROWER is subset of entity class LIBRARY USER, which is subset of the class PERSON)

Attributes: *<u>Membership Number</u>* (*<u>MemNo</u>*); *NameOfUser* (*UserName*); *Address; PhoneNumber (PhoneNo)*.

* **Relationships**

We find that the following **Relationships** exist among the above mentioned entity-types

RELATIONSHIP: R-1 Between entity-type E-1 and E-2: A particular copy, volume or issue of an individual Biographic Item can be on loan to NONE or ONE Library User. (*See* Figure (a)). Alternatively we can say that ONE Library User may borrow NONE, ONE or MORE numbers of Bibliographic Items (copy, volume or issue of a particular bibliographic document) for specific time (*See* Figure (b)).

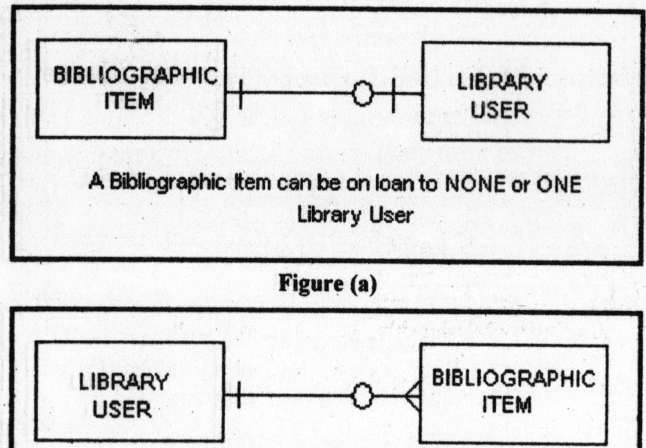

Figure (a)

Figure (b)

RELATIONSHIP: R-2 Between entity-type E-1 and E-2: ONE or MORE Bibliographic Items-On-Loan may be overdue from ONE or MORE Library Users

RELATIONSHIP: R-3 Between entity-type E-2 and E-1: A Library User may have NONE, ONE or MORE Bibliographic Items overdue with him.

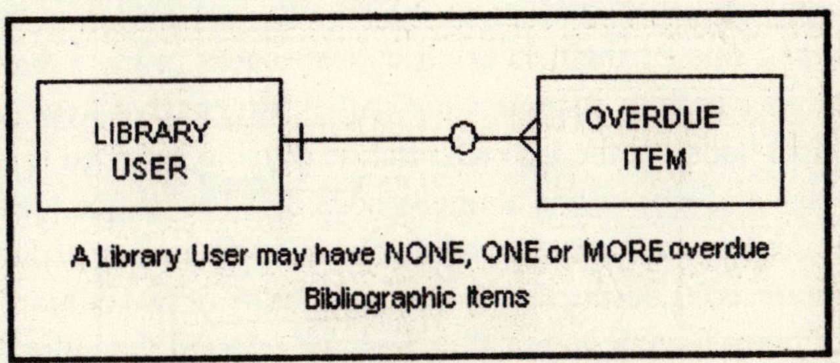

4.5 Relation Schema of the Illustrative System

4.5.1 Rules for Defining a Relation or Table

While defining a relation or table of a relational model one has to fulfil the following requirements:

1. Each Relation or Table must be given unique heading, e.g., a relation or table called BIBLIOGRAPHIC_ITEM. (Use uppercase for relation/table names).
2. Each attribute (column) of a Relation/Table must be given a name, also referred to as ***key***, tag, or ***field***. (Use BiCapitalisation (CamelCaps) for attribute names
3. Each tuple of a relation, corresponding to a row in the table, must have an attribute or combination of attributes which serves as unique identifier, referred to a ***primary key*** (or simple ***key*** for brevity) of entity tuple/row/record, which allows us to identify uniquely an entity in entity set.

a. For example, consider the following relation or table for entity-type USER of a Library.

***Relation**: USER*

USER (*Entity-type*): [***MemNo*** (*Primary* or *key attribute*), *Name, Address, PhoneNo* (*non-key descriptive attributes*)]

The attribute named *MemNo* (Membership No) of the above relation or table is the primary key whose values *uniquely* identify a specific entity tuple/record in the table, while USER is the heading of the relation or table.

Often, more than one attribute within a relation or table may be unique. When this occurs, each of the attributes is called **candidate key**, and one of them is arbitrary chosen as primary key. The remaining unique attributes are called **alternative keys**. As an example consider the USERS relation or table, referred to above. The name of a person is normally considered as unique identifier. Thus, *Name* of a library user could become primary key of the table. However, considering that there is possibility of two or more users of a library having identical names, we selected the unique code ***MemNo***, assigned by a library, as a primary key of the relation USERS. In this case, we can say that both the attributes are candidate keys, as *MemNo* is chosen as primary key, then the *Name* becomes alternative key, and vice versa.

At times, in a relation no single attribute of the relation can play the role of unique identifier. When this is the case, the key must be constituted by combining one or more than one attributes. This type of primary key is called **concatenated key**. For example, consider the following table:

LIBRARY BRANCH: [*LibName + BName* (concatenated key), *BAddress* (non-primary key – descriptive attribute).

(***Note***: A branch of a particular library, out of many libraries, can only be identified by the attributes *LibName* (Library Name) and *BName* (Branch Name); as such combination of two attributes is chosen as primary key. Such a key is referred to a *concatenated key*.)

1. A Relation or Table must have fixed format. This implies that a relation representing an entity type must have a specific number of attributes (i.e. a row or tuple must be made up of fixed number of columns or fields).
2. A Relation or Table must be homogeneous; that is, all the rows or tuples in the table be of same kind. However, no two rows or tuples may have identical data. This is because row or tuple represent fact or data about distinct set of entities instances of entities. Identical tuples or rows (i.e., having identical data) shall imply redundancy.
3. All values of attributes in a tuple, row or record should be elementary; that is, they need no further division or splitting. Further, each entry in the table must be single-valued; no repeating group are allowed.

4.5.2 Normalization of Relations

In the relational model, normalisation of relations is a process of applying progressive transforming to achieve intended normal form. At the out set the initial conceptual design (ER model) is converted into a set of relations or relational tables in *First Normal From (1NF)* by assigning a unique key to each entity-type and removing repeating groups (multivalued attributes) from the relation by splitting each into two or more attributes whose data values are atomic. First normal form is essentially just description of basic table. The set of relational tables in 1NF may be changed into set of tables in **Second Normal Form (2NF)** by removing partial *functional dependencies* within relations (tables). This is again accomplished by splitting of these dependencies into new separate relations (tables). In the 2NF a table must be in 1NF, and have all non-key attributes/ columns/fields fully functionally dependent on the primary key. (A non- key attribute is one that does not form part of the primary key, such as <u>CallNo, MemNo,</u> or <u>CallNo</u> + <u>MemNo</u>. If need be, the set of tables in 2NF may be converted into a new set of relations (tables) in **Third Normal Form (3NF)** by eliminating transitive dependencies. To be in 3NF a table must be in 2NF (and hence first), and all non-key attributes/columns/fields have to be non-transitively dependent on the primary key. If one finds there exist dependencies for which the determinant is neither the key nor an alternative key then the tables may be converted into set of table in **Boyce-Code Normal Form (BCNF).** By removing multiple, multi-valued dependencies relations tables can further be changed to **Forth Normal Form (4NF)** and so on. **5NF** is known as Project-Join/ Normal Form (PJ/NF). and last one the **Domain Key/Normal** (DK/ NF). Tables are changed from one normal form to another for purpose of improving the relational database design. The goal being, given a conceptual design for a system, translate the design into a set of relations (tables) in which data duplication is *minimized*, and in which certain problems associated with the maintenance of tables are eliminated; that is, these tables have reasonable properties with respect to data management.

4.5.3 Functional Dependence between Attributes

Within one relation or table we consider a set of attributes which defines the entity-type, a particular attribute representing the specific facet or fact about the entity-type with which we may be concerned in a given context. For instance, a person can be member of a library, at the same time a staff member. In case, we are involved in defining staff database then we are only concerned with a particular person, who is a staff-member not do consider his other facet or the capacity, such as his being user of the library, if he is one. Further, each row or tuple of a table represents data for an instance of entity, object, or event and constitutes of two parts - *the ruling part attribute(s)*, and the attributes which provide data regarding the particular entity, object, or event - *the dependent part*.

Consider the relation USER as shown below:

USER (*Relation/Entity-type*): [***MembershipNumber (MemNo)*** (*Primary* or *key attribute*), *Name, Address, PhoneNumber* (*non-key descriptive attributes*)]

While creating database records of relation (entity type) USER, each row or tuple in the USER table represent data for individual library user and for a given particular value for *MembershipNo*, the value of the borrower's *Name, Address*, and/or *PhoneNumber* is automatically determined. For example, specifying **'M1'** as a member's identification number one automatically determines the value for the *Name* attribute, the value for *Address* attribute, and/or the value for *PhoneNo* attribute of the concerned library user or member. In this context, we can say that the attributes *Name, Address*, and *PhoneNo* are functionally dependent upon on attribute *MemNo.* Because given a particular value of the attribute *Membership Number*, there exists precisely one corresponding value for each the attribute; *Name, Address* and *PhoneNo.* As such, we can define the concept ***functional dependency*** in following terms:

> "An attribute **B** is said to be **functionally dependent** n the attribute **A** if the value of attribute **A** always determines the value of the attribute **B.**"

These dependencies are shown symbolically as follows:

MembershipNo → Name

MembershipNo → Name, Address, and Phone Number

Or A → B

The symbolic representation A à B is read as: **A** is determinant of **B**; or B is *functionally dependent* on **A**. This symbolic representation can also be read as: **A** *identifies* **B** or if value of **A** is known the value of **B** can be determined. The statement MEM-NO à *Name, Address, PhoneNo* can be similarly interpreted.

A functional dependency may involve more than two attributes. As an example, consider the relation MONGRAPH, given below, in which the primary key is concatenation of two attributes *ClassNo* + *BookNo* and we note that the non-primary key attributes *Author* and/or *Title* are *fully* dependent on the group of attributes (or concatenation of two attributes) namely — (*ClassNo* + *BookNo*). Because of the fact that only knowing the value of *ClassNo* and

BookNo we can determine the value of non-key attribute. All non-key attributes refer to the entire concatenated key and there is no non-key attribute that is dependent on only a subset of the concatenated key. For instance we can not determine the exact value of the attribute *Author* of a particular tuple (bibliographic item) by using the value of the attribute *Class-No/Subject* only; that is to say *ClassNo/Subject* à *Author* (i.e., Class_No à determines Author) in not true; as two authors may have written books on the same subject. Similarly two or more BIBLIOGRAPHIC ITEMS or MONOGRAPHS may have same *Title (*at least each volume of a multi-volume books have same title). Further, libraries, quite often, have more than one copy of a document.

> **MONOGRAPH** (Relation): [(***ClassNo*** + ***BookNo***) (*Concatenated Key Attribute* – Identifier). *Author1* (*Attribute*), *Author2* (Attribute), *Author3* (Attribute), *Title* (*Attribute*), *PublishedBy* (i.e., The Name of the Publisher (*Attribute*), *PlaceOfPublication* (*Attribute*)

Further, in the above RELATION, we find the attribute *PlaceOfPublication* does not dependent on the primary key attribute directly, in the sense that *Place* is primarily dependent on the attribute *PublishedBy*, which in turn is functionally dependent on *ClassNo* + *BookNo* (key attribute). This type of dependency is referred to as **transitive dependency**.

4.6 Schema Mapping from the Conceptual Model of the Document-Loan System to the Relational Model

4.6.1 Introduction

The representation of the entity types identified in the conceptual model (ER-model) into relational model results into a set of relation definitions, in which each relation is defined having a primary key and a set of non key attributes. Further, we cannot use external identifiers (links) in relation model; we transform them into internal identifier or key of a relation. Each defined relation corresponds to either entities or relationship and must be in normal form.

For each entity type identified in ER model, we create a relation that includes all the simple attribute of the entity, and only simple attributes of composite attribute are selected. On attribute simple or concatenated attribute is chosen as primary key.

In relational model, the composite and multivalued attributes are modelled in terms of simple, single-valued attributes. We can handle the composite attributes in two ways: (i) all the constituents of this attribute are considered as an individual attributes, or (ii) the entire attribute is considered as a single attribute. For example, let us take the case of composite attribute *address* of the entity type PERSON, LIBRARY MEMBER or INSTITUTION, this attribute constitutes of the following distinct components or data elements, *Building; Street/ Locality; Village/Town/City/; Tehsil; District; Region; State; Country; Postal Code.* In this case have two alternatives available to us: (i) either treat the entire composite attribute *address* as a single attribute having no as distinct components, in this case components lose identity; or (ii) treat all its constituent components or data elements as an individual attributes of the entity PERSON, LIBRARY MEMBER or INSTITUTION.

Multivalued attributes requires new entities/relations to be introduces, in which it can be represented as a single valued attribute, so that each multivalued attribute can be represented as single valued attribute of a particular entity/relation. The new entity/relation is comprised of the multivalued attribute plus the primary attribute of original entity. Alternatively the components of a multivalued attribute can divided treated as individual single-valued attributes. Let take the example of the attribute *NameOfAuthor* of the entity BIBLIOGRAPHIC ITEM→MONGRAPH or ARTICLE. We know that one or more persons can be authors of BIBLIOGRAPHIC ITEM → MONGRAPH or ARTICLE. In this case the attribute *NameOfAuthor* is an multivalued attribute, and the name each author can be considered as an individual attribute and defined the entity BIBLIOGRAPHIC ITEM → MONGRAPH or ARTICLE possessing attributes namely, *NameOfAuthor1, NameOfAuthor2; NameOfAuthor3,* and so forth.

For each week entity identified in the ER model associated with an owner entity, create a relation of the week entity by including all simple attributes, and simple components of composite attributes, as attributes the relation In addition include primary key (s) of the owner relation (s) that correspond to the owner entity type(s). The primary key of relation (of week entity) is the combination of the primary key (s) of the owner relation (s) and an attribute of the week entity treated as key (this key is called partial key of the relation).

Rules for Conversion of One-to-One, One-to-Many, Many-to-Many other types Relationships between Entities from ER Model to Relational Model.

Conversion of One-to-One, One-to-Many, and Many-to-Many relationships between entities are handled, either collapsing them into one relation (table) or defining separate relationship relation. One has also to consider whether two entities have total participation in the relationship; or one or both have partial participation in the. In principle, if the two entities A and B participating in the relationship results in separate relations, however this is not always true. For example, in a One-to-One relationship, a record in Relation / Table A can have only one matching record in the corresponding Relation B and a record in Table B can have one only matching record in Table A. As such, in case of One-to-One relationship, if the participation of both the entities in the relationship is total or partial, both the entities are collapsed into one relation by combining all the attribute of both entities, including primary keys of one (if the keys are same), or both (if the keys are distinct). 1:1 and 1:M relationship type of ER model are transformed into single relation with merger of all keys

Conversion of One-to-Many relation between entity types A and B is accounted for by including the primary key of entity type A in the relation corresponding to entity type B as a simple attribute (or attributes). The primary key in B is external identifier (foreign key). However if the entity B at many side has partial participation in the relationship and there is possibility of having null value in the external identifier (foreign key), a better alternative is to set third relation called relationship relation (Refer relation 3 below)

Many-to-Many relations require defining of separate relations. In a many-to-many relationship, a record in Table A can have many matching records in Table B, and a record in Table B can have many matching records in Table A. This type of relationship is only possible by defining a third new relation or table (called a junction table) whose primary key consists of two fields — the foreign keys from both Tables A and B. Let us consider a many-to-many relation EnroledIn between the entities STUDENT and COURSE. We create the two relations or tables for the two entities STUDENT and COURSE add to it another table ENROLLED_IN, which has primary key the pair (STUDENT_ID-COURSE_ID). In this junction table, the primary key fields function as foreign keys. You can add other fields to the junction table, just as you can to any other table. In the junction table, set the primary key to include the primary key fields from the other two tables.

Other remaining two types of relation are: (i) n-ary (n > 2) relationships and recursive relationship. N-ary relationships follow the same rule to convert ER model to relation model as Many-To-Many binary relationships: the relation inherit all the identifier (primary attributes) of n entities (which form the key of the new relation. A recursive relationship or looped relationship from entity A to itself is modelled as a new relation including two attributes; they both correspond to the primary key of entity A, and the names of two roles of entity A. In figure the recursive or looped relationship Manages is mapped to a relation MANAGER_OF, whose attributes are [<u>*EmployeeId*</u> + <u>*SubordinateId*</u> (*Primary* or *key attribute*), *NameOfManager* (*non-key descriptive attribute*), *NameOfSubordinate* (*non-key descriptive attribute*.).

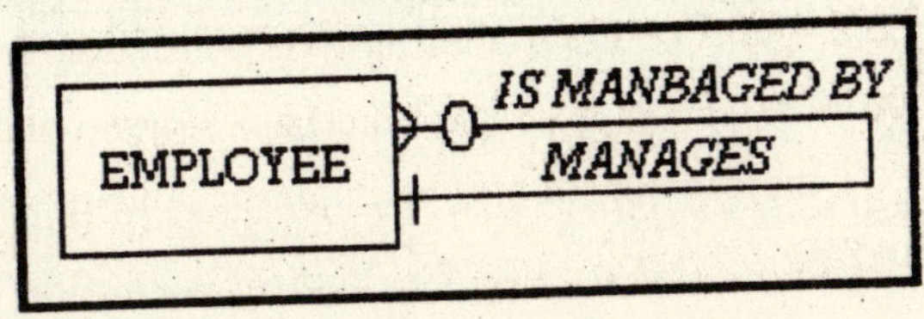

4.7 Relation: Employee

If Many-to-Many Relationship then

1. **R1:EMPLOYEE** [<u>*EmployeeId*</u> (Primary or key attribute), *EmployeeName* (Non-key descriptive attribute), *DateOfBirth* (Non-key descriptive attribute), and so forth].

OR

1. **R1: EMPLOYEE** [<u>*EmployeeId*</u> (Primary or key attribute), *EmployeeLastTName* (Non-key descriptive attribute), *EmployeeFirstName* (Non-key descriptive attribute), *DateofBirth* (Non-key descriptive attribute), and so forth.]
2. **R2:MANAGER_OF** [<u>*EmployeeId*</u>+<u>*SubordinateId*</u>(Primary or key attribute), *NameOfManager* (Non-key descriptive attribute), *NameOfSubordinate* (Non-key descriptive attribute)].

If One-to-Many Relationship then

1. **R1:EMPLOYEE** [*EmployeeId* (Primary or key attribute), *EmployeeLastTName,* (Non-key descriptive attribute), *EmployeeFirstName* (Non-key descriptive attribute), *DateofBirth* (Non-key descriptive attribute), and so forth.].
2. **R2: MANAGER_OF** [<u>*SubordinateId*</u> (Primary or key attribute), *NameOfSubordinate* (Non-key descriptive attribute), *NameOfManager* (Non-key descriptive attribute)].

4.7.1 Transformed Relation Schemas of Illustrative Document Loan System.

RELATION 1: USER

USER: [<u>*MembershipNo*</u> *(Primary or key attribute), NameOfUser* (Non-key descriptive attributes), *Address* (Non-key descriptive attribute), *Phone Number* (Non-key descriptive attribute)].

RELATION 2: BIBLIOGRAPHIC ITEM

BIBLIOGRAPHIC ITEM: [<u>*CallNumber*</u> (Primary or key attribute) ; *PrincipleAuthor* (Non-key descriptive attribute); *Title*

(Non-key descriptive attribute); *Edition* (Non-key descriptive attribute); *VolumeNumber* (Non-key descriptive attribute); *IssueNumber* (Non-key descriptive attribute); *Publisher* (Non-key descriptive attribute); *PlaceOfPublication* (non-key descriptive attribute); *AccessionNumber* (Non-key descriptive attribute). (The list of attributes is not exhaustive)]

(***Note***: Author of a book when treated as an attribute, constitutes a *multivalued attribute*. The reason being that more than one author may be associated in writing a bibliographic item, particularly a monograph or an article. In relational database, multivalued attributes require introducing new entities; each multivalued attribute requires an entity in which it can be represented as single-valued attribute. Alternatively, a multivalued attribute is to decompose into a set of single valued attributes such ***Author1, Author2, Author3***, and so on. In first case we, can resolve the problem by treating AUTHOR as an entity or relation, which we are not considering here. We have also not followed second alternative and have resolved the problem by following AACR rule for the choice of author of a publication. However, most of the time the result this decision may not prove very effective or user friendly.

RELATION 3: BIBLIOGRAPHIC ITEM_ON_LOAN

BIBLIOGRAPHIC ITEM_On_LOAN: [*<u>CallNumber</u>* (Primary key), *MembershipNo* (Descriptive attribute – Foriegn Key), *Title (Descriptive attribute), DueDate* (Descriptive attribute), *MemName* (Descriptive attribute), etc.]

Note: This relation schema is defined to represent the one-to-many relationship: BIBLIOGRAPHIC ITEM **BorrowedBy/LoanedTo** LIBRARY USER, between the entities BIBLIOGRAPHIC ITEM and LIBRARY USER. The relationship between the entity LIBRARY USER and BIBLIOGRAPHIC ITEM is of ONE-to-MANY type. In this case both the entities are related in partial relationship – *zero, one or many* type, as a book may be on loan or may be on loan to a library user. To avoid the null values and to represent entities as well as the relationship we created the relation **BIBLIOGRAPHICITEM_ON_LOAN,** *by* including the foreign key attribute, *MembershipNumber* of the relation LIBRARY USER in addition to primary attribute *<u>CallNumber</u>* of the relation

BIBLIGRAPHIC ITEM, and other pertinent non-primary attributes from both the relations. This relation or table is formed by as joint operation and enables us to identify the items due from the users, or to identify a user to whom a particular item is issued at given point in time, from the tuples of this relation that contains value of <u>CallNo</u> and *MemNo*, along with other descriptive attributes of the particular overdue item.

Further, both the tables BIBLOGRAPHIC ITEM and LOANED_ BIBLIOGRAPHIC ITEM describe bibliographic items. The LOANED_ BIBLIOGRAPHIC ITEM contains a subset of all bibliographic items – those loaned out or borrowed by users. In this case the set of call numbers in the tuples of BIBLIOGRAPHIC ITEM_On_LOAN relation is always included in set of call numbers in the tuples of BIBLOGRAPHIC ITEM relation. This reference relationship constraint between two relations is called an **inclusion dependency** of <u>*CallNumber*</u> in BIBLIOGRAPHIC ITEM_On_LOAN on <u>*CallNumber*</u> in BIBLOGRAPHIC ITEM.

RELATION 4: OVERDUE_BIBLIOGRAPHIC_ ITEM

OVERDUE_ BIBLIOGRAPHIC ITEM: [<u>*CallNo*</u> + <u>*MembershipNo*</u> (Primary or key attribute), *Author* (Descriptive attributes), *Title* (Descriptive attribute), *OverdueDate* (Descriptive attribute), *MemberName* (Descriptive attribute), etc.]

Note: *The relationship between the entities LBRARY USER and OVERDUE_ BIBLIOGRAPHIC_ITEM and is of type Many-to-Many, as many library members may have one or more overdue bibliographic items with them. As such we created a new relation OVER DUE BIBLIOGRAPHIC ITEM having primary key that is formed by combining primary keys of both the relations LIBRARY USER and LOANED_BIBLIOGRAPHIC ITEM and, and adding to it pertinent non key attributes of the relations. In this case <u>CallNo</u> + <u>MembershipNo</u> are the primary key of the relation formed by combining the primary keys of the BIBLIOGRAPHY ITEM and LBRARY USER having one-to-many relationship: BIBLIOGRAPHIC ITEM **BorrowedBy/LoanedTo** LIBRARY USER.*

* We now look at the process of creating or modelling a one-to-many join table.

- We decide we need a table that contains information about two entities LIBRARY MEMBER and OVERDUE BIBLIOGRAPHIC ITEM.
- The relation between these entities is One-to-Many relationship. That is, a library member may posses zero, one or more bibliographic items overdue items with him.
- Thus, we create one table, each for entity type (class) - LIBRARY MEMBER and OVERDUE BIBLIOGRAPHIC ITEM. Each of this table will be assigned a primary key – *MemNo* and *CallNo* + *OverdueDate*, respectively.
- In order to make this relationship possible, we will need a ***foreign key*** in table which is at the 'many' side of relationship – in this case OVERDUE BIBLIOGRAPHIC ITEM (a subset of bibliographic item-on-loan table).
- Therefore, we add the key *MemNo* to the table OVERDUE BIBLIOGRAPHIC ITEM.

4.8 Physical Database Design of a Relational Database

4.8.1. Data-Definition

The data definition implies that the physical characteristics or data type of each attribute, data element or fields of each of the entity-type or relation specified in the relational schema must be described. The **data type** is the characteristics of a field that determine what type of data it can hold. Data types include. ***Integer, Fraction, String (Character Type), Length of Each Field, Long, Single, Double, Boolean, Date, Currency, and Variant.*** We must also specify whether the particular field is vital/essential or elective/optional, and repeating or non-repeating. The physical characteristics or data types of the attributes/data elements/fields pertaining to each of the above listed entity-types or relations are listed in the following tables:

RELATION (Entity Type): BIBLIOGRAPHIC ITEM - MONOGRAPH

Attribute	*Key Attribute or Non Primary Attribute*	*Field Name*	*Data Type*	*Length (No of Characters)*	*Mandatory or Non Mandatory (M/NM)*	*Constraints*
Class number	Key Attribute (Part 1)	*ClassNo*	Alpha-n	60	M	Coded by Colon Classification Scheme. Edition. 7
Book Number	Key Attribute (Part 2)	*BookNo*	Alpha-n	15	M	Coded by CC Book Numbering System.
Collection No	Key Attribute (Part 3)	*CollNo*	Alpha-n	10	M	Local Code
Heading		*Heading*	Alpha-n		M	Rendered as per CCC (Ed 5) Rules
Title Statement	Non-Key Attribute	*Title*	Alpha-n	150	M	
Edition	Non-Key Attribute	*Ed*	Alpha-n	20	M	If Ist. edition then Null Value
Volume	Non-Key Attribute	Vol	Alpha-n	8	M	Null Value Possible
Publication Date	Non-Key Attribute	*PubDate*	Date	15	M	
Publisher	Non-Key Attribute	*Pub*	Alpha-n	150	M	
Place of Publication	Non-Key Attribute	*Place*	Alpha-n	15	M	
Series	Non-Key Attribute	*Series*	Alpha-n	100	M	Null Value Possible
Imprint	Non-Key Attribute	*Imprint*	Alpha-n	20	M	

RELATION (Entity Type): LIBRARY MEMBER/USER

Attribute	*Key Attribute or Non Primary Attribute*	*Field Name*	*Data Type*	*Length (No of Characters)*	*Mandatory or Non Mandatory (M/NM)*	*Constraints*
Membership Number	Key	***MemNo***	Character String	8	M	Coded Form
Name of Member	Non Key	MemName	Character String	80	M	
Address	Non Key	Address	Character String	200	M	
Email Address	Non Key	EMail	Character String	20	M	If available
Phone (Residence)	Non Key	Phone(R)	N	12	M	If available
Phone (Office)	Non Key	Phone(O)	N	12	M	If available

RELATION (Entity Type): BIBLIOGRAPHIC ITEM-On-LOAN

Attribute	*Key Attribute or Non Primary Attribute*	*Field Name*	*Data Type*	*Length (No of Characters)*	*Mandatory or Non Mandatory (M/NM)*	*Constraints*
Class number	Key Attribute (Part 1)	ClassNo	Alpha-n	60	M	Coded by Colon Classification Scheme. Edition. 7
Book Number	Key Attribute (Part 2)	BookNo	Alpha-n	15	M	Coded by CC Book Numbering System.
Collection No	Key Attribute (Part 3)	CollNo	Alpha-n	10	M	Local Code
Membership No	Key Attribute (Part 4) – Foreign Key	MemNo	Alpha-n	8	M	Local Code
Due Date	Non-Key Attribute	DueDate	Date	15	M	
Heading		Heading	Alpha-n	100	M	Rendered as per CCC (Ed 5) Rules
Title Statement	Non-Key Attribute	Title	Alpha-n	150	M	
Edition	Non-Key Attribute	Ed	Alpha-n	20	M	If Ist. edition then Null Value
Volume, Part No	Non-Key Attribute	Vol	Alpha-n	10	M	Null Value Possible
Publication Date	Non-Key Attribute	PubDate	Date	20	M	
Name of Member	Non Key	MemName	Character String	80	M	
Address	Non Key	Address	Character String	200	M	
Email Address	Non Key	EMail	Character String	20	M	If available
Phone (Residence)	Non Key	Phone(R)	N	12	M	If available
Phone (Office)	Non Key	Phone(O)	N	12	M	If available

BIBLIOGRAPHICAL REFERENCES

1. Ansi/X3/Sparc, Database Management System Study Group. *Interim Report*. American National Standards Institute, Washington, D.C. 1975.
2. Bachman, C. W. Data Structure Diagrams. *Database,* 1(2); 1969.
3. Batini Carlo, Ceri Stefano, and Navthe, Shamkant B. *Conceptual Database Design: an Entity-Relationship Approach.* Benjamin/Cumming Publishing Company Inc., Redwood city, California. 1992.
4. Casanovo, M. A. Mapping Uninterrupted Schemes in Entity-Relationship Diagrams: Two Applications to Conceptual Schema Design. *IBM Journal of Research and Development*., 28; 1984; p. 82-94.
5. Chen, Peter Pin-Sen. The Entity Relationship Model - Towards A Unified View of Data. *ACM Trans on Database*. 1(1); 1976; p. 9-36.
6. —. **Ed.** *Entity-Relationship Approach to Information Modeling and Analysis*. North-Holland, Amsterdam. 1983.
7. Codd, E. F. A Relational Model of Data for Large Shared Databanks. *Communication of the ACM*, 13(6); 1970; p. 377-87.
8. —. Extending. The Database Relational Model to Capture More Meaning. *ACM Trans on Database Systems*, 4(4); 1979; p. 397-434.
9. —. Relational Database: A Practical Foundation for Productivity. *Communication of the ACM*, 25(2); 1982; p. 109-17.
10. —. Is your DBMS is Really Relational and Your DBMS run by the rules. *Computer World*., Oct 14 & Oct 21, 1985.
11. —. *The relational model for Database Management—Version 2*. Addison-Wisely, 1990
12. Date, C. J. *An Introduction to Database Systems*. Ed 3. V 1. (Indian Student Edition). Norsha Publishing House, Delhi, 1986.
13. —. *An Introduction to Database Systems*. Ed 5. Addition-Wisely, 1986.
14. Dean, S. M. *Principles and Practice of Database System*, 1985.
15. Fagin, R. Normal Form and Relational Database Operators. *Proceedings of the ACM Sigmod International Conference on Management of Data.* 1979, p. 153-60.
16. —. A Normal Form for Relational Databases That is based on Domains and Keys. *ACM Transactions on Database Systems,* 6(3); 1983; p. 387-415.
17. Elmasri, Ramez and Navathe, Shamkant B. *Fundamentals of Database Systems.* 1994. Second Edition, Benjamin/Cumming, Redwood City, CA, 1994.
18. Frank, Lars. *Database Theory and Practice*. 1984, p. 162.

19. Hughes, John G. *Database Technology: A Software Engineering Approach.*, 1988, p. 17.

20. Kashyap, M. M. Data Processing and Computer Application in Library. *Journal of Library and Information Science,* 7; 1982; p. 61-83.

21. Korth, Henry F. and Silberschatz, Abraham. *Database System Concept.* McGraw-Hill, New York, 1986.

22. Lusk, E. L., and others. A Practical Design Methodology for the Implementation of Ms Database, Using Entity-Relationship Model. *Proceedings of the ACM Sigmod International Conference on Management of Data,* 1986, p. 9-21.

23. Litton, Gerry. M. *Introduction to Database Management Systems: A Practical Approach.* W C Brown, Ubuque, Iowa, 1987.

24. Lusk, E. L., and Others. A Practical Design Methodology for the Implementation of Ms Database, Using Entity-Relationship Model. *Proceedings of the ACM Sigmod International Conference on Management of Data.* 1980, p. 9-21.

25. Maier, D. *The Theory of Relational Databases.* Computer Science Press, Rockville, Maryland, 1983.

26. Martin, James. *Computer Database Organisation.* Ed 2. (Eastern Economy Edition). Prentice-Hall, 1975.

27. Oxborrow, E. *Database and Database System,* 1986.

28. Teorey, T. J., and others. Logical Design Methodology for Relational Database. *Computing Survey,* 18(2); 1986.

29. Tsichriztis, D. C. and Klug, A, **Ed.** The Ansi/X3/Sparc DBMS Framework: Report of the Study Group on the Database Management Systems. *Information System,* 3; 1978.

30. Wang, S. Normal Entity- Relationship Model - A New Method to Design Enterprise Schema. *Proceedings of the IEEE International Conference on Computer Applications,* 1984.

J
Decision Tables

1 INTRODUCTION

Every organisation is involved in varied and complicated patterns of decisions. From broad decisions about the mission and objectives of the organisation to more specific decisions about day-to-day operations of the organisation.

Decision-making is the basic process to carry out the key functions necessary for managing an organisation — namely, planning, organising, staffing, directing, co-ordinating, and controlling. All these functions involve decision-making. *Planning*, for example, is in itself a decision making process. It is the process of deciding in advance: What is to be done? Who is to do it? When it is to be done? Moreover, how it is to be done? It provides a framework to decide about future actions. Similarly, in *organising* we have to decide which activities should be grouped to constitute a sub-unit of an organisation, who should be its in-charge, and what authority should be vested in him/her. *Staffing* involves deciding whom to employ or to promote. Co-ordinating implies taking such decision and actions that harmonize all the activities of an enterprise to simplify its working, and its success. *Control* implies observation and measurement of performance of the staff, to see whether the set objectives, plans, and procedures of an institution are being achieved and complied with. If not, decisions about what actions need to be taken to improve the situations.

While performing these functions, a manager has to face decision-making problems of one sort or the other. Consequently, *information* scientists consider decision-making as the most vital and central activity of managers. **Herbert A Simon**, an eminent *system* theorist has even expressed that "decision making is synonymous with managing" [16].

Today libraries are growing in an environment quite different from that which prevailed twenty or thirty years ago. With the rapid growth of literature and *multimedia* in recent times, the collection and the staff to manage it in libraries have increased. The demand for varied, effective and efficient services has grown; with the result there is a growing trend to introduce *information* technology for rapid processing of bibliographic data and providing quicker *information* services to library users. This pace of rapid growth and ever increasing application of *information* technology in libraries and *information* centres has made the job of librarians more complex and challenging. It seems reasonable to predict that modern librarians cannot function effectively without a solid foundation in decision-making skill. Today we need library managers who possess a combination of intelligence, professional competence, vision, and perseverance enabling them to handle varied simple to complex decision-making situations effectively. They are not only expected to possess the skill to find the right decision in a given situation but also the talent to persuade others to accept it. Viewed from this perspective, we explain the scientific approach to decision making.

2 TYPES OF DECISIONS

In every human organisation, be it a library system, an *information* organisation, a business enterprise, or a hospital, managers (decision makers) at all level decide what is to be doneand how. They employ programmed and non-programmed strategies in response to the problems they face. A programmed strategy is used when the manager can solve a problem by the application of a rule, program, routine or procedure that has been previously used to solve such a problem.

Programmable Decisions

The decisions that people make in response to repetitive and routine problems are called programmed decisions. According to **Simon** "decisions are programmed to the extent they are repetitive and routine, to the extent that a definite procedure has been worked out for handling them so that they do not have to be treated *de novo* each time they occur" [**Simon**, 17]. Such decisions have also been described as "completely specified." [**Bradford**, 1]

Programmable decisions are also called **structured decisions** because the standard policies or guidelines to execute such decisions are already established. An example of a programmable decision is whether to give a serial on-loan to a certain category of user. The standard policy or guideline to execute this decision can be pre-determinated. In fact, all the procedures, processes or operations that are repetitive and routine in nature having well-defined parameters, fall in this category. Examples of such procedure are: documents charging and discharging process, bill payment system, inventory control system, etc.

The decision situations involved in this category of procedures and processes are simple and can be solved by the straightforward application of decision-making process. To carry out the repetitive decisions their decision logic can be totally defined and described clearly as a '**decision table**'. This enables the staff to carry out decisions easily and effectively on a routine and involuntary basis.

In an organisation, the execution of programmed decisions is usually entrusted to subordinates, and they follow the instructions given to them by the managers very meticulously. The directives or guidelines either for making appropriate decisions, or choosing specific course of action, or the way in which decisions have to be carried out by the staff in certain situations, are generally given to them either orally or in narrative form.

Oral instructions and narrative forms have their drawbacks. One is likely to misunderstand or partly forget oral instructions. In the narrative forms, very often, it is difficult to organise the directions in a concise and logical way. As a result, it becomes difficult to interpret what is communicated.

The use of computers for handling clerical and other operations has caused the necessity of presenting complex decision logic in such a way so that it is easy to express, comprehend and is used by others. Computerisation of operations or systems demands that their relevant procedures involving decision situations (or conditions) and rules for taking specific action or set of actions in a given situation, are explained in such a way such that it becomes easy to grasp the system's logic and develop computer programs.

System analysts and computer programmers use graphic techniques besides narrative form to clarify the logic of the procedures they seek to automate. One is called *logicalor decisions flow-charting technique* and other *decision tables*. Both the graphic techniques have been valuable aids in understanding, describing and improving manual and automated procedures.

A decision table is used to express complex decision logic in a tabular form. This tabular approach helps system analysts and computer specialists to reduce complex decision logic or a procedure to its simplest form, by arranging and presenting logically alternative course(s) of action to be taken under various conditions, as a decision table. A decision table defines all conditions (the prerequisite for an action) and separates them from all actions. Further, it relates given conditions to the appropriate actions, with some columns of entries that forms the rules. Any alternative condition that results in other actions constitutes other rules written side by side. Tables may be produced in limited, extended or mixed entry form.

We find that "a flow chart is time ordered and decision table is simultaneous presentation. As a result a decision table is more compact and more flexible with respect to a permissible course of action, while a flow chart is less compact and more rigid." [**Hartman**, 7] Further, it is more convenient and suitable than the logical flow chart to develop and display the decision algorithm of a program or procedure with the aid of a computer program. A decision table can be used independently or to complement a flow chart to express a complex decision logic graphically.

The basic ideas of decision tables and most of the conventions for developing decision tables in system analysis, procedure design, and documentation are discussed in the next part.

Non-programmable Decisions

Decisions are termed **non-programmed** or **unstructured decisions** when they are made for uncommon and unstructured problems. When a problem has not arisen earlier or in the same manner before, or is complex and important that requires a non-programmed decision-making strategy. Non-programmed strategies are creative responses to unstructured problems that cannot be solved by set rules, guidelines or routines.

"Decisions are non-programmed to the extent they are novel, unstructured, and consequential. There are no cut and dry method of handling the problem because it has not arisen before, or because its precise nature and structure are elusive or complex, or because it is so important that it deserves custom-tailored treatment" [**Simon**, 18]. This type of decision has also been called "*ill-structured*" [**Simon**, 19] or "non-specifiable." [**Bradford**, 2]

Decision processes of such decisions cannot be specified in advance for future uses. Decision-makers resolve each problem every time, based on intuition, experience, judgement, and two different decision-makers may reach two different conclusions or solutions. Making such a decision is very challenging and a highly creative process. Examples of such decisions are those regarding computerisation of library services, library co-operation and networking, and expansion.

Levels of Decision-Making

Decisions are also categorised as:

* Operational
* Tactical, and
* Strategic level decisions.

Operational decision

Operational decisions pertain to executing specific routine tasks and assuring that they are carried out efficiently and effectively. Primarily lower-level managers or supervisory staff make these decisions. Policies and standard practices are pre-set for operational decisions. Supervisors or low-level managers are expected to make operational level decision, and these are the decisions that keep the day-today operations in line with predetermined standards or normal practices. Examples of operational decision making situations are accepting or rejecting supply of equipment, assigning jobs to staff, sending reminders for overdue supply, and so on.

Tactical decision

Tactical decision-making pertains to short-term administrative operational activities and carrying out the decisions made at strategic level, including allocating resources to pursue organisational objectives. The tactical decision-making is generally involved in areas, such as formulation of budget, allocation of budget, and personnel problems.

Strategic decision

Strategic decision-making involves establishing objectives for the organisation and making long-range plans for attaining these objectives. Strategic decisions are future-oriented and characterised by a great deal of uncertainty. Strategic decisions are concerned with future development, policymaking, and attaining total effectiveness for the organisation.

3 PROCESS OF DECISION-MAKING

Developing Decision-Making Skill

Good decision-making constitutes an essential and indispensable quality of a capable manager. A successful decision-maker is one who makes right decisions, has courage to take the (harsh) but appropriate decisions and ability to get them accepted and implemented by the staff willingly.

The effectiveness and value of a manager's decision largely depend on his/her mental and analytical ability. One can get these decision-making capabilities and skills through education, training, and experience. Too often, people assume that decision-making qualities in a manager are innate and they cannot be learnt. However, the belief that a good decision-maker is born and not made is not absolutely true. A good decision-maker is born "when a man with some natural endowment (intelligence and some capacity for interacting with his fellow men) by dint of practice, learning and experience develops his endowment into a mature skill." [5].

Decision-Process Model

Considering that good decision-making involve both applications of empirical methods of science and intuitive judgement by decision-makers, some authors have made efforts to develop the science of decision making in the discipline of management science.

The credit of developing first decision-process model goes to **Herbert A Simon** [16] He divided the process of decision-making into the following three phases:

1. Intelligence (detection) activity phase.

During this phase the environment inside and outside the organisation is scrutinised for conditions (problems or opportunities) requiring decisions and information is gathered concerning those conditions. Simon representing the military meaning of intelligence (i.e., getting information or knowledge about the opponent forces or surroundings) uses the term "intelligence".

2. Design activity phase.

During this phase, one identifies the possible courses of action, specifies and analyses them to find their relative value as solutions to resolve the decision problems.

3. Choice activity phase

This phase involves selecting a satisfactory course of action from those identified. Decisions are the mechanisms by which a decision-maker or manager seeks to achieve some desired state. Often managers go through several stages of reassessment or analytical study that help them to think through the problem, develop alternative potential strategies or solutions to the problem, and selecting one deemed the most suitable.

Every decision is the outcome of a dynamic intellectual process influenced by multitude of conditions or variables. In simple terms decision can be defined as "a chosen course of actions selected out of all perceived or available alternatives by the decision maker based on some criteria and in the light of objective(s) or purpose(s) to be fulfilled" [**Kashyap**, 11]. One must differentiate between *decision as a process* from the *decision as a product*, which is a resolved action or a set of actions, chosen because of individual or collective deliberation or thought. In other words decision-making is process of thoughtful deliberation that results in a decision or a choice of a course of action that one needs to follow to achieve the set purpose, or objective. The process influences how good the decision is likely to be or how much effective will be the result of a decision, when carried out. [*Also refer to*, **Simon**, 16-20; **Brown**, 3; **Nutt**, 14].

Decision Making Activity

Decision-making activity is a cyclic process involving several rounds of deep analysis of the problem before you find a solution or solutions to the problem. It is a method of problem resolution (i.e., Solving a disagreeable or an undesirable situation, or finding an opportunity of carrying out a critical decision), constituting a series of interactive activities carried out by a decision-maker, to articulate and implement a satisfactory or most suitable decision in a given situation - may be to convert the present less desirable situation into a future situation, judged to be more desirable.

The decision process begins when a person perceives that there is a gap between what is and what should be in a given situation. He/she, then tries to conceive the problem in clear terms, puts forth efforts to find what needs to be done about it or what will be the best solution to overcome the problem. Thus, we can visualise the process of deciding as a decision system constituting of cyclic (interactive) activities or steps, as listed below:

1. Identification and crystallisation of a decision problem or situation.
2. Determination and formulation of goals (to be met by the decision) and environmental constraints.

3. Recognition and articulation of possible courses of actions — the search for alternative solutions.
4. Determination of outcome, value and utilities of each identified alternative solutions.
5. Establishment of criteria for evaluation of available alternatives and assessment of their outcomes as to costs and benefits.
6. Resolution of decision process — the act of choosing a satisfactory course of action.
7. Carrying out the selected course of action.
8. Re-appraisal and improvement of the executed course of action.

4 DECISION TABLE DESIGN

Purpose and Use of Decision Table

As described earlier, the purpose of a decision table is to provide information concerning a decision pattern in a concise tabular format, which is easy to read and understand. This tabular approach can be used not only to express the decision logic in its simplest form but it can also be of immense help in the analysis of a decision problem. The decision table preparation process forces the decision-maker to think through a problem logically. One can clearly point out relationships that exist between conditions affecting a decision and the consequent actions to be taken.

The decision table can be an effective instrument for communication between the librarian and computer programmer as it helps to clarify the logic of the procedures to be automated. This tabular representation of decision logic process is more effective than narrative approach because its statements are concise, explicit and show ordered arrangements of the procedure with nonessential information truncated.

Decision tables can be used "throughout the organisation to document all decision-making deemed worthy of documentation. This includes top-level policies, middle management directives and computer program routine or models." [**Fergus**, 2] In other words the decision table can be a valuable aid in describing, understanding and improving both manual, or automated library procedures, and related policies.

The decision table approach can be very useful in problem analysis and aid a library operation on a daily basis. For example, while cataloguing documents due to conflict in authorship or otherwise, many possibilities exist that influence the proper choice of heading and other access points. One needs to examine each possibility carefully to ensure that the cataloguing of documents is done consistently according to set rules, conform to existing practices and that future records will be consistent with the records prepared today. One needs to identify all the possible alternative choices relating to choice and rendering of heading identified and then prescribe entry rules as a decision table. Old and new staff can quickly and easily pick up the cataloguing procedure and conventions with the help of such a decision table or a set of decision tables. The use of a decision table by staff helps to bring consistency in the library catalogue despite frequent changes in the staff working in a cataloguing department.

Decision Table Structure

The decision table relates, in a matrix form, all the possible *conditions* (i.e., factors to be considered in making a decision) or combinations of conditions and the consequent actions, or series of *actions* or steps to be taken when certain combinations of conditions exists.

The main body of a decision table (Figure Chapter I-1) consists of four major sections divided by intersecting horizontal and vertical double lines. In addition there is a table heading section and note section.

The upper-left half of the table formed by double horizontal lines (called the *condition stub* or *area*) lists the *conditions*. The conditions are expressed or stated as questions. The upper-right half of the table (called the *condition entries' area)* lists all possible responses to the questions.

The lower-left half of the table (called as the *action stub* or *area*) lists all possible actions to be taken. The lower-right half of the table (called as *action entries' area*) indicates whether action is to be taken in the particular case.

The left half, formed by double vertical lines, is called *stub* and the right half *entries' section*. All the four sections are named: I - Condition Stub, II - Action Stub, III - Condition Entry Grid, IV - Action Entry Grid. The grids III and IV together comprise Rule Grid.

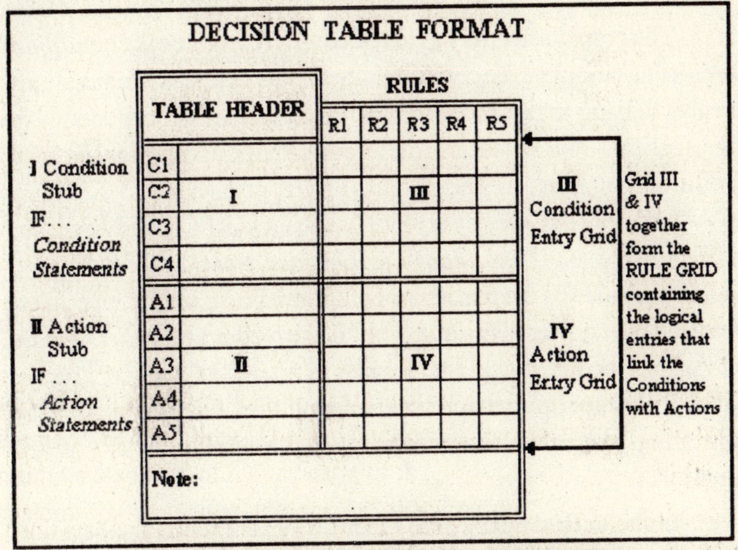

Figure I-1: An Example of Decision Table Format

In the **condition stub** (Section I) is listed all the ***conditions*** to be considered that might affect the decision outcome. The condition and action statements are logically formulated as: "**If** .... **Then** ...."; and, "If .A....and....B **then** X....Y....Z" statements. Such as: "**If** an employee comes late consecutively for three days **then** deduct his one day leave", "**If** the member is a teacher and document is serial **then** issue it for one week", and so on

The first part of the statement starting from *if up* to *then* is called ***condition statement*** (i.e. statements that introduces one or more conditions). These statements are written in the form: (IF)

Reader is a student; (IF) Documents is a periodical publication; (IF) Document is manuscript, etc.

(**Note:** *The term IF is not written in the table but implied*).

In the **action stub** (Section II) are listed all possible ***actions*** that may be taken to solve a decision problem. The actions' statements, which introduce one or more actions, are usually formulated as THEN statements and written in the form: (THEN) Issue the document for one week; (THEN) Issue the document for one month; (THEN) Do not issue the document, etc. (Note: The term THEN is not written in the table but is implied).

The **condition entry grid** (Section III) contains the ***condition entries*** that complete the condition statements. All possible situations or rules that are to be considered in reaching a decision are listed in this section. The rules are different situations applicable to a condition, such as - YES or NO, TRUE or FALSE, VALID or INVALID, ON or OFF, CORRECT or INCORRECT and so on; or, = (*Equal to*), < (*Less than*), > (*Greater than*). Alternatively, whichever rule fits the particular condition. For example, in a given situation the answer to the question 'Is the reader a teacher?' can be Yes or No; or the statement 'Reader is a teacher' can be True or False. Rules are unique and independent; they do not duplicate or contradict one other. Therefore, one rule applies in any given situation.

In the **action entry grid** (section IV) are listed the decision rules for the actions and sequence of actions to be followed when particular conditions are satisfied. Within a rule an '**and**' relationship exists between valid applicable conditions and actions. That is, for a rule to satisfy the first application condition *and* second application condition *and* the third applicable condition, and so on may exist. Similarly, every rule must have an action entry or set of actions associated with it. The actions to be taken are specified by **X** (*Cross Mark*). An action not to be taken is specified by a *dash* (-) or the column is left ***blank***. Any other wording may be used to complete the action statement.

The table is vertically divided into two sections. The left side forming of **Stubs** II and II) contains listing of conditions and actions. The right side forming the **rule grid** contains logical entries that link the condition to the action. That is, condition entry section and action entry section taken together form a **rule grid**, showing a specific combination of conditions and the actions to be taken under those conditions. Rules simply show that under a given condition or set of conditions, specific action or set of actions must be taken. In other words, the conditions and actions are linked through rules and within a rule.

The entire condition statement is written in the stub, in such a way, that it must be either True (T) or False (F). Consequently, the entries are limited to Y's (or T's); N's (or F's); or blanks. Similarly, each action is completely described in the stub. It is either to be executed or not to be executed. Consequently, the entries are limited to X's or blanks relationship exists between conditions and actions. That is, ***IF*** certain condition exits ***(Yes or No) THEN*** certain action or actions are to be taken.

The relevant entry characters used in the rule grid are specified below:

For conditions:

·	Y or Yes	Condition satisfied or exists.
·	N or No	Condition not satisfied or exists.
·	= or ET	Equal to.
·	> or GT	Greater than.
·	< or LT	Less than.
·	Dash (-)	Exclude.
·	Blank	Irrelevant.

For actions:

·	X (Cross)	Execute.
·	Blank	Do not execute.

The **table heading section** (or **Header**) is used to show the table number and/or the table name, the project name and/or code identifying the table. It may also include a name of a system or procedure, a name of analyst, or any other information that explains the purpose of the table.

A single horizontal line through the stub and entry parts of the table is called a row. These lines are used to specify conditions and actions; and the grid formed by the horizontal line and vertical lines in the entry sections is used to specify condition's rules and action's rules. The table shown in Figure Chapter I-1 has four condition rows (C1, C2, C3, C4) and five action rows (A1, A2, A3, A4, A5) and seven rules (R1, R2, R3, R4, R5).

The **note section** is used to write comments or to clarify some items in the table.

5 TYPES OF DECISION TABLES

There are three types of tables and are classified according to approach taken to represent condition entries. These are known as (a) Limited Entry Table, (b) Extended Entry Table, and (c) Mixed Entry Table.

Limited Entry Table

In a limited entry table (Figure Chapter I-2) all the conditions and the action statements are fully specified in the stub side of the table. The condition entry and the action entry sections are limited to showing, for each case, whether particular situation is True or False, or not present (represented by Y or N, or blank).

The symbols used to represent rules in a *condition entry grid* are: (a) Y (Yes), which implies that the condition *exists* or is fulfilled, (b) **N** (No), which implies that the condition does *not exist* or is not fulfilled, (c) **blank,** specifying that the value of stated condition is *irrelevant*, or the condition does not apply, or the condition is impossible, or it makes no difference whether the condition exists or not. The notations **T** (i.e., True), or **F** (i.e., False) or - (dash) are also used in the condition entries for Y, N, and blank respectively.

The symbols used in the *action entry grid* are (a) **X** (cross), specifying that the stated action is to be executed; (b) **blank** specifying do not execute the action (in some table the symbol - (dash) is used for blank).

An example of a limited entry table, about a decision situation in a document issue procedure, consisting of four conditions, five actions, and involving five rules, including 'Else' rules, is shown in Figure Chapter J-2.

LIMITED ENTRY TABLE

TABLE1: Procedure to issue a bibliographic item on loan	R1	R2	R3	R4	R5
C1 Member is a Teacher	Y	Y	N	N	E
C2 Member is a Student			Y	Y	L
C3 Item for loan is a Monograph	Y	N	Y	N	S
C4 Item for loan is a Serial		Y		Y	E
A1 Issue for one month	X				
A2 Issue for two weeks			X		
A3 Issue for one week		X			
A4 Do not issue				X	
A5 Go to Table 2					X
Note: Verify whether the person obtaining the item on loan has valid membership. Check his/her membeship card					

Figure J-2: An Example of Limited Entry Table Format

Extended Entry Table

An example of the extended entry table is given in Figure Chapter I-3. In this table the condition statements and action statements in stub portion of the table are not completed, but are extended into the entry portion.

EXTENDED ENTRY TABLE

TABLE: 1 Procedure to issue a document on loan	R1	R2	R3	R4
C1 Member is a	Teacher	Teacher	Student	Student
C2 Document is	Monograph	Serial	Monograph	Serial
A1 Issue the document for	One month	One weeek	Two weeks	Do not issue

Note: Verify whether the person obtaining the item on loan has valid membership. Check his/her membeship card

Figure J-3: An example of Extended Entry Table Format

Mixed Entry Table

An example of a mixed table is given in Figure Chapter I-4. A mixed entry table is exactly what the name implies. While the limited and extended entry format can be mixed within a table, only one form may be used within a condition statement entry or an action statement entry. In this table the limited and extended entry forms are mixed. As can be seen, while the table contains both types of forms, still each individual row is either entirely limited or entirely extended. In the table rows C1 and A2 have limited entry format.

MIXED ENTRY TABLE

TABLE 1: Procedure to issue Serials on loan	R1	R2	R3	R4	ELSE
C1 Member has	Red Tickect	Blue Ticket	Green Ticket	Any of the 3 tickects	
C2 Document is a serial	Y	Y	Y		
C3 Document is a monograph				Y	
A1 Issue the serial for	2 Weeks	1 Week	Do not Issue		
A2 Refer to Table 2					X

Note: Red tickects are issued to Techers. **Blue** to Ph.D. Students and **Green** tickccts t M. A./B.A. Students

Figure J-4: An example of Mixed Entry Table Format

One can always change an extended or a mixed entry table into a limited entry table. Limited entry table is more precise; facilitate logical analysis and development of decision procedures, then other types. However, an extended or a mixed entry format can be useful in solving a problem or displaying information when few rules are involved.

6 TABLE CONSTRUCTION METHOD

To construct a table the problem must be outlined in detail. Then all possible conditions and appropriate actions to be taken are identified and listed in standard language. In the next step, rules to be followed are decided — that is the combination of conditions calling for different actions and their sequences are specified. Finally the conditions and the actions as well as rules to be followed are written in a tabular format.

While presenting the procedure description in a tabular format, one should also see that duplication contradiction and redundancy in the statements and in the rules are eliminated.

Expanded or Full Version of the Decision Table

To check that a table is complete — that all combinations of conditions that can occur have been considered and the appropriate actions specified for them — one must first design the expanded version of the table to allow for all the possible combinations of conditions whether they occur or not (as shown in Figure Chapter I-5) and then check out each rule for appropriate action.

The total number of rules needed to satisfy all possible combinations is always equal to *the number of value raised to the number of conditions* {i.e. V^c = number of unique conditions. Where V = **number of possible values a condition may possess** (e.g., YES and NO - two values; or > (greater than), = (equal to), < (less than) - three value) and **c = number of conditions**}. For instance, in the table (Figure Chapter I- 5) four conditions are listed. Each condition has two possible values - Yes or No. Therefore, the total possible condition combination or condition rules come to 2^4 (i.e. 2x2x2x2) = 16. In case two conditions have three possible values, then in this case the total possible condition combination comes to $3^2 = 3x3 = 9$.

Let us examine the prototype table (complete or expanded version Figure Chapter I-5) to identify and remove duplications, contradictions and redundancies in the rules. To read the table, we shall examine a single rule at a time together with the statements to the left.

While going through the logic of first rule, we find that the rule is a contradictory rule. As, a ***library member is enrolled only under one category not in two or more***, by a library. Further, a library normally treats ***a particular document or bibliographic item either as a monograph or serial.*** The first rule column of stub III contains answer Y (Yes), for all the corresponding rows of stub-I. In this case the logic of table implies: (i) Is the reader getting the bibliographic item is teacher? The corresponding answer to the question is Yes; (ii) Is he student? The answer to the question is Yes, (iii) Is the item being taken on loan is monograph? The answer to the question we get is Yes; (iv) Is the item being taken on loan is serial? The answer is—Yes. This compound statement or declaration is irrational. In other words, the condition combinations of the rule are impossible or contradictory. Therefore, the rule is an invalid rule and one should not consider it as candidate for inclusion in the final diagram of a decision table. Similarly, while going through the logic of rule numbers R2, R3, R4, R5, R8, R9, R12, R13, R14, R15 and R16, we find that the condition combinations stated in each rule is either redundant, contradictory, impossible, or invalid.

The rule 6 is the first is logically valid rule. As can be seen, the condition combination stated in the rule R6 is logically valid and the rule can be paraphrased as: IF a Member is a Teacher (value Y) and not Student (value N), and the Document for issue is Monograph (value Y) and not Serial (value N), THEN issue the Document for One Month (X). The other valid rules involving logical condition combination are 7, 19 and 11. Thus, we find that four rules would be required to represent the real world situation, and other rules that do not satisfy the table logic must be ignored. The table completeness, by displaying all possible condition combinations, helps us, not only, to locate illogical statements but also to check the accuracy of policy or procedure documented in narrative form.

In the table all the contradictions and redundancies (invalid rules) are shown as **shaded area**. After removing these impossible, redundant, or invalid rules and keeping only valid or logical rules (or condition combination s), we draw a final table keeping those combinations that are found appropriate or representing only the valid rules. Such a table is shown in Figure Chapter I-2, above.

TABLE : 1 Documents issue Procedure	1	2	3	4	5	6	7	8	9	10	11	12	13	14	15	16	17
C1 Member is a Teacher	Y	Y	Y	Y	Y	Y	Y	Y	N	N	N	N	N	N	N	N	E
C2 Member is a Student	Y	Y	Y	Y	N	N	N	N	Y	Y	Y	Y	N	N	N	N	L
C3 Document is a Monograph	Y	Y	N	N	Y	Y	N	N	Y	Y	N	N	Y	Y	N	N	S
C4 Document is a Serial	Y	N	Y	N	Y	N	Y	N	Y	N	Y	N	Y	N	Y	N	E
A1 Issue for one month						X											
A2 Issue for two weeks										X							
A3 Issue fior one week							X										
A4 Do not issue											X						
A5 Go to Table 2																	X

Note: Shaded area indicates invalid or impossible condition combination

Figure J-5: An example of Limited Entry Table with complete 24 (16) Rules

REFERENCES AND READING LIST

1. Bradford, K. J. *Information system in management*. Reston Pub Co., Reston, Virginia. 1973, p. 13.
2. *ibid.* p. 30.

3. Brown, Ray. *The intuitive manager*. 1986. Little Brown, Boston.

4. Fergus, Raymond M. Decision tables — what, why and how. **In** COUGER (J. Daniel) and KNAPP (Robert W), *Ed. System analysis techniques*. John, New York, 1974, p. 177.

5. *Ibid.* p. 171.

6. Gildersleeve, Thomas R. *Decision tables and their practical application in data processing*. Prentice-Hall International, London, 1970.

7. Hartman, W; Others. *Management information system handbook*. McGraw-Hill, New York. v. 6-2; 1972; p. 7.

8. Hayes, Robert M; Becker, Joseph. *Handbook of data processing for libraries*. Becker and Hayes, New York, 1970, p. 157-60

9. Heinritz, Fred J. Decision tables: A tool for Librarians. *LRTS*. v. 22; 1978; p. 42-6.

10. Hughes, Marion L; Others. *Decision tables*. McGraw Hill; New York, 1968.

11. Kashyap, M. M. Decision making for library managers and system analysts: A systematic approach. *Journal of Library and Information* Science. v. 3; 1978; p. 140-55.

12. McDaniel, Hermann. *An introduction to decision logic tables*. Wiley, New York, 1966.

13. Montalbano, Mike. *Decision table*. Science Research Associates, Chicago, 1974.

14. Nutt, Paul c. Types of organisational decision process. *Administrative Science Quarterly*. 1984; p. 414-50

15. Pollock, Solomon L.; Others. *Decision tables: Theory and practice*. Wiley, New York, 1971.

16. Simon, Herbert. The new science of management. 1960. p. 1.

17. *ibid.* p. 5-6.

18. *ibid.* p. 6.

19. Simon, Herbert. The structure of ill-structured decision processes. *Artificial Intelligence*. v.4; 1973; p. 181-201.

20. — *Reasons in human affairs*. Stanford University Press, Stanford, Calif, 1983.

K
Network Technique PERT/CPM

1 ORIGIN

The term Network Technique refers to the method of planning, scheduling and controlling of progress on various components of a project. The network concept has its origin in graph theory, and has developed in an evolutionary way over many years. "Scientists and Engineers have been visualising network and networks' concepts since the earliest days of industrial revolution" [*cf.*, **Archibald**, 1]. However, the modern concept of Network Planning and Critical Path Analysis was developed during 1957-58 concurrently, by two research teams, one developing '***Program Evaluation and Review Technique***' [*cf.*, **USA, Department of Navy**, 18; **Malcolm**, 12] and the other '***Critical Path Method***' [*cf.*, **Kelly**, 7; **Kelly and Walker**, 9]. PERT was originally devised in 1958 for POLARIS Fleet Ballistic Missile Program by the Program Evaluation Branch of the Special Project Office of the US Navy and CPM was conceived and devised jointly by **Morgan R Walker** of E I Dupont Company and **K E Kelley** of Remington Rand Univac (USA) in 1957.

The basic objectives and foundation for PERT and CPM are the same. There are other techniques that have since been developed differing only in nonessentials from CPM/PERT. All these techniques are treated as a whole and the term '*Network Analysis*' or PERT/CPM is used to describe the general approach. The underlying basis of both PERT and CPM is network chart or diagram. Network representation of project activities has its basis in *Milestone chart,* which is the modified and the improved version of ***Gantt chart,*** developed by **Henry L. Gantt** from 1911-1919. [**Gantt**, 4]

1.1 Need and Purpose of Network Analysis

Due to time and resource constraints for conducting a Library Systems Study Project, the system analyst has to pre-plan the time schedule for its completion. Such constraints could be caused due to the limitation placed by the authorities to finish the project within a given time and due to financial, technological and manpower limitations. It is not only essential to find out the optimum project duration but also to control the performance time by a series of activities of the project to finish it on schedule. *Not controlling* the schedule implies an increase in the sum of direct and indirect cost. For this purpose, one has to plan and establish time estimates for completion of each activity of the project. Fix target times for its start and finish. Synchronise schedules of concurrent and successive activities of the project.

Network technique, known under different names such as Program Evaluation and Review Technique (PERT) and Critical Path Method (CPM), is well-developed management tool, which systems analysts can effectively used the for above stated purposes. The PERT and CPM techniques are concerned with planning of a set of activities that must be completed to achieve the objectives of a project.

These project management techniques are based on network model, and are used for developing a workable plan of a project involving

* Activities that make up the project, including specification of their interrelation.
* Time estimates for the completion of each activity within the complete project and total time required completing the entire project.
* Controlling, synchronising and co-ordinating the sequences of activities of the project.
* The sequence of activities that will consume the most time in reaching the end event is called '***Critical Path***'.

A network model is a diagram with which one may present a complete picture of a project plan showing logical sequence of the activities and events and interrelationships of various activities of the project. An activity is any segment of a project that consumes time and resources and has a definable beginning and ending. Commonly used terms synonymous with *activity* are *'task'* and '*job*.' An event means the beginning and end of an activity and does not consume time. It shows a noteworthy or significant point in a project. For example, in a library system receipt of books and book bills are starting events, which trigger further actions. To list a purchased book in an accession register is an **activity** and an accessioned book is an **end event**.

The advantages of a Network Analysis are summarised as follows:

a. It forces a thorough preplanning of the task.

b. It increases co-ordination.

c. It identifies trouble spots, often in advance, and pinpoints responsibilities.

d. It refines thinking and increases the user's awareness of the problems involved, and their relative importance in the total operation.

e. It focuses the management's attention on those activities that are or likely to be in difficulties, rather than on to activities that are progressing smoothly and therefore need no attention.

f. It facilitates the hand over of the information during changes in management and is a valuable aid when issuing orders.

g. It shows optimum start and finish times for each activity in an operation.

h. It enables the plan to be revised in the best way to suit changed circumstances.

i. It suggests where alternative methods should be sought.

j. It allows progress reporting and the issue of orders without complete loss of security.

k. It allows certain operations that follow a set pattern to be partly pre-planned, thus speeding up the final planning.

l. It is an important means of training personnel in the techniques of handling operations.

m. It forms a useful comprehensive record that requires a minimum of storage space.[**Engineer,** 3]PERT/CPM can be effectively used in detailed planning and scheduling of library projects, such as analysing the library systems or operations and improving their performance; construction of a library building; shifting library collection to a new location; transferring library staff from one place to another; making major changes in the working of a library department, planning and reorganisation of different departments of a library, and so on.

Thus, we find that network analysis is the tool that systems analysts can use for:

* Breaking down the project into a series of *activities* and events and arranging them in a logical network to accomplish the objective of a project successfully.
* Estimating the duration and resource requirements of each activity, drawing up a schedule and finding which activities control the completion of the project to increase the chance of completing the project by target date.
* Re-allocating money, men or other resources to improve the schedule and do rescheduling to reduce the total time required for completing the project.
* Controlling and monitoring progress as the project proceeds

1.2 Conventional Planning and Control Methods

As described earlier, the network design is essentially an outgrowth of the Gantt Chart. Before we discuss the fundamentals of network technique, it will be useful to explain the important features of the Gantt Chart and bring out its deficiencies that led to the development of PERT/CPM network.

Gantt Chart

Gantt Chart, also known as ***Bar Chart*** was designed to show the duration of a job and to control the time elements of a project. It is essentially a two-dimensional picture describing the relation between jobs and time and takes the form shown in Figure Chapter K-1. It consists of two co-ordinate axes. The vertical scale shows the set of activities to be performed and the horizontal scale shows scheduled start and finish time of the activities and their current status. An activity is represented as a line or bar the length of which is proportional to the duration of the activity and the position of bar indicates a schedule of start and finish of the activity.

In any project, some activities can be started ***concurrently*** and some can only be started after some preceding activity or activities are completed. In **Gantt Chart,** bars running parallel represent concurrent jobs and bars running serially, that is, one beginning after another bar ends, represents sequential jobs. For example, in Figure Chapter K-2, activities A, B, D, is shown to start at the same zero time and go on concurrently or parallel and they take different time intervals for their completion. The bars representing D and E are shown to run serially, it implies that activity E can only begin when activity D is over.

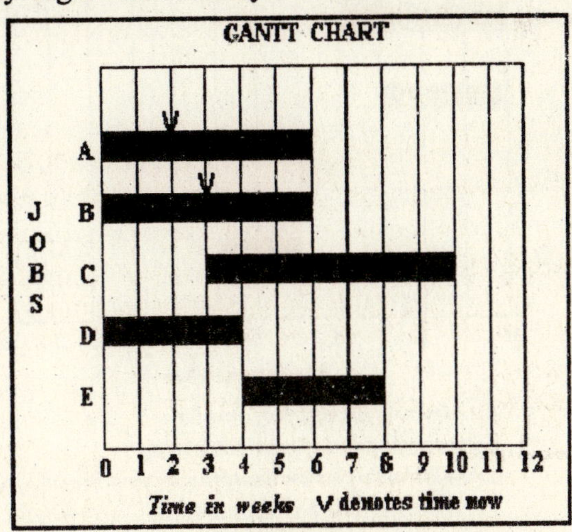

Figure K-1

Let us now consider an example to illustrate graphically the time schedule of library project activities with the help of Gantt Chart. Suppose that the book collection of a library is to be shifted from present location to another in the same building and the project consists of following set of activities:

Activity	*Estimated Time Scale*
A - Making suitable bundles of books for transportation	4 weeks
B - Installation of new set of book shelves at the new location	3 weeks
C - Shifting of books to new location	1 week
D - Opening the bundles of books and arranging them on the shelves at new location	2 weeks

The bar chart for this project is shown in Figure Chapter K-2. In this chart, the activities listed above are shown along the vertical axis and estimated duration of time required completing the activities shown along the horizontal axis.

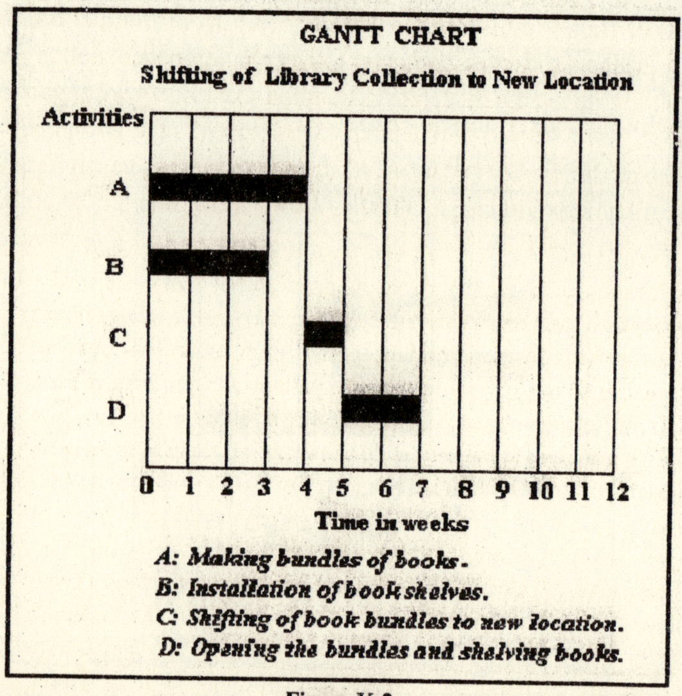

Figure K-2

The Drawbacks of the Gantt Chart

Gantt Charts do show duration in time, and each bar represents a succession of activities performed by one man or one team. However, in the Gantt chart there are no cross connections to show directly the interdependence of one activity on others explicitly. The mere fact that two or more activities are started simultaneously or have overlapping schedules does not make them related, or interdependent, or completely independent. Consider for example, the project represented in Figure Chapter K-2. The activities A, C and D have been shown to run sequentially. That is, activity A must be completed before the activity B can begin, and B must end before C can start. The activities A and B have been shown to go on simultaneously and appear to be independent activities. On making, a deeper analysis shows that all these activities have dependency relationship. It is obvious that shifting of books and their shelving can be done soon after some shelves are fitted and a segment of books are bundled up. The bars representing such activities are not allowed to overlap. Further, the making of books' bundles, shifting of book, opening cum shelving of books should not take 7 weeks in total as it appears in the Gantt chart (*see* Figure Chapter K-2).

One weakness of bar chart is that it is not able to show dependency relationship or interdependencies and the interrelationships between the project's tasks, exactly. Another weakness is its inability to reflect or predict: (a) the total span of time required to complete the project; and, (b) the effect of delay in one area on another and on the project as a whole.

2 NETWORK CHARTING TECHNIQUE

2.1 Introduction

The shortcomings of bar chart, such as: (a) not being able to show dependency relationship between activities and (b) its inability to reflect the uncertainty or tolerance in duration time estimates for various activities, efforts were made to modify it by adding new elements. These successive modifications culminated as PERT/CPM network charting method. The important features of these methods are that "they expand the capabilities of the Gantt Chart to show interrelationships among tasks (particularly time dependencies) to reflect uncertainties in schedules or costs, and to predict problem area." [*cf.*, **Hayes** and **Beker**, 5]

PERT/CPM Network diagram became more important and useful than Gantt Chart, because of the fact that the dependencies of activities upon each other are displayed more explicitly than in bar chart. "For modest sized programme one can incorporate the dependencies on a bar chart implicitly. However, because of the enormous size of many present days' programmes that contain thousands, of significant activities, taking place in widely dispersed locations, it is no longer possible to treat interdependencies implicitly with the help of *Gantt Chart*. This is also true for relatively small projects subjected to very detailed planning."[*cf.*, **Moder** and **Philip**, 13]

2.2 Network Diagram

As explained earlier, PERT/CPM techniques based on a network diagram have been developed to aid management in planning and controlling the set of activities that must be accomplished to reach objectives of a project. A PERT/CPM network model represents graphically these activities. In a network diagram, as shown in Figure Chapter K-3, an arrow represents each activity of a project and its associated time. The nodes are events. The beginning node of an arrow shows the start of associated activity or activities, and ending node, its or their completion. This example of PERT network diagram, containing eight events (number 1 to 8) and eight activities of the proposed project listed along arrows, represents a network model of planning and conducting a ***library survey project.***

A PERT Network Diagram

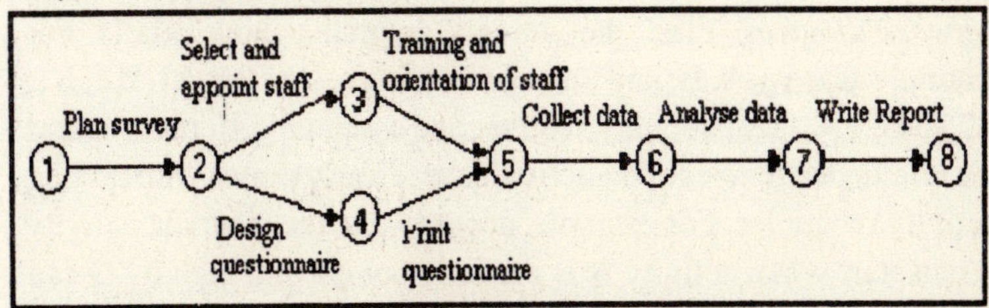

Figure K-3

We also present the following PERT network diagrams (Figure Chapter K-4 and Figure Chapter K-5), one drawn to scale and other not drawn to scale. These charts pertain to the project earlier drawn in Figure Chapter K-2 with the help of Gantt chart.

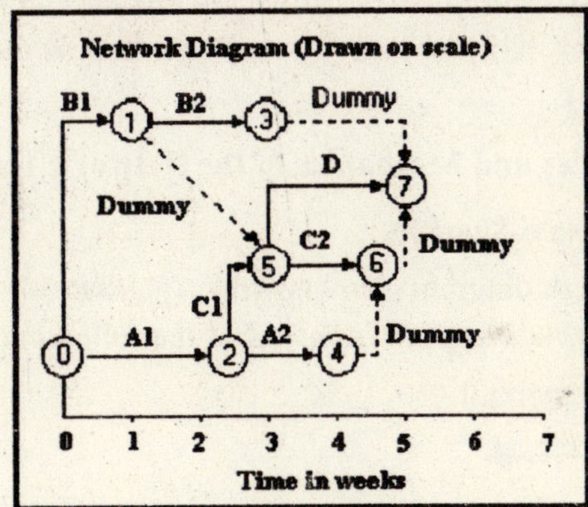

Figure K-4

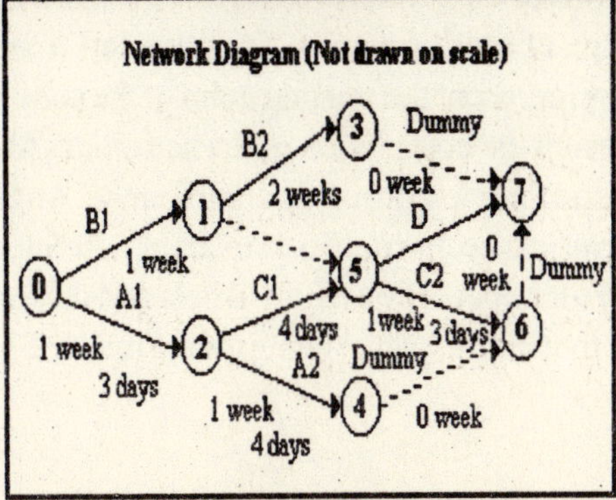

Figure K-5

The above network diagrams (Figure Chapter K-4 & K-5) illustrate the major differences between the Gantt chart and the *network diagram.* First, the network diagrams show details. For example activity A, B, and C are broken into activities A1, A2, B1, B2 and C1, C2 respectively. The second essential difference is that the interdependencies of the activities are clearly shown with revised activity schedules. For example, according to the diagram, activity C can start when activity A is partially completed; activity D can start when activities B and C are partially completed; activity D cannot be completed unless activities B and C are completed, etc. (*This concept will become clearer when details of network will be discussed.*) The third difference is that the network diagram shows 5 weeks as total project completion time (which is correct representation) to complete the project, while the Gantt Chart (*see* Figure Chapter K-2) shows 7 weeks (*which is an* incorrect *representation*).

2.3 Principles and Mechanics of the Network Techniques

Network Diagram Symbols

A network diagram also known as '***Activity on Arrows***' or merely an '***Arrow Diagram***' consists of the following symbols:

(a) Activity symbol

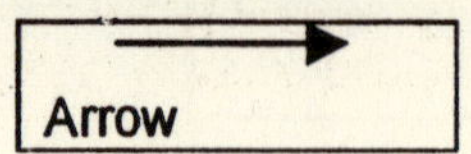

An arrow represents an **Activity**. The arrowhead shows the direction or flow of time. An arrow is drawn left to right. The tail ends of an arrow represent the starting point of the activities whereas the heads represent the completion of the activities. Arrows are not drawn to scale and their length has no significance. Angles of arrows also have no significance. In a network diagram, activities are labelled by letters of the alphabet. The activity labels and the time estimates of respective activities are written along the arrow (*see* Figure Chapter K-6).

(b) Event Symbol

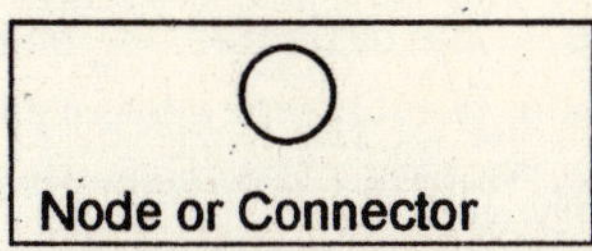

A node represents an ***Event*** or ***Milestone***. In network diagrams events are labelled by numerals.

(c) Dummy Activity Symbol

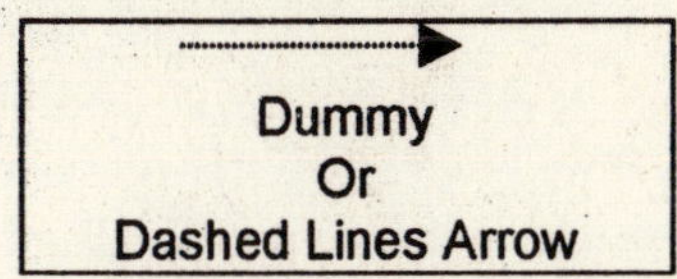

A dashed line arrow represents Dummy Activity or Zero Time Activity.

Note: *A solid arrow shows only such task sequences as are logically inseparable. Dashed line arrows show dummy activity (or zero time activity) and a situation in which the start of activity is constrained by the completion of another activity both being logically separable. A node, at the beginning of an arrow represents a start event and a node after the arrowhead an end event.*

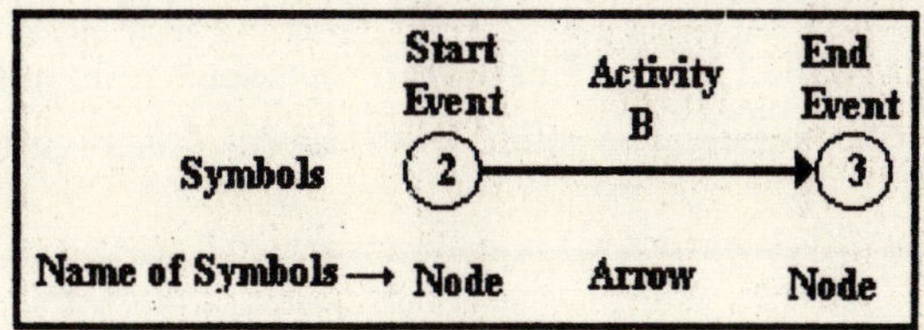

Figure K-6

2.4 Network Concepts

A Network is a graphic plan or model of all those tasks to carry out to complete a project. The model also represents interdependencies and interrelationships among the defined tasks of the project. The components that make up a network are '***Events***' and '***Activities***'.

2.5 Event

An Event is a specific definable accomplishment in a project plan at a particular instant of time — the definable beginning and end of an activity. It is an instantaneous point in time and not passages of time. Event is also referred to as ***Node*** or ***Connector***. Events do not consume time or resources and are represented on the network by circles.

Certain key events are called **Milestones** and they are represented by ***rectangles*** in a network. Events common to two or more networks are called **Interface Events.** When such situations arise while drawing a network diagram of a large project then by using interface event symbols, individual small networks are tied together logically at the appropriate interface points. (*See* Figure Chapter K-7)

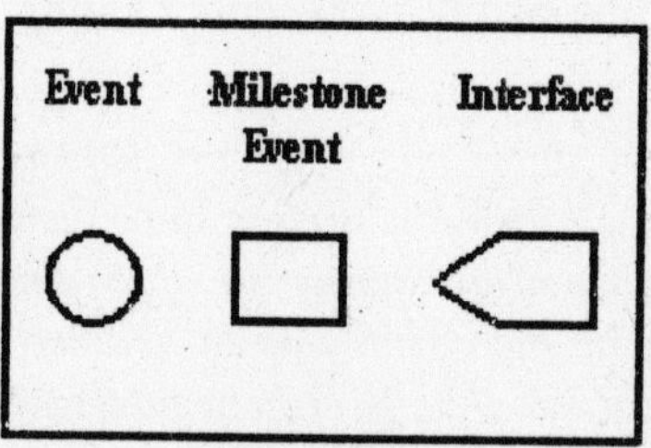

Figure K-7

If an event represents the joint completion of more than one activity, it is called **Merge Event.** If it represents joint initiation of more than one activity, it is called **Burst Event.** (*see* Figure Chapter K-8)

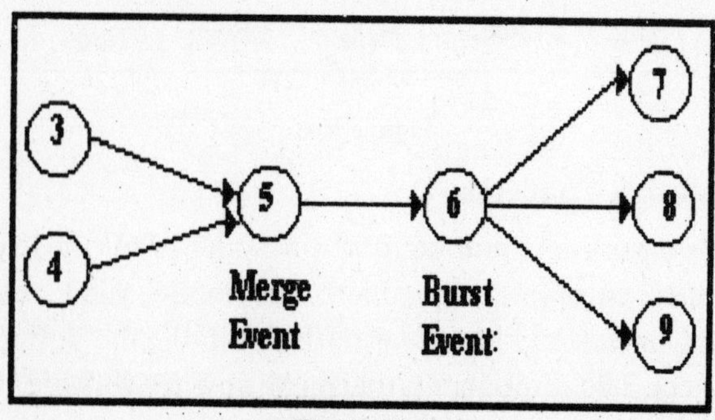

Figure K-8

2.6 Activity

An activity is defined as the work necessary to progress from one point in time (i.e., from a predecessor event) to another point in time (*successor event*) in a project. An activity cannot start until event preceding it has occurred. Activities consume time and resources.

One can decompose any project into a series of *Activities*. One considers a project completed when all the activities of a project have been executed and completed in appropriate sequence. Some of the activities of a project are executed one after another in some sequence and some others simultaneously.

All the activities of a project are related in varied ways. These types of relations are called *sequential relations*, *parallel relations* and *dependency relations*. Depending upon the type of relationship, the activities are called: Concurrent or Parallel Activities, Sequential Activities, Dummy Activities, Composite Activities, Aggregated Activities, Lead-time Activities, and End Time Activities. We give detailed description of these activity types in the succeeding sections.

Sequential Activities

In a project if an activity **A** precedes activity **B** or activity **B** follows **A,** then **A** and **B** are called **sequential** *or* **serial activities** (*see* Figure Chapter K-9).

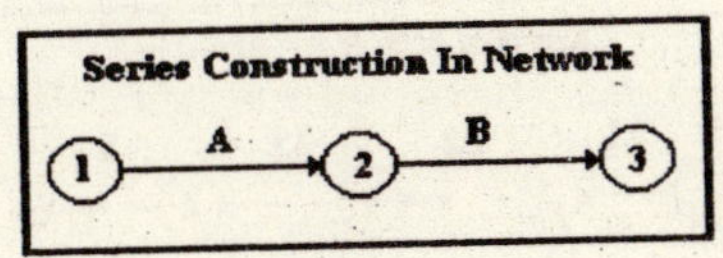

Figure K-9

Concurrent or Parallel Activities

It can happen that two or more interrelated activities must begin at different events and end at the same event. They may start from the same event end at different events. Such activities are called **parallel or concurrent activities**. For example, as shown in Figure Chapter K-10 activities A and B are concurrent activities.

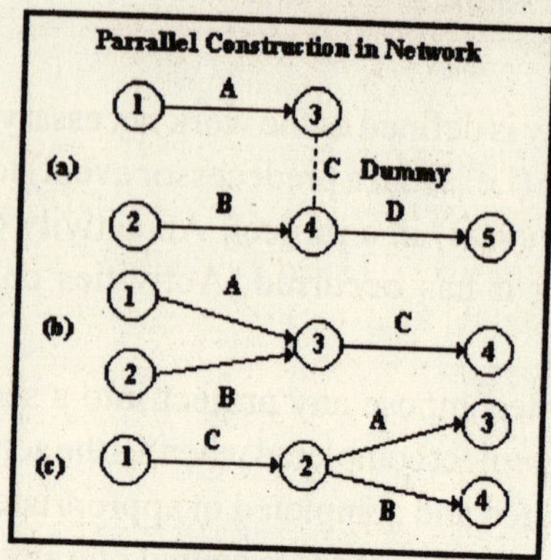

Figure K-10

Composite Activities

Suppose in a project two activities A and B are such that A is the predecessor activity of activity B, and actually, B could begin when A is partially completed. We may say that A and B are partially concurrent activities. More generally, many activities can be started at different stages of completion of A. In this situation the activity A is considered composite of many activities. For example, if activity C can be started when A is one-third completed, activity D when A is two third completed, and B when A is fully completed then A is considered composite of three different activities A1, A2, A3 and is to be represented in the network diagram as illustrated in Figure Chapter K-11

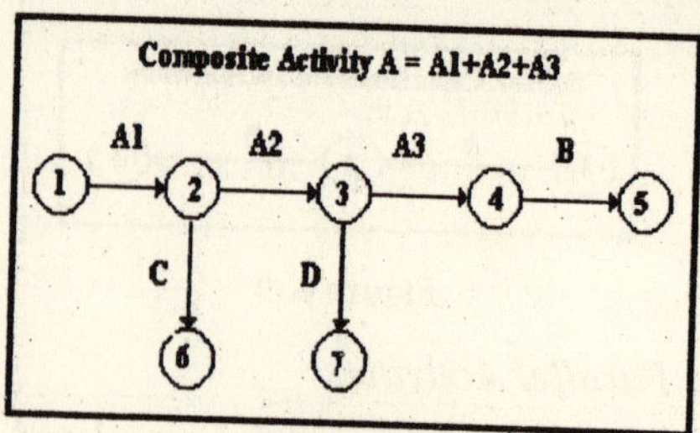

Figure K-11

Dummy Activities or Zero Time Activities

Dummy activity is a Network activity that represents the dependency of a successor event on a predecessor event. Dummy activity does not consume time, manpower, and financial or other resources. In a network diagram if one wishes to establish that a particular *event—i* cannot occur before some other event j, although no specific activity occurs between the two, then in such a case, a ***dummy activity*** is inserted to show dependency relationship. For example, consider a project involving the installation or starting of a Reprographic Unit in a library for providing photocopies of documents. Let us assume that the project constitutes of following activities:

Activity A = Advertise for operator's post.

Activity B = Appoint Operator.

Activity C = Train Operator on the machine.

Activity D = Purchase reprographic machine.

Activity E = Install Machine.

One might attempt to draw network diagram of the project as shown in Figure Chapter K-12:

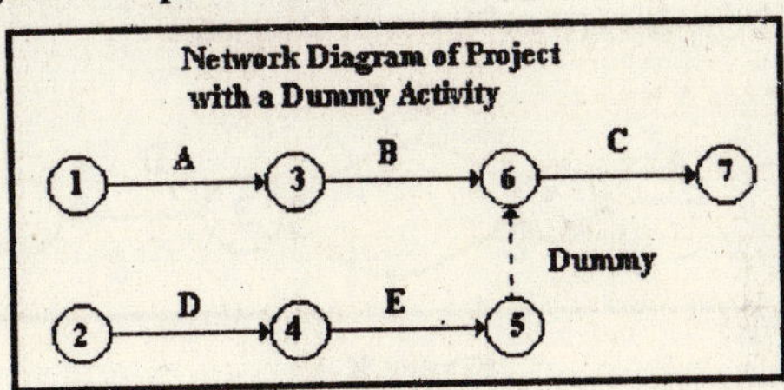

Figure K-12

Comments:

1. In the above Figure Chapter K-12, activity A precedes B and B precedes C. This figure shows the network path in series.
2. Activities A and D, as well B and E are concurrent. This shows the network path in parallel.
3. In this figure use of the dummy activity shows that the activity C cannot be started unless events '5' and '6' occur. It implies that the training of an operator on the machine cannot be started until the machine is installed. It indicates that the true dependency for starting the activity logically depends not

only upon completion of direct linked activity B but also upon dummy activity F starting from event '5'. It also does not imply that C must follow E.

As has already been said, an activity is defined by its beginning and end events. Dummy arrows help to avoid ambiguous cases that might otherwise occur. For example, it can happen that two or more activities begin and end at the same events in a project. This situation is ambiguous, since all these activities would have the same designation numbers, as shown in Figure Chapter K-13, below. To eliminate this ambiguity we consider all but one of the two activities to be composite of two activities. One is the activity itself while the other is a fictitious activity or ***dummy***. This situation is illustrated in Figure Chapter K-14. Dummy activity F is introduced to distinguish between B and C but still maintaining the required sequencing of the activities. Zero time duration is assigned to dummy activity F. [*cf.*, **Kelley, P 8-301**]

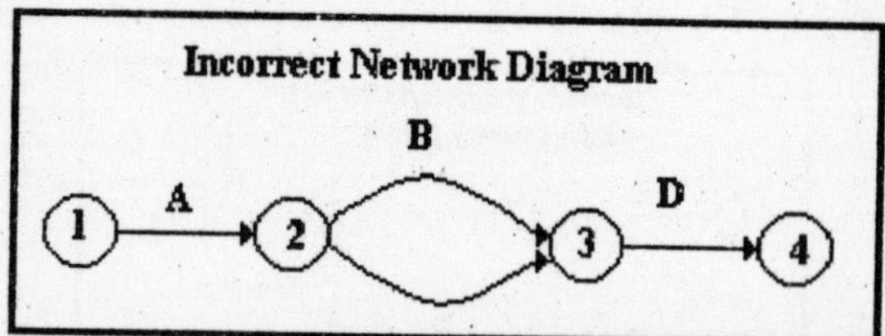

Figure K-13

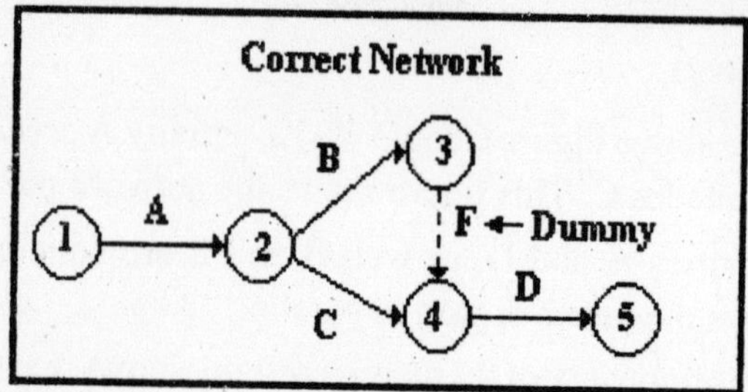

Figure K-14

Aggregated Activities

Sometimes, a certain group of activities can be considered as one activity. This type of aggregation in a major project may be desirable for certain purposes, such as, simplification of the network diagram. When this type of situation arises, a dummy is substituted for the whole group of activities. As shown in Figure Chapter K-16, ***dummy*** X is substituted for activities B, C, D, E and F of the network diagram, shown in Figure Chapter K-15.

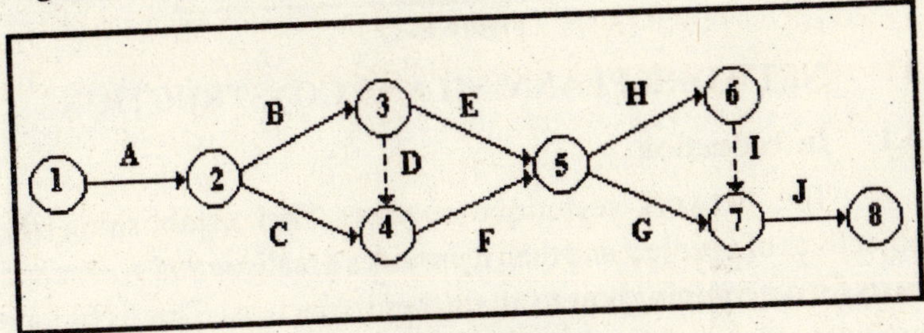

Figure K-15

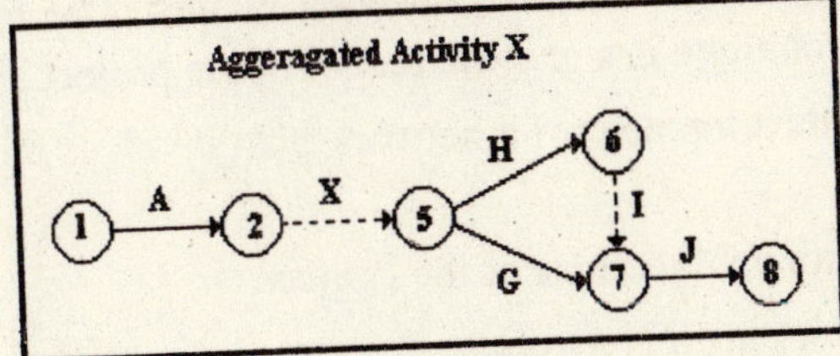

Figure K-16

Lead Time and End Time Activities

Lead-Time Activity is by definition on that must precede all other activities. It is a purely fictitious activity, much the same as dummy, as shown in the Figure Chapter K-17, which starts at the zero date on the calendar or has zero time duration and terminates at the start of the project. It may be used to aggregate certain administrative matters, actually that must be taken care of before the actual start of the project, such as receiving final approval of the project.

An ***End Time Activity*** is the one that follows all other jobs. Like Lead-Time Activity, it may also be purely fictitious or dummy activity, as shown in the Figure Chapter K-17, purpose being to tie up the loose ends of a network.

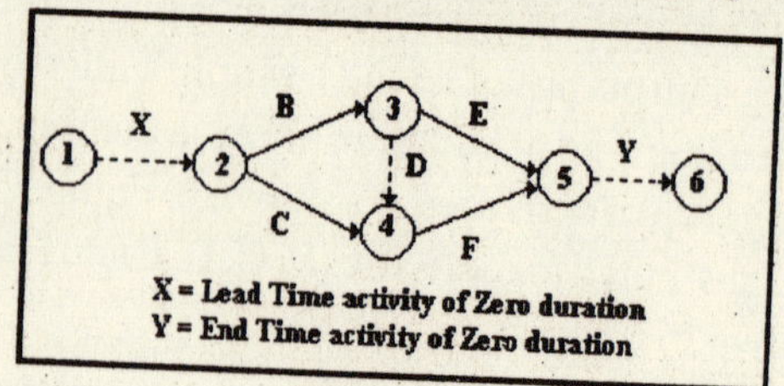

Figure K-17

3 NETWORK PLANNING AND CONSTRUCTION

3.1 Introduction

The network technique requires first establishing the objectives of a project and then it provides a realistic and systematic basis for determining how to attain these objectives. This technique provides a clear and concise way of documenting and communicating project plan, schedule, time and cost factors. The backbone of Network technique is a graphic model of the project activities.

The development of a network plan involves the following steps:

1 Defining Objectives of the Project.
2. Developing a Network.
3. Project Time Estimates, Schedule and Identification of Critical Path.

Defining Objectives of the Project

Developing a Network plan implies *defining the project objectives* as a first step. Establishing objectives provides the basic framework from which the required network can be prepared and various activities of the project identified and correlated.

Developing a Network

To develop a network diagram, we must first identify all the activities (or tasks) and the logical interconnection between these activities (or tasks), to be performed, to accomplish a project, say, design and development of a computer-based library information system. At this stage: (a) specific events as significant points in accomplishing the project are identified; (b) activities making up the project are defined, and (c) logic of the activity relationships is accurately established to develop a framework of the network diagram.

The analyst can build up the network physically in the following two ways:

(a) To follow *forward planning procedure*. That is, starting from initial event proceeding forward, building up the activities and events in chronological sequence until the end event is reached. In this process as we move through the project we consider:

* What activity or activities follow this event?
* What event or events come next? and,
* What activities can take place concurrently?

(b) To follow *backward planning* procedure. In this process we work backward from that end event through the project, to achieve its objective:

* What should have taken place? This means, having an end objective in view, work back if we want to achieve this; what should have taken place? That is, going backwards from the end event of the project we must ask:
* What activity or activities precede this event?

In this manner starting from the terminal event through systematic analysis of the project, we come to the initial event.

Often planners employ a combination of these techniques, working back and forth until the entire project network plan is worked out.

After identification of all the activities and logical interconnection between them a network diagram is prepared. In developing the network diagram there are certain ground rules to be observed to maintain correct topology. These are:

* Each activity must have a preceding event and a succeeding event. Similarly, each event must have a preceding and succeeding activity, except the starting and final events.

* No activity can start until its predecessor event is completed. No event can be considered complete until all activities leading to it are complete.
* Normally, an event once having occurred cannot occur again; that is, there is no looping back to the previously accomplished event.

There are no other formal rules to aid the construction of the network diagram except that logical sequence.

The most common system to rank an event number is called 'i—j' numbering system, where the number of the predecessor *event—i* should be less than the successor *event-j*. The numbers are assigned using a count of 10; 20; 30, etc., in the first numbering. The utility of this gap numbering system is that at a later stage if an activity has to be inserted in the network; an appropriate new node number can be allocated without renumbering the entire network. Without contravening the 'i-j' rule, one can also follow the following steps for sequential numbering of events:

1. Consider an initial event, which has arrows emerging out of it and none entering it, number it '10'.
2. Cancel mentally all arrows emerging from event 10 and then identify the next event(s), which seems to be the initial event(s) as per definition given in step 1.
3. Number the new initial events '20, 30 and so on'.
4. Again, drop mentally the emerging arrow(s) from this/these numbered event(s), which will create a new initial event or events.
5. Follow or repeat step 3
6. Continue till a situation is reached when one finds that the event that has no arrow emerging from is arrived at, this event is the end event of the project. (*see* Figure Chapter K-14)

4 TIME ESTIMATES, SCHEDULING AND IDENTIFICATION OF THE CRITICAL PATH TIME

After the planner has decided and drawn the network, the next step is to develop the schedule of the project. This involves estimating the time required for performing each activity, calculating how long it will take to complete the planned project and devise means to control the total duration of the project.

As we know, "each activity takes time to perform. Thus, it will have duration associated with it. The time at which an event occurs is the maximum of the duration of the inwardly — directed paths (arrows) to the event, since all of the activities directed into the event must have been completed. The project duration is then the maximum of the elapsed times along all paths from the origin to the terminal node (the event marking the completion of the project). The path with the longest duration is called '***Critical Path***' and the activities on it '***Critical Activities***'. Any delay in a critical activity will obviously cause a corresponding delay in the entire project." [*cf.*, **MacMrimmon**, 11]

Thus, to control the duration of the project or reducing the duration, a systematic method of detecting the 'critical path or paths' and estimating the time for performance of project activities becomes a necessity. To achieve this, the analyst can use either PERT statistical approach method or CPM schedule calculation procedure.

The PERT schedules calculating method and CPM method have many points in common. However, they differ in the following ways:

(a) PERT method is event based and CPM is activity based. This does not mean that PERT completely ignores activities or CPM, the events. It is a question of emphasis.

(b) PERT scheduling computations are based upon 'three time estimates' and CPM scheduling computation is based upon 'single time estimates'.

(c) PERT statistical approach is appropriate for scheduling and controlling project comprising primarily of activities whose actual duration time are subject to a considerable amount of random variation.

According to the studies made by **Moder** and **Rogers** [16], it was found that the *'single time estimate'* applied in CPM method results in slightly biased estimate of the mean on the other hand '*three time estimate method*' used in PERT gives unbiased estimates of mean activity time. However, **Klingel** [10] believes that if the network has multiple parallel paths with relatively equal means and large variances in the calculation time estimates, then the PERT calculations give biased results. In such cases, the simulation method can be effectively used to estimate the distribution of completion time.

Pert Scheduling and Project Completion Time Calculation Procedure

We have so far discussed the basic concepts, rules and method for developing a network for a project. On the network so developed, we can calculate Time aspects and cost aspects of the project. These estimates can be calculated either using manual calculation method or computerised PERT programs. We will explain the procedure to calculate the time aspects of a project based upon manual calculation method using PERT statistical approach.

PERT statistical procedure is based upon "probability theory for managerial decision making. Scheduling systems have, traditionally, been based upon the idea of a fixed time for each task. In the PERT system, three time estimates are obtained for each activity - an optimistic time, a pessimistic time, and a most likely time. This range of time provides a measure of the uncertainty associated with actual time required to perform the activity sometime in future." [**Moder and Phillips**. 14, P 275]

By means of PERT procedure, it is possible for a decision-maker

1. To calculate expected activity duration time from the three-times estimate,
2. To find the critical path within a network, and

3. Calculate the shortest time to complete the entire project.

Once a project is underway these duration time estimates, as well as critical path networks serve as a guide to the completion of each activity in proper sequence and on schedule. However, activities will seldom begin or end exactly according to planned estimates. With the help of PERT network, these time estimates can be updated.

"There are four functions performed in the process of updating the schedule alone (without regard to cost.) These are:

1. Denoting actual progress on the network.
2. Revising the network logic or time estimates of uncompleted activities.
3. Recompiling the basic schedule of earliest and latest allowable time.
4. Revising the scheduled activity start times and denoting new critical path." [Moder and **Philips**, 15. P 327]

Three Time Estimations

We derive an expected activity duration or mean time for an activity with the help of the following formula:

$$t_E = \frac{a + 4m + b}{6}$$

The formula was derived in the original PERT summary Report Phase I [15]. In this formula, the symbol '**a**' denotes ***optimistic time***; '**m**' denotes ***most likely time***; '**b**' denotes ***pessimistic time*** and the symbol 'tE' denotes ***estimated activity duration time***.

Optimistic Performance Time = a

This is the estimate of the shortest possible time required for the performance of an activity. This estimate is based on the assumption that the activity is performed in better than normal condition. That is, no unforeseen problem arises during its performance.

Most Likely Time = m

Most likely time is the time that lies between the optimistic and pessimistic time estimates, subject to or assuming that the activity is executed in the normal way, with a few setbacks, no dramatic breakthrough and so forth. This is the estimate, which experts think; the activity shall normally take, if the activity is performed many times under the same conditions. It is the modal value of the distribution or the value that is likely to occur more than any value. (*Note*: This estimate is the only estimate taken when single time estimates are used in CPM Network.)

Pessimistic Performance Time = b

This is the estimate of the maximum possible or longest time it might take to complete an activity. The pessimistic time estimate is made keeping in view all abnormal situations or uncertainties excluding natural calamities such as fire, labour strikes and technological break down like power failure, and so forth.

Expected Activity Time = tE

The time calculated as a mean (not average) value from the three estimates for an activity.

Once, using the above given formula, the expected activity duration t_E of all the network activities are calculated then these estimated can be entered on the network. Normally the activities are described over the arrow and the activity time estimates are shown below the arrow.

From the three time estimates, we are not only able to calculate t_E—that is, meantime for the completion of an activity—but also, some measure of its dispersion (or variance of the activity performance time) and standard deviation of the project. We can compute it according to following equations:

$$(1)\ (V_T)2^{1-j} = \frac{(b-a)^2}{(6)^2}$$

Where the symbol V_T denotes the degree of variance (uncertainty) associated with the deviation of the expected time.

(2) Standard Deviation SD for the project

= Sum of variance $(V_T)2$ along the critical path

$$\text{or } V_T = \frac{b - a}{6}$$

With the help of these equations, we can find the probability of occurrence of an event on or before some *scheduled date* or *time* denoted by the symbol **Ts**.

The **Critical Path**, which is the longest duration path through the network, and time estimate for completion of the entire project can be calculated with the help of the *earliest expected time*, denoted by the symbol $\mathbf{T_E}$, the ***latest allowable time***, denoted by the symbol $\mathbf{T_L}$ and the ***slack*** denoted by the symbol **S**.

Schedule Computation Example

Let us take as example of the PERT network diagram, as shown in Figure Chapter K-18, to understand the concept of drawing the Network diagram and scheduling aspects of a project.

To draw a Network diagram of a project, as a first step, we have to identify all events and the activities to be performed to complete the project. We have assumed that the project constitutes of ten events and twelve activities. These activities are arranged in the sequence in which to perform them. In this way the Network diagram is drawn. The ten events are numbered 10, 20, 30, 40, 50, 60, 70, 80, 90, 100; and the twelve activities labelled A, B, C, D, E, F, G, H, I, J, K, L. The numbering of the events is according to procedure discussed in an earlier section. Further, the Start Event and the End Event of the project are marked as ***milestone events*** (rectangles). Circles show the other events. The ***optimistic time estimate - a, pessimistic time estimate* - b**, and the ***most likely time* - m**, for each activity are given or written along the respective activity arrow.

Computation of Expected Activity Time

The expected activity time for each activity of the Network is calculated by the three time estimates, according to PERT formula:

$$t_{Ei\text{-}j} = \frac{a + 4m + b}{6}$$

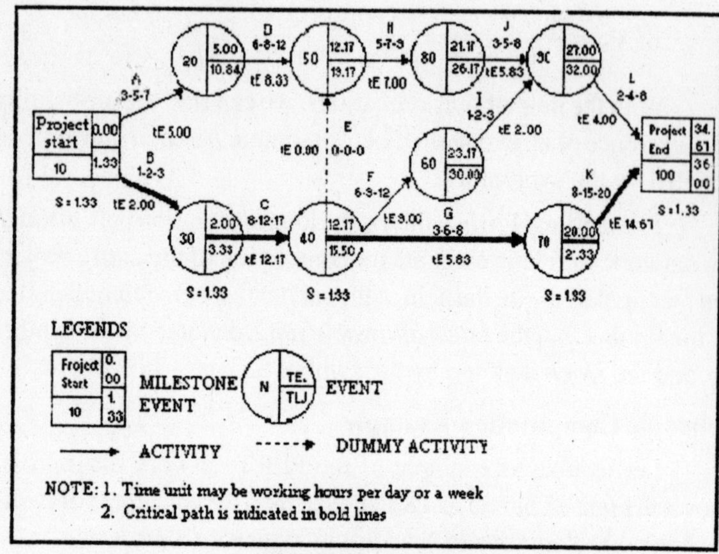

Figure Chapter K-18

For example for the activity L between event 90 and 100 (*see* Figure Chapter K-19) the ***optimistic time estimate*** **a** = 2, ***pessimistic time estimate*** **b** = 6 and the ***most likely time*** **m** = 4:

2-4-6

(90) ——→ (100)

L

Figure K-19

The expected activity time for this activity is calculated as follows:

$$t_E^{90\text{-}100} = \frac{2 + 4 \times 4 + 6}{6} = \frac{2 + 16 + 6}{6} = \frac{24}{6} = 4 \text{ units time}$$

Similarly t_E of all the Network activities is calculated and their vales are given in Table 1 below:

*Table 1: Calculation s of tE of the Network Activities**

Activity			Expected Activity Time
90	L	100	04.00 *Unit Time*
70	K	100	14.67
80	J	90	05.83
60	I	90	02.00
50	H	80	07.00
40	G	70	05.83
40	F	60	09.00
40	E	50	00.00
20	D	50	08.33
30	C	40	12.17
10	B	20	02.00
10	A	20	05.00

* **Note:** It is convenient to start calculations for tE from the terminal event. The end event 100 is entered first in successor event column 2 of the Event-Activity Table (see **Annexure I**). As this event has two predecessor events 90 and 70, two entries are made for this event in the table. Further successor events along with their predecessor events are entered in the respective columns and rows according to the decreasing order of their numerical value.

The data for **a, m, b** and $\mathbf{t_E}$, for the activities that comprise the Network is also recorded in tabular form in the **Event-Activity Scheduling Table** (*see* Annexure I).

Comments:

As may be seen that the network (*see* Figure Chapter K-18) contains 4 paths from the start event to terminal event. After calculating the sum of $\mathbf{t_E}$ of each path, as shown in the Table 2 below, the critical path of the network can be established.

Table 2

S. No.	Path	Activities	Σt_E	Unit Time
1	W	O -A→ O -D→ O -H→ O -J→ O -L→ O	5.00+8.33+7.00+5.83+4.00	= 30.16
2	X	O -B→ O -C→ O -G→ O -K→ O	2.00+12.17+5.83+14.67	= 34.67
3	Y	O -B→ O -C→ O -E→ O -H→ O -J→ O -L→ O	2.00+12.17+0.00+7.00+5.83+4.00	= 31.30
4	Z	O -B→ O -C→ O -F→ O -I→ O -L→ O	2.00+12.17+9.00=2.00+4.00	= 29.17

From the above calculations, we observe that path X, which takes longest time to complete, that is 34.67-unit time, is the **Critical path** of the network. The activities lying along this path are critical in the sense that their occurrence cannot be delayed if the scheduled completion time, say a 36-unit time is to be met.

Calculation of Earliest Expected Event Time (T_E)

The **Earliest Expected Event Time** is the time or date when a successor event j of an activity i-j can be expected to be completed. Thus, we can say it is the earliest finish or completion time for any activity i-j. It is denoted by the symbol $\mathbf{T_E}$. $\mathbf{T_E}$ for a path in network is computed by adding the $\mathbf{t_E}$'s of the activities of a path leading to the end event. Symbolically we can say TE = $\Sigma \mathbf{t_E}$.

The formula for calculations of $\mathbf{T_E}$ of all the events in the network is:

$\mathbf{T_{Ej}}$ (successor event) = **maximum of** $\mathbf{T_{Ei}}$ (predecessor event) + $\mathbf{t_{Ei\text{-}j\ (activity)}}$

i.e., $\mathbf{T_E}$ (of successor event) = $\mathbf{T_E}$ (of predecessor event) + $\mathbf{t_E}$ (of activity)

One starts the computations of earliest expected event times (of TE's) from the initial event and end with the terminal event of the network. This procedure is called forward pass.

Therefore, for calculating $\mathbf{T_E}$'s of events of the network example (**Figure K10-18**) we work with the ***scheduling table*** (**Annexure 1**) from the bottom upwards and compute the $\mathbf{T_E}$ of each event as shown below:

$\mathbf{T_E}$ of Event 10 = 0 unit time

$\mathbf{T_E}$ of Event 20 = $\mathbf{T_E}$ Event 10 + tE (activity 10->20 or A activity) = 0.00+ 5.00 = 5.00 unit time

According to PERT rules, when two or more activities combine at a particular Event, the earliest expected time must be calculated through all the activities and the highest of all the values is declared as earliest expected time of the particular event.

We have calculated earliest expected time through all activities and according to the given formula and the $\mathbf{T_E}$ of each event derived after computations are given in the **Table 3**. The highest value of the $\mathbf{T_E}$ of an event, having more than one value is printed in italics. This value (i.e., printed in italics *) is taken as the valid earliest expected time of the particular event and recorded on the network diagram (*see*).

Table 3. Calculations of Earliest Expected Event Time T_E

$\mathbf{T_E}$ Event 10		= **00.00** unit time
Event 20	= $\mathbf{T_E}$ Event 10 + $\mathbf{t_E}$ Activity A	= **05.00** unit time
Event 30	= $\mathbf{T_E}$ Event 20 + $\mathbf{t_E}$ Activity B	= **02.00** unit time
Event 40	= $\mathbf{T_E}$ Event 30 + $\mathbf{t_E}$ Activity C	= **14.17** unit time
Event 50*	= $\mathbf{T_E}$ Event 20 + $\mathbf{t_E}$ Activity D	= 13.33 unit time
Event 50*	= $\mathbf{T_E}$ Event 40 + $\mathbf{t_E}$ Activity E	= *14.17* unit time
Event 60	= $\mathbf{T_E}$ Event 40 + $\mathbf{t_E}$ Activity F	= **23.17** unit time
Event 70	= $\mathbf{T_E}$ Event 40 + $\mathbf{t_E}$ Activity G	= **20.00** unit time
Event 80	= $\mathbf{T_E}$ Event 50 + $\mathbf{t_E}$ Activity H	= **21.17** unit time
Event 90*	= $\mathbf{T_E}$ Event 60 + $\mathbf{t_E}$ Activity I	= 23.17 unit time
Event 90*	= $\mathbf{T_E}$ Event 80 + $\mathbf{t_E}$ Activity J	=*27.00* unit time
Event 100*	= $\mathbf{T_E}$ Event 70 + $\mathbf{t_E}$ Activity K	= *34.67* unit time
Event 100*	= $\mathbf{T_E}$ Event 90 + $\mathbf{t_E}$ Activity L	= 31.00 unit time

These calculations are also entered in column 7 of the ***scheduling table*** (Annexure 1). The valid Earliest Expected Event

Time (T_E^j) values written in bold letters and in italics are entered in columns 8 of the ***scheduling table*** (Annexure 1).

***Note**:*As pointed out earlier, according to PERT rule when an event j has more than one predecessor event the maximum of T_E^j value is considered. In the above calculations: (a) Event 50^j has two predecessor Events, 20 and 40; (b) Event 90^j has two predecessor Events, 80 and 60; and (c) Event 100^j has two predecessor events, 70 and 90. Therefore their respective, maximum value of T_L^j (printed in italics) is considered and recorded the column 7. The value of all printed in bold and italics are then written in column 8 of scheduling table Annexure 1 as valid values of T_L^j.*

Calculation of Latest Allowable Event Time (T_L)

The next step of the network analysis is to determine the latest date or time which each Event can be accomplished without interfering with the scheduled date or time for completion of the project. The latest date (T_L) for an Event is determined by the amount of time on the longest path between the End Event of the project and the Event being considered. It is, therefore, a similar calculation to be carried out as for earliest expected event time (T_E), but in reverse, starting at the End Event and working backward through the network. This can be explained again using the example network.

The Scheduled **Time** = T_S fixed by the sponsoring authority, or management, or analyst for completion of a project and refers to the occurrence of End Event is entered on the network as Latest allowable End Event Time. This can be more than or equal to or less than the project estimated or derived duration. In the case of the example Network, we have assumed TS = 36.00 unit time. This date is entered as end date on the network.

The latest allowable date or time the preceding Event (T_L) is calculated by taking the latest date of the succeeding event and subtracting the time of the activity, which is connected with both the Events. Thus, the latest allowable finish time of activity i-j can be calculated by the following formula:

$$T_L^i = \text{minimum of } (T_L^j - t_E^{i\text{-}j})$$

Or $\mathbf{T_L}$ (predecessor Event) = $\mathbf{T_L}$ (successor Event) - $\mathbf{t_E}$ (activity)

According to PERT rules, when a preceding Event has more than one successor Events the minimum value of a successor Event is considered for calculation of $\mathbf{T_L}$ of the predecessor Event.

The calculations of $\mathbf{T_L}$ are started from the terminal Event and end at the start of Network. The procedure is called *backward pass*. Therefore for calculating the $\mathbf{T_L}$'s of the events of the network example (Figure Chapter K-18) we will work the ***scheduling table*** (Annexure 1) from top downwards, and these calculations are given the Table 4.

Table 4: Calculations of Latest Allowable Time (T_L)

T_L Event 100	= $\mathbf{T_L}$		**= 36.00 unit time**
T_L Event 90	= $\mathbf{T_L}$ Event 100-$\mathbf{t_E}$ L	= 36.00-4.00	**= 32.00 unit time**
T_L Event 80	= $\mathbf{T_L}$ Event 90-$\mathbf{t_E}$ J	= 32.00-5.83	**= 26.17 unit time**
T_L Event 70	= $\mathbf{T_L}$ Event 100-$\mathbf{t_E}$ K	= 36.00-14.67	**= 21.33 unit time**
T_L Event 60	= $\mathbf{T_L}$ Event 90-$\mathbf{t_E}$ I	= 32.00-2.00	**= 30.00 unit time**
T_L Event 50	= $\mathbf{T_L}$ Event 80-$\mathbf{t_E}$ H	= 26.17-7.00	**= 19.17 unit time**
T_L Event 40*	= $\mathbf{T_L}$ Event 70-$\mathbf{t_E}$ G	= 21.30-5.80	***= 15.50 unit time****
T_L Event 40*	= $\mathbf{T_L}$ Event 60-$\mathbf{t_E}$ F	= 30.00-9.00	= 21.00 unit time
T_L Event 40*	= $\mathbf{T_L}$ Event 50-$\mathbf{t_E}$ E	= 19.17-0.00	= 19.17 unit time
T_L Event 30	= $\mathbf{T_L}$ Event 40-$\mathbf{t_E}$ C	= 15.50-12.17	**= 03.33 unit time**
T_L Event 20	= $\mathbf{T_L}$ Event 50-$\mathbf{t_E}$ D	= 19.17-8.33	**= 10.84 unit time**
T_L Event 10 *	= $\mathbf{T_L}$ Event 30-$\mathbf{t_E}$ B	= 3.33-2.00	***= 01.33 unit time****
T_L Event 10 *	= $\mathbf{T_L}$ Event 20-$\mathbf{t_E}$ A	= 10.18-5.00	= 05.84 unit time

These calculations are entered in column 9 of the ***Scheduling Table*** (Annexure 1)

Comments

1 As per PERT rule, a given scheduled time or date for completion of the terminal Event (i.e., the project's scheduled time) determines the latest allowable time for the project. In case, management does not make available scheduled completion time (i.e., **Ts**), then one should consider $\mathbf{T_L^j}$ equal

to T_E of the terminal Event. Here we have however, assumed **Ts** = 36.00 unit time as given scheduled completion time.

2 As per rule when an event i has more than one successor event then minimum of $T_L{}^i$ is taken as appropriate value for $T_L{}^j$. In the above calculation, (a) **Event 40** has three successor events 70, 60 and 50; Event **10** has two successor events 30 and 20. Therefore, their respective minimum value recorded in italics * in column 9 are considered as valid value for calculating $T_L{}^j$.

3 Later, in the column 10, the appropriate values of **TLj**, recorded in bold and italics in column 8 are entered against the respective events.

4.1 Calculation of Event Slack

The difference between the Latest Allowable Time ($T_L{}^I$) and the Earliest Expected Event Time (T_{Ej}) is called ***Event Slack***. Thus, slack time or float time is the amount of time by which the actual completion time of an activity exceeds the earliest expected time T_{Ej} without causing the duration of over-all project to exceed its scheduled completion time **Ts**. There are the three conditions of slack: negative, zero, and positive. If expected time T_E**j** exceeds the allowed time T_{Lj} then there is negative slack. If allowable time T_{Lj} exceeds the expected time then there is positive slack. If allowed time T_{Lj} and the expected time T_{Ej} are equal then there is zero slack. The computation of **Slack (S)** for an activity (i—j) is done according to the formula:

$$S^j = T_L^j - T_E^j$$

The calculation of **slack time S** in completion of the activities of the Network example (Figure Chapter K-18) is done according ***the*** given formula and shown in the Table 5 below:

Table 5: Calculation of Slack Time (S)

S (Event 100) T_L^j (Event 100) - T_E^J (Event 100)	= 36.00-34-67 = **1.33** u t*
S (Event 90)	= 32.00-27.00 = *5.00* u t**
S (Event 80)	= 26.17-21.17 = *5.00* u t**
S (Event 70)	= 21.33-20.00 = **1.33** u t*
S (Event 60)	= 30.00-23.17 = 6.63 u t
S (Event 50)	= 19.17-14.17 = *5.00* u t**
S (Event 40)	= 15.50-14.17 = **1.33** u t*
S (Event 30)	= 0 3.33-02.00= **1.33** u t*
S (Event 20)	= 10.80-05.84 = *5.00* u t**
S (Event 10)	= 01.33-00.00 = **1.33** u t*

The slack time of each activity is entered in column 12 of the ***Scheduling Table*** (Annexure 1)

Comments

After calculating slack times for various activities of a project we can also find out the ***critical path*** in the project, which consists of consecutive events having minimum slack times. Referring to ***Table*** (Annexure 1), we may note that the events 10, 30, 40, 70, 100 are the events of the network having minimum slack times namely, ***1.33 unit time*** *. This path is the **Critical Path** of the network. For the network the following is the critical path:

10 ⟶ 30 ⟶ 40 ⟶ 70 ⟶ 100

The above critical path is also *the longest path through the network*. Besides determining the critical path through the network, we can identify various sub-critical paths that have varying degrees of slack. Arranging the next groups of events according to the magnitude of their total slack, we find that events 20, 50, 80, 90 have ***5 unit slack*** ** each. Hence, the path connecting these events is ***near critical path*** or ***semi critical path*** of the network.

4.2 Computation of Dispersion or Variance of Activity Performance

The computation of variance $(V_T)^2$ for an activity: i-j is done according to the formula:

$$(V_T)^2\ i\text{-}j = \frac{(b-a)^2}{(6)^2}$$

After calculation the variances of all the activities of the network are given in the following Table 6:

Table 6: Calculation of Variance

Activity		Variance
L	$= \frac{(6-2)^2}{(6)^2} = \frac{(4)^2}{(6)^2} = \frac{(2)^2}{(3)^2} = \frac{4}{9}$	= 0.44 unit time
K	$= \frac{(20-8)^2}{(6)^2} = \frac{(12)^2}{(6)^2}$	= 4.00 unit time
J	$= \frac{(8-3)^2}{(6)^2} = \frac{(5)^2}{(6)^2}$	= 0.69 unit time
I	$= \frac{(3-1)^2}{(6)^2} = \frac{(2)^2}{(6)^2}$	= 0.11 unit time
H	$= \frac{(9-5)^2}{(6)^2} = \frac{(4)^2}{(6)^2}$	= 0.44 unit time
G	$= \frac{(8-3)^2}{(6)^2} = \frac{(5)^2}{(6)^2}$	= 0.69 unit time
F	$= \frac{(12-6)^2}{(6)^2} = \frac{(6)^2}{(6)^2}$	= 1.00 unit time
E	$= \frac{(0-0)^2}{(6)^2} = \frac{(0)^2}{(6)^2}$	= 0.00 unit time
D	$= \frac{(12-6)^2}{(6)^2} = \frac{(6)^2}{(6)^2}$	= 1.00 unit time
C	$= \frac{(17-8)^2}{(6)^2} = \frac{(9)^2}{(6)^2}$	= 2.25 unit time
B	$= \frac{(3-1)^2}{(6)^2} = \frac{(2)^2}{(6)^2}$	= 0.11 unit time
A	$= \frac{(7-3)^2}{(6)^2} = \frac{(4)^2}{(6)^2}$	= 0.44 unit time

The *data variance* of performance of each activity given in Table 6 is entered in column 5 of the ***Scheduling*** Table (Annexure 1).

Comments

With the help of variance $(\mathbf{V_T})^2$ and standard deviation **SD** = /$(\mathbf{V_T})^2$ of the critical path, earliest expected completion time ($\mathbf{T_E}$) and scheduled time (**Ts**) of the network, we can calculate probability of completion of the project on scheduled date.

Calculations

The ***variance*** of the critical path of the project can be determined by summing up the variance of the following activities along the critical path.

10 ⟶ 30, 30 ⟶ 40, 40 ⟶ 70, and 70 ⟶ 100

The ***critical path*** of the network is:

10 ⟶ 30 ⟶ 40 ⟶ 70 ⟶ 100

and the variance of the each activity on the path is:

Activity	*Variance*
10 ⟶ 30	0.11
30 ⟶ 40	2.25
40 ⟶ 70	0.70
70 ⟶ 100	4.00

Thus:

The variance of the critical path = 0.11+2.25+0.70+4.00

= 7.06 Unit time

Standard deviation (SD) for the project = /7.06 = 2.65 unit time

Scheduled completion time for the project Ts = 36.00 unit time

Earliest expected completion time for the project T_E

= 34.67 unit time

The normal deviate of project from **Ts** from $\mathbf{T_E} = \frac{T_s - T_E}{SD}$

$$= \frac{36.00 + 34.67}{2.65} = \frac{1.33}{2.65} = \frac{1}{2} \textit{ approximately}$$

Referring to the table of 'Normal Distribution Function' probability of completion of the project within scheduled time **Ts** comes to **69.2 per cent.**

REFERENCES AND READING LIST

1. Arhibald, Russell D; Viloria Richard L. *Network-based system (PERT/CPM).* 1958; p. 10.
2. Dhirendra Rao, M. K. PERT/CPM - its application to library and information systems. *Annals of Library Science and Documentation.* v.25; 1978; p 31-71.
3. *Engineer Planning and organisation of work.* 1964. Technical Training Group, REME, Chatham, England. p 3.
4. Gantt, J. L. *Organization of work.* 1919
5. Hayes Robert J; Beker, Joseph. *Handbook of data processing for libraries.* Ed 2. 1970. p. 7.
6. Kashyap, M. M. Network analysis: A library project management tool. *Journal of Library and Information Science.* v. 1,2; 1976; p. 199-231.
7. Kelley J. E. Critical path planning and scheduling: Mathematical basis. *Operation Research.* v. 9; 1961; p. 296-230.
8. —. *op cit.* P 301.
9. —; Walker, Morgan R. Critical path planning and scheduling. **In** EASTERN JOINT CONFERENCE (1959). *Proceedings.* 1960; p. 150-73.
10. Klingel, A. R. Bias in PERT project completion time calculation for real network. *Management Science.* v. 13; 1966; p. B194-B201.
11. MacMrimmon, K. R.; Kyave, C. A. An analytical study of PERT assumption. *Operation Research.* v. 12; 1964; p. 17-37.
12. Malcol D. G.; *et al.* Application of technique for R and D program evaluation (PERT). *Operation Research.* .7; 1959; 546-69.
13. MODER (Joseph J) and PHILIPS (Cecil R). *Project management with CPM and PERT.* Ed 2. 1970. P 7.
14. – and – *op cit.* P 275.

15. – and – *op cit.* P 327.
16. – and ROGERS (E G). Judgement estimates of the moment's PERT type distribution. *Management Science*. 15; 1968; B76-B83.
17. PRATAP LINGAM (P). Library and information systems: planning scheduling and control through the PERT/CPM. *Library Science with Slant to Documentation*. 18; 1981; 248-62.
18. USA, DEPARTMENT OF NAVY, SPECIAL PROJECTS OFFICE. PERT summary report phase I. 1958. Government Printing Press, Washington D C.

ANNEXURE 1: EVENT-ACTIVITY SCHEDULING TABLE: PART I

1	*2*	*3*	*4*			*5*	*6*
Activity	***j NODE Successor Event***	***iNODE Predecessor Event***	***3 point estimates***			***t_EMean***	***$(V_T)^2$ Variance***
			a	***m***	***b***		
L	100	90	2	6	4	04.00	0.44
K	100	70	8	15	20	14.67	4.00
J	90	80	3	6	8	05.83	0.69
I	90	60	1	2	3	02.00	0.11
H	80	50	5	7	9	07.00	0.44
G	70	40	3	6	8	05.83	0.69
F	60	40	6	9	12	09.00	1.00
E	50	40	0	0	0	00.00	0.00
D	50	20	6	8	0	08.33	1.00
C	40	30	8	12	17	12.17	2.25
B	30	10	1	2	3	02.00	0.11
A	20	10	3	5	7	05.00	0.44
Start	10	-	0	0	0	00.00	0.00

Part II

$7T_E^i$	$8T_E^j$	$9T_L^J$	$10T_L^J$	11Ts	12S
31.00	34.67	32.00	36.00	36.00	**1.33***
34.67		21.33			
27.00	27.00	26.17	32.00		5.00**
25.17		30.00			
21.17	21.17	19.17	26.17		5.00**
20.00	20.00	15.50	21.33		1.33*
23.17	23.17	21.00	30.00		6.83
14.17	14.17	19.17	19.17		5.00 **
13.33		10.84			
14.17	***14.17***	01.33	03.33	15.50	**1.33***
02.00	02.00	01.33	03.33		**1.33***
05.00	05.00	05.84	10.84		***5.00*** **
00.00	00.00	0 0.00	01.33		**1.33***

***Critical path** = 10 → 30 → 40 → 70 → 100

L
Bibliographic Database: Content Description, Organization And Retrieval

This chapter briefly discusses: 1) the cataloguing contents of the records containing descriptive elements of bibliographic items, including metadata of bibliographic databases; 2) methods of indexing contents and techniques and tools for organizing the contents; 3) strategies for search and retrieval of records; and 4) problems in searching and retrieval.

A more detailed discussion on content development organization and retrieval is planned to be published separately.

1 CONTENT DESCRIPTION

The description, analysis, preparation of indexes to and organization of the contents of a database are crucial to the rapid identification, and efficient retrieval of pertinent information responding to the requirements of the end-user.

In manual cataloguing of a document, codes and rules, such as the Anglo-American Cataloguing Rules (AACR2), the International Standards for Bibliographical Description (ISBD) and S.R. Ranganathan's Classified Catalogue Code have been used. Recent revisions of some of these guides (e.g. AACR2 rev. 1998, ISBD(ER)) cover the bibliographic description of electronic resources also. Unesco's Common Communication Format (CCF/B), Indian Standard (IS:11370-1985) — Guide for Data Elements and Record Format for Computer Based Bibliographic Data Bases for Bibliographic Description of Different Kinds of Documents and

Library of Congress Machine Readable Catalogue (MARC) formats* are widely used in selecting fields and their tags for bibliographic records. (*See also* 1.3.4.2.4)

(*Note:* All USMARC products have become MARC 21 products. The first to be published were *MARC 21 Format for Bibliographic Data Including Guidelines for Content Designation (1999)* and *MARC 21 Format for Authority Data,* followed by the other formats and code lists. The Library of Congress, the British Library, and the National Library of Canada synchronized the USMARC, UKMARC, and CAN/MARC formats, and have now joined their MARC documentation to form MARC 21)

A widely accepted bibliographic record structure to facilitate exchange of records among databases is ISO2709. The structure of ISO2709 data format is described in the CCF/B manual.

1.1 Metadata

Metadata, in a broad sense, is data about data or information about information. With reference to the Internet, metadata refers to data describing the attributes of an electronic resource. This implies that metadata refers to another piece of information existing in a separate physical form from the item it refers to or represents. However, increasingly the term metadata is used to specify records that cite or refer to any digital or no digital information resources.

Metadata is defined by **Hodge** as "structured information that describes, explains, locates, or otherwise makes it easier to retrieve, use or manage an information resource." (*cf.*, **Hodge, Gail.** (2001). Metadata Made Simpler: A guide for libraries . National Information Standards Organization (NISO), Bethesda, MD 20814.). Another definition of Metadata is "data associated with objects which relieve their potential users of having to have full advance knowledge of the existence of characteristics" (*cf,* **Demsey and Heery** (1998)).

Thus we find that the term metadata is used differently in different contexts. Some use it to refer to records that describe electronic or internet resources, while in the library environment metadata is commonly used for any formal scheme of resource description, applying to any type of bibliographic item, digital or non-digital.

The use of metadata facilitates identification and accessing relevant information resources on the Web in a seamless way irrespective of the type of resource – text, image, museum object, scientific data, etc. – and its location.

Thus metadata assists in:

* Resource identification and location by relevant criteria
* Resource documentation
* Resource selection, evaluation and assessment
* Bringing similar resources together
* Distinguishing dissimilar resources
* Improving the quantity and quality of search results
* Content reuse
* Efficient content development and archiving
* Protecting intellectual property rights
* Electronic commerce through encoding of price, terms of payment, etc.

1.1.1 Characteristics of Metadata

* It is readable by both humans and computers.
* It takes a variety of forms, both specialized (Visual Resources Association(VRA)) Core Categories and general (Dublin Code(DC)), and may be part of a larger frame work (Text Encoding Initiative(TEI)).
* New metadata formats may emerge as the networked digital information resources grow and matures.
* Metadata differs from conventional catalogue data in certain respects. These differences relate to the nature of electronic resources on the Internet as differentiated from the physical (hard) items in, say a library, or electronic resources, such as, CD, held in a LAN environment. Almost any one can publish on the Web and there is virtually no control over it. Hence,

in web publishing there is little attempt to conform to any norms of resource description. Other differences to note include:

* A metadata record usually holds the location information within the record in such a way as to allow direct document delivery from appropriate application software. This implies that the record may contain detailed access information and network addresses. For using networked resources other access information, such as, access restriction or support contact addresses, may be required in addition to the URL (Uniform Resource Locator). This does not apply to location details in a conventional catalogue record.
* The Internet electronic data environment where metadata services are used change and develop rapidly.
* The location information given in a conventional catalogue entry in a library OPAC (Online Public Access Catalogue) typically refers to the location in that library. On the other hand, the metadata record information may refer to a remote location often not associated with the library / institution. Therefore, the metadata record has to provide information about access methods to the remote location, e.g. whether FTP or HTTP, and about access restrictions, such as, password.
* An Internet resource may be accessed from a growing number of different locations on the Net, more like a union catalogue.
* In the electronic form one and the same document may exist in different formats, for example, ASCII text, PDF, Postscript, MSWORD, etc. Usually metadata formats allow for different versions of the same document to be described in one record. In the hard copy or print version these are regarded as different editions or versions of the document.

* Data on the Internet is relatively short-lived as files are moved from one web server to another, making the original URL for the resource obsolete.
* Authors may change and develop documents with an existing URL. Thus many documents on the Internet may simply be working documents.

1.1.2 Metadata Format Types

Recognizing the limitations of search engines for the Internet resources, projects have been initiated for developing metadata formats and these will become increasingly important for retrieval of data from the Internet. It is unlikely that a single format will be adequate and universally acceptable for description of all types of information resources. There already exist widely used cataloguing codes for traditional library catalogue and other bibliographic records. Typical descriptive attributes include Name of Author(s) / Person responsible for the thought content of the work, Title of the Work, Indication of the Subject or Intellectual Content of the Work, Publisher, etc. Additional data fields may be required to describe other kinds of information resources (non-document). Client requirements may vary. A catalogue of documents of a publisher or of publishers may give price of the item, the distributors name, and terms of availability.

Researchers may wish to have more or extended documentation about an information resource. Again, some resources may exist on the Web for a short period only, while the others may be scholarly communications of more enduring interest and yet others may be of archival value. The first category may get only a simple catalogue description, whereas the others may warrant fuller description. Metadata may be embedded within the object described (e.g. databases accessed online from remote sites) or it may exist externally as a database of metadata records (e.g. catalogue database).

The Machine Readable Catalogue (MARC) family of formats were formulated even before the Internet and the extensive use of the Internet world-wide necessitated formulation of an Internet-compatible metadata format. The Dublin Core (DC) format was formulated specifically for describing Internet resources. The Text Encoding Initiative (TEI) has emerged out of the efforts to standardize electronic texts. The VRA Core Categories is a metadata element set developed to describe visual materials such as buildings, photographs, paintings and sculptures (http://www.gsd.harvard.edu/~staffaw3/vra/vracore3.htm). There are attempts to bring together different metadata formats under a common semantic network. We will briefly describe the three formats DC, TEI and MARC.

1.1.3 Dublin Core (DC)

The Dublin Core Metadata Element Set arose from discussions at a 1995 workshop sponsored by OCLC and the National Center for Supercomputing Applications (NCSA). As the workshop was held in Dublin, Ohio, the element set was named the Dublin Core. The original objective of the Dublin Core was to define a set of elements that could be used by authors to describe their own Web resources. The originally thirteen core elements were included, which were later increased to fifteen: *title, subject, description, source, language, relation, coverage, creator, publisher, contributor, rights, date, type, format,* and *identifier*. The detailed description of these elements is given below:

The Dublin Core Elements

Element Name	***Definition & Comments***
1. Title	A name given to the resource, by which the resource is known
2. Creator	An entity (a person, an organization, or a service) that is primarily responsible for making the content of the resource.
3. Subject	A topic of the content of the resource, which may be expressed by keywords, key phrases or classification codes that describe a topic of the resource using

	a controlled vocabulary or a formal classification scheme.
4. Description	An account of the content of the resource. Typically, an abstract, table of contents, and the like may be used to indicate the content of the resource.
5. Publisher	An entity (a person, an organization, or a service) that is responsible for making the resource available. Typically, the name of a Publisher is to be used to indicate the entity.
6. Contributor	An entity (a person, an organization, or a service), other than a creator, who makes certain contributions to the content of the resource. Typically, the name of a Contributor is to be used to indicate the entity.
7. Date	A date of an event in the lifecycle of the resource. Typically, Date will be associated with the creation or availability of the resource. Recommended best practice for encoding the date value is defined in a profile of ISO 8601 [W3CDTF] and includes (among others) dates of the form YYYY-MM-DD.
8. Resource Type	The nature or genre of the content of the resource. Resource type is indicated by the terms describing general categories, functions, genres, or aggregation levels for content. Recommended best practice is to select a value from a controlled vocabulary (for example, the DCMI

Type Vocabulary [DCT1]). To describe the physical or digital manifestation of the resource, use the FORMAT element.

9. Format — The physical or digital manifestation of the resource. Typically, Format may include the media-type or dimensions of the resource. Format may be used to identify the software, hardware, or other equipment needed to display or operate the resource. Examples of dimensions include size and duration. Recommended best practice is to select a value from a controlled vocabulary (for example, the list of Internet Media Types [MIME] defining computer media formats).

10. Resource Identifier — An unambiguous reference to the resource within a given context. Recommended best practice is to identify the resource by means of a string or number conforming to a formal identification system. Formal identification systems include Uniform Resource Identifier (URI), the Uniform Resource Locator (URL)), the Digital Object Identifier (DOI) and the International Standard Book Number (ISBN).

11. Source — A Reference to a resource from which the present resource is derived. The present resource may be derived from the Source resource in whole or in part. Recommended best practice is to identify the referenced resource by

	means of a string or number conforming to a formal identification system.
12. Language	A language of the intellectual content of the resource. Recommended best practice is to use RFC 3066 [RFC3066] which, in conjunction with ISO639 [ISO639]), defines two- and three-letter primary language tags with optional sub tags. Examples include "en" or "eng" for English, or "en-GB" for English used in the United Kingdom.
13. Relation	A reference to a resource related to the primary resource. Recommended best practice is to identify the referenced resource by means of a string or number conforming to a formal identification system.
14. Coverage	The extent or scope of the content of the resource Typically, Coverage will include spatial location (a place name or geographic coordinates), temporal period (a period label, date, or date range) or jurisdiction (such as a named administrative entity). Recommended best practice is to select a value from a controlled vocabulary (for example, the Thesaurus of Geographic Names [TGN]) and to use, where appropriate, named places or time periods in preference to numeric identifiers such as sets of coordinates or date ranges.
15. Rights	Information about rights held in and over the resource. Typically, this

element is represented by a rights management statement for the resource, or reference a service providing such information. Rights information often encompasses Intellectual Property Rights (IPR), Copyright, and various Property Rights. If the Rights element is absent, no assumptions may be made about any rights held in or over the resource.

Description of a monograph resource metadata, in Dublin Core format, is given below:

Title: Online Database Searching and Retrieval - Strategies, Procedures, Commands, and Problems: a Brief Guide

Creator: Neelameghan, A.

Subject: Online Database; Search Strategies

Description: Describes Search Strategies for Retrieving Information from Online Databases

Publisher: Sarada Ranganathan Endowment for Library Science, Bangalore.

Organization: Sarada Ranganathan Endowment for Library Science, Bangalore.

Date: 1995

Type: Text

Format: Text

Language: en

The Dublin Core metadata element set is a standard for cross-domain information resource description. Here an information resource is defined to be "anything that has identity". This is the definition used in Internet RFC 2396, "Uniform Resource Identifiers (URI): Generic Syntax", by Tim Berners-Lee et al. There are no fundamental restrictions to the types of resources to which Dublin Core metadata can be assigned.

The DC metadata standard is being coordinated by OCLC and NCSA. It is a simple set of fifteen elements covering the description of a range of network resources. The semantics of the fifteen elements of the standard have been established by an international, inter-disciplinary group of professionals representing library science, computer science, text encoding, museums and other related fields. The decisions are arrived at in DC workshops. The continuing development of the Dublin Core and related specifications is managed by the Dublin Core Metadata Initiative (DCMI) (http://dublincore.org/). The DC home page is maintained by OCLC at the URL http://purl.oclc.orf/metadata/ dublincore.

Each DC element is optional and may be repeated. A limited set of qualifiers, that is, attributes for use to further refine the meaning of an element is available. The DC is essentially for application to document-like objects but it may be used to describe similar or cognate entities, such as, profiles of persons, institutions, and research projects. DC is relatively simple, international in scope and may be extended as need arises.

1.1.4 Text Encoding Initiative (TEI)

The TEI (http://www.tei-c.org/) is an international project to guidelines for preparation and marking-up electronic texts for interchange with a view to support scholarly research and for a broad range of uses by the language industries. The sponsors of TEI are: the Association for Computers and the Humanities (ACH) and the Association of Literary and Linguistic Computing (ALIC), with support from the U.S. National Endowment for the Humanities (NEH), the Commission of the European Communities (CEC-DG-XIII), the Andrew W. Mellon Foundation, and the Social Sciences and Humanities Research Council of Canada. The TEI covers problems of describing encoded work such that the text itself, its source, encoding, and revisions are properly and completely documented This is achieved by the Header component of TEI which defines both a core set of elements and additional tag sets that may be used as extensions when necessary. The components of the TEI Header are:

* A file description containing full bibliographic description of the electronic resource including the sources from which the electronic text was derived.
* An encoding description of the relationship between an electronic text and its source(s).
* A text profile, containing classificatory and contextual information about the text, for example, the subject of the work.
* A history of the revisions.

The TEI Header can become lengthy and complex or quite simple. TEI headers may also be used as free standing documents.

1.1.5 MARC Format

The Machine Readable Catalogue (MARC) format consists of a family of formats. Having been started in the 1960s for meeting the opportunities offered by the computerization of library catalogues, the MARC has had a longer history than the other metadata formats. All of these have similar record structure and similar method of tagging data. However there are differences in their implementation. MARC was initially intended mainly to provide a framework for the exchange of catalogue records. The MARC format conforms in structure to the ISO2709 format and has four components:

* The Record Label (Leader);
* Directory;
* Data Fields; and
* Record Separator.

The MARC format essentially covers documents, videos, sound recordings at the object level. Given the fact that almost anyone or any organization can be a publisher on the Internet, retrieval of the information would become more efficient and convenient if these publishers incorporate metadata into the electronic publications. In this context it is highly desirable to identify and agree upon a minimal set of core metadata elements to be adopted by publishers of electronic information. Agreement on more elaborate and comprehensive metadata formats is also necessary for detailed descriptions of electronic records on the Internet.

1.2 Authority Lists / Files

As mentioned above, cataloguing codes and rules are useful guides in ensuring consistency of choice and rendering of various elements (e.g. Names of Persons, Corporate Names, Names of Meetings, Title of Documents, Title of Series, Names of Publishers, Names of Countries, etc.) in catalogue / database records. Additionally authority lists of such elements, with necessary cross references, can facilitate in ensuring consistency. The cataloguer / indexer should be able to consult such lists in and preferably use them online. This would minimize the need to type / key-in long and complex names, and hence reduce chances of typing errors. The ISBD manual and CCF manual give a list of codes for languages, and for countries. These can be consulted manually or databases of these can be created and consulted online at the time of data entry in a database. Examples of an authority list of corporate body names and serial titles from the IDRC's MIBIS database is given in Annex 3.

1.3 Subject Content Organization and Indexing

S.R. Ranganathan defined a work as consisting of three components: The **soul**, that is the ideas embodied in the work; the **subtle body**, that is the language of expression, the method of exposition, the style etc.; and the **gross body**, that is the physical carrier. This view applies irrespective of the physical medium in which the ideas are embodied. An organized body of ideas constitute a subject. Users of databases (electronic resources) are primarily interested in retrieving subject(s) embodied in information resources. The relevance of the records retrieved in satisfying the subject interest needs of the user depends in a great measure on how well the content has been analyzed and ideas of potential interest to users have been identified, selected and indexed. for quick retrieval.

The analysis of the subject content of an information resource should preferably be done by a person familiar with the subject, its specialized vocabulary, etc. Alternatively and in addition the cataloguer may take the help of appropriate subject specialist(s). The analysis and selection of concepts for indexing (and abstracting) can be assisted with the use of relevant classification scheme, thesauri, subject heading lists, concept maps, and other vocabulary management tools. Text mining and text analysis software can facilitate the analysis, synthesis (preparation of abstract) and selection of terms for indexing of text.

2 SEARCH STRATEGY

2.1 Introduction

The objective of a search and the associated search strategy is to obtain the best search results. That is the retrieved data / information matches with the inquirer's information requirement as fully as possible. All the records / information in the system that meet the user's interests at the moment are retrieved, and no irrelevant information is retrieved. The search result should be available when the user needs and with minimal effort and cost on his / her part.

A search in a database is an interactive, iterative and heuristic process. It is often a trial and error exercise in which the searcher in conversational or dialogue mode with the system and, if necessary and possible, with the participation of the end-user, attempts at successively refining and reformulating the search strategy and the initial search expression on the basis of responses of the system and end-user's reactions to the intermediate search results.

Searching in and retrieval of records / information from, a database may be done by the end-user directly, alternatively, an information professional – an intermediary e.g. reference librarian - may perform the search and retrieval operations for the end-user. In either case the success of an online search for and retrieval of, information from a database can be affected by a number of factors.

In a large measure it also depends on the searcher's understanding of the search languages and of the characteristics of the databases accessed and his/her ability to interact with the system, to formulate a search expression in the search language of the database service(s) to precisely represent the information need. If an information intermediary is involved in performing the search for the end-user, then the intermediary should be able to effectively interact with the end-user.

2.2 Principal Stages of the Search

The principal stages in database search may be summarized as follows:

1. Recognition of an information need and defining that need by the end-user in terms of a specific subject, type of information / document desired (e.g. bibliographic reference with or without abstract, numerical data, articles in periodicals only, documents in a particular language only, whether full-text would be required, translations requirement, to be kept updated, etc.), how soon the information is needed and other particulars.
2. Communication of the information need to the database service centre (in person, by letter, telephone, e-mail, or through another person), especially if the search is to be carried out by an intermediary.
3. Recording of the search request in a Search Record Form (online or printed form).
4. If necessary and if possible, the reference librarian / information specialist should arrange for a discussion with the end-user with the view to specifying as precisely as possible, the various aspects of the end-user's information need. Aids, such as, a scheme for classification or a thesaurus covering the subject of the query, subject map, known documents or a specialist in the subject of the query can help in the interview with the end-user. The display of these aids can be done online for the end-user to view. (cf, A. Neelameghan, 1995).

5. Selection of appropriate database(s) likely to yield best results.
6. Formulation of the query in the search language of the database and the software used in the creation of the database. This implies, adoption of search strategy and search expressions appropriate to the structure, organization, search language and capabilities of the system. Vocabulary management tools, such as, thesaurus, classification scheme, subject heading lists, etc. associated with the database(s) to be searched can assist this step. If possible, the end-user should be enabled to participate at this stage to obtain good search results.
7. The search operation: Fast access files, such as inverted / index file(s) created by the system should be used. The Any File of CDS-ISIS is also a fast access file. The end-user can assist in the evaluation of the initial / intermediate search results and provide feedback.
8. If necessary, modification of search strategy and refinement of the search expression on the basis of the successive end-user feedback on the successive intermediate retrieval results.
9. Selecting the most relevant references / abstracts and arranging for copies of the documents as desired by end-user.
10. Recording / logging the query (e.g. in a Search Request Form), the search procedure adopted and the results obtained for future use and analytical studies.

The flow chart (Figure Chapter L-1 in Appendix) is a schematic representation of the search procedure. (cf, Guinchat and Menou, 1990)

2.3 General Features of a Search Language

The documents represented by surrogates (e.g. catalogue entries, bibliographic citations) in the database are assigned index terms preferably selected from a related vocabulary tool, such as, a thesaurus, classification scheme, subject headings list, Wordnet, subject map, etc. Often these tools indicate the nature of relations (hierarchic and non-hierarchic associative relation) among concept

/ terms. Such tools can not only aid in the indexing of documents at the cataloguing / data entry stage nut also in the correct specification and representation of user's query and in evaluating and refining the search expression to begin with and on the basis of evaluation of intermediate search results as mentioned earlier. The index terms should be selected by a trained indexer and / or subject specialist. The vocabulary tools can also be used online while entering data in a database or formulating search expressions searching in the database. This can be done with CDS-ISIS (DOS version) using the Pascal programme VOCON.PAS, and also with WINISIS the database management systems of UNESCO.

Terms in the search expression are matched with the index terms assigned to document surrogates to effect retrieval of relevant records. The retrieved references are deemed to represent documents pertinent to the end-user's query and those not retrieved are deemed not pertinent.

Database systems generally permit the following types of search:

1. **Index-based search strategy**

   1.1 Display the index and select appropriate terms

   1.2 Enter the search terms (without selecting them from the index) but the system will scan the index for matching terms, and if found, will select them for search in the database.

   In the index-based search, much like looking up the index to a book, the system will directly identify the matching documents, if any (random access)

2. **Free-text search** (not using the index) strategy. Here the search will be sequential, record by record from the first to the last, much like going through page by page of a document to find the match. Hence free text search is relatively a longer process..

3. **Combination of (1) and (2)** strategy

   Generally the terms in the fields frequently searched by users are indexed (Canon of Recall Value), e.g in a bibliographic database, Name of author, Title words, Series title and/or words from the title of the series, Subject descriptors, Keywords, etc. Search by date of publication, name of publisher, place of publication, physical description etc. may be required only very occasionally. Hence contents of such fields may not be indexed. However, should the need arise, search in any one of these fields can be carried out using free text search. For example, all documents published in 2002; all documents in microfilm form, etc.

Combination of index-based search and free-text search is useful in responding to queries such as the following:

* Documents by C.R. Rao published during 1999 and 2002.
* In this case the author field will normally be indexed but not the date of publication field.
* Videocassettes on 'Environmental pollution'.
* In this case the subject descriptor field and / or keywords fields are usually indexed, but may not be the 'Type of material' field.
* The indexed field search is carried out first and then a free-text search in the output of the first search.
* Obviously the combination search strategy is useful when the number of records retrieved (or number of hits) by the indexed-based search is large and a further selection from the set may be made by free-text search – e.g. year or period of publication.

2.4 Search Operators

Search languages permit the use of various operators in formulating search expressions in order to improve the search results; firstly, retrieve all relevant references and not retrieve non-relevant references; secondly, enable evaluation of the retrieved references and organize or rank them in a sequence of decreasing relevance.

Boolean Operators: The widely used Boolean search operators include:

OR, AND, AND NOT

In the search expression for a particular software each of these operators may be represented by a symbol. For example in CDS-ISIS: OR by +; AND by * and NOT or AND NOT by ^

The search expression: aves **OR** birds (aves + birds in CDS-ISIS)

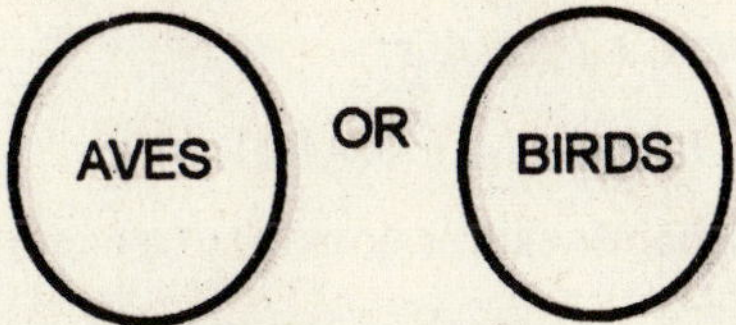

Fig. Boolean OR

Implies that the retrieved records may contain either of the terms 'aves' or 'birds'

The search expression: India **AND** Religions.

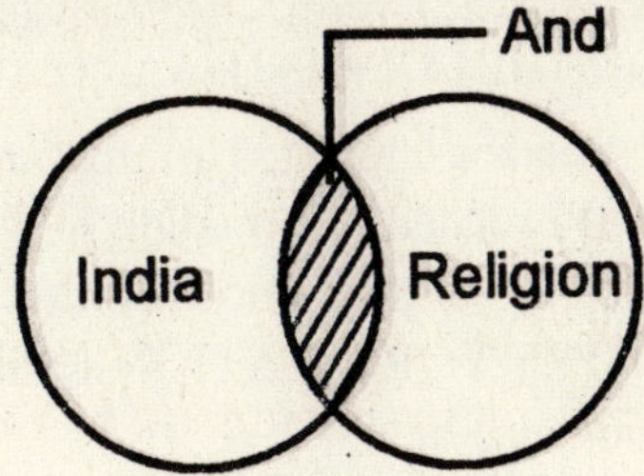

Fig.: Boolean AND

Implies that the retrieved records must contain both the terms 'India' and 'Religions'.

The search expression: oil NOT mineral oil.

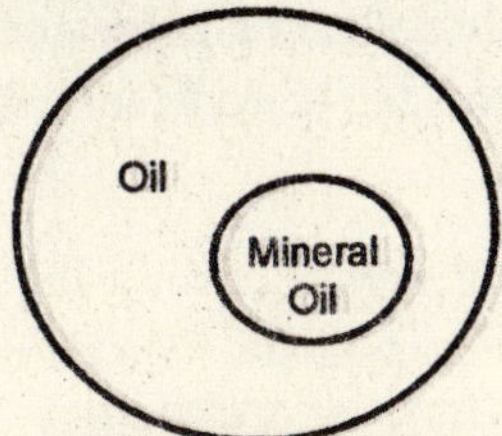

Fig: Boolean NOT

Implies that the retrieved records should contain the term 'oil' but should not contain the term 'mineral oil'

Other operators:

Parentheses are used to shorten the search expression and also ensure that the combination of terms in Boolean expressions are correctly applied. For example, the information need Pollution in Bihar, Orissa, and Tamil Nadu may be expressed as three separate search expressions:

POLLUTION * BIHAR

POLLUTION * ORISSA

POLLUTION * TAMIL NADU

The three separate expressions may be combined (using CDS-ISIS operators) as:

POLLUTION * BIHAR + POLLUTION * ORISSA + POLLUTION * TAMIL NADU

Using parentheses, the search expression may be made compact as:

POLLUTION*(BIHAR + ORISSA * TAMIL NADU)

Truncation: A person interested in information on 'FOREST' may also find useful / related information in documents that are indexed under each or combination of the terms FOREST, FORESTS, FORESTRY, FORESTATION. Using the OR operator the search expression, can be:

FOREST + FORESTS + FORESTRY

However, most retrieval software permit truncation, for instance, by suffixing a character (other than those that may normally occur in the search terms) to a common root of the search terms. CDS-ISIS uses $ (single dollar character) for the purpose. Thus, the above search expression can be represented as:

FOREST$

Care should be taken regarding the position in the string where the $ is placed. For instance, FORE$ will also OR terms such as FOREMAN, FOREIGN, FOREWORD, etc. which will lead to considerable noise in the retrieval. (retrieval of irrelevant documents)

Some software use? (question mark) as the truncation character and also allow specifying the number of characters that may be present after the truncation character. For Example:

RAMA RAO, K.?1

This means, the matching term in the record may contain just one character after K. For example, RAMA RAO, K.N, RAMA RAO, K.T will be a match, but not RAMA RAO, K.A.N.

Masking: The role of masking is somewhat similar to that of truncation but normally not suffixed but placed within a term to mask a character. For example:

NORMALI?ATION

This will OR the terms NORMALISATION and NORMALIZATION

Field Specific Search: If a user wishes to retrieve references to documents on S.R. Ranganathan but not to works by him, then it may be necessary to specify in the search expression that the search term Ranganathan, S.R. should occur in the Subject Keyword / Descriptor field only. The use of an operand qualifier in the search expression can be a solution. The search expression can be RANGANATHAN,S.R. /(field tag for subject descriptor) or SU=RANGANATHAN,S.R

Adjacency: In order to improve precision in retrieval with search expression(s) containing two or more terms, it may be necessary to specify that selected:

Two terms should follow one after the other with no other term separating them

The two terms may be separated by one, or two, or three...or n other terms only

The two terms may be separated by not more than one, or two, or three or ... n other terms.

CDS-ISIS prescribes adjacency operators $ **(dollar), . (dot)** for the purpose.

2.5 Limitations of Boolean Logic

The Boolean retrieval process generally uses the inverted or index file to the Database (s) being searched. Some of the limitations of this mechanism are as follows: (Gerrie, 1983)

1. A query must me fully and precisely state as a logical expression compatible with the indexing practrice of the database, irrespective of whether the index is made up of derived or assigned terms. This implies that an incomplete or open-ended search expression is not permitted.
2. The Boolean mechanism tends to have an all-or-nothing quality, that is, if the logical search expression is true for a specific document, the corresponding document / entry is retrieved; otherwise it is not retrieved; there is no partial matching.
3. The logic of sets compels value-judgment regarding a document into a binary scale – that is, either relevant or not relevant.
4. There is no order of preference within sets of retrieved records, each document retrieved is taken to as important as any other in the set.
5. Although a query can be precisely expressed using Boolean logic, the set of retrieved documents is not arranged in any sequence in terms of relevance to the query. A single retrieved set can be ranked after the retrieval.
6. With Boolean logic it is difficult to vary the depth of a search in order to vary the number of records or quantity of information required unless terms are either grouped in classes so that they can be automatically substituted for one another or the searcher is willing to study the properties of the index language in order to construct the right kind of query.
7. Boolean algebra or calculus of sets is not suited for considering doubtful classes or variable product classes. String ABC may represent a different class (BAC) in a different context. For

example, the three terms *Paint, Destruction, Microorganisms* in combination may connote either.

Destruction of Paint by Microorganisms

Or

Destruction of Microorganisms by Paint

2.6 Mismatch Between Information Need and Search Results

Problems of online searching identified in Fenichel's study (1980-1981) are summarized below:

Approaches to searching vary considerably, from one searcher to another even on the same system and database.

Major problems of most searchers are with the search strategy and not with the mechanics of the retrieval system.

Many searchers perform simple searches and do not browse the retrieved references to check the adequacy of a search formulation or to improve a search, that is, they do not make full use of online interactive facilities.

The online search process tends to be sensitive to and affected by many factors – including economic considerations, administrative policies, the search environment, the charging policy - in addition to the skill of the searcher and the nature of the question.

The major causes for the deviation between the actual information need of end-user and search results occurring at different stages of the search procedure include the following (Guinchat and Menou, 1990, p.314):

Problem recognition and actual information need of end-user

Information need as perceived by end-user

- Definition of problem
- Knowledge of available information
- Knowledge of information sources

Information need as expressed in end-user's query

- Communication means used (letter, phone, e-mail, in person, etc.

- Conscious retention of the exact parameters of the problem
- Communication ability of end-user

Information need as interpreted by Information specialist (IS)

- Subject / domain knowledge of IS
- IS's understanding of end-user's needs
- IS's aptitude for effective dialogue with end-user
- IS's capacity for expression

Query formulation in the language of the system

- Knowledge of search language of system
- Capabilities of the search language

Formulation of search expression and strategy

- Searcher's experience in searching particular database
- Adequacy of the search logic

Search and retrieval operations

- Capacity and flexibility of system
- Structure and organization of database

Intermediate results

- Adequacy of database

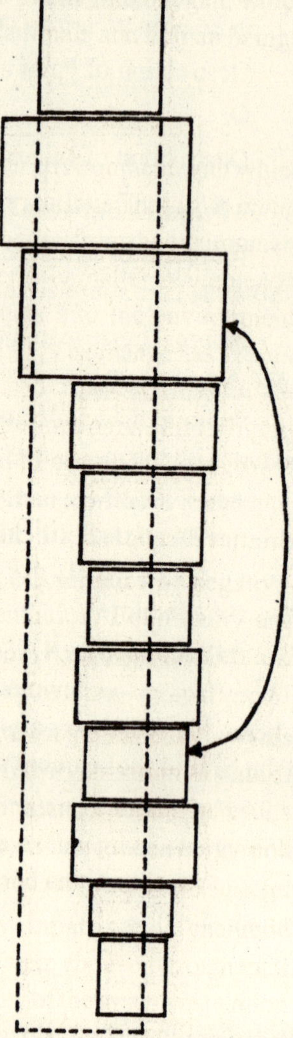

Fig: The Search Process

- Validity of judgement of pertinence

Final result

- Refinement of search expression
- Modification of search strategy

The unsatisfactory search results can arise from inadequate und-user/information specialists interaction. Selection of inappropriate database(s), inadequacy of and / or inadequate understanding of the search language of the database resulting in less effective searcher-system interface, etc. Therefore, a knowledge about and an understanding of the characteristics of the database system, the search language, formulation of search expression and searching, and specification of user needs can assist in adopting measures and techniques to improve search results vis a vis end-user needs.

Some of the differences between databases and errors within databases may not affect significantly searching in a printed page but they do so when searching online. For a searcher without adequate knowledge of the design and structure of the searchable fields, the capabilities of the query language, of the indexing language, the search engines, etc. obtaining satisfactory search results can be quite difficult. Variations can occur across database files, across the searchable indexes, and across the query languages used. When a number of databases are to be searched in different online services or websites. the difficulties may be compounded.

2.7 Major Approaches in Search Strategy

Major approaches in searching are (Markey and Atherton, 1981; Harter, 1986, chapter 7; Hartley, 1990, p. 170-71):

1. Briefsearch
2. Block-building method – reducing a request to a series of sub-problems
3. Successive fractions method – incolving iterative refinement of a broad starting strategy

4. Citation pearl growing method – a form of prototype matching
5. Starting a search with the most discriminating facet first;
6. Starting the search with the lowest posted or the most specific term as measured against the file; and
7. A combination of two or more of the above methods – usual in actual practice of searching.

2.7.1 Briefsearch

A Briefsearch is a quick and relatively less expensive way of getting a rough idea about what a database holds about a subject. Usually it involves a single search formulation, a Boolean combination of a few search terms, without spending time to use a vocabulary control tool to select synonyms, related terms etc. There may be minimal interaction between the searcher and the system. Recall ratio may be low.

Example: Birds AND India

Schools AND Karnataka

One may not adopt the Brief search approach for a full-fledged search. However if appropriate specific terms are used in formulating the search expression, it may result in high precision (relevance ratio) and also reasonably high recall. Example: biodiversity AND antarctica. Brief search can be useful to examine the terms used (e.g. descriptors) in a database for a particular concept; to select additional terms to build further search steps as in the Building Block Method and Pearl Growing Method. Brief search will also be useful to retrieve a record for a document known to be relevant to the query, for example, by words in the title, name of author, etc. Such a record can provide additional terms to build up a more in-depth or complete search strategy.

2.7.2 Building-block Method

In the Building-Block strategy each concept of the query is enlarged or enriched by synonyms and related terms (say, taken from a thesaurus) using Boolean OR to build smaller blocks which are then ANDed together to produce the answer set. The principal steps in the strategy after query formulation, formulation of objectives of the search and selecting appropriate database services and databases accessible include the following:

1. identification of major concepts and facets and the interrelationship among them;
2. formulating search strings that represent the concepts: words, phrases, descriptors, identifiers, qualifiers, etc.;
3. determining database fields to be searched;
4. for each component of the search expression a set of posting will be created; the sets are then Ored;
5. the sets resulting from step 4 are then combined using Boolean AND and NOT operators;
6. the intermediate results are evaluated and search terms and strategy modified if necessary and the process is iterated to obtained desired results.

Example: Query: Microcomputer software packages for information retrieval

Building blocks: s1 computer OR microcomputer OR PC
s2 software OR packages OR software packages
s3 information retrieval
s4 s1 AND s2 AND s3

This strategy is logical in construction but takes time in keyboarding and requires knowledge of the appropriate vocabulary. Use of a vocabulary control tool is advisable. It is a good way of conducting a comprehensive search requiring high recall.

2.7.3 Successive Fractions Strategy

The Successive Fractions approach is a way of reducing a large set created by using AND or NOT.

Example:Query: Swimming and physical fitness of women

Search sets: s1 swimming AND (wom?n OR female?) 620 postings s2 s1 AND fit? 42 postings

s3 s2 AND yr >= 1995 7 postings

Terms specifying date of publication and / or language(s) are useful to reduce the number of documents retrieved.

If the search retrieves too few or no records at all or the terms used in the search expression appear to be ambiguous, then the strategy may have to be changed. Two successive facet methods are available for the purpose – most specific concept first and fewest postings first. These are closely related to the Successive Fractions Strategy. All these methods start with a search expression that results in high recall and proceed to reduce the set to a smaller number of postings. They differ slightly in the method for selecting the initial set of postings.

2.7.4 Citation Pearl Growing Method

The Citation Pearl Growing method begins with a very small initial set, even a single item known to be relevant to the query. The initial record(s) set may be by Name of Author, a known specialist in the subject. The record(s) retrieved can provide additional relevant terms from the title, descriptors, abstract, etc. These can be used to cary out further searches on the subject. The Citation Pearl Growing method can be helpful in searches on subjects that are not familiar to the searcher and those in which vocabulary control tools are not available.

Prototype matching technique is similar to Citation Pearl Growing strategy.

2.8 Formulation of Search Expression

Formulation of a search expression consists of translating the concepts of the search request into the language of the database or information retrieval service selected. If the database has an associated vocabulary control tool, such as, list of subject headings, a thesaurus, and/or classification scheme, then it should be referred to, if not already done so while preparing the search request, in order to select appropriate near-synonymous or equivalent terms, and broader, narrower, and related terms.

Example: Query: References on Hyperactivity in Children

Key concepts selected: Children, Hyperactivity

Reference to a related thesaurus gives:

Children	Hyperactivity
Young children	Hyperkinesis
Infants	
Neonates	
Adolescents	

Boolean Expression:

(hyperactivity OR hyperkinesis) AND (children OR young children OR infants OR neonates OR adolescents)

The search expression means that the retrieved records / documents should contain at least one of the terms from each set of ORed terms (terms placed in parentheses)

When a search in a broad subject area is desired, consultation of the documentation on the database will indicate whether such a feature for search is provided for. For example:

* by DDC number in MARC records
* by Biosystematic Codes in BIOSIS
* by Section Code in CAS Online, Sociological Abstracts etc.
* by Subfiles in CAB International and TOXLINE

Example with ***Sociological Abstracts***

Section Code 1900 'The Family and Socialization' a search expression could be:

? ESH=1900

Ref	**Items**	**Index-term**
E1	225	SH=1844[SH = Section Heading Code]
E2	3456	SH=19
E3	8615	*SH=1900
E4	2356	SH=1900/38

E5	2345	SH=1900/39
E6	1654	SH=1900/40

...... more....

The searcher may select one or more of the Section Heading Codes, for example, **E5 Adolescence and Youth** for use in a search expression

The EXPLODE feature in relation to the terms in the hierarchical structure of MeSH terms in the *Medical Subject Headings – Tree Structure*, the EXPAND feature in DIALOG, and ZOOM on ESA-IRS can be used for a similar purpose, that is, for searching a broad subject area.

Example: SEARCH (EXPAND DE/CHILDREN)

CHILDREN	785
ADOPTED CHILDREN	73
MIGRANT CHILDREN	107
YOUNG CHILDREN	128
INFANTS	3679
PRESCHOOL CHILDREN	115
NEONATES	235
PREMATURE INFANTS	189
RESULT:	3175

If the term(s) of the vocabulary control tool does not adequately represent a concept, the database may use natural terms as index terms – free terms, text words, identifiers, etc, that may be applied in addition to or instead of, the controlled vocabulary terms. The following example illustrates such use.

Query	:	Effect of meditation on hypertension
Database searched	:	MEDLINE
Vocabulary tool	:	Medical Subject Headings (MeSH)

Let us say the term 'Meditation' does not occur in MeSH. Therefore, the search expression may be:

HYPERTENSION AND MEDITATION(TW)

[TW denotes Textword]

At this stage, the retrieval may be limited or narrowed down by language and/or date of publication of the papers and other parameters. Alternatively, these can be introduced at a later stage if the initial search expression retrieves a large number of records.

2.8.1 Improving Search Results: Recall and Precision Devices

Precision value is the ratio of the number of records retrieved to the number of relevant records present in the database. Precision devices are used to restrict the number of records retrieved. Such devices enable the coordination of linking information at various stages of document indexing, search, and retrieval processes. These devices include logic, syntactic, weighting devices, and bibliographic coupling.

2.8.2 Recall devices

Recall devices are used to increase the number of relevant references retrieved by a search expression. The more important of such devices are synonym control, hierarchical term linkage, associative term linkage, document clustering, control of word forms, summation of document sets, and bibliographic coupling so as to be able to retrieve related materials relevant to the subject of the query which may otherwise be missed.

Each of these devices can be implemented in different ways in online search. A summary of the implementation of these devices is given in Annex 1:

2.8.2.1 Synonym control

The searcher has no control over the indexing language, method or depth of indexing used by the producers of databases or the online services on which the databases may be accessed. However, if the software used has a facility for mapping of terms, then the searcher may use a non-preferred term from the vocabulary control tool associated with the database but will be guided or directed to the preferred term. In some systems, such as, MEDLINE, it is not advisable to use concurrently two search aids, e.g. expanding (exploding) an access term and the mapping facility. It may result in a 'NO POSTINGS' message.

Terms that are not truly synonymous are treated as such (e.g. FLATS and HOUSES), it may result in loss of term discrimination in the search language.

In some systems synonym control is implemented by confounding synonymous and near-synonymous terms, using different terms in indexing but they may be taken as synonyms in searching. The SAVE Search command in most information retrieval systems can emulate this feature. Judicious use of truncation can help, for example: LAW? can take care of LAW, LAWS, LAWYERS, LAWMEN, LAW SUIT, etc.

2.8.2.2 Hierarchical term linkage

Hierarchical Term linkage refers to the linking of the selected descriptor to its broader terms (BT) and narrower terms (NT) (super-ordinate and sub-ordinate terms). For example ***see also*** references in subject heading lists and BT and NT in thesauri. Establishing such relationships should preferably be done while formulating the search expression, say, with the help of appropriate vocabulary control tools. The EXPAND / EXPLOTE facility of the search software automatically matches generically related search terms taken from the controlled vocabulary. At time this can lead to the inclusion of noise (irrelevant) terms in the search expression.

2.8.2.3 Associative term linkage

Associative Term linkage represent non-hierachic associative term relations for a given descriptor, for example, the RT terms in a thesaurus. About thirty such relationships have been identified (Neelameghan, 2001; Neelameghan and Ravichandra Rao, 1974).

2.8.2.4 Document clustering

Associative and probabilistic indexing apply statistical techniques to produce clusters of keywords that form the basis for automatic derivative classification for retrieval. The associative groups are used in cluster-based retrieval (van Rijsbergen, 1979). The searcher controls the search and decides on the stopping point, to produce a list of retrieved documents in a sequence ranked according to their closeness to the query.

2.8.2.5 Control of word forms

Such control is essentially based on the prescriptive use of vocabulary in indexing. Judicious use of truncation enables matching of words with a common root. For example:

NETWORK? will match with NETWORK, NETWORKING and NETWORKS

LEGISLAT? will match with LEGISLATION, LEGISLATIONS, LEGISLATIVE, LEGISLATOR. LEGISLATORS, and wrongly spelt words, such as, LEGISLATOIN:

Control of word forms at search point provides the searcher different search options. However, the flexibility provided by truncation will be lost if confounding of word forms is done automatically at the indexing stage.

2.8.2.6 Summation of document sets

Most online retrieval services allow the use of Boolean operators. Different word forms can be ORed together. For example:

NETWORK OR NETWORKING OR NETWORKS

With CDS-ISIS, the ANY FILE and ANY FILE SEARCH provide for this facility extensively.

Gerrie's remarks are noteworthy in this connection:

"Under certain circumstances, the Logical expression A AND B may be too constraining, in that not all wanted documents explicitly contain B. Recall can be improved by identifying alternatives for B or by simply omitting B from the search and identifying some undesirable concept C. (A AND B) or (A NOT C), which will retrieve those documents that contain A and explicitly mentioning B while rejecting those explicitly mentioning C.

Quorum logic, in which retrieval is based on "n out of x terms" is also equivalent to Boolean logic and is useful when retrieval of a polythetic group is required but the actual term combinations are unimportant. Both weighted retrieval and quorum logic have the advantage of being able to express a retrieval function in a concise way when the retrieval objective is clear"

2.8.3 Precision Devices

Precision ratio is the number of recoras / documents retrieved to the number of records / documents judged to be relevant to the user's query. Precision devices are used for limiting the number of records retrieved and involve the coordination or linking of information at various stages of the indexing of documents, searching and retrieval processes. Online retrieval provides a variety of linkages and pre-coordinate index terms may be broken up for post-coordinate retrieval, the distinction between pre-coordinate indexing and post-coordinate indexing becomes hazy in online retrieval. The major precision devices may be grouped into logic devices, syntactic devices, weighting devices, and bibliographic coupling. A summary of the implementation of precision devices is given in Annex 2.

2.8.3.1 Logic devices

Logic devices include Boolean operators (AND, and AND NOT as distinct from OR NOT), and appropriately applied quorum logic (a retrieval specification "7 out of 10" terms will retrieve fewer records with a higher probability of relevance than a specification "5 out of 10"). Logic devices are based on post-coordinate contextual analysis , an extension of Boolean logic, and takes into account positional information in the retrieval process for enhancing the associative strength between terms so as to improve the precision.

2.8.3.2 Syntactic devices

Links and roles are used with syntactic devices. Links show which concepts are related by assigning a common letter or a number code to each of them or by using fixed tags and subfield code combinations so as to avoid false coordination or terms. As there are other methods of avoiding false coordinations there is relatively less interest in the use of links and roles. PRECIS as a pre-coordinate indexing system has been using role indicators.

2.8.3.3 Weighting devices

Term weighting technique is used for presenting search results in a ranked sequence. Weighting applied at the stage of indexing a record is based either on the intuitive judgment of a human indexer identifying concepts as major or minor or based on a statistical assessment of a term's weight depending on a calculated frequency of occurrence of terms. Retrieval based on such weights regard weighted occurrences of terms as more specific subsets of the whole set, both weighted and unweighted.

Weighting at the stage of searching permits the searcher to express an interest in a term over another for reasons unrelated to the actual use of the terms in the set of documents. A user interested in the subject "Comparative export potential of software from Hong Kong and Taiwan" may give greater weightage to a document that presents export figures for the two countries than to separate documents that deal with software industry in Hong Kong and software industry in Taiwan. There are several approaches to ranking of the retrieved sets (Hartley and others, 1990, p. 350-355; Gerrie, 1983, p. 154-155).

2.8.3.4 Bibliographic coupling

Bibliographic coupling is a measure of concept / subject association determined by the number of cited works that documents have in common. The measure remains over time once the documents are published.. Bibliographic association may be used to increase precision in retrieval in a scoring search.

The search begins with retrieval of a document known to be relevant to the query. Documents in a file or database in which the cited documents do not match in any way those in the document chosen are rejected. Documents with matching cited items are presented in a ranked sequence of their decreasing commonness of items with those in the bibliography of the chosen document.

2.9 Sensitivity to Errors

Most database systems require almost perfect input of data in cataloguing / indexing, search statements, command, etc. regarding spacing, punctuation, and spelling. Errors in typing and those relating to understanding of procedures and protocols specific to the particular system / software / service being used are common. Some types of typing errors are:

Character insertions	infformation
Character omission	infomation
Character substitution	imformation
Character reversal	informatoin

The system's lack of sensitivity to such simple human errors can lead to mismatch of search terms with the terms in the record or the index. This can result in recall or precision failures. The chances of retrieval of no records due to misspelling, incorrect usage of punctuation, spacing etc., are quite high. Such failures can be due to the searcher not using all possible approaches to retrieval or the search language used by the searcher not being fully compatible with that of the indexer of the system (Lancaster and Fayen, 1973)

Some systems (cf MEDLINE) ignore superfluous spacing and punctuation in the input. Right truncation can help in some cases as indicated earlier. The use of an abbreviated entry form for lengthy word form can offset the chances of errors in typing longer words

Some systems do not report error in input the search expression. As mentioned earlier, Boolean combinations of terms can be interpreted in more than one way, unless the components are properly enclosed in parentheses.

BIBLIOGRAPHIC REFERENCES

1. Dempsey, L. and Heery, R. (1998). Metadata: a eurrent view of practice and issues. *Journal of Documentation*, 54(2); p. 145-172.
2. Guinchat and Menou, (1990). *Sciences et techniques de l'information et de la documentation, Introduction generale*. Paris: Unesco. 5, p.224.
3. Hodge, Gail. (2001). *Metadata Made Simpler: A guide for Libraries*. National Information Standards Organization (NISO), Bethesda, MD 20814.

4. Neelameghan, A. (1995). *Online Database Searching and Retrieval - Strategies, Procedures, Commands, and Problems: a Brief Guide*. Sarada Ranganathan Endowment for Library Science, Bangalore. p. 150.

Annex 1: Recall Devices

Device	*Implementation*	*Remarks*
Synonym control	a) Prescriptive use of an index language while indexing	Possible loss of term discrimination
	b) Prescriptive use of an index language while indexing with term mapping while retrieving	
	c) Confounding synonyms	Advantageous to have relationshipsdefined by searcher
Hierarchical linkage of terms	a) Indexing documents both specifically and generically	Difficult to control search level
	b) Explosion by automatically linking generically related search terms at point of search	Spurious/undesirable genericspecific relationships in search expression
Associative linkage of terms	a) Automatic keyword classification	
	b) Associative probabilistic indexing	
Document clustering	a) Cluster-based retrieval	
Control of word forms	a) Truncation and suffixing	Control of word forms at point of search provides for a variety of search options
	b) Prescriptive use of an index language search options	
	c) Confounding word forms	

Device	*Implementation*	*Remarks*
	d) String searching	
Summation of document sets	a) Boolean OR b) Weighted retrieval c) Quorum logic	Qualitative retrieval and brevity of search expression
Bibliographic cycling	a) Forward cycling b) Backward cycling	Links between documents may be spurious; on the other hand associations that would otherwise remain hidden are revealed

Annex 2: Precision Devices

Device	*Implementation*	*Remarks*
Logic devices	Boolean AND, AND NOT a) Quorum logic x out of n b) Contextual logic	Reformulation of a search to increase precision is easier with quorum logic
Syntactic devices	Links a) Roles	
Weighting	a) At the point of indexing b) At the point of search c) At the point of retrieval d) At the point when document enter the system	Easier to vary the specificity of a search by assigning theshold and cut-off values. Weighting at the point of search provides more flexibility including the retrieval of a contiuous set of documents in a sequence of their probable relevance
Bibliographic coupling	Measures association among documents by their co-citation frequency	

Annex 3: Example of Authority Lists

Fields of the database (as in IDRC's CDS-ISIS based MIBIS database)

Tag	*Name*	*Repeatable*	*Subfields*
901	Corporate body		abcd
902	See reference(s	R	
903	Other language version(s)	R	
904	Former name(s)	R	
905	Later name(s)	R	
911	Serial title		
912	ISSN		
913	See reference(s)	R	
914	See also other language edn(s)	R	
915	Former title(s)	R	
916	Later title(s)	R	
921	Supplier authority code		
922	Supplier name and adder		abcd
997	Authority record notes		
998	Authority date		

CORPORATE BODY

International Development Research Centre, Ottawa, ON, CA.

SEE REFERENCE(S) : IDRC.

OTHER LANGUAGE VERSION(S) : Centre de Recherches pour le Developpement International.

Centro Internacional de Investigaciones para el Desarrollo.

Authority record notes : Source: its annual report.

Authority record date : 1988-01-14.

Centre de Recherches pour le Developpement International, Ottawa, ON, CA.

SEE REFERENCE(S) : CRDI.

OTHER LANGUAGE VERSION(S) : International Development Research Centre.

		Centro Internacional de Investigaciones para el Desarrollo.
Authority record notes	:	Source: its annual report.
Authority record date	:	1988-01-14.

Centro Internacional de Investigaciones para el Desarrollo, Ottawa, ON, CA.

SEE REFERENCE(S)	:	CIID.
OTHER LANGUAGE VERSION(S)	:	International Development Research Centre. Centre de Recherches pour le Developpement International.
Authority record notes	:	Source: its annual report.
Authority record date	:	1988-01-14.

OECD, Development Centre, Paris, FR.

OTHER LANGUAGE VERSION(S)	:	OCDE. Centre de Developpement.
Authority record date	:	1988-08-10.

OCDE, Centre de Developpement, Paris, FR.

SEE REFERENCE(S)	:	Centre de D,veloppement de l'OCDE.
OTHER LANGUAGE VERSION(S)	:	OECD. Development Centre.
Authority record date	:	1989-02-23.

OECD, Paris, FR.

SEE REFERENCE(S)	:	Organisation for Economic Co-operation and Development.
OTHER LANGUAGE VERSION(S)	:	OCDE.
Authority record date	:	1989-02-23.

OCDE, Paris, FR.

SEE REFERENCE(S)	:	Organisation de Coop,ration et de Developpement Economiques.
OTHER LANGUAGE VERSION(S)	:	OECD.
Authority record date	:	1989-02-23.

SERIAL

WHO chronicle

ISSN	:	0042-9694
OTHER LANGUAGE EDITION(S)	:	Cr¢nica de la OMS Chronique OMS

Authority record date : 1988-08-04

Cr¢nica de la OMS

ISSN : 0250-8591

OTHER LANGUAGE EDITION(S) : WHO chronicle Chronique OMS

Authority record date : 1988-08-04

Chronique OMS

ISSN : 0373-3556

OTHER LANGUAGE EDITION(S) : WHO chronicle Cr¢nica de la OMS

Authority record date : 1988-08-04

Canadian woman studies

ISSN : 0706-8204

SEE REFERENCE(S) : Cahiers de la femme

EARLIER TITLE(S) : Canadian women's studies

Authority record notes : Name changed with v. 3, no. 2, 1981.

Authority record date : 1987-04-01

APPENDIX

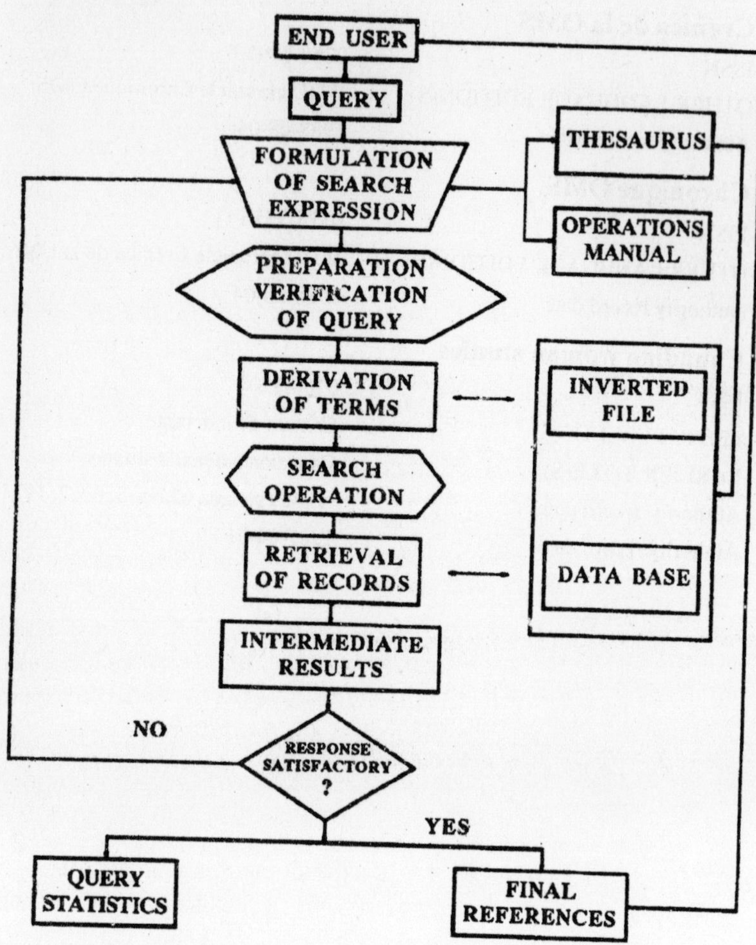

Figure L-1

Index

L

M